WHAT DID HE SAY?

A PASTOR'S NOTES ON THE NEW TESTAMENT

By Dr. Peter G. Law

ALL RIGHTS RESERVED PUBLISHED BY POT BELLY PRESS 2021

ISBN: 9798516759635

Peter Law is the author of:

A Devotion of Caritas

Adventures in Dirt Creek

Jim Bauer; The Prodigal Foreman

The Author lives in Memphis TN with his wife, and spends much of his spare time caring for his children and grandchildren. His pastoral service was in Minnesota. In retirement, he continues his study of the Bible, and teaches an adult Bible Class at Emmanuel United Methodist Church.

Acknowledgments:

        Passages quoted from the Bible, except where noted, are from the NIV or NRSV, used by customary permission.

For my sons. -P

FORWARD

I think we are in a time of transition. I am old enough to have read systematic theologies that are now considered silly. For instance, "God is Dead", and "Process Theology". I do not pretend to be a Bible Scholar in the old sense. Discoveries like the correction of Champollion's chronology have given us proof that the Old Testament is historically accurate. That Genesis is theology, not science is a major insight. I don't care how many editors were involved in the Bible. I want to know what the final author wanted his readers to understand. Why did he write? What was the issue? Who were his opponents? I have limited ability in Greek. Instead, I have approached the scriptures as might an English teacher. And, in that guise, only as an amateur. I have asked myself, **What is the author of this Gospel or Epistle really trying to say?**

While I was a doctoral student, I encountered a visiting professor who insisted that I outline Ephesians in order to "boil down" what Paul really intended his readers to understand. That encounter has been the basis for all my later studies.

Some years ago, while working through Romans, I realized that almost everything I have read about that letter has passed through the lens of Martin Luther (Salvation by Grace through Faith). And while Luther was absolutely correct, it is not the message of Paul's Letter to the Romans. (To see what I think is the real message, read the chapter.)

So, I offer these notes in humility. Some will scoff. Others will say it isn't scholarly. I readily admit that. However, students in the Adult Bible Class in the congregation where I volunteer my efforts, have appreciated my efforts.

The reader, if you get that far, will notice that I have not included notes on Revelation. That is on purpose. I don't propose to know much about that book, other than it tells me things will get worse and worse until the Lord intervenes. Anything else I might put to ink would be highly questionable speculation.

Finally, a word about English usage. I hate grammar books. They seem to me faulty. For instance, proper nouns should be initiated with upper case letters. Habitually, grammarians treat Heaven as if it were not a proper noun, in other words it has no reality. I take umbrage at the usage that fails to distinguish the word earth as dirt, and Earth as the place we live. So, I have adopted my own usage. For instance, most scripture quotes will be in **bold print**. -P

MATTHEW

AN ALTERNATIVE VIEW

Preparatory Cautions:

Most scholars suggest that M. was written about and for "the Jews". Some suggest that as an Apostle, M. (the tax-collector), would have had to write it prior to 70 AD. Dr. James Buchanan believed that much of it was put to paper prior to 70 and edited post 70 (and the first destruction of Jerusalem by Rome). This is my assumption also.

One of the serious characteristics of a parable noted by (for instance) John Dominic Crossan is that it contains a truth so troubling that, if it were fully understood by those to whom it was told, the teller would be put to death immediately. Parables, like metaphors, are always open to more than one understanding. Indeed, the following ideas are not intended, and do not constitute a challenge to current and traditional understandings of the Gospel.

We see an example of caution at 13:10-11 [the disciples came and asked him, "Why do you speak to them in parables?" He answered, "To you it has been given to know the secrets of the kingdom of heaven, but to them it has not been given.] . The Apostles ask the Lord why He speaks in parables. He answered that the general hearers are not supposed to understand, and that He would explain His teachings to His closest followers.

Most certainly true is the postulate that the dramatic theme of Matthew consists of the antagonism between Jesus and several of the Jewish religious groupings, e.g., Pharisees and Sadducees. Even though he wrote his Gospel in Greek, most scholars think he addressed a Jewish audience. He fails to elucidate Jewish custom. Even though some Gentile Christians have taken his Gospel as fodder for antisemitism, Matthew, a Jew, was certainly not anti-Semitic. He must have meant to confront certain groups within Judaism.

My Problem:

All my life I have been troubled by an uncomfortable association of the Gospel and the role of my Nation in God's Plan of Salvation for the World. Born during the worst month of World War II, I have been bothered by what I perceive to be the "quietism" of Jesus, especially toward Rome. The United States has affirmed, again and again, it's role as the New Israel. Ideas like Manifest Destiny, and the glorification of our role as a "Light Shining in the Darkness", and the "Alabaster Cities" are not possible without an identification of the Nation with the Salvation Program of God. Can this Gospel help me understand the role of the Kingdom of God within our world?

The Main Idea:

The Destruction of Jerusalem was most certainly the second traumatic event within the life of M. The first, of course, was the Crucifixion of Jesus. He may have had of other traumas, for instance, the torching of Christians in Rome following the great fire of 64 AD. Trauma has the affect of focus. Taking the two major traumas in M's. life, the Crucifixion and the Destruction of Jerusalem, I can see how he may well have focused on the dynamic antagonism of the Kingdom of God vis a vis the established powers of the World (Rome and/or Jerusalem).

The parables may well be aimed toward those powers. Not only do they offend the worship and relational ideas of the common Jew of His day (for instance the Lost Lamb); they rub most abrasively against the Pharisees and Sadducees. The Lord singles out the Scribes and

Pharisees in Chapter Twenty-three. His denunciations are horrific; Blind guides, hypocrites, inward filthiness, etc. No other group, religious or secular, rates this treatment. They were also singled out by John the Baptist and excluded from the "Baptism of Repentance". Like Jesus, John considered them to be beyond redemption. The Scribes were a part of the Pharisees' sect. They saw, as their religious duty, to explain, and *amplify* the Law of Moses. Thus, they added to the burdens of the Law, while not, in the view of the Lord, amplifying the relationship of the Seeker and "The Father". The larger grouping (Pharisees) is accused of insisting on external obedience to esoteric rules while ignoring inward righteousness (which, according to Jesus, is the basis for a correct relationship with God). The Sadducees were the ruling elite. Their higher loyalty was to the status quo, and not to an immanent breaking in of the Kingdom of God. Rome might well be reprehensible; but as long as the Sadducees were allowed to maintain their status and influence, Rome was acceptable to them. Jesus was considered a vital danger, by them, because He threatened this dance of power.

My Thesis Statement:

The Gospel of Matthew was directed against the two cultural powers of Judea: Pharisees and Sadducees. They were fundamentally antagonistic toward the Gospel of the Kingdom of God.

The Ancestry and Birth of Jesus:

Beginning with Chapter One, the lineage of Jesus illustrates two very pointed ideas.

There is no mention of Moses. Jesus is descended from Abraham both literally and theologically. Matthew, mirroring Paul, wrote that Jesus taught an inward righteousness apart from the Law of Moses. Interestingly, He [I will always begin a pronoun that referenced Deity with an upper-case letter] is the product of four unmarried women: The twice widowed Tamara (who played the prostitute to be impregnated by her father-in-law Judah), the widow Ruth (a non-Hebrew Moabite), Bathsheba (who married David only after being impregnated by him and after David essentially had Uriah murdered), and Mary (who was impregnated by the Holy Spirit). To the Pharisee and Sadducee, these ideas are offensive. The Messiah could not have had these lapses of strict adherence to the Law of Moses in his lineage.

One of my favorite passages is the second chapter of Matthew, as it leads us to an approximate date for the Birth of the Lord [See my notes on the Christmas Star(s). Nativity Dec. 7 BC, return from Egypt 4 BC (Death of Herod).]. However, that focus blinds us to the offensive nature of the account. To Matthew, Herod seemed as if he were the younger brother of Satan, and his devoted servant. Herod, as representative of Rome (whom St. John called "the Great Whore"), unknowingly served God by his witness that Jesus must be born in Bethlehem. And note that Herod said that he wanted to "worship" Jesus. That word would not have been used if Jesus were only a king. This Advent was witnessed by Hebrew exiles (the Magi) before Jesus became an exile in Egypt. Clearly, one should expect nothing but evil from the representatives of worldly governments. The Magi's gift of gold financed the expedition to Egypt. Might Matthew be saying that within this world of political intrigue, God is still able to accomplish His goals. God can even use an evil man like Herod in order to accomplish the goal of the Kingdom.

The Baptism of Jesus:

John announced that **the Kingdom of Heaven is at hand** [3:20]. As noted later, John denied baptism to the Sadducees and Pharisees [3:7]. He denounced their claim to be children of Abraham [3:9]. He denounced their outward righteousness and inward sinfulness [3:8]. They have no place in the Kingdom of Heaven.

The Temptations of Jesus:

One of the Spiritual Dynamics [Please note: Spiritual Dynamics and "in-order-that" have a major place in my interpretation of the entire New Testament] evident in the life of Jesus, and applicable to His followers, is that immediately following a great blessing, will come a deep temptation. That temptation is often related to the most pressing issue to face the Disciple. In this case, Jesus was deeply troubled about the nature of the Kingdom of Heaven; is it inward and spiritual, or is it part of a worldly structure? His decision is obvious.

Jesus lived in Capernaum [4:13]. The Gentiles **have seen a great light** [Isaiah 9:2]. What does this mean within the context of the Temptations? It is related to the Temptations, because the first thing Jesus did, after casting away Satan, was to move from Nazareth to Capernaum (a people living in darkness/lacking understanding). The Temptations [4:1-11] had as their inner subject, authority within this world. Jesus understood the Kingdom of Heaven to be within the person, and not, as per the Pharisees and Sadducees, a moral structure within the world. Matthew's. Gospel relates this dynamic antagonism to the history of Judea from the advent of Jesus to the Resurrection (with antecedents to Abraham and his Faith). His first ministry was among Samaritans and in Syria, that is among those who were not central to the Jewish cultus. His "first sermon" demanded that his listeners **"Repent, for the kingdom of heaven has come near"** [4:17]. In other words: the Kingdom is not in Jerusalem but in the Presence of Jesus. He called the Apostles from among those unidentified with the authority of Jerusalem; indeed, of the world.

The Sermon on the Mount:

As Jesus details the characteristics of "the blessed" [5:1-12], they are in stark contrast, implied and specific, to the Pharisees and Sadducees. The fortunates who enter the Kingdom of Heaven are: poor in spirit, humble, those who mourn over this present world, who hunger for righteousness, the merciful, peacemakers, and the persecuted (by the Pharisees and Sadducees?). Finding the inward Kingdom of Heaven, they are to rejoice greatly because they are a lamp on a stand, and salt to the world.

Jesus asked the worth of salt that has lost its flavor [5:13-16]. Salt was spread over the floor of an oven. Bread was baked over the salt. Any salt remaining after the baking was removed was spread on the pathway to prevent the growth of weeds, and thus, was trampled day by day and had only one use. Just so, the Jewish expression of God within the world had lost its use. The Jewish People were fit only to be trampled by Rome. God had ceased to support their nation because it had lost its ability to present a cogent impression of God for the world.

The Beatitudes present, then, not only the character of the Saint, but also the character of the Kingdom of Heaven. It is inward, peaceable, humble, meek, righteous, *and persecuted.*

Jesus then pokes His finger in the eye of the Scribes. He said, **"Do not think I come to abolish the Law and the prophets. I have come to fulfill them"** [5:17]. They (Scribes) amplified the

Law in-order-to "perfect" it. Jesus saw the Spirit within the Law, and within the ministries of the prophets. It was that inward Spirit which fulfills the Kingdom of Heaven.

The following "you have heard it said...but I say" all relate to the erroneous teachings of the Scribes [5:21-48].

A person whose character reflects the inward meanings of these teachings also reflects the Character of God, and is thus "perfect(ed?)" [5:48]. It is character rather than performance of the law that makes perfect.

Whoever violates the least of these instructions of Jesus will be least in the Kingdom [5:19]. That is to say, the Scribes who considered themselves to be the arbiters of the Law (a sort of Supreme Court of the Law of Moses) but who were blind to the inward nature of the Law, will be fully undone in the Kingdom of Heaven. Thus, anger is murder and violates one's sacred offerings [5:21ff.]. That is, one's relationship to the Almighty is broken because while one has been outwardly righteous, inwardly he or she has violated the character of the Kingdom. Likewise, adultery is of the heart, and not of the body [5:31ff.]. One cannot be faithful to God while unfaithful to one's spouse. [And, not to dwell on the subject; there is no such thing as divorce. Divorce is the expression of faithlessness. If one violates Earth's most sacred covenant, how might one expect to maintain the Covenant with God? The good news, observed by others, is that divorce is not listed as one of the unforgivable sins against God.

Swearing by the altar, is an example of the unhelpful reasoning of the Scribes [5:33ff.]. While the Commandments list false witness as a grievous affront to God, the Scribes had missed its real meaning. Jesus expected fundamental honesty in all things, not simply an avoidance of misrepresentations. The honesty of the Saint is to be of such quality that an oath is not required in any instance. Jesus also treated the prohibition of vendetta ["eye for an eye" 5:38ff.]. Jesus requires the saint to be of such peaceable character that an attack is not resisted in any way, ever [See Romans 12:19: Do not take revenge, my dear friends, but leave room for God's wrath, for it is written: "It is mine to avenge; I will repay," says the Lord.] He went on to require a double response to an unjust demand; for instance, the taxation of one's coat, or the requirement by a Roman soldier to carry his pack for a mile. One might extrapolate (but not necessarily) from obedience to a Roman to one's non-resistance to Evil. One might equally equate a Roman with a representative of the Jewish state. If one is deeply spiritual (that is, intimate with the Holy Spirit of God) one will see these impositions as an opportunity, no matter how hidden, for God to interact with the unrighteous one who makes the demand. It naturally follows that one must Love (agape) one's so-called enemies [5:43] in-spite-of the universal human tradition of hatred. Hatred, even directed against one's opponents, violates the relationship of the Saint and God. That relationship is of greater worth than an eye or a hand [M. 5:29ff].

In this regard, God's-Love (agape)-made-flesh is the perfection expected of a follower of Jesus [5:48].

Chapter six opens with an attack on the hypocrisies of the Pharisees. Like the bronze plaques marking a large (though not sacrificial) gift by a wealthy donor, the Pharisee might have a trumpet call announce a special gift at the Temple [6:1ff.]. Prayer and charitable gifts are to be done in such a way as to not draw attention to the giver or supplicant because it must come from the heart. The reward is one's own heart-felt satisfaction.

Even the prayer given to the disciples is revolutionary and would be offensive to the Pharisee. [*As an aside: John Wesley was condemned by the officials of the Anglican Church, not for ordination, or for preaching outdoors, but because he prayed from the heart, extemporaneously rather than from the Book of Common Prayer.] Prayer contains all that is required, and unlike the law, is simple. Unlike our liturgical prayer, the Lord's Prayer ends with the request that evil be avoided. His teaching, however, continues.

The first unforgivable sin is a heart that cannot forgive. That is: one that is without mercy [6:14-15]. The Pharisee, Sadducee, and Scribe might seek justice, or even advantage, but seldom would they seek mercy. Jesus sought the purity of a spirit unburdened by resentments. One is to live with such a light dependence on the things of the flesh [6:19; treasures on Earth] that the corruptions of Earth don't matter. One's reliance upon God should be of such magnitude and awareness, that more than a daily bread is unnecessary. If one is concerned about the things of Earth, one will not be able to disenthrall from the viewpoint of the Sadducees and Pharisees [6:24; no one can serve two masters]. Rather, one is to pay attention to the things of the Spirit, and God will take care for the things of flesh.

The Sadducees continually contrived to seek advantage in politics, wealth, prestige, influence, and so on. They judged what was helpful from a worldly point of view. Jesus presented a different viewpoint. For Him reliance on the "Father-God", an intimate, caring Eternal Personality, was of greater worth than a temporary advantage or comfort [7:7-12; the Father in Heaven will give good gifts].

Jesus closed His sermon with a startling dichotomy. The way to destruction and loss, is the way of the Sadducees and Pharisees. Matthew saw this borne out in history. Instead, the narrow way (the way of inward righteousness [7:12; golden rule] would lead to inner wealth and life [7:13-14; it is hard, and few find it]. He, again, pointed out the enemies of "life": the wolves disguised as sheep. Rather than name His enemies, Jesus simply stated that their fruits betray them [7:15-20]. They will claim to be foremost in the Kingdom, but they will be rejected by God because they trusted outward righteousness rather than an inward relationship with a Father-God [7:20-23; Not everyone who says "Lord, Lord, will enter the Kingdom].

His final parable: the strong and weak foundations [7:24-27] would be recognized by any Christian after 70 AD. Remember that a parable includes a truth so dangerous that it would lead to the death of its teller. Were Jesus to predict the destruction of Jerusalem forty years before the event would certainly be a dangerous venture.

"Therefore, everyone who hears these words of mine and puts them into practice is like a wise man who built his house on the rock. The rain came down, the streams rose, and the winds blew and beat against that house; yet it did not fall, because it had its foundation on the rock. But everyone who hears these words of mine and does not put them into practice is like a foolish man who built his house on sand. The rain came down, the streams rose, and the winds blew and beat against that house, and it fell with a great crash."

The Pharisees and Sadducees had led the nation to entire destruction. At the same time, the Way had spread out across the Roman Empire and had become a subversive spiritual community.

The Authority of Jesus as Messiah:

The Sermon on the Mount ends with M's. evaluation that the people were astonished at the authority of Jesus [7:28-29]; an authority beyond that of the Scribes and even against them. The Scribes always quoted an earlier authority. Jesus simply asserted His Truths, mostly without attribution. Matthew continued with a full list of powerful acts which expressed the greater authority of Jesus.

The healing of a leper was an extraordinary thing. No leper was healed by ritual in the Temple. Indeed, the only function of the priest, in this regard, was to certify that the leper *had been* healed and was clean. By reporting that Jesus had healed a leper [8:1-4], Matthew elevated Jesus above the hierarchical priesthood. Jesus has a greater authority than that of Moses, because Moses never healed a leper. [He did ask the Lord to heal his sister Miriam (Num. 12:13), and the Lord responded.] The healing in Matthew was clearly of a different magnitude. Jesus held authority within Himself. By a simple command, "Be clean", the leper was made clean.

A Centurion came to Jesus requesting health for his servant [8:5-13]. While many would believe the subject is "faith", it is more appropriately understood as authority. The Centurion understands authority, because he daily exercises it. Matthew takes pains to present this because even a representative of the Great Evil Empire was able to witness to the authority of Jesus. [An aside: Could this man be the same one who witnessed the Crucifixion, and the same one who was baptized by St. Peter? Following principles of historical research, I am tempted to affirm it.] Jesus avers that such a man will enter the Kingdom of Heaven [8:11-12] well ahead of those who think they are at the head of the line (i.e., the Sadducees).

Jesus entered the house of Peter whose Mother-in-law had a fever [8:14-15]. In healing her, he gave her the ability to serve. That in itself is a great lesson. Those who are healed by Jesus have a witness to share about the authority of the Name.

Matthew seals his testimony by quoting Isaiah. Isaiah [II] was the great prophet of Messiah. His dialogue between the prophet, Israel, God, and the Messiah stands as the source material by which the character of the Savior must be judged. Having fulfilled the prophecy [8:17], **He healed our diseases and took our infirmities**, Matthew announced that Jesus is, in fact, the predicted Messiah, and thus has Messianic Authority.

Matthew is aware that at least one Scribe became a Disciple of Jesus (and thus does not condemn all "the Jews"). This extraordinary Scribe wanted to follow Jesus even beyond the boundaries of Israel. Jesus refused [8:20] with the confusing statement that "foxes have holes". There is only one other use of the word "fox" in the New Testament. Luke quotes Jesus in-reference-to Herod [Luke 13:32], **tell that fox**. Does Jesus believe that the Scribe is a "fox", a representative of the Sadducees, and thus unworthy of trust? Does Jesus believe that the Scribe is a "plant" or a "spy"? He associates "fox" with "birds" [bids have nests], which we will see is an allusion to Rome (the Eagle). Interpreted thus Jesus says: "Sadducees have their place, Rome has its place, but the Messiah has no place to lay his head" [8:20]. A friend pointed out another valid interpretation. Jesus may be using folk idioms to point out that the Son of Man is not the leader of a great army.

Yet another hearer asked leave to bury his father. The Lord's reference to the dead burying the dead [8:22] suggests that all who are not His followers are spiritually dead. They (the spiritually dead) have no value equal to that of the Kingdom of Heaven which is present in the preaching and teaching of Jesus. Those, already dead, are those who have followed the established traditions of Judea.

In the boat, Jesus demonstrated his Messianic Authority over nature by calming the storm and saving the Apostles [8:23-27]. Of interest in these verses is the Greek word *seismos,* which is translated "storm", but which refers to earthquakes. Apparently, an earthquake brought up tremendous waves. Jesus was unconcerned. His reality was/is in the Greater Realm, rather than in the world of natural disasters. This is yet another tough one for us to bring into our own lives. He would ask us: Where do you live: this world or the Greater World?

And finally, Jesus has an authority greater than the demons [8:28-34]. Matthew illustrated this authority with the charming account of condemning unclean spirits into unclean animals who then commit mass suicide: the dead leading the dead to death.

The Messianic Authority of Jesus Tested:

While exercising His great Authority by healing a paralytic, Jesus forgave sins which were apparent to him though not to us [9:1-8]. He didn't call the paralytic sinner evil; instead He called the Scribes "evil" [9:4] - Knowing their thoughts, Jesus said, **"Why do you entertain evil thoughts in your hearts?** because they, who should have understood and gladly received Jesus, called him a blasphemer. But this led to greater miracles. The crowds, the unnamed common folk, glorified God. They understood that they had seen the Power of God at work in Jesus.

And an even greater miracle took place. Matthew was converted [9:9-17]. Matthew saw the Power of God in Jesus, while the Pharisees judged. They saw the outward actions of a collector of Roman taxes. Jesus saw a man whose heart was hungry for holiness [Cf Sermon on the Mount: 5:6 Those who hunger for righteousness.]. Matthew saw grace in the Lord's interaction with "tax-collectors and sinners". The Pharisees only saw disgrace. In one of those mildly sarcastic asides for which Jesus became famous, He referred to Himself as a physician. The Pharisees obviously didn't need a doctor since they were all above criticism, that is, they all felt they were "clean". Matthew knew he needed forgiveness. He rejoiced when Jesus said that He had authority to forgive sins [9:6]. To the Sadducees, Jesus said: **God desires mercy, not sacrifice** [9:13]. They, who were in charge of the sacrifices of the entire community, were not known to be concerned for inward repentance.

Matthew took the opportunity to associate his [Matthew's] calling with a number of teachings. Obviously, having dinner with Jesus seemed like a wedding celebration [9:15]. Jesus is the Bridegroom, and the Kingdom of Heaven is the Bride. Associating with the wedding celebration, Jesus took a chance to chastise the Pharisees [9:16], who put new interpretations on old laws. Jesus increased the distance between the Pharisaical understanding of the Law, and the Kingdom. Putting the righteousness of the Kingdom into the old, establishment endorsed, idea of righteousness is like putting new wine into old wineskins. The original wineskins are unable to hold the new wine, and the old law is unable to support the new interpretations/additions. He then instructed the Sadducees: God desires mercy rather than sacrifice! Try to fit that into your teachings about the law! The new wineskins were the common folk who accepted Jesus. The old wineskins were both the old Law and those who taught it.

The remainder of the chapter [9:18-38] constitutes only one teaching: Because Jesus has demonstrable Authority, the authority of the Pharisees and Sadducees is undone. Jesus journeyed to heal a child who had, to those who looked on, seemed to have died [9:18-19, 23-26]. While on this journey, He was interrupted by a ritually unclean woman [9:20-22]. While the Pharisees and Sadducees would have even refrained from touching her, and would have denounced her for touching them, Jesus was not offended. To the Pharisees and Sadducees, the power of the unclean infiltrates the clean making both unclean. To Jesus, cleanness is a power that went out of Him, cleansing the unclean woman. He has Authority over uncleanness, while they have none. Jesus continued His trek to the home of the comatose girl, and, raising her up, demonstrated His Authority over the boundary between life and death. Again, the Law of Moses prohibited touching the dead. She was beyond the help of the Pharisees, Sadducees, and Priests, but not of Jesus.

As He left that house, two blind men asked for forgiveness. This is a common theme in the Gospels. There are two kinds of blindness: physical and spiritual. In several of the healing accounts the two are conflated. In this instance [9:27-31], the blind men are asked: Do you think I can do this? That is to say; "Do you believe I have Authority over the blindness of your eyes, and of your spirit?" Answering in the affirmative, He granted their healing according to the faith they held in His Authority. That this Authority is the subject of the pericope is found in two ways; His question, and in the growth of His fame "throughout the district".

After healing yet another demoniac, this one dumb, and demonstrating His Authority, again, over the whole of nature and spirit, the Pharisees accused Jesus of casting out by demonic authority. They had begun to understand the nature of the contest: their authority verses His Authority. The crowds of common folk said in awe: [9:36] **"We never saw anything like this!"** And Jesus had compassion on them, because while He undermined the authority of the Pharisees and Sadducees, they were left without a shepherd guide [9:36-38]. His response to their need was in the sending out of the Apostles!

Jesus Dispenses Authority to His Disciples:

Jesus extended his Messianic Authority to His Twelve (the minimum requirement for the establishment of a Synagogue or worshiping community) over disease, demons, and infirmity [10:1]. If this were important, so must be the naming of those men to whom the authority had devolved [10:2-4].

The conditions upon which this new mission depend were spelled out [10:5-15]. They are: an utter dependance on God for sustenance, an authority derived from Jesus over death, demons, disease, and especially leprosy. [A twenty-first century Christian might note that authority over nature, history, or Wall Street is not in the list.] Their orientation was toward only the "Lost Sheep of Israel" [10:6], excluding those who were unaware of their lostness [Pharisees and Sadducees].

Matthew, remembering the destruction of Jerusalem by the Tenth Legion in 70 AD, related the instructions of Jesus to the Twelve. Clearly Matthew 10:15-22 reflects that sense of Divine Judgment on the Jerusalem "establishment". It was, indeed, more tolerable for Sodom and Gomorrah [10:15], and for Tyre and Sidon [11:21-22] than for Jerusalem. The latter escaped the full destruction wrought by Rome's professional destroyers.

The revolt against Rome began in 66 AD. Vespasian was sent by the Emperor Nero, who was assassinated in 68. Vespasian, becoming Emperor, left his son Titus in charge to finish the work. His troops killed 1.1 million persons, according to Josephus, and took sixty to ninety thousand prisoners to Rome where they built the Coliseum. The revolt had been led by the Zealots, who split into three groups and fought each other as intensely as they did the Romans. It was a house divided against itself [12:25]. The Romans desecrated the Temple with corpses and offal before demolishing completely everything on what we call Temple Mount.

The rejection of the Gospel by Israel led to the persecution of the Apostles and Disciples. Yet this persecution had a purpose. Though full of pain and tragedy, it gave to the Saints the opportunity to witness among the Gentiles [10:16-20], and that is part of the Great Plan of God for the Kingdom of Heaven. The emphasis is not on the rejection, but rather on the Power within the Kingdom of Heaven to overcome all obstacles. Have no fear (regard?) of the Pharisees and Sadducees, or, indeed of Rome. God is greater than their earthly powers. God has Authority over both life and the existence beyond death [10:28].

Verses thirty-two through forty-two reflect the experience of the Saints during the First Revolt against Rome. Indeed, parents and children were divided. Many Christians lost their lives. And, just as the Revolt began, the Holy Spirit instructed the Christian Church to flee from Judea [24:16]. While the Saint is of great worth in the Kingdom of Heaven, he or she is not immune to the frailties and ravages of this sinful world. Jesus counseled the Saints to be faithful, enduring to the end (their death) [10:22; you will be hated by all because of my name. But the one who endures to the end will be saved.] for the reward of the Kingdom. If one has found the Life within the Kingdom of Heaven, should one turn away from it? Those confronted by a choice, should take to heart the **fear of Him who can cast into Hell** [10:28].

That Jesus had come not for peace, but to provoke judgment was apparent to the Saints of 70 AD. They saw clearly, that the Kingdom has a reality beyond the governmental structures of Earth. Unlike the Modernists of the Twentieth Century, they understood that the Kingdom comes on Earth not through the moral efforts of the Saints, but rather, by the intrusion of the Savior at the End of Time (or, of the Era). The Authority to "create" the Kingdom of God on Earth was not granted to the Apostles. Authority over disease, death (both physical and spiritual -but mostly spiritual) and uncleanness (sin) is the (only) great possession of the Body of Christ.

Jesus Identifies the Kingdom to John the Baptist:

Jesus shared the evidences of Messianic Authority with the Disciples of John the Baptist. They are: the blind see, the deaf hear, the lame walk, lepers are cleansed, the dead are raised, and, perhaps of greater importance, **the poor have good news preached to them** [11:4-5]. Jesus, according to Matthew, referenced Malachi's final verses (now, but not then, the final verses of the Old Testament) to substantiate His Messianic Authority. Malachi quoted God as sending His Messenger to announce judgment against Israel [Mal. 3:1,5], and described the issues upon which the judgment is to be decided. The prophecy concludes with a promise that God will send Elijah before the terrible day of judgment [Mal. 4:5]. Jesus asserted that John the Baptist is Elijah "re-incarnated". Of greater interest to those who had ears to hear, were the other parts of the promise. He (John? Or perhaps Jesus?) will turn the hearts of the parents and the child toward each other. This is in direct contrast to the division of parent and child in Matthew 10:21[children will rise against parents and have them put to death]. Those who repent, according to Malachi, will skip like calves in the springtime [Mal. 4:2] and see the "Sun of Righteousness rise".

Jesus was aware that He was gaining the same sort of notoriety that resulted in the imprisonment of John. When He asked about the "present generation" [11:16], he pointed to the reaction both John and He received. They (the Pharisees and Sadducees) accused John of demonic influence, and Jesus of gluttony [11:16-19]. We know that the "they" refers to the Pharisees and Sadducees because of the accusation "He associates with tax-collectors and sinners" [11:19].

Matthew took pains to suggest that the poor, the common people of Israel, accepted Jesus as the Messiah, and that the Establishment did not. The rest of the chapter deals with the judgment rendered by God in 70 AD (as noted above).

While the Pharisees and Sadducees derived their authority from Moses, it was God the Father who gave Messianic Authority to Jesus. Not only that, the Establishment groups were blinded. They do not know God as Father. Only Jesus reveals that secret [11:25-27].

One must note that the final verses of Chapter Eleven promise an easy yoke to those who accept Jesus as Messiah [11:28-30]. Thus far the evidence suggests something else. The Saints face persecution and betrayal, oppression, and the destruction of their nation. Yet, inwardly, they face a joyful future, set free from want, fear, and the "second death". And, within this context, they are freed from the odious burdens which the Sadducees and Pharisees would place on one's shoulders.

End lesson one

Jesus Challenges the Law of Moses:

Jesus directly confronted the Pharisees and Sadducees by twice violating the Law of the Sabbath [12:1-14]. The Pharisees understood the challenge and took counsel how to "destroy" Jesus. His Disciples ate grain from the field on the Sabbath, and Jesus healed a man with atrophied hand. In the first case, Jesus declared the Disciples innocent, and challenged the Pharisaical notion that sacrifice was of greater importance than inward innocence [12:6].

Of greater importance is the announcement that something greater than Sabbath is here [12:6]! Every Jew understood that Sabbath was the first and greatest creation of God [Gen 2:3]. The only way a "greater than Sabbath" could be present, would be for the Creator Himself to be Present. That is exactly what is meant by Jesus!

So, Matthew presented the legal argument against the Law of Sabbath *as interpreted by the Pharisees*. A human being is of greater worth than a sheep, which, if it fell into a ditch on the Sabbath, would certainly be pulled out (and with innocence) [12:11-12].

Matthew called on the authority of Isaiah to support the claim that One greater than Sabbath was present. Isaiah [II] presented the Messiah as One for whom the "coastlands" (the Gentiles) hungered [Is. 42:1-4], and One who would "execute Justice"! Here, in Jesus, one finds clarity of wisdom and judgment. His judgment is clearly superior to the amplified interpretation of the Law of Moses by the Pharisees and Sadducees.

The idea that Satan would cure one whom Satan had afflicted, is untenable and illogical. If by the Holy Spirit Jesus was able to heal a blind, mute, demoniac, the position of the Pharisees is untenable. If the Pharisees and Sadducees denounce the work of the Holy Spirit, they are guilty of one of only two unforgivable sins. The first [noted at 6:14-15] is an unmerciful heart; the second is blasphemy against the Holy Spirit [12:31]. Jesus placed before the Pharisees a logical judgment they could not ignore. They recognized, in Jesus, the most serious threat to their authority [12:22-32]. Jesus threw down the challenge in the form of a judgment from the bench [12:33-37]: having judged their Law as unjust, they would be judged and held responsible for every careless word. Since they are without mercy, God would have no mercy for them.

Faced with the logical outcome of their own Law, the Pharisees asked for a sign that Jesus was Messiah [12:34]. His answer was a prediction of the death and resurrection [12:39-40]. Sheba and Nineveh are of greater innocence than the Pharisees and Sadducees, because they responded to the invitation of God, while the Pharisees reject it.

An infamous event offered Matthew a chance to point to the Saints as the "family of Jesus". His family wanted Him declared mentally unfit, and that He be committed to their care. Jesus responded that those who do God's Will, and recognize Him as Messiah (as did His brother James after the Resurrection) are the truly sane, while those who reject Him are not mentally (or spiritually) well [12:46-50].

The Dangerous Wisdom of Jesus taught in Parables:

With that before me, I begin this deeper look into the Gospel, preparatory to a look at the Parables of Jesus presented by Matthew in Chapter Thirteen. I remind you that the purpose of a parable is to present an idea that is so revolutionary and dangerous that the hearers would want to destroy the speaker.

The Parables of Jesus:

The Value of the Kingdom:

Hidden Treasure: 13:44

The Pearl of Great Value: 13:46

Faith:

The Mustard Seed: 13:31

The Leaven: 13:33

The Mustard Seed and the Mountain: 17:14-20

Judgment:

The Strong and Weak Foundations: 7:24-27

Weeds and Grain: 13:24-30

The Great Catch of Fish: 13:46-50

Real and Supposed Defilement: 15:10-20

Lost Sheep: 18:12-14

Workers and Wages in the Vineyard: 20:1-16

The Withered Fig Tree: 21:19-22

The Two Sons: 21:28-32

The Wedding Feast: 22:1-13

The Budding and Withered Fig Tree; 21:19-22

Ten Virgins: 25:1-13

The Talents: 25:14-30

The Sheep and the Goats: 25:31-46

Parables in other Gospels:

The Lost Coin

Lost Son

Lazarus

The Good Samaritan

The Two Debtors

Unforgiving Servant

The Disturbed Neighbor

The Unjust Judge

The Pharisee and the Publican

The Rich Fool

The Vineyard

The Great Banquet

The Good and Faithful Servants

Building on Sand or Rock

The Hidden Lamp

The Unjust Steward

The Parable of the Sower of Seeds:

Matthew gathered the Lord's teachings into the second of the great sermons of Jesus.

In the Parable of the Sower [13:3-9] (Jesus) broadcasts the Word of the Kingdom of God. Some of it falls among weeds and thorns. The cares of the world crowd out the good news. The Sadducees were more concerned with the things of this world than with a Kingdom "not of this World" (though Matthew does not include this quotation) or a Kingdom which is "at hand" (as per John the Baptist), and most certainly not a Kingdom among the poor and sinners, the meek and sorrowful.

Some of the seeds fall on shallow soil: a person without deep spiritual roots. An Evil one, the Demonic in the person of a Pharisee, comes and dissuades the new follower. Because he has few spiritual resources, he is unable to contend with the established tradition of the Pharisee with its legalistic view of salvation through obedience to the Law of Moses (and the amplified regulations of the Scribes).

Yet, if the seed falls on deep spiritual soil, it sends down strong rootage and will bring forth an abundant harvest in due time.

In between the parable and its explanation, Matthew placed two other parables: The Leaven and the Mustard Seed.

Leaven, as used here by Matthew is an evil. For instance: **Take heed and beware the leaven of the Pharisees and Sadducees** [16:6]. In 13:12, we are led to understand that "leaven" equates to the teachings of the Pharisees and Sadducees. Thus, leaven is identified with an evil pharisaical theology.

One troubling interpretation of the parable of the leaven in the bread dough, is that Pharisees and Sadducees have polluted the dough with their evil ideas. Unleavened bread is the true bread, as per Passover. On the other hand, one could argue that the Kingdom of Heaven is subversive [like yeast] among the teachings of the Pharisees and Sadducees, and in the midst of Roman oppression.

In 13:31, Jesus taught about the Mustard Seed. Our translators have had difficulty with the verse, identifying the full-grown mustard plant as a tree. Classified as an herb, it must have been the largest plant within its classification (as available to Matthew). Rev. Kevin Presley suggested that the seed of the Mustard is so tiny that it becomes an invasive problem (like dandelion). The Kingdom is invasive, and was surely a problem to the Scribes, Pharisees and Sadducees.

What is noteworthy is that the birds come and build nests (homes) within its branches. The revolutionary and dangerous idea presented here is that the attitudes and actions of the Establishment have led directly to the domination of Judea by Rome. The only foreign bird to make a home in Judea was Rome, whose symbol was the Eagle. The Kingdom of Heaven, by contrast, is tiny, invasive and impossible to destroy/defeat. And Angels roost among and in its branches.

Thus, within the context of the parable of the Seeds, Jesus identified his opponents as the Pharisees and Sadducees, on the one hand, and Rome, on the other.

The Parable of the Weeds and Grain:

Having set forth His "Enemies List", Jesus announced a judgment [13:24ff.]. This parable has other insights too. The "man" who planted is, of course, God. While humanity failed to notice, God's enemies (We may include others, but Matthew intended his readers to understand: Pharisees, Sadducees, Scribes and Priests) planted weeds within His [God's] field (the Jewish faith). These evil additions will remain until the time of the harvest, at which time they will be destroyed. Clearly, Matthew thought the sack of Jerusalem in 70 AD constituted such a judgment. [A note: Unfortunately, based on the readings of the New Testament, the Church took from this a nasty antisemitism. However, for Matthew, the Judgment was not against all Jews, for many (if not most) of the early Christians were Jews. It was against the ideas of the Sadducees and Pharisees.]

The Parable of the Great Catch of Fish:

Jesus re-illustrated the teaching of the Judgment with this parable [13:47-50]. The Fisherman (Jesus) casts a wide net, proclaiming a Kingdom *available* to all. It appears that the divorce between those who held the theology of the Apostolic Council in Jerusalem, and those who followed the "Salvation by Grace through Faith" theology of St. Paul was about to (or had already) taken place.

Parables of the Kingdom:

Following the identification of His enemies, Jesus turned to the subject of His Subversive Kingdom [13:44ff]. Judea, and the Jewish culture, are identified as a "field". Within this field, a merchant (that is: a person seeking wealth), discovers the pearl of greatest worth: The Kingdom of Heaven. That Kingdom is of greater worth than any tangible asset. In-order-to possess this pearl, the Merchant places himself in danger from want. He has no protection, no source of income, no place in the world. He has sold all that he has. Rome and the Sadducees are irrelevant to the Merchant because he has the pearl of greatest value. The Pearl is a "hidden" or "covered up" treasure, available to anyone who would seek it.

Interestingly, selling all that one owned and giving the proceeds to the Church was the practice of the early Christian Community in Jerusalem. They anticipated an early return of the Lord, and thus had no "place" in this world.

The Scribe who interprets the Law of Moses, would be wise to understand the value of God's teaching within the Law, as well as what is newly presented, i.e., the Kingdom of Heaven [13:52]. He would be trained for entry into the Kingdom. Perhaps Matthew held out an olive branch to some within the Community of Faith who wished to hold onto parts of the Law of Moses, e.g., the Jerusalem Council Christians. Perhaps he likened them to a Scribe who brings forth from both the old and the new. This is in contrast to Matthew 7:6; **do not cast pearls before swine, and do not give the sacred to dogs**. The swine and dogs are, to Matthew, the Pharisees and Sadducees. They are the ones responsible for both the traumas of Matthew's lifetime: the Crucifixion and the Destruction of Jerusalem.

A final note on Chapter thirteen:

That His own people rejected Jesus amplifies this interpretation as pertaining to the community divorce following 70 AD. One of the more encouraging statements of Jesus, and one which seems most in accord with the personality ascribed to him by all the Apostles, is found at 11:6 **"And blessed is he who takes no offense at me"**. Most certainly the Scribes, Sadducees and Pharisees took offense. If one hears and understands the hidden meaning of these parables and is not offended, one is blessed. The poor, ill, tax-collectors, and other social outcasts did not. Even one of Rome's Centurions did not.

Evidence of the Present Kingdom of Heaven:

Herod's execution of John the Baptist [14:1-12] is, in an unusual way, evidence that the Kingdom of Heaven is present, and that the Israel is judged. Matthew has taken great pains to show the divergence of opinion between the common people and the elite. Were Herod willing, John or Jesus "might-could" have expressed grace to him. Unlike Herod, the common people were so hungry for the Word, that they came out to hear Jesus preach, and did not leave with enough time to get food for themselves [14:13-21].

Of course, the feeding of five thousand is also a demonstration that the Kingdom is present; whether Jesus multiplied the food, or the thousands shared. In either case, the community gathered around the Word is unlike any previous Jewish community.

Likewise, the miracle on the sea [14:22-33; Jesus walks on water] demonstrates the power of the present Kingdom of Heaven. In today's terms, it is as if the dimensions of nature and the Dimension of Spirit have blended. The Biblical notion of nature is quite amenable to such a mixing. Nature, according to Genesis, is the product of Spirit [Gen. 1:1; Note: I am frustrated at the academicians who translated "Ruach" as "wind" rather than "Spirit". They continue to show an agnostic attitude toward scripture.].

When Jesus used the term, "it is I" [Gk. lit. ego: emphatic "I", eimi: "I am"], most scholars agree that He was using the pronoun for deity. This might well be understood by the Apostles. They were well aware of the traditional association of God and sea; the Spirit hovered, vibrated, swept, or trembled over the deep [Gen. 1:1]. God led the Hebrews out of Egypt through the Sea. Noah confronted God in the depths of the sea, and so on. No other interpretation accounts for the willingness of St. Peter to leave the safety of the boat. He learned the lesson that the power of the Kingdom extends over and throughout nature. There is nothing within this world that should frighten a Disciple of Jesus.

Even the Gentiles at Gennesaret recognized the Presence of the Kingdom and were greatly blessed [14:34-36]. How different this reception from those who urged Him "to the leave them" [Luke 8:37], and yet not so different as it seems. Luke concluded that the Gerasene's had been overcome by "fear". In either case, the people must have been awe-struck.

A different group of Pharisees, these from Jerusalem [15:1], had come out to test Jesus. Apparently, the word had been passed up the chain of command. The rural Pharisees must have reported their understanding of the danger Jesus posed to the establishment. The "beltway experts" had come out to judge for themselves. Again, the resistance of the Established powers to the power of the Kingdom of Heaven, is presented as evidence of its (the Kingdom) presence [15:1-9; Whatever support you might have had from me is given to God,' then that person need not honor the father. Followed by: The heart of this people is far from me.].

And again, Matthew presents the basis on which the Judgment of God was to fall on Jerusalem. Rather than washing the hands before eating (exterior), inward righteousness is what is required. The contrast between tradition, and Command is emphasized [15:2-3; And why do you break the commandment of God for the sake of your tradition?]. There is a "one-upmanship here. The Pharisees attacked Jesus over the violation of tradition, and Jesus responded with their violation of Commandment. The Sadducees and Priests had misrepresented the meaning of the Law, again for their own benefit. They had ruled that those who avoid the commandment "Honor your father" in the Decalogue, by giving that financial support to the Sadducees and Priests were not to be considered guilty. Jesus called it a human concept concocted without the authority of God (or, indeed, of Moses).

Jesus called on the common people to witness His response to the Pharisees [15:10-12]. In His parable, Jesus explained that non-Kosher food cannot defile a person, but evil thoughts can. The Pharisees, in their cunning, had tested Jesus, only to find themselves judged and found wanting [15:13-14]. Not only are they blind themselves, but because they are blind, they lead others astray. We must take note of verse 13. It is often overlooked. **Every plant that my heavenly Father has not planted will be uprooted. Let them alone.** Jesus seems to have been tired of announcing judgment against his antagonists.

The incredulous Apostles asked Jesus if He were aware that He had offended the important representatives of the Jerusalem establishment. And. of course, He was fully aware. His use of the *parable* of real and supposed defilement is evidence of the danger He felt. Again note: Jesus used parables to teach, when the Truth contained within was so dangerous that, if understood correctly, the listeners would have executed Him immediately. In this case, He suggested that the Pharisees were fit only for the sewer (NRSV). The word translated "pit" is "bothunos" a derivative of "bathuno" which referrs to a deep cistern pit...a sewage dump.

The Enlarged Nature of the Kingdom:

The Canaanites were anathema to a Jew. They were ancient enemies, akin to the Palestinians of the present day. A Pharisee or Sadducee would not speak to one.

Here a Canaanite woman, out of love for her daughter, fear of a demon, and hope for a Savior, approached Jesus, calling **Have mercy on me!** [15:21-28]. His response extends the boundary of the Kingdom to faith-filled despised persons beyond the Jewish community.

While the geography makes little sense, going from Gennesaret to Sidon, and returning to the Sea of Galilee (Capernaum?), and thence to Magadan, the association of events has an interior logic. The association of a second feeding of a multitude or repeating a second account of a single event [15:29-38], demonstrates the power and breadth of the Kingdom of Heaven.

The Signs of the Times:

In the district of Magadan (on the shore of the Sea of Galilee), yet another test was put forth by Pharisees and Sadducees [16:1-4]; they asked for a sign from Heaven (or, from God). His retort dwelt on the signs of the times. Matthew understood the signs, having the benefit of historical knowledge. The sign of Noah obviously referenced the Garden Tomb. One asks whether Matthew introduced a new meaning, or that Jesus expected a prophetic utterance to be remembered. I do not know the answer to the question, but assert that before the Gospel was published, this "sign of the time" was confirmed in Matthew's mind by the events of 66-70 AD. Had he lived to 135 AD, his opinion would have been doubled. In that year Jerusalem was destroyed yet again, a pagan temple built on the Temple Mount, a plow run across the residential area, all Jews and Christians expelled, and the name of the city changed to Aelia Capitolina. The province was renamed Syria Palestrina, and remained a pagan city until at least 390 AD.

Matthew took this opportunity to reinforce the judgment of Jesus against the Pharisees and Sadducees: Beware of their yeast or leaven, their teachings and/or influence [16:11]. The Bread of the Kingdom of Heaven, that is, the Bread with which Jesus fed the five thousand and the four thousand, gives life. The leaven of the Pharisees does not [16:5-12].

The climax of this "ministry section" of the Gospel is in the affirmation of St. Peter that Jesus is the Son of God [16:16]. That statement confirms all the judgments against the Pharisees and Sadducees. They have, by continually testing Him, declared that they are not "with Him" [12:30;

Whoever is not with me is against me, and whoever does not gather with me scatters.], and thus are "scatterers" rather than gatherers. The statement also confirms the Messianic Authority of Jesus.

Upon that statement the Kingdom of Heaven is made real. It does not confer *special* messianic authority on St. Peter, as is demonstrable by the denunciation by Jesus in the following verses. That is to say: The Kingdom of Heaven is made real, or noticeably present, when a person confesses that Jesus is the Messiah, the Son of God.

St. Peter's response to the idea of a Cross is like that of the Pharisees and Sadducees [16:23; **You are a stumbling block to me; for you are setting your mind not on divine things but on human things."**]. Peter, like them, had thought in human terms rather than from the Divine perspective.

The pericope about taking up one's cross is not directed toward only Peter, but to all that hunger for the Kingdom [16:24-26]. Of note, Jesus might be saying that the Sadducees and Pharisees (who already "have their reward") are of a type unwilling to take up the burdens of the Kingdom (i.e., the Cross).

The person who confesses Jesus as Messiah, must also be willing to suffer for the Kingdom. The Cross is the greatest of the "Signs of the Times". Jesus had taken pains to point to Noah, elsewhere to Daniel, and to Isaiah as prophets whose predictions are fulfilled in the Cross.

Prophecy Fulfilled and unfulfilled:

Two statements need clarification. When the Son comes with the Angels, He will repay those who deny the Kingdom, and who persecute the Saints [16:27]. From the post 70 AD perspective, Jesus' prophecy was fulfilled. The Sadducees as a ruling group were greatly displaced. Matthew probably expected an immediate return of Jesus in the short period after 70 [16:28; **"There are some standing here who will not taste death before they see the Son of Man coming in his kingdom."**].

The Transfiguration recalls, and perhaps predicts, the return of the Shekinah (Pentecost). Jesus' face shone "like the Sun" [17:2]. The face of Moses shone in the same way when he spoke to God, face to Face. The Shekinah, most scholars agree, is an Old Testament presentation of the Holy Spirit: a sign of the Presence of God. Of course, James, John and Peter were fully aware of the role of the Spirit in prophecy, and Matthew was fully aware of Pentecost.

Peter's offer to build three booths, either elevates the prophets, or demotes Jesus. That the Shekinah Cloud of the Father overshadows them is perhaps a reference to Moses on the Mount of the Law. One suspects an irritated voice from the Deity: (very roughly translated) "Don't you get it, Peter? This is my Son, not just another Prophet. Pay attention to what He says, Dummy!" [17:5]. The Apostles were terrified, and with good reason! Jesus had to reassure the Apostles [17:7], for two reasons: they were terrified by the Voice in the Cloud, and potentially they would be afraid of Jesus following this revelation. The Transfiguration is proof that Jesus fulfills the "Law and the Prophets" [5:17 and 22:40].

The Apostles asked why the Scribes insisted on a return of Elijah prior to the Messiah. As noted above, Elijah's return was predicted by Malachi. Here, Jesus re-affirms that John was Elijah returned, but He added that He expected to be treated by the establishment as badly as was His cousin [17:10-13].

Matthew habitually placed a healing between a parable and its interpretation. He did so here with the father of the epileptic son. The teaching moment arrived when the Apostles were unable to cast out the demon. Jesus upbraided, not only the Apostles, but an entire generation of the Jewish People [17:17; "You faithless and perverse generation ... How much longer must I put up with you?"]. Jesus claimed that if the People would have even a miniscule faith, a mountain could be moved from one place to another [17:20]. What made this such a dangerous parable? Herod the Great had completed the Herodium, a vast fortress within a huge man-made mountain, three miles southeast of Bethlehem. Its inner area had a two-hundred-foot diameter, not including the earth-berm which surrounded the fort. He had literally built a mountain. The demonic king had faith enough to build a mountain, while the people had not the faith to cast out a demon. Again, the established powers had faith in their own power, while the People had no faith in themselves, or in the unseen but present Kingdom of Heaven.

An historical note: while the outcome of the Revolt of 66 AD was a foregone conclusion (Rome was not the same as the Seleucid Empire), the Roman victory was made much easier by the disunity of the three Zealot parties. Matthew certainly knew that disunity destroys power [cf.13:15 and 15:8].

Jesus followed the explanation of the parable with a prediction that He would be placed under the power of those whom He denounced as "human hands" [17:22]. In Matthew, is this the result of the little faith of the People, or is it part of God's intention? If the former, it fits His denunciation of their lack of faith. If the latter, God would demonstrate the greater power of the Kingdom through the Crucifixion and Resurrection. That "they [the Disciples] were greatly distressed" [17:23] could signify either a reluctance to see their Master in the hands of their opponents; or it could mean they felt His denunciation of their lack of faith.

Jesus paid His Temple Tax with a shekel coin from the mouth of a fish. He declared that the **sons** (children?) **are free** [17:26]. Free from what? Free in their personal relationship to the Father-God, as opposed to the established idea that one had to pay to support an official relationship.

The Nature of the Kingdom:

Children are unlike adults, but that is obvious. Less obvious is the difference between **"these little ones who believe in me"** [18:6] and the established powers. Adults, and the Pharisees and Sadducees calculate, ponder, scheme. Children just do. Jesus claims that one must simply "do" the Kingdom thing, because it comes out of a clean heart. One must not be looking for advantage. If one is simply humble enough to behave within the Kingdom as a child does naturally, one will be the "greatest" [18:4] in the Kingdom. Weak child-like faith is closer to what God intended in the creation of humanity, than all the human traditions of adults and the powerful.

Whoever leads astray one of the "little ones of Jesus", that is, His Disciples, will be harshly judged [M. 18:6-10]. Certainly, the prediction was manifestly true in 70 AD. It would, indeed, have been better to be drowned than to endure the siege and destruction of Jerusalem.

And more so, if one of the little ones is led astray, the Father-God will search for him. God will rejoice over a restored follower of Jesus, more than over all who never fell to the temptations of the Pharisees and Sadducees [18:12-14]. (An alternative interpretation: God is more concerned to find the lost sinner, than is He with the faithful in the Synagogue/Church. Another alternative:

God is willing to search for a lost Pharisee or Sadducee and would rejoice greatly over his conversion to the Kingdom of Heaven.)

However, that the subject is concerned with fellow members of the Body of Christ, is evidenced by the next verse, which is the rule by which a believer can be restored to fellowship [M.18:15-17] **"If another member of the church sins against you, go and point out the fault when the two of you are alone. If the member listens to you, you have regained that one. But if you are not listened to, take one or two others along with you, so that every word may be confirmed by the evidence of two or three witnesses** [See 2 Corinthians 13:1]. **If the member refuses to listen to them, tell it to the church; and if the offender refuses to listen even to the church, let such a one be to you as a Gentile and a tax collector**. Matthew, the tax collector, must have felt an inward twinge as he wrote that an unrepentant apostate must be **as a... tax-collector to you.** One must inquire: does that mean one who is beyond redemption, or (as in his own case) one who is sought with even greater intensity?

I think it is the latter case. If even two persons wish to bind a reprobate apostate, Jesus will join them, and he will be saved, **For where two or three are gathered in my name, I am there among them** [18:20].

A congruence occurs when St. Peter asks how often one must forgive a fellow Disciple **Then Peter came and said to him, "Lord, if another member of the church sins against me, how often should I forgive? As many as seven times?" Jesus said to him, "Not seven times, but I tell you, seventy-seven times** [18:21-22]. This becomes the occasion for the parable of the unforgiving servant [18:23-35]. Here is an echo of the unforgivable sin noted at [6:14-15]. One wonders who might have caused such a rupture within the ranks of Disciples. It is enough to suggest that the entire chapter dealt with how an apostate is to be treated by the fellowship of Disciples. Certainly, the challenge of 66-71 AD would have caused enough fear and even instances of betrayal within the fellowship. Jesus predicted a falling out within the fellowship, **do not judge** [7:1-5] and, **Do not think that I have come to bring peace to the earth; I have not come to bring peace, but a sword** [10:34]. Did Matthew think the disaster of 70 AD was the predicted sword of judgment?

Because of the prominence of His demand for forgiveness during a time of great disturbance, Matthew thought the Lord required a willingness to restore the apostate within the fellowship must have primary importance.

Getting the Point about Perfection:

The Pharisees tested Jesus yet again. This time their ironic choice was divorce [19:3-9]. The Lord's response illustrated, yet again, the difference between God's intention, and the Law of Moses. The Pharisees and Sadducees viewed the Law as perfect. Jesus saw the *intention of God* as perfection. Thus, the Sermon on the Mount, and the advice to the young man [19:21]: divest yourself from the concerns of this life and follow me. The establishment saw the concerns of this life as central, and the Law as the guide to a perfect application of God's Will. Jesus saw the concerns of this life as antithetical (perhaps even irrelevant) to the concerns of the Kingdom of Heaven.

On the subject of divorce, the teaching of Jesus is very clear. There is no such thing as divorce. The legal fiction of divorce is applicable only after the offense of adultery. That is to say, a spiritual relationship cannot be broken. A relationship may be adjusted legally after one or the other violates one of the Ten Commandments. Yet, this is a concession from God, because men (and women) are hard-hearted and rotten sinners [19:8]. Human affection is untrustworthy. To a divorced and remarried pastor, who has found extraordinary grace in the "God of a Second Chance", this teaching is absolutely correct. One must note the part of the teaching *not expressed*: divorce is not on the list of unforgivable sins. See also, the teachings about the restoration of a fallen brother (or sister).

The reaction of the Disciples is puzzling [19:10-12]. Becoming an eunuch is rather further than "celibacy in singleness". One must delve into the mindset of the Pharisaical life. To them, every Jewish man was intended by God to be a husband and father. Every woman was intended to be a wife and mother. Those roles defined human fulfillment (along with obedience to the Law of Moses and the traditions of the Pharisees and Sadducees). To not become a husband and father is, whether surgical or not, to, in effect, become an eunuch. Jesus, like St. Paul, admits that the cares of marriage and family have the power to distract from the concerns of the Kingdom of Heaven. Yet Jesus (again like St. Paul) permits choice in the matter **For there are eunuchs who have been so from birth, and there are eunuchs who have been made eunuchs by others, and there are eunuchs who have made themselves eunuchs for the sake of the kingdom of heaven. Let anyone accept this who can** [19:12]. Some scholars assume that St. Paul was a widower. Here, [I think] the comparison is between the perfect relationship and the imperfect; and that God's intention is associated with the perfect.

Little children, on the other hand, occupy a different place in the heart of Jesus: **Let the little children come to me, and do not stop them; for it is to such as these that the kingdom of heaven belongs** [19:14]. They are naturally part of the Kingdom of Heaven, because they do not concern themselves with the troubles of the day and are not subject to the heavier restrictions of the Pharisaical life. Most little children do not worry about what they will wear, or what they will eat tomorrow. They live from moment to moment. These, it seems, are characteristics of the Kingdom of Heaven.

Clearly, the teaching about the children and the teaching about the wealthy young man [19:16-22; **If you wish to be perfect, go, sell your possessions, and give the money to the poor, and you will have treasure in heaven; then come, follow me.**] are related. In His explanation, Jesus ties them together: **It is easier for a camel to go through the eye of a needle than for someone who is rich to enter the kingdom of God** [19:23-30]. The rich are concerned about today and tomorrow; about the things of life and wealth. Those concerns tend to interfere with entry into the freedom of the Kingdom. Only the Power of God makes such an entry possible for the wealthy [19:26; **With God all things are possible.**].

St. Peter's question is more than just personal. He requested a "cost/benefit" analysis of the Kingdom. ...**when the Son of Man is seated on the throne of his glory, you who have followed me will also sit on twelve thrones, judging the twelve tribes of Israel. And everyone who has left houses or brothers or sisters or father or mother or children or fields, for my name's sake, will receive a hundredfold, and will inherit eternal life** [19:25-30]. And, of note, Jesus answered that the Kingdom is one-hundred-fold better than the life of the wealthy establishment. That is quite a cost/benefit.

One might ask for some examples of that assessment. Jesus was happy to comply. The parable of the workers in the vineyard presents a rather socialist view of the Kingdom, but only in economic terms. If the subject continues to be "perfection", as it has been to this point, the moral of the story is that the Landowner (God) gives perfection to all who enter, whether early or late [20: 1-16; For the kingdom of heaven is like a landowner who went out early in the morning to hire laborers for his vineyard.].

One may have a different insight to this parable. The Pharisees and Sadducees might have grumbled that Jesus was suggesting an easier way to Heaven. They had restricted themselves, refused many of the delights of life (as, for instance the abstinence of Methodists, or the Baptist prohibition against dance), and these sinners who had not kept the Law of Moses were to be given the same reward?

Continuing the discussion of perfection, Jesus predicted (yet again) that He would suffer at the hands of the powers in Jerusalem [20:17-19]. The mother of James and John ["sons of Zebedee": 10:2] asked for Him to grant that her sons sit next to Him at the "Heavenly Banquet" [20:20-28; my term]. This, essentially, is a request for Him to declare them perfect. Jesus declined, and used the moment to teach about what constitutes perfection within the Kingdom of Heaven. It is, of course, the willingness to serve. That could be the message within the Parable of the Workers and Wages. But it is more. He associated perfection with martyrdom: **the cup** [20:22; Are you able to drink the cup that I am about to drink?]. Martyrs resign everything of this life for the Kingdom of Heaven, just as Jesus was preparing Himself to do. Just as had John the Baptist done. And, just as most of the Apostles had done prior to 70 AD.

Knowing themselves as less than perfect, two blind men, ironically, had the sight to call on Jesus for mercy [20:29-34]. Gaining their sight, they followed Jesus. That is, as blind men, they must have been poor beggars. They had nothing of worth in this world, and all to gain in the Kingdom of Heaven. They chose the perfect way; the way the wealthy young man was unable to grasp.

END LESSON TWO

The Entry of the King of Heaven:

The Palm Sunday account is highly dependent on Zechariah, especially chapters nine to fourteen. Though it is not part of this study, certain things should be noted. Zechariah is a prophecy of the *restoration of Israel, after the rejection of the Messiah King*. Zechariah 9:9 predicts that the King will enter Jerusalem on a colt. Also worthy of note is that the tradition of Judah was that the King was only another brother withing the clan. He was to rise out of the brotherhood of Judah. Thus, the King was to ride a donkey *up* into the City of David from the Kidron. Jesus rode the donkey down from the top of the mount. It was as if to say, this King does not arise from among the brotherhood, but rather comes *down* from Heaven.

God is angered by the leaders/shepherds [Zechariah10:3-6] because the people have no real leaders [Zechariah 10:2-3]. The People (sheep) wander and have no water, they (the shepherds) give empty consolations. God will judge them but *will have compassion on Judah* [Zechariah 10:6].

Zechariah also predicts that the Shepherd (Messiah) will command peace [Zechariah 9:10; and he shall command peace to the nations; his dominion shall be from sea to sea,], but He will be rejected by the People, and will be abused. His value is thirty pieces of silver [Zechariah 11:10-14]. The Covenant shall be broken, as will the relationship between Judah and Israel.

What is noteworthy here, is that the theme of the prophecy is the rejection of Messiah, and the judgment against the leaders of the People. The prophecy is very confused (in the sense that many unrelated things are blended together). It deals with the sixth century BC, the fourth century BC, the time of Jesus, and our present day. Let us leave to others a decoding of its message (and get back to Matthew).

Suffice it to say that the passage predicts, and Jesus fulfills, a triumphal entry into Jerusalem on a colt, followed by a rejection of Messiah, followed by His ultimate triumph.

The Confrontation:

To initiate the confrontation, and identify the opposition, Jesus cleanses the Temple precincts, saying **You (Sadducees) have made it a den of robbers** [21:13]. In stark contrast, Jesus heals or cleanses *without charge* [21:14; The blind and the lame came to him in the temple, and he cured them.]. This (providing services without charge, and the praise of the People) angered the Chief Priests [21:15], but they were apparently silent. His retort was a quote from Psalm 8:2 and 4, which deserves quotation in full (RSV): **Thou whose glory above the Heavens is chanted by the mouths of babes and infants, Thou hast founded a bulwark because of Thy foes, to still the enemy and the avenger. --- What is man that thou art mindful of him, and the *son of man* that thou dost care for him?**

The Psalmist compared the praise of infants, and God's "care" for Messiah, but ignored the prayers and praise of the Priests. That the verse is not a pleasant acceptance of the praise, but rather an indictment of the Priests as the "enemy" of God. See: praise is everywhere...and the Priesthood is silent.

The Fig Tree is the symbol of Israel [21:22]. Jesus' curse against Israel is the hidden meaning in the parable. Israel is never again to bear fruit. Jesus pointed to the southeast at the Herodium, visible on the horizon. By contrast, He said, if His followers have faith, they will be able to cast that man-made [cf. M. 21:19-22] mountain into the sea. That is another way of saying that the Disciples will be able, by prayer, to overthrow Herod's government (and by implication, Rome?).

If this was written after 70 AD, when sixty thousand Jews were enslaved to build the Colosseum in Rome, that is quite a claim!

Demonstrating their lack of vision and insight, the Chief Priest and Elders, are unable or unwilling to identify the source of authority in John the Baptist, and Jesus refused to share with him (them) the Source of His Authority [21:23-27]. However, He voiced another parable of condemnation [21:28-32]: Two sons asked to work in the fields, one said yes and didn't go, the other "no" but went. He, obviously spoke to the Priests, in the presence of the People. The two sons are clearly identified. The Priesthood was called, and failed to do God's Will. Jesus, the other Son, responded and is fulfilling the Will of God. Here is an interesting and useless aside: Prior to His baptism, did Jesus struggle with His calling as Messiah?

He told yet another parable of condemnation [21:33-41]. The Landlord is angry with the tenants, the Jewish Establishment, who do not provide for Him the expected fruits. Having sent His Son, Jesus predicted they will treat Him as their predecessors treated the prophets.

And finally, Jesus expected the Kingdom to be taken away from the establishment of Judea, and given to the Saints [21:42-46; The rented-out vineyard, the cornerstone rejected, etc.]; a People willing and able to produce the fruits of righteousness. To fully understand this prophecy, one must look at the Christian Community of 70 AD. By that date, the divorce between Mosaic Jews and Gentile

Christians had been completed. The "fruits of the vineyard" were evidently produced by the Early Church.

The challenge was accepted by the Priesthood. The People continued to listen to Jesus.

Speaking to the People, Jesus compared the Kingdom to a wedding feast [22:1-13]. This was a dangerous parable, because, as M. noted, the Pharisees were also listening. Those whom God had called and invited to His Feast, had failed to respond, had resisted, had declined His grace. God had then invited any and all sundry. They had responded. However, one of the many failed to appear appropriately. He was ejected from the Festival, and placed (bound) in the outer darkness (which, in the descriptions of Heaven contemporary to M., is the area outside, and separate from, the City of God; a place of damnation). The wedding robe is symbolic of the righteousness of faith (or of acceptance of Jesus as Messiah). In other words, His Disciples had been given the invitation first addressed to the Establishment (Priests, Pharisees and Sadducees). Yet, even they must act appropriately, and be clothed in righteousness. One man, Judas Iscariot, was at the Feast, but was cast out into damnation.

The Pharisees might well have understood His saying: **Many are called, but few are chosen** [22:14]. They felt themselves to be called *and* chosen. Jesus was saying they were not chosen (by God). They tried, once again, to trip Him up. They wanted to upset the popularity He had with the People [22:15-22]. They asked Him whether Rome had authority to tax Judeans. Withholding or cheating on taxes might well have been one of the ways they resisted Rome. In any case, Roman taxes were very unpopular. Jesus cleverly dodged the issue with a higher one. Give the property of the Emperor back to the Emperor. Give to God what belongs to God [22:20]. The Pharisees were willing to do neither, in the view of Jesus.

Having dumb-founded the Pharisees, the Sadducees tried their hand at tripping Jesus [22:23-32]. They denied the resurrection of the dead. They asked a clever, but somewhat childish, legal question. Which husband of seven is married to the six-time-widowed woman? Again, Jesus supplanted one issue with a higher one. God is not concerned with such issues. Marriage is for Earth, not for Heaven. In Heaven, human beings are "like the Angels", that is: beyond physical sexuality. They are spiritual. Within this context, "the living" refers to the spiritual; and the dead [as before at 8:22] are physically alive but without relationship with God. If Abraham, Isaac and Jacob are alive to God, then there must be a life after death, a resurrection. The Sadducees could not fail to understand that Jesus considered them "dead" to God.

The Pharisees had one more chance, in this duel of wits. They asked about the greatest of the commandments [22:34-40]. Of course, Jesus answered with the First of the Ten: **Love God with all your heart, mind, soul and strength**. Perhaps they thought it a peace offering to the Rabbi from Galilee. Jesus would have none of that. His second commandment was a direct challenge to their outward righteousness: **You shall Love** [agape] **your neighbor as yourself. On this hangs all the Law *and* the Prophets!** Here is a statement of deeper spirituality. Only as the Spirit of God grants it, may a person Love his/her neighbor as him/herself. The Pharisees paid strict attention to the amplified Law but ignored the message of the Prophets.

The stunned silence that must have followed such an interchange gave Jesus a chance to ask His question. They all thought they had asked Jesus "unanswerable" questions. In this game of one-ups-man-ship, Jesus proved He had the superior mind, as well as insight. Not only had he already asked them a question they refused to answer [21:23-27], re: the authority of John the Baptist, now He asked another [22:42-46]: Whose son is the Messiah?" They all agreed that Messiah was to be descended from David. Jesus quoted Psalm 110:1.

> **The Lord says to my lord:**
> **"Sit at my right hand, til I I make your enemies your footstool."**
>
> **The Lord sends forth from Zion your mighty scepter (Jesus is the Power of God).**
> **Rule in the midst of your foes!**

The Psalm is clearly a messianic poem. Not only does the Lord God speak of the Lord *over* David, He promises to make Messiah a priest after the order of Melchizedek [22:4; The Lord has sworn and will not change his mind, *"You are a priest for ever after the order Melchizedek*]. Since the Letter to the Hebrews was written prior to Matthew's Gospel, we have the assistance of insight into how the Church interpreted this idea [Tertullian thought the author was Barnabas. So do I.].

Melchizedek was the King of Salem [Genesis 14:8]. He was "Priest of the Most High God". It was, according to tradition, a priestly order of one. There were no priests before, or after, Melchizedek. Barnabas made the case that, as such, Jesus was able to make the one perfect and sufficient sacrifice for sin, thus ending the penalty of the Law of Moses. So, Jesus is greater than David, greater than Melchizedek (who made the offering to God for Abraham), and greater than Abraham. Since He is the fulfillment of the Law of Moses, He is also greater than Moses. All this was implied in the simple quotation of Psalm 110:1.

Jesus Condemns the Scribes, Pharisees, and Sadducees:

Having defeated them in this vigorous debate, Jesus turned to the crowd and condemned His opponents. He was, first, careful to distinguish between the teaching of the Law and the doing of the Law [23:2-12]. At first glance, there seems to be an incongruence between His previously spoken attitude toward the Pharisees, and His urging His Disciples to learn from them and to do the Law [23:3; do whatever they teach you and follow it; but do not do as they do]. However, this may well be within His understanding of the Law as God-given, and the distinction between inward spirituality and outward behavior. Or Matthew may have been aware of how St. Paul had challenged the Christians to complete the law...an impossible task. In any case, these verses are the subject statement for the curses that follow.

Jesus called on the Apostles and Disciples to have no teacher of God [Rabbi] other than He [23:10], and no earthly Jewish father authority [23:9]. Since the sin of the Pharisees is self-confidence and pride, His Disciples and Apostles must elevate other over self. This has interesting implications for religious education and worship leadership. Each one is to be led into understanding by Messiah [after the Resurrection, by the Holy Spirit], and each one is to be led in worship by (or through) Jesus. Therefore, teaching and worship leaders must understand their role with deep humility. It is the Divine, not the leader who is in charge.

The five curses that follow, identify and limit the differences Jesus had with the Pharisees. They are zealous teachers of falsehood [23:13-15], who, by teaching "human traditions" and emphasizing the amplified details of the Law, prevent their students from learning inward righteousness. They engage in esoteric scholastic arguments with no real-world basis [Consider some theological arguments of our day], often in a vain attempt to excuse their own behavior [23:16-22]. They find overly scrupulous means to support the religious hierarchy, while paying too little attention to the true issues of justice and mercy [23:23-27]. In this regard, they pay too little attention to the witness of the Prophets, who, inspired by the Spirit of God, spoke holy words to Israel. Today, too, there are voices of moral legalism that contrast sharply to the Voice of the Love of God. The result is a self-indulgent sense of personal righteousness; the opposite of a righteousness that comes from the Spirit. They fail to value the Voice of the Prophets. Their daily life, values and priorities demonstrate the opposite [23:28-33].

The curse of Jesus is instructive insofar as concerns the Pharisees [23:34-39]. Jesus calls on those who have ministered through the influence of the Holy Spirit: the Prophets, [including the Priest Zechariah who exhorted the People to rededicate themselves to completion of the Temple during the time of Darius] to witness against the Pharisees. However, in vs. 36, the definition of "you" changes from the Pharisees to the entire People of Jerusalem. They will all suffer the judgment against the Pharisees, and by implication any and all who resist the work of the Spirit of God [23:32-33; Fill up, then, the measure of your ancestors. You snakes, you brood of vipers! How can you escape being sentenced to Gehenna?], especially the work of the Spirit in and through Jesus. The blessing of God is removed from them until and unless they will bless the One who comes in God's Name, i.e., Jesus [23:39; For I tell you, you will not see me again until you say, 'Blessed is the one who comes in the name of the Lord.].

END LESSON THREE

Jesus Predicts the Destruction of the Temple:

Many scholars believe that the prediction of destruction, and the instruction to flee, is not authentic to Jesus, but, rather, is the content of an Holy Spirit prophecy and warning given to the Church sometime after 65, but before 70 AD.

The Church may well have preserved an authentic prophecy by Jesus at 24:1-2; **not one stone will be left here upon another**. Matthew 24:32-35 ["From the fig tree learn its lesson: as soon as its branch becomes tender and puts forth its leaves, you know that summer is near. So also, when you see all these things, you know that he is near, at the very gates. Truly I tell you, this generation will not pass away until all these things have taken place. Heaven and earth will pass away, but my words will not pass away.] is possibly another of the authentic prophecies of Jesus. His words will not pass away or disappear, even though the Fig Tree (Israel) is judged and will be destroyed.

Many of the Jerusalem Christians fled Judea at some time during the Zealot revolt against Rome. Matthew 24:15-22 constitutes that first warning to flee.

Matthew 24:3-14 seems to be a post 70 AD reflection on the bitter experience of the Community during those dangerous years: false prophecies, especially of the immediate return of Christ, Roman torture and executions, betrayal, apostasy, anarchy and fear. One finds the distress of the Church reflected today in the persecution of Christians in many places. One can imagine the disappointment of the Christian Community at the failure of the Messiah's return. Faced with such immense violence, they surely hoped and prayed for deliverance. However, after the city's destruction, the Community revalued its expectations. **The End is not yet** [24:6]. The mission of the Church remains, and is, indeed, enlarged. The Good News must be expressed to the ends of the Earth before the Christ will return [24:14].

Matthew noted the relationship between this prophetic warning, and the prophecy of Daniel 9:25-27. The Prophecy called "Weeks of Years", most current scholars believe, was ancient (the time of the Exile), and clearly references Rome as the fourth empire, and at 483 years after the restoration proclamation of Cyrus, predicts the day of the Crucifixion. The prophecy also noted the pouring out of wrath, a desolating sacrilege. The Early Church clearly understood Daniel to refer to their time, and the judgment against Jerusalem (and the Jerusalem Establishment) [the 3 ½ years].

It is very possible that, under the influence of the Holy Spirit, Matthew (himself) felt the Savior speaking to him and quoted the Lord in Matthew 24:23-31. Indeed, such an experience could well be the motivation for the entire composition of the Gospel. While the Lord delays the Return, He expresses it with a new grandeur. Vs. 30 is an unfortunate, though long traditional translation. Coming on the clouds could have been properly translated, "coming with the Spiritual Giants" [Nephilim: cf. Gen. 6:4]. The Nephilim are associated with angelic beings and are strong warriors.

Matthew 24:31 [And he will send out his angels with a loud trumpet call, and they will gather his elect from the four winds, from one end of heaven to the other.] follows with a command to send out these angelic warriors to gather the Elect from "one end of Heaven to the other", i.e., the total of Heaven and Earth. This way of translating vs. 30 avoids the obvious difficulty of all the Earth seeing the return at the same time, as well as the questionable use of water-vapor as a mode of transportation. Verses. 36-42 continue the prophecy of the Return and are yet another indication that the Nephilim are the intended companions of the Lord (rather than clouds). Today, more often than not, we interpret these verses as meaning that the Return will be sudden and unexpected. This is surely proper but ignores the relationship of the prophetic story of Noah to the Nephilim. Both humanity and "the sons of God" along with their offspring were judged. By implication, the Return will be a judgment, not just of Earth, but of the total of Heaven and Earth (cf. Revelation to John).

The final paragraph of chapter twenty-four is so out of character with both Jesus and Matthew that one wonders the conditions that produced it. The idea that Jesus would speak of dismembering his opponents, or that Matthew would decry one who eats with drunks, betrays immense distress. Does he intend to criticize the steward of the Jerusalem Community who, perhaps, failed to properly distribute foodstuffs within the Community? However, the warning remains pertinent. The Return is a promise with an indefinite date.

Greeting Messiah:

These are, according to most scholars, authentic (to Jesus) parables. They fit His character and message, though Matthew may have placed them in a context other than the original. We should interpret them with caution because, by doing so, he may well have changed the meaning of the parables.

The Parable of the Wise and Foolish Virgins [25:1-13] is used by Matthew with a sharp edge of judgment against Jerusalem. Preached prior to the arrest, the meaning could well have been: Messiah is here; how will you receive Him? It could have been an appeal to the wise virgins. With the benefit of hindsight, Matthew has transfigured this parable into the emphasis on the foolish virgins who are now in the outer darkness. The changed (and now negative) emphasis demonstrates, yet again, how Matthew felt about the Sadducees and Priests.

The second parable is also considered authentic to Jesus. The Parable of the Talents [25:14-30] may also show a changed meaning. In the original instance, Jesus may have meant that the Jerusalem Establishment (Priests, Sadducees and Pharisees) had failed to produce the fruits of the Kingdom of Heaven, and thus is to be thrust aside. In the latter circumstance, the parable stands as a challenge to the Christian Community to produce the sacred fruits of faith. It may also reflect Matthew's. conclusion that the Christian Community is, in fact, the faithful stewards who enter into the joy of their Master. Even if one chooses the latter interpretations, they must be juxtaposed against the earlier, in which Jesus expressed an "if-then" evaluation of the Jerusalem Establishment. The parable, in that form, would have been very dangerous to the continued good health of Jesus (the definition of a parable).

The third parable is very clearly one of judgment [25:31-46]. The sheep and the goats are placed before Messiah, who must select those who belong to His flock. There are two questions implied: who are the sheep, and who are the goats, and why are some selected while others are not.

There are, again, a number of possible answers. In the original instance, Jesus may have meant the difference between His Disciples, and those of the Pharisees. Both purport to be doing the Will of God. Given the differences between them, one group must be in error. In that case, Jesus points out the guiding principles of the approaching judgment. They are basically a generous philanthropy from within, rather than from obedience to an exterior commandment. One must feed the hungry, clothe the naked, greet the alien, visit the imprisoned, and tend the sick. All of these require a personality of giving, a personality of humility; the kind of person described in the Sermon on the Mount [5:2-12; The Beatitudes].

On the other hand, "the nations", that is all humanity, gather before the Lord. On the basis of the philanthropic heart, Jesus judges each person as a sheep of His fold, or a goat to be cast away. Matthew may well have seen this as a test to be applied to Gentile Christians as well as Jewish Christians.

If Jesus used the term "nations", the sheep may be His Disciples, while Rome and Judea, along with many another state may be the goats. Most likely however, Jesus expanded the role of judgment attributed to the Messiah. He would certainly have been familiar with Isaiah 49:6; that it is too small an assignment that Messiah should go only to Israel. Instead, Messiah is instructed to be a **light to the nations, that My salvation may reach to the end of the Earth.**

This idea was attractive to the Early Church. It informed their sense of mission, and it predicts the Great Commission [28:19-20]. If so, there is yet another perspective on the parable. Like the wheat and the weeds, Matthew has turned his attention to the Christian Community, and especially the apostate element around the time of the Jewish Revolt. They, indeed, cry out "Lord, Lord", but have turned their back on the needs of the Community. As refugees, the Christian exiles from Judea would have experienced great need along the line Jesus laid out. They were the aliens in need of clothing and food, visitation and medicine, etc. Perhaps there were Christians (or Jews?) who refused to share. In view of the socialist organization of the Christian Community [having all things in common; Acts 2:44], this would have been a serious violation. That this final idea is most appropriate to Matthew might be seen within the final judgment, that whoever cares for the needs of **one of My brothers or sisters** [24:45; as several translations have it] is blessed.

A final note on this chapter of Matthew's. Gospel: vs 31 must be consistent with 24:30 (the Son of Man coming "on the clouds" or with the Angelic Host). Here Jesus specifically notes that He will come with the Angels, the Spiritual Giants, the "Sons of God" [Noah; Genesis 6:1-4].

The Passion of Jesus:

Unless someone (e.g., Joseph of Arimathea) who was present shared this information with the Church, [26:2-5] is purely surmise. Matthew is not specific here. One might easily believe that High Priest Caiaphas met with the Elders to draw up a warrant against Jesus, but the attribution of this journalistic enterprise is missing.

How typical of Jesus, that He should be staying at the home of Simon the Leper [26:6-13]. And, how wonderfully appropriate that an unnamed woman should anoint Him. Most preachers will identify this woman with other women in other Gospels. Again, documentation is missing. One seems a bit fussy about this, because the historical discipline allows attribution in other circumstances, but not in this. Prior to cross-referencing, or a report of a meeting is presented, some kind of evidence is required that a reliable witness was present. And when a woman does something as spectacular as this, her name ought to be remembered. One notes that Matthew can't (or doesn't want to) remember the name of the landlord where the Feast of Preparation was to take place [25:18] and calls him "a certain man".

What is of greater importance is that these two events are the background for the real drama of the day: Judas Iscariot betrayed the Lord for thirty pieces of silver [26:14-16], recalling the prophecy of Zechariah [11:10-14]; The Lord's Last Supper [26:17-29, 36-30] recalling the first Passover; The Time of Temptation in the Garden of Gethsemane [26:36-46] recalling the Temptations in the desert [4:1-11]; the Protestations of the Apostles [26:21-25, 31-35]; The Arrest [26:47-50, 55-56]; Disciple's Violence [26:51-54]; The Indictment Hearing [26:57-68]; and Peter's Denial [26:33-35, 69-75]. Along with these vignettes, Matthew presented a theme: These events fulfill prophecies [26:2, 13, 30-32, 54-56a, 74].

In previous decades, scholars insisted that these events are literary constructs, designed by Matthew (or others) to justify their status as a redemptive community. Those scholastics (a majority) were openly agnostic about the Resurrection. However, in the past thirty years or so, majority opinion among professional researchers has changed. The consensus now is that these events are historically correct. They reason that the combined accounts create a narrative so dangerous (just like the parables) that he [Matthew] could have faced the immediate and cruel persecution of Rome. Something like meeting the Risen Jesus is the only plausible explanation for his daring to write such a document. One is reminded that Nero was Emperor when Matthew began his task, and Vespasian or Titus ruled when he published. None of the three would have welcomed his work.

Perhaps that is reason enough for his emphasis on the fulfillment of prophecy. Matthew presented what he considered to be the evidence that One who is more powerful than the Emperor has come, and that, indeed, all earthly powers have been (or are about to be) overthrown.

The account of the Feast of Preparation is notable in Matthew as he emphasized the betrayal [26:20-25]. Matthew seems to indicate that the betrayal was anticipated and expected by Jesus. Moreover, Judas' sin is symptomatic of the later denials and betrayals of all the Apostles (they all fled at the time of the arrest). This is one side of a literary tension, one of defeat.

The other side of the tension (one of victory) in this account is the statement that Jesus would not drink wine until the Kingdom comes [26:29]. One suspects that Matthew expected to see Jesus almost immediately after the destruction of Jerusalem.

The time of prayer in the Garden is presented as an inward struggle by Jesus to be obedient [26:36-46]. Indeed, obedience is a major part of "perfection" [Cf. 5:48 and 19:21]. Luke is different insofar as he presents the same narrative but sets it out as a time of temptation. One notes in Luke 4:13, that Satan departed until a "more opportune time". The Garden, in Luke, seems to be that time. Matthew reflected the inward struggle, making Jesus more "human" and understandable to those who struggle with the same sort of issue, especially at the end of the sixth decade.

The arrest and the protestations of the Apostles continues a narrative that connects the Christians of 66-70 AD with the person of their Lord. Would the Lord approve of a violent response to the oppressions of Rome? Would Jesus endorse the revolt by the Zealots? Matthew answers, "no" [26:52-54]. This is of critical importance to us as the world confronts the continued and appalling violence of Evil. Muslim violence leads many Christians to consider a violent response. Any such consideration must include this radical difference between Jesus and Mohammed. Matthew asserts that God would send four times the number of legions as Rome employed against the rebels of Judea, should Jesus ask it. The difficult question for His followers, then and now, is whether to ask Him for that kind of support or not.

This is precisely the point at which my faith is troubled. Has the Church of Jesus Christ compromised His position to the point of non-compliance, just as had the Pharisees and Sadducees compromised the Law of Moses by amplification? Would Jesus have us endure the persecutions, calling on the Legions of Angels, and trusting our God even to the point after death? The shoe hurts when it is on my foot.

The indictment hearing is notable in two respects. First is the historical witness that Jesus had already been beaten when He was turned over to the Romans [26:67-68]. Of interest to historians is the recent awareness of the juridical procedures in Jerusalem at that time. The description perfectly fits what we have learned, much to the amazement of a previous generation of Biblical scholars. Only when the Priest put Jesus under oath, did Jesus respond to the accusations. Mark adds the words "I am" at the beginning of Jesus' response [Mark 14:62], which would have been the Holy Name of God. It would have been even more offensive to the Priests than His claim that he would return with the Nephilim [26:64]. Even here Matthew presents the theme of prophecy and fulfillment. Those at the hearing demanded that Jesus prove His credentials as Messiah, as if all He had already done was not enough [26:68]. Matthew's remark, that **"when morning came"** [27:1] the priests conferred and ruled, is not just a passing notation. Jewish law prohibited a hearing or trial during the night. They had to wait until dawn to pass judgment.

Little needs to be said of Peter's Denials. Peter's execution was to Matthew a recent event. Martyrs have an effect. Even one's denial of the Lord may lead to higher discipleship. Those whose denials under threat at the time of the Revolt were given by Matthew a second chance to serve. One must repent with tears, and (as St. John put it) feed the sheep.

Matthew returned to his theme of prophecies fulfilled:

- 26:2: Jesus predicts that the Son of Man will be sacrificed as the Passover lamb.

- 26:13: the woman is, in fact, remembered in the Gospel of Matthew, just as Jesus said it would.

- 26:30-32: Zechariah [13:7] predicted that the Shepherd Messiah would be struck and that the sheep would scatter, just as they had done after the death of Stephen and in 66-70 AD

- 26:54-56a: Jesus asked how the prophetic scriptures could be fulfilled unless He be arrested and executed.

- And finally: 26:33-34 and74: Jesus predicted Peter's three denials, and after the third denial the cock crowed. These fulfillments, placed as they are, provide a backdrop to the supra-cosmic events.

All Heaven and Earth are united in Jerusalem as Jesus is Tried, Crucified, and Resurrected.

Pontius Pilate is known in Roman history as one of the most violent of Procurators. His wife is remembered by the Orthodox as having become a Christian and a Saint [27:19]. Shortly after dawn the Priest convened a court ("conferred") and voted a bill of indictment against Jesus. He was then transferred to Pilates' authority for judgment [27:1-2].

Even Judas Iscariot gives witness [27:3-10] to the innocence of Jesus (meaning that Judas understood that what Jesus had said and done proved that He was Messiah). Matthew noted, as he had previously [26:14-16], that what Judas was doing was also predicted by Jeremiah [Jer. 32:9 And I bought the field at Anathoth from my cousin Hanamel, and weighed out the money to him, seventeen shekels of silver.]. Matthew combined several prophecies, one from Zechariah (in which no field is mentioned) and Jeremiah (who bought a field for burial purposes). Some think that Matthew associated the notion of "blood-money" and Jeremiah's field in order to make a prophetic point.

That Pilate asked Jesus whether He was the King of the Jews [27:11], indicates the nature of the indictment. The so-called crime of Jesus, that which so offended the High Priest, was that He used the Holy Name in reference to Himself. That would not have been a crime under Roman Law, and so they accused Him of sedition against Caesar. Jesus apparently refused to "enter a plea" [27:12]. Whether that was wisdom, a refusal of the Holy to relate to Evil, obedience to Jewish Law (to not have social interchange with non-Jews, a Law He broke when speaking to the Samaritan Woman, for instance), or that He was already exhausted (by this time He had been awake for 28 hours, and without food for twelve [?]) cannot be determined. Pilate next asked Jesus whether He was aware of the list of indictments [27:13; "many charges"]. This is pro-forma legal detail not often noted by Bible Scholars. That Jesus refused to answer may have been the best defense, because Pilate had no idea how to proceed [27:14]. Grasping at an available excuse, Pilate offered to release Jesus or (according to tradition) a Zealot who was guilty of murder [27:15]. There is a great pun in the linking of the two names: Yeshua Son of God, or Yeshua son of a father (or Yeshua the bastard). The crowd chose the violent revolutionary rather than the non-violent resister [27:20-23]. Pilate had, thus far, acted legally. Faced with an angry mob, during the Passover celebration (as per, police facing a mob on Mardi Gras), Pilate began to act from his police authority rather than as a judge. He thought that no one would object, and he tried to release Jesus [27:24] into their custody (as might a Sheriff release to the mob for a lynching). Matthew had seen or heard of the massacre at Jerusalem in 70 AD. The gutters flowed with blood up to the ankle. He saw that as God's reprisal against the people who had condemned the Lord. Thus, Matthew included that very unfortunate phrase: **His Blood be upon us and our children** [27:25]. It is unfortunate because, while Matthew condemned only the Established parties, the Christian Church has, on all too many occasions, seen fit to condemn all Jews. And the penalty has already been paid out in full [70AD].

Unlike his attention to the observance by the Priest and Council of the niceties of Jewish law, Matthew's account of the torture of Jesus [27:26-31] does not include a legal rationale. One might note that it was not exactly extraordinary. It was, however, brutal. Because the Roman flagrum had three straps, each with a lead barbell at the end, Jesus was struck one hundred twenty times. Evidence suggests that two soldiers, one on His right and one on His left administered the whipping, which would extend from His shoulders to his calves. Each time the lead struck His skin, a piece of flesh from the size of a dime to that of a quarter would explode from His body. Jesus was greatly in danger of death from this experience. A non-Roman would not pass thirty-nine strokes for fear of the death of the victim, which would be counted as a homicide. This on a man who had been awake now for thirty hours, and without food or water for eighteen [?]. Yet Matthew paid little attention to the brutality of the flogging, paying greater attention to the mocking by the soldiers [27:27-31]. He apparently considered that to be the greater sin: The Evil (demonic) authority of Rome mocking the Ultimate Authority of God embodied in Jesus. Even here, Matthew turned his Gospel into a "political" treatise: Jesus was hailed as King of the Jews, which, of course, He was and is. Not only that, had the soldiers been aware, Matthew believed, they would have known Him to be their King as well.

Simon of Cyrene is named [27:32]. As a historian, I can only conclude that he became a Christian, and is one of the sources of the Crucifixion Account. Considering the brutality of the flogging (the open wounds to shoulder, back, and legs), physicians have never attributed His inability to carry a beam, weighing perhaps one hundred pounds, to weakness. His injuries were already so great that He was near death.

Crucifixion was well known to persons who lived within the bounds of the Roman Empire. Everyone knew how it was done, what was anticipated, and so on. Before nailing Him to the crossbeam, the soldiers offered Him a drink of wine with gall [Gk: "chole" -an acidic poison, sour] intended to deaden the pain a bit, and hasten death [27:34]. He refused the poison, Matthew perhaps believed, because He was fulfilling prophecy, and was not intended to die by poison [27:33-44]. Again, Matthew continued the theme of mockery. The soldiers printed a sign with the charge against Him: "Yeshua Rex Jude", confirming the charge made by the Priest [27:37]. The common people mocked, as did the Priest and Elders who came to witness their judgment. If they said what Matthew quotes, the meaning can be either mockery or an attempt to self-justify [27:41-43]. It could have been their attempt to prove to themselves that their judgment was correct. If the judgment were false, they could have, perhaps, ushered in the poltical kingdom they expected (as opposed to the one Jesus preached).

The Death of Jesus:

Historical notation: Some historians have noted that (according to our calendar) April 3, 33 AD was a Friday upon which Passover began at Sundown; that there was an eclipse of the moon on that day, and that a moderate earthquake occurred in the area [27:45, 51].

Since Jesus had already provided proof of His Authority over death, it seems plausible to Matthew that tombs should be opened at the moment of His death [27:52]. However, reason is lacking in this verse, as prior to the Resurrection, there were no Saints. This may have been, instead, a note of encouragement for his own generation of Saints, and thus fit his theme.

Jesus cried out about His feeling of abandonment [27:46]. Most scholars link this to a theology of judgment; that Jesus (looking into Hell) felt Himself separated from the Father-God. St. Peter touched this theme [I Pe. 3:19; he went and made proclamation to the imprisoned spirits—]. Matthew paired it with the "too-little-too-late" hope that Jesus was calling Elijah. The irony in this pairing is that Jesus had already taught that John the Baptist was Elijah returned, and this, then, was the moment of Judgment.

Jesus **cried out with a loud voice** [27:50] and **breathed His last**. Many of the physicians who have studied the Crucifixion believe that Jesus died of a heart attack caused by either a blood clot from the torture, or from stress on the heart itself. Some, however, notice that by hanging the body from the wrists, and nailing through the heel, the entire weight of the body was supported by the diaphragm. After three hours, and considering the violence the body had already experienced (not to mention the dehydration), Jesus may well have been aware that His ability to breathe was coming to an end due to paralysis. He, therefore, lifted Himself one last time, and screamed out all the air in His lungs, bringing death within five more minutes.

I have speculated that the Centurion [27: 54] might well be Cornelius whom Peter baptized [Acts 10:1ff]. My reasoning is that the terror he felt witnessing the earthquake and eclipse at the time of the Lord's death, witnessed to by Matthew, may well have led him into the fellowship of Christians. His name would be remembered. All the more so after 70 AD, as if to note that not all Romans were Evil. By 70 AD, of course, more Christians were Gentiles than Jewish. It is, however, only speculation.

Matthew continued with a list of those who witnessed the Crucifixion, including Mary Magdalene, Mary (wife of Zebedee) and Joseph of Arimathea [27:57-60]. He has listed persons who enjoyed some fame among the Christian Community. Joseph stands out for an act of daring. It was no small thing to declare himself a disciple [talmid] of Jesus on the day of His execution. Joseph fulfilled the Law by having Jesus removed from the cross and buried before the beginning of Passover. (The NRSV has it: **When it was evening** [27:57]. However, the Complete Jewish Bible (CJB) translates it: **Towards evening....**) Apparently, the Early Church considered the testimony of the two women to be valid (A feminist point?). Matthew said **they provided for him** [27:55]. Some scholars suggest that they [the women] were the source of financial support. However that may be, the CJB translates the same passage as **they helped Him**. They testified that they watched the burial [27:61].

Matthew insisted that the Priest testified against himself [27:62-66]. By placing a guard at the Tomb, he guaranteed that the Disciples did not steal the body. There is more than a hint of irony in Matthew's. assertion.

The Resurrection:

An aftershock of the Friday earthquake rolled the stone away from the Tomb, and the guards fainted (either from fear of the earthquake or from the appearance of an Angel whom they saw roll the stone back) [28:1-2].

The Angel announced the Resurrection to the two Marys, and (to add to the confusion of the scholars) said that the women would see Jesus in Galilee [28:5-7; But the angel said to the women, "Don't be afraid. I know you are looking for Yeshua, who was executed on the stake. He is not here, because he has been raised — just as he said! Come and look at the place where he lay. Then go quickly and tell the *talmidim*, 'He has been raised from the dead, and now he is going to the Galil ahead of you. You will see him there.' Now I have told you." CJB]. Our usual translations seem to suggest that Jesus was to precede the Apostles. According to Luke/Acts, they didn't leave Jerusalem until after Pentecost. Still, this doesn't help, because Jesus met the women with a "Shalom" and instructed the Apostles to go to Galilee [28:9-10]. Matthew reported that the Apostles did so, and met Jesus on the Mount of the Transfiguration [28:16-17]. He does not say that they went immediately. Perhaps some of the Disciples went, and others stayed in Jerusalem. They may have gone at a later date. In any case, his account differs from Luke/Acts.

Matthew completed his account of the subterfuge of the Priests with a bribe to the guards and a lie to the public [28:11-15]. That the guards told the Priest **everything that had happened** [28:11], doubles the guilt of the Priests, because they perjured themselves knowingly. They rejected the true report of their own guards. This accusation, post 70 AD, is a final denunciation of those who had, in the opinion of Matthew, brought such a disaster to Judea and especially to Jerusalem.

The Great Commission:

The Great Commission [28:18-20] transfers Messianic Authority to the Apostolic Church; from the Jerusalem Community to the Gentile Community; from Jewish Jerusalem to "the world"! It is the voice of the Judge declaring the consequence of the great sin of the Pharisees, Sadducees, Scribes, and Elders of Jerusalem.

One question intrigues me. What does the Lord mean by "the age"? Clearly a new age has begun. But is it post 33 AD, or post 70 AD? How long did Matthew expect the "age" to last? And, of course, does it matter what he thought at all?

Peter's Conclusion:

Matthew presented his Gospel as good news for the Post-Pauline Gentile Church. While some Jews remained within the fellowship, most left after 70 AD. The Gospel is, among other meanings, a polemic against the Jerusalem Establishment. Matthew condemns the hypocrisy of outward righteousness and inward sin. He condemns the Establishment: those who are not inwardly righteous but met the expectations of the amplified Law of Moses. They were beyond the boundary of God's Community. He condemned the lack of spiritual power within the Establishment evidenced by the miracles of Jesus in contrast to the rituals of judgment within the Temple Community. To Matthew the blessed of God were the poor: those who desired inward righteousness; those who had no influence in the "world of affairs" and few financial resources. He approved hose who withdrew from the politics of the day into a life of grace and generosity; a life that was content to pass each day within the Fellowship of Jesus' Friends, and, most especially, those who held no moral debts against anyone.

A noteworthy question: How does Matthew define the Kingdom of God/Kingdom of Heaven? What are the relative portions of Earth and Heaven within the Kingdom? Is it primarily an Earthly Fellowship with the spiritual presence of Jesus, or, is it primarily a spiritual realm with an Earthly (anticipatory) Fellowship?

Matthew raised questions beyond the scope of his Gospel.

- Was Matthew aware of St. Paul's [Rom. 12:18] **In so far as it depends on you, live peaceably with all**?

- Or of Romans chapter three, in which the Apostle describes sinners who have not known "the Way of Peace", and are eager to shed human blood?

- Did Matthew expect that Christians would (and ought) flee from bloodshed and war?

- Was, to Matthew, the only proper response of a Christian, to turn the other cheek?

- Was Jesus' message, according to Matthew (and did he represent the entire Christian Community in this), a message of complete non-resistance to the evils of the world (apart from continually evangelizing)?

- Is the *quietest* message of Matthew appropriate for Christians today, especially as we face the continuing violence of Islam?

OR:

- Was Matthew's. message intended only for his contemporaries?

- Was the Church willing to take other measures for defense?

  ☐ Historians suggest they did not.

- Should we, today, feel bound by Matthew's message of peace?

GOSPEL OF MARK

I am a runner. I had the beginnings of heart disease, and my doctor told me, "Peter, you will run or you will die". Rather strong encouragement, don't you think? I started running later in life. My first workouts were really hard. I was unable to run a quarter mile (one lap at the track) without walking to catch my breath. But I knew that, if I were to live, I must run. A year later, I ran my first marathon.

Mark tells us the same thing: "Run or die". His words are different, and also the definition of "die"; but the meaning is the same. Start running now, or you will not be ready when running is demanded.

The day of the race has been set. Just as I had a set amount of time to prepare for that first twenty-six-mile race, so you and I have a set time to prepare to live or to die. We'd better be working out regularly, or we will not be prepared for the race.

Mark doesn't begin his Gospel with stories about the Birth of Christ, or His childhood, or the genealogy of the Lord's family. He undoubtedly knew all those things, since he was one of the Apostles [Though not one of the original twelve]. Obviously, he just didn't care about those things. He had something much more important on his mind. He thought, I must get this word out to people, because the time is short.

And so, Mark began with an abrupt announcement. This book is **the good news about Jesus the Messiah,** [Greek: Christou] **the Son of God!** He is the One about whom Isaiah spoke hundreds of years earlier, saying; [Isaiah 40:3] **Prepare the way for the Lord, make straight paths for him.** In plain words: The predicted Christ has arrived, and you (reader) have a short time to accept Him.

He was preceded, not only by Isaiah, but by John the Baptist. Like Mark, the Baptizer demanded an immediate decision. John knew that the One was coming. But even he was surprised when his cousin Jesus stepped into the water next to him. They had known each other since early childhood [see Luke chapter one]. We need not be surprised to learn that John had no idea that Jesus was the Messiah. Apparently, even though Jesus was an extraordinary boy, the moment of decision and acceptance occurred to him at the shore of the Jordan River. From that moment on, Jesus was committed to the ministry of the Messiah, the Christ.

Mark didn't dwell on the Temptations of Christ, as did Luke [4:1-13]. He simply mentioned them. Mark had more urgent matters before him. His concern wasn't so much what happened to Jesus, as much as the requirement for you and me to IMMEDIATELY come to a saving faith in Him.

Take note of the urgency with which Mark related his message. He used the word for immediately twelve times.

[1:30] **they immediately told Jesus about her** (Simon's Mother-in-Law was ill and Jesus healed her).

[1:42] **Immediately the leprosy left him and he was cleansed.**

[2:8] **Immediately Jesus knew in his spirit that this was what they were thinking in their hearts**

[5:29] **Immediately her bleeding stopped**

[5:42] **Immediately the girl stood up and began to walk around**

[6:27] **So he immediately sent an executioner with orders to bring John's head.**

[6:45] **Immediately Jesus made his disciples get into the boat** (Jesus walks on water)

[6:50] **they all saw him and were terrified. Immediately he spoke to them and said, "Take courage! It is I.**

[9:20] **When the spirit saw Jesus, it immediately threw the boy into a convulsion.**

[9:24] **Immediately the boy's father exclaimed, "I do believe; help me overcome my unbelief!"**

[10:52] **said Jesus, "your faith has healed you." Immediately he received his sight.**

[14:72] **Immediately the rooster crowed the second time.**

Each of these passages relates to the Authority of Jesus. Whatever he does or says brings about an immediate response. Now back to Mark's account.

He skipped over the first portions of the other synoptic gospels [Matthew, and Luke] to the point at which John was arrested by Herod. Mark used that event as a signal. **Jesus went into Galilee, proclaiming the good news of God. "The time has come," he said. "The kingdom of God has come near. Repent and believe the good news"** [1:14-15]! Indeed, the time has come. Respond now, before it is too late.

And with that sudden proclamation, Jesus began to assemble the group of Apostles. There is no account of Andrew inviting Peter to meet Jesus. Jesus simply invites Andrew and Peter to **follow me, and I will make of you fishers of men** [1:16-18]. And **without delay** he called Zebedee's sons, James and John [1:19-20].

Not only that, according to Mark's chronology on the first Sabbath [Q: does "first Sabbath" have hidden meanings?], His teaching inspired fear in an impure spirit who called out, **"know You…You are God's Holy One** [1:24]. At this, Jesus commanded that the demonic spirit leave the man. Shrieking [dramatic word; Gk: phonesan phone; cried out in a loud voice], the demon left him [1:26]. And, the people were amazed by His Authority [1:28]. Barclay has it: "Personal Authority". When Jesus taught, He didn't quote earlier "authorities". Mark implied what Matthew made plain in the Sermon on the Mount: **You have heard that it was said to the men of old… But I say to you** [Matthew 5: 21-22]. The demon understood His Authority, but the congregants didn't. They questioned among themselves, **What is this? A new teaching** [Mark 1:27]?

So, Mark's chronology has less to do with the proper order of events than that it is concerned with a dramatic announcement. Here is the Messiah. Recognize Him. Worship Him. Serve Him. He has never-seen-before Authority.

Jesus healed the sick with that amazing Authority, and his fame spread rapidly. So rapidly, in fact, that He felt He had to command that people stop talking about it [1:44], a command that was readily disobeyed.

When he returned to Capernaum, and the paralyzed man was dropped through the roof on a pallet, Jesus healed him by saying, **Your sins are forgiven** [2:5]. This is the beginning of the controversy that would lead to the crucifixion and resurrection. Apparently, the people were content to have a "healer", but forgiving sins was the function of the religious establishment. To forgive sins, by simply announcing that they had been forgiven, was too much [note Catholic/Protestant difference on priest/pastor forgiving sins]. They considered it blasphemous [2:6].

Jesus responded by declaring that "the Son of Man" has Authority over sins and forgiveness [2:10]. A great deal of ink has been applied to the term "Son of Man". One easy meaning is that Jesus is the "representative man" through which humanity will be restored to its proper (Edenic) relationship with God. [**Commentary Critical and Explanatory on the Whole Bible**; Robert Jamieson, A. R. Fausset and David Brown, 1871] The term has references in Ezekiel and Daniel, and was used extensively by Jesus.

We have a second name for Matthew at 2:17: "Levi son of Alphaeus" [Saint Matthew]. His calling is the opportunity for the announcement of a great spiritual dynamic. **It is the ill who need a physician** [2:17]. That is to say, only those who are aware of their separation and alienation from the God of

Love, the Father, the Creator; only those who are aware of their need which may be reached by the saving grace of Christ. If one denies his/her sinfulness, he/she may not be saved.

Thus far, Mark has told us: This is the Savior. He has Authority over illness, demons, and sin. You'd better pay attention, because sinners and demons recognize Him.

With that, Mark turns toward the content of the controversy between Jesus and Jerusalem: the law.

Jesus has a new message. It can't be fit into the old system of legalistic obedience to the enlarged rules of Moses. You mustn't put new wine into old wineskins [2:21-22], and **The Sabbath was made for man, not man for the Sabbath** [2:27]. These insights put the light on all that is to come. They are a direct challenge to the Jewish system of the Jerusalem establishment.

Jesus was angered by the indifference to suffering among those who observed the Sabbath legalistically [3:1-6]. His violation of "Sabbath rest" in the healing of a man with a palsied hand, led the Pharisees to plot against Him with the Herodians. In Mark's eyes, Jesus was intentionally challenging them. And they understood the challenge.

With that challenge, Jesus began to assemble his "team". He chose the twelve Apostles: [3:14-19] **that they might be with him and that he might send them out to preach and to have authority to drive out demons. These are the twelve he appointed: Simon (to whom he gave the name Peter), James son of Zebedee and his brother John (to them he gave the name Boanerges** [say: bo-an-erg-es]**, which means "sons of thunder"), Andrew, Philip, Bartholomew, Matthew, Thomas, James son of Alphaeus, Thaddaeus, Simon the Zealot and Judas Iscariot, who betrayed him** [Note: Levi has become Matthew, and apparently his brother, James the son of Alphaeus, has joined the group].

Against this backdrop, Mark points out that His family thought He had **lost his mind** [3:20-21], and the representatives of the Jerusalem establishment thought he was **possessed by Beelzebul** [3:22]!

Verses 23-25 give an answer to a very old question; what are the unforgiveable sins? Matthew gave us one, **For if you forgive other people when they sin against you, your heavenly Father will also forgive you. But if you do not forgive others their sins, your Father will not forgive your sins** [Matthew 6:14-15]. Mark gives us the only other: **whoever blasphemes against the Holy Spirit will never be forgiven; they are guilty of an eternal sin** [3:29]. The context sheds light on the question. The people from Jerusalem attributed the Authority in Jesus to Beelzebul, not to the Holy Spirit active in the Christ. In other words, one who, in the face of the evidence, attributes evil to the work of Christ stands unforgiven. Reject Christ, and you reject all possibility of salvation.

This insight is the light by which we are able to view the following parables of Jesus.

A parable is a teaching which is so offensive and revolutionary, that, were it understood, the hearers would immediately react with violence. Unless we are able to see the deep offense in each parable, we have not understood what Jesus was teaching.

To understand the offense in the parable of the sower [4:3-8], one must identify the soils. So, Mark shares the interpretation given to the Apostles. **Some people are like seed along the path, where the word** ["word" does not occur in the text] **is sown. As soon as they hear it, Satan comes and takes away the word that was sown in them** [4:15]. These are the people who reject Jesus out of hand, for instance the Pharisees. **Others, like seed sown on rocky places, hear the word and at once receive it with** joy. But since they have no root, they last only a short time. When trouble or persecution comes because of the word, they quickly fall away [4:16-17]. These are Mark's contemporaneous Christians who renounce their faith in the fear of Roman Persecution. Still others, like seed sown among thorns, hear the word; but the worries of this life, the deceitfulness of wealth and the desires for other things come in and choke the word, making it unfruitful [4:18-19]. These people are contemporary to us. They claim the faith, but do nothing about it. They claim to be faithful, but are not disciples. They are useless to the coming Kingdom, and Mark wants nothing to do with them. As the Spirit said to the Church at Laodicea [Revelation 6:14-16] because you are lukewarm—neither hot nor cold—I am about to spit you out of my mouth. And finally, the faithful are praised: like seed sown on good soil, hear the word, accept it, and produce a crop—some thirty, some sixty, some a hundred times what was sown [4:20].

But this is not enough. Mark emphasizes the urgency of choice. As soon as the grain is ripe, he puts the sickle to it, because the harvest has come [4:29]. And he pointed to the rapid spread of the Kingdom People in the parable of the mustard seed. Mustard is an invasive plant. Its tiny seeds spread everywhere, just as did the Christian Fellowship. Jews and Gentiles had been incorporated far across the Mediterranean World by the time Mark published his Gospel.

LESSON TWO

The event on the Sea of Galilee has several layers of meanings [4:35-41]. While Mark and Luke used a Greek word for "violent storm", Matthew used a different word. He used "seismos" [8:24] from which we derive earthquakes. In any event, the meaning is that, not only does the demonic obey Jesus, so does all of nature. However, in context with what follows, we have yet another meaning. Jesus was on his way across the lake to visit an area habituated by Gentiles and demons. The storm may be seen as demonic resistance to His Gentile Ministry.

While there, Jesus healed "Legion" and destroyed a herd of pigs. As an event, this is yet another demonstration of the Authority of Christ. And that Authority is applied to Gentiles as well as Jews. Yet the pigs are perhaps a metaphor for the judgement of Gentiles. By faith in the Christ, the demonic is cast out. Resistant Gentiles will be destroyed.

Mark related two events that enlarge the extent of Jesus' Authority, and offer to us yet another spiritual dynamic. First the account of the raising the daughter of Jairus [5:21-24, 35-43]. Jesus demonstrated his Authority over death and life. But hidden in the midst of this event, is the healing of an "unclean" woman [5:25-34].

The Pharisees believed that what is unclean pollutes the clean, as putting mud in clean water. But Jesus taught that the power of the clean purifies the unclean. And so, as the woman with a menstrual flow touched Him, power went from Him to her and she was (not just healed) made clean. In other words, our faith is the Power by which God cleanses us from our sinful nature.

Jesus had reached yet another turning point. We must note a reference to the family of Jesus. He had several brothers and sisters. Among them, James, Joseph, Judas and Simon [6:3]. While the resistance of family and familiars continues, Mark noted a limit on the Authority of Jesus. It is another statement of one of the previous spiritual dynamics. Where faith in Christ is rejected, miracles don't happen. Stated the other way, miracles happen only to and among the faithful. Thus, the continual and urgent demand, "have faith and believe!"

The obverse to this dynamic is clear: when the faithful are called and sent, when we are obedient to His commands, miracles *do* happen. Thus, the twelve were sent out and performed many miracles [6:7-12]. They were amazed to discover that His Authority extended to and through them.

As a means of demonstrating the increasingly intense demonic resistance to the Authority of Christ, Mark related the execution of John the Baptist [6:14-29]. Christians, early and late, are both cautioned and alarmed at the potential of evil in the power of governmental authority. Herod had the power to execute John. He did not have the power to quell or even limit the Authority of Christ. And it is that Authority, that miracle-working Power, which continues to be asserted in Believers. That is the mark of the Kingdom. John's death is a powerful (excuse the pun) reference to Mark's undefeatable message: **The time has come! Repent and believe the Good News** [1:14]. Not even his execution could slow down the rapid growth of the Kingdom.

The same is true today. Governments the world over try to control the Kingdom of God. In many places Christians are openly restricted and persecuted. In others, so-called governmental authorities attempt to "regulate" worship and ministry. There are too many examples to even provide an illustration.

In stark contrast to governmental authority, Mark reported the feeding of the five thousand. While the direct meaning is this contrast of the "authority to punish" against the Authority to feed by Miracle Power. One is tempted to point to the difference between our government's ability to feed the hungry without reference to the things of the spirit, and the untapped power of the Church to feed spirits and change lives.

The miracle of Jesus walking on the water as they crossed the Sea, again illustrates how hard it was for the Apostles to grasp the depth and breadth of Jesus' Authority. **They were completely amazed,** *for they had not understood* **about the loaves; their hearts were hardened** [6:52]. However, the Gentiles understood. They had seen Legion healed. Now, they placed their ill wherever Jesus might walk and many were healed [6:53-56].

While in the Gentile community, Jesus was confronted by Jewish authorities from Jerusalem. Mark clearly defined the fault line between the new "Christian" definition of defilement, and the older "Pharisaic" definition. They asked why the Apostles didn't ritually sprinkle water on their hands, cups and plates, before eating. Please note that this requirement had nothing to do with disease or germs. To answer their question Jesus invoked Isaiah [29:13]:

These people honor me with their lips,
  but their hearts are far from me.

They worship me in vain;
  their teachings are merely human rules.

His disciples didn't quite understand, and so, in private, he explained his position. **"Are you so dull?"** he asked. **"Don't you see that nothing that enters a person from the outside can defile them? For it doesn't go into their heart but into their stomach, and then out of the body." (In saying this, Jesus declared all foods clean.)** [7:18-19] Jesus explained that uncleanness comes from within the heart of a person. Then He listed **sexual immorality, theft, murder, adultery, greed, malice, deceit, lewdness, envy, slander, arrogance and folly** [7:21-22] as examples of what is truly unclean.

The next cleansing and exorcism took place in Tyre. A Greek mother begged Jesus to heal her daughter [7:24-30]. This was followed a trip to the Decapolis, another Gentile area, and by the "opening" of a deaf man's ears and tongue [7:31-37]. Clearly, Mark wants the reader to know that Jesus ministered to Gentiles as well as Jews.

Chapter Eight opens with the "Feeding of the Four Thousand" [8:1-9]. Whether an event or not (scholars debate this) is of little importance. The hidden meaning in the event can be clearly pointed out. Mark was surely aware that his contemporary Christians used fish and bread loaves as symbols of their community. Mark clearly intended his readers to see that, when the "hungry" are gathered together, the Miracle Power of the Christian Community will "feed" them. "Feeding" has a dual meaning. It is not just the physical that is fed. More importantly, they are fed spiritually by, with, and through the Gospel of Christ.

This "meaning" is lifted up by the response of Jesus to the demand for a "sign from Heaven" [8:11-13]. Jesus sighed and told them that no sign would be given. Clearly it had already been given. He was exasperated by his Disciples. They couldn't understand the demonstrations of the Heavenly Miracle Power they had just seen. Jesus asked about the surplus of bread after the feeding of the two massive multitudes. They answered "seven" and "twelve". Both those numbers have meaning for the Church. Seven means enough, and twelve is the number of men required to form a worshipping congregation. With the Power of Heaven, the early Christian Community had more than enough Authority to meet any need.

LESSON THREE

With these developments, Mark transitioned from a "Presentation of the Messiah" to a preparation for the Passion of Christ.

He began with a question: **Who do people say I am** [8:27]**?** Obviously, the people were confused. The Apostle Peter responded with his famous affirmation: **You are the Messiah** [8:29]. To this affirmation, Jesus began to teach his Apostles what they ought to be prepared to accept [8:31-32]. This is the pivot point of the Gospel. **He then began to teach them that the Son of Man must suffer many things and be rejected by the elders, the chief priests and the teachers of the law, and that he must be killed and after three days rise again. He spoke plainly about this.**

Peter objected and was called "Satan" by the Lord. He was perilously close to blaspheming the Holy Spirit as Jesus predicted the details of the crucifixion and resurrection. Jesus responded with a warning to Peter and to us. **You do not have in mind the concerns of God, but merely human concerns** [8:33]. The warning was extended to his disciples and us in the next teaching. **Whoever wants to be my disciple must deny themselves and take up their cross and follow me. For whoever wants to save their life will lose it, but whoever loses their life for me and for the gospel will save it** [In those days, this was interpreted literally.]. **What good is it for someone to gain the whole world, yet forfeit their soul** [8:34-36]**?** Mark also included a promise: [9:1] **Truly I tell you, some who are standing here will not taste death before they see that the kingdom of God has come with power.**

The meaning of the Transfiguration [9:2-12] is intriguing and multi-layered. As we look at the theme of Mark's Gospel, we need look only at one insight. Jesus appeared with Abraham and Moses, and the Apostles wanted to build memorial booths. However, God corrected them. If I may paraphrase His words, a dangerous thing to do, I think Mark intended for us to understand them with his dramatic theme in mind. So, to give it a try: "Listen, Dummies, this is My Son...not another great religious figure". Now, that is not what Mark wrote, but I think we understand it better this way. In Mark's Gospel, the Apostles never quite "get it" until after the Resurrection.

The account of the healing of a boy with a convulsive affliction reinforces what Mark had already written about the availability of Miracle Power to the Disciples and Apostles. [9:23] **Everything is possible for one who believes.**

This affirmation is followed by another spiritual dynamic and promise. The Apostles argued about greatness, but Jesus rebuked them to say that Miracle Power is not about greatness, but about service. We believers must become like a child in our faith [9:35-36], *and* in our relationship to power. Children are powerless and trust the power of the adults around them. Just so, you and I are powerless. We are to have absolute trust in the One who works through us.

Once more, we ought to distinguish between the kinds of power that influence our lives. There is the power of nature. We have some limited authority in this field. We may build levies, or situate our house on high ground, for instance. A big enough flood will overtop our efforts. Our power is limited. Then there is the power of government. Jesus seems to have had utter disdain for that power. He viewed it as irrelevant to the really important matters of our life. We focus so much attention on the activities of the government that we are sometimes blinded to the much more important spiritual events. To which of these three powers is Miracle Power directed most often? Which will be more important to you an instant after you die; the income tax rate or the extent of your ministry during your life? God is the Lord of History, but my personal contribution to the Kingdom of God is much more important to my spirit, than any action by the UN.

Mark emphasizes the point about faith and Miracle Power by yet again quoting Jesus: **He said to them, "The Son of Man is going to be delivered into the hands of men. They will kill him, and after three days he will rise"** [9:31]. Jesus expressed little concern over the tax rate, the estate He would leave to His Earthly family, or even whether Israel would face a famine. He was focused on the Miracle Power; **after three days he will rise.**

And again, in the next teaching. This one was about Miracle Power exercised by a "non-ordained" or "unauthorized" person. If anyone casts out demons, it is the Holy Spirit working through that person. The Holy Spirit does not work against the Kingdom.

The next lines are referenced in the other Gospels [9:42-50]. They are authentic teachings by Jesus. Mark uses them but without the context present in the other Gospels.

The first was directed against false teachers [Luke 17:1]. If you cause His Disciple to fall from grace, it would be better that you had never been born. The second was directed toward every Disciple. If you value a sin more highly than the Kingdom of God, cut it off. The Kingdom is of greater worth than your hand or eye. In other words; one's condition in this temporary life is of little worth compared to the Life Eternal. Any expense in this temporary life is more than compensated in the Real Life. One may face a horrific and painful martyrdom, but be of good cheer, the reward of faithfulness is beyond calculation. Miracle Power is greater than any earthly power. His unique contribution is this: **Everyone will be salted with fire** [9:49]. He meant, of course, that even disciples will suffer.

Chapter Ten treats a subject of tremendous contemporary importance: divorce. There are Christians who are deeply troubled and think that, no one who is divorced and remarries without the incident of adultery, can be saved.

It may be that divorce is the most potent illustration of broken loyalty. And that makes sense as we try to understand the other teachings in the chapter.

Let me be clear: No one ought to affirm divorce as a spiritual good. However, by the same token, no one should claim that divorce or adultery is the "unforgiveable sin". One enters Heaven as an individual, not as a half, or a third, or a quarter, or a fifth of one's marital relationships. The marriage contract is between two individuals and the state. Its concern is over property and the care of children. Matrimony is a relationship that involves God, and the violation of that relationship is a very serious matter. And, all sin affects the condition of one's spirit. Divorce is not a good. At best it is a response to a very difficult situation. Both the situation and the response affect the condition of one's spirit. If this were a parable, the meaning would be, "a person with a divided loyalty cannot enter the Kingdom"!

That Mark intended us to take this message might well illuminate the next pericope. **Truly I tell you, anyone who will not receive the kingdom of God like a little child will never enter it** [10:15]. A child is "all in" with loyalty and trust. And so must we. I am not sure whether this is a third unforgiveable sin. It is surely a spiritual dynamic.

The subject of "loyalty" is furthermore illustrated by the encounter of the "Rich Young Man" [10:17-27]. He was unable to make a complete commitment to the Kingdom by setting aside his wealth. Saint Peter's question enables the bold contrast and affect. "We have left everything. What do we get" [My paraphrase]? Jesus promises **"No one who has left home or brothers or sisters or mother or father or children or fields for me and the gospel will fail to receive a hundred times as much in this present age: homes, brothers, sisters, mothers, children and fields—along with persecutions—and in the age to come eternal life** [10:29-30]. Mark was especially aware of the troubles that accrue to Disciples as he illuminated the blessings of Kingdom Life and Miracle Power.

Mark used the recurring announcements of the crucifixion as book-marks on each of these teachings. The Lord again explained to the Apostles that He would not be accepted as Messiah and would be persecuted to the death [10:32-34]. This is followed by yet another set of teachings.

The values of temporary life are opposite and antithetical to the values of Real Life (I use "Real Life" to distinguish our earthly life from Eternal Life, in that Real Life includes both our present life and the Life to come). In this life we seek to be served. In order to be "served" in Real Life we must be of use to the Kingdom, we must "serve" the interests of the Kingdom. And we cannot do that if we seek our own welfare, our own glory [10:35-45].

Mark ends what we might call the "Presentation of Christ" with the healing of Bartimaeus. It is another demonstration of Miracle Power; another "book mark".

Chapter eleven begins Mark's account of the Passion of Christ. Rather than teaching, Jesus is "doing" the Messiah Ministry, the Ministry of Miracle Power.

Interestingly, Mark is not much concerned about the Palm Sunday procession. Unlike the other Gospels, he simply mentions it, and passes on to the subject of importance. Palm Sunday, to Mark, is just another "book mark".

What is of importance to Mark is God's Judgement against Israel. The fig tree [11:12-15,20] is the symbol of Israel, as the Stars and Stripes are symbolic of America. **May no one ever eat fruit from you again** is a particular judgement against the religious establishment of Jerusalem. **'My house will be called a house of prayer for all nations'. But you have made it 'a den of robbers'** [11:17; ref. Jeremiah 7:11], is a judgement against the money changers AND the priestly establishment that endorsed it. It is yet something more. Mark's ministry among Gentiles suggests that he used Jeremiah's prophetic statement as an indictment of the inward-looking nature of the Jewish religious leaders. Thus, the universal nature of the Church (a House of Prayer for all nations) is announced to the readers. The Good News is intended for all; Jew and Gentile. The old Jewish Establishment has literally been destroyed. From those days until the present, the Jewish Jerusalem Priestly Establishment has had no function in salvation history.

They exercised no real power. Real power is Miracle Power. **"Have faith in God," Jesus answered. "Truly I tell you, if anyone says to this mountain, 'Go, throw yourself into the sea,' and does not doubt in their heart but believes that what they say will happen, it will be done for them. Therefore I tell you, whatever you ask for in prayer, believe that you have received it, and it will be yours** [11:22-24].

Apparently, the sin behind the failure of the Jerusalem Establishment was a failure of faith. Jesus could point, from the summit of the Mount of Olives, toward the Herculaneum. It was literally a man-made mountain. Herod had constructed it as a fortress. Herod had demonstrated the power of government, while the Priests had not established the Miracle Power of the Kingdom. They had not even provided for real forgiveness of sins. Which is why the Christian must forgive others from the depths of his/her heart. Mark quotes Jesus, just as did Matthew [6:15], providing us with perhaps the most important of spiritual dynamics. If we are unable to forgive others, God is unable to forgive us. This is in sharp contrast to the sacrifice of a lamb with no alteration of one's heart (attitude).

Perhaps the most important issue of the Gospel is presented in a question by the "Teachers of the Law": **"By what authority are you doing these things?" they asked. "And who gave you authority to do this"** [11:28]? Mark's quotation of Jesus' response would be humorous, were it not so tragic. **"John's baptism—was it from heaven, or of human origin** [11-30]?" While their response was intellectually correct, spiritually it was the most tragic of possible answers. By saying they did not know the answer, they testified to their absolute ignorance of the Kingdom. The authority question posed the contrast between a ritual performed with heart-changing faith, and a ritual with no heart-faith involvement. John's Baptism changed the lives of people. Sacrifice at the Temple, apparently, changed no hearts. Thus, John prepared people for entrance into the Kingdom, and had Miracle Power. The rituals in the Temple were devoid of Miracle Power and changed nothing. Have you attended Christian worship services that have no life-changing power?

Jesus responded to their lack of faith with parables. Recall that a parable is a metaphor so dangerous that, were it understood, the hearers would kill the Teacher. The Vineyard [12:1-12] was understood by the Establishment representatives. They would have killed Jesus immediately, were that possible. Instead with understanding, they began the crucifixion plot. His parable illustration was of a rented vineyard whose tenants refused to produce the fruits required by the contract [see: Covenant]. It pointed to the death of the prophets who complained of the fruitlessness of the Covenant Society. And it predicted the attempted destruction of the Christ/Messiah. They "got it" and plotted His arrest [12:12].

Their first failure was the question concerning paying the Roman tax. This question allowed Mark to continue his narrative of the Vineyard. "Pay to Caesar what is his, and to God what belongs to God" [12:17]. We all understand that our life is on loan from God, not from the government. We are to obey the temporal authorities in all the irrelevant and unimportant issues of the day, while obeying God in all the things of Ultimate Significance. That is, whatever conditions one encounters in this life requires our obedience to *God's* Authority.

The second failure was in the question about multiple marriages [12:18-27]. Many have misunderstood this discussion because it seems so clearly to be about marriage. But it has a deeper meaning. **He is not the God of the dead, but of the living** [12:27]. The dead were standing in front of Jesus. The Living were, and are, those who have entered the Kingdom by faith.

Their third pitch came close to a strike. They inquired about the greatest law of Moses? And, they had it correct, **Love your neighbor as yourself** [12:31; Ref: Leviticus 19:18]. And Jesus said **You are not far from the Kingdom** [12:34].

As examples, pro and con, of this "love of neighbor", Jesus pointed out the pride of the "Teachers of the Law" who enjoy public stature and wealth through the donations of widows. Then he pointed to the selfless love of a widow who put her entire wealth into the offering plate [12:38-44]. Of the two, the widow's faith was shown to be the greater -and more honest.

LESSON FOUR

The key to understanding the entire thirteenth chapter is found in verse fourteen: **'the abomination that causes desolation'.** It is a reference to Daniel 9:27; 11:31; and 12:11. Daniel experienced a dramatic vision. He was taught by Gabriel. A code of years and events was given to him. Gabriel predicted that 434 years after Cyrus sends out a proclamation returning the Hebrew People to Jerusalem, the Messiah would arrive. He will be put to death **but not for himself** [Daniel 9:26]. Then there will be a pause, followed by three and a half years of terrible destruction [9:26-27]. Those who study apocalyptic prophecy suggest that one period of three and a half years of terrible destruction has yet to be fulfilled. However, between late 65 A.D. and 70 A.D., the Roman Army destroyed Jerusalem, the Temple, and much of Judea. They find Daniel's prophecy singularly accurate. Some scholars suggest that Mark is the author of this chapter (not Jesus), and that he had already experienced that destruction, or that it was so clearly about to happen, that anyone could predict it. Their presupposition is that God does not exist, and certainly doesn't "send angels to predict human events". But the same scholars are caught in a dilemma. They write that Mark is the earliest Gospel. They also know that Matthew was written between 65 and 75 A.D. So, let us accept that Jesus, who predicted his own death by crucifixion, was also able to predict the destruction of the Holy City.

With that before us, we can understand Mark's urgent demand for faith and loyalty. The Christian Community would be fractured by persecution and fear. Rumors and actual destructive events will frighten to the inner being. However, the events of the latter first century are not the hope of Christians. That hope is contained in the remaining three- and one-half years of Daniel's prophecy. It has not yet happened. **At that time people will see the Son of Man coming in clouds with great power and glory. And he will send his angels and gather his elect from the four winds, from the ends of the earth to the ends of the heavens** [13:26-27].

At this point I must ride my personal hobby-horse. The translators render the word "clouds" from the Greek "Nephos". It is the word which is similar to the Hebrew "Nephilim"; which means "spiritual giants". They are the Angels, whom He will send to gather in the faithful.

This warning may well have been the final urgent appeal of Mark. Make your decision now, because five minutes from now may be too late. **But about that day or hour no one knows, not even the angels in heaven, nor the Son, but only the Father. Be on guard! Be alert! You do not know when that time will come** [13:33].

The final pages of Mark's Gospel, might be styled, "Pictures of the last days of Jesus". I will call them "pictographs" or word portraits. That is, they are the brief word pictures; each with a dramatic message. Sometimes we look too closely, and we miss the dramatic message.

The first is "a portrait of a desperate love" [14:1-9]. A woman poured a tiny jar of nard oil on the head of the Lord. She loved Him enough to lavish a year's wages on one act. She had already accepted the invitation of God. She had responded to the urgent appeal of the Apostle.

The second "pictograph" is of the Last Supper. Mark's is the most brief of all the accounts, and the most pointed. This portrait is the dramatic counter-point to the Woman of Bethany. This is "the portrait of rejection" [14:10-26]. While presenting the most accurate details, Mark's emphasis is on the betrayal by Judas Iscariot. Here is a follower whose heart is unlike the Woman of Bethany. The source of his betrayal was in his disappointment that Jesus refused to fulfill Judas' earthly expectations. He demanded that Jesus meet his expectations, rather than the other way around.

The third "pictograph" is "Peter's Nap at Gethsemane" [14:32-41]. Jesus' anguished prayer is set next to Peter's unconcern. That unconcern would quickly become betrayal. Peter, along with the others, ought to have been praying with and for his Lord. Instead, his head was heavy...not his heart.

The fourth "pictograph" is "the arrest" [14:41-51]. The contrast in this portrait is between the violent reaction of one of the followers [14:47], to which Jesus' response was intolerable: **"Am I leading a rebellion," said Jesus, "that you have come out with swords and clubs to capture me? Every day I was with you, teaching in the temple courts, and you did not arrest me. But the Scriptures must be fulfilled"** [14:49-50]. To Mark, this isn't so much a theological statement about the Kingdom, as it is about the earthly reaction to his words: **Then everyone deserted him and fled** [14:50].

Possibly the most interesting line of the entire account, is verse fifty-one and fifty-two. **A young man, wearing nothing but a linen garment, was following Jesus. When they seized him, he fled naked, leaving his garment behind** [14:51-52]. Many scholars believe this to be the signature of Mark. If so, he was an eye-witness to all these events. And Mark fled too. He too left Jesus in the hands of the earthly authorities. Here is a portrait of "fearful Mark".

In this collection of portraits, the next one is central [14:53-65]. At the indictment hearing before the High Priest, Jesus is silent until the one and only important question is asked: **"Are you the Messiah, the Son of the Blessed One"** [14:61]? And, of course, the response is the most important sentence in this entire Gospel: **"I am," said Jesus. "And you will see the Son of Man sitting at the right hand of the Mighty One and coming on the clouds of heaven"** [14:62]. We will call this the portrait of "Truth".

The sixth "pictograph" is the portrait of "weeping": Peter's denial [14:66-72]. Peter led the way. He was the first of the followers to weep. But his weeping was for himself, not for his Lord. Peter wept at the loss of his manhood. He wept because he feared for his own safety more than he cared about his Lord. Mark must have wept too, though not at this moment. Everyone who loved Jesus, and witnessed His execution, must have wept. The unspoken contrast is between the example of Jesus, who undoubtedly feared the pain, but whose Spirit was unbroken, and the fear of his followers.

The next is the portrait of "rejection" [15:1-15]. Though Mark was a Jew, his record shows that the Jewish Jerusalem Establishment fully rejected the **Messiah, the Son of the Blessed One** [14:61]. One may not shout **"Crucify Him"** [15:14]! without a demonic hatred. The crowd hated Him so much that they demanded the release of Barabbas (literally: the son of (a) father).

Mark's picture of "false worship" is different from the other Gospels [15:16-20]. He doesn't mention the flogging. Perhaps the details of Christ's torture meant less to Mark than the attitude of the soldiers. False worship is as demonic as hatred. The soldiers falsely bowed down to Jesus in contrast to the true worshippers.

One must add a footnote to the next picture [15:21-32]: the portrait of "acceptance". Simon of Cyrene, and his son Rufus, are mentioned as carrying the crossbar for Jesus. Two possible reasons for their inclusion in the account of all three of the synoptic gospels is that they became well-known members of the Christian Community, and the undeniable picture of a disciple actually carrying his cross. Simon responded immediately and completely to the needs of his Lord.

He, however, is not the only one carrying a cross. The "repentant thief" was probably carrying his own cross to Golgotha. His plea to Jesus, in the last moments of his life, was enough to gain redemption and salvation.

The portrait of "judgment" is next [15:27-37]. This does not appear as one picture, according to our rules of grammar. However, the paragraphs are connected by the attitude of the people near the cross: **Come down from the cross and save yourself!** [15:30] and the Centurion who affirmed **Surely this man was the Son of God** [15:39].

The information in the account allows us a clue as to a possible date for this Pivotal Point of Human Life. The darkness from noon to three is a reference to an eclipse. One occurred on April 3, 33 A.D. It, according to Mark, was accompanied by an earthquake. That is harder to date, but we might note that Jerusalem's height rises from one of the most active fault-lines of the Earth.

Perhaps the most startling pictograph is of the women. They are the heroes while the Apostles are the cowards. So, this one might be called "Portrait of Heroes" [15:40-16:13]. The Apostles are contrasted to the women who had come to Jerusalem from Galilee with Jesus [15:40-41]. They seem to have been fearless, though they must have been burdened with terrible grief. They are the picture of faithfulness within this portrait of judgment. They go about the work required of them without regard to the power of the Romans or the power of the religious establishment. When Joseph of Arimathea was granted the body of Christ, the women took note of the tomb. And early the morning after Sabbath, they returned to anoint His Body. They did the "disciple thing", while the Apostles huddled in a fearful room.

The final portrait is the one of "singular command" [16:9-18]: **Go into all the world and preach the gospel to all creation. Whoever believes and is baptized will be saved, but whoever does not believe will be condemned.** And surprisingly, they did so! **Then the disciples went out and preached everywhere, and the Lord worked with them and confirmed his word** [Gk: logon meaning Holy Spirit-words] **by the signs that accompanied it** [16:20].

So, there you have it. Mark's Gospel demands an immediate response *from you*. Jesus is the Son of God who will return with glory and unimagined Miracle Power. If you have not yet accepted Him as Lord, let it be known to you that a particular time has been set for the last moment at which you may respond to His invitation. The thief on his cross took advantage of that moment. This may be your last moment. Do not be a coward, denying Him. Accept Him now, or face the terrible consequence.

And if you have already given your life to Him, you know that you must carry your cross, not just one of endurance, but one of obedience and Miracle Power. His Power is extended through you...through your acts of obedient faithfulness. Mark took note of the denial by himself and the other Apostles. That is a grace to you. Have you failed to take up your cross of obedience? Now receive the urgent appeal of Saint Mark: do the "disciple thing" and take note of the Miracle Power in your hands and prayers.

Everyone here has been extended Mark's Urgent Appeal. Respond now, he intended you to understand, before it is too late.

THE GOSPEL OF LUKE

The basic idea expressed in Luke's Gospel is that Jesus was a perfect (sinless) human being, *and* a perfect representation of the Character of God. His theme in Acts, and the reason that it is a separate book, is the historical development of the Christian Sect from a Jewish enclave to a fellowship of both Jews and Gentiles. Further, the locus of Christianity moves from Jerusalem to Rome, and from the Apostles to a second generation of leaders. It is not an urgent appeal, as was Mark. It seems to be a book of instruction for Luke's contemporary Christians. Most scholars suggest that the Gospel was written between 59 and 62 A.D. That is, near the time of the martyrdom of Saints Peter and Paul. Liberal theologians prefer a date after 70 AD; the time of the destruction of Jerusalem.

Luke, after his introduction, began with the birth of John the Baptist. One wonders why. He understood John to be the fulfillment of the prophetic predictions. Luke wanted to present the birth of Christ in an atmosphere of holiness and sanctity. Zechariah met the Archangel Gabriel at the second holiest place on Earth; the altar just in front of the curtain that shrouds the Holy of Holies. The Altar of Incense was the place where the Priest offered a holy sacrifice for the "blood of the sacrifices". That sacrifice was the most important of all. It made the shedding of blood at the High Altar, pure and blameless.

The location and conversation, between Angel and Priest, suggests the subject of the Gospel: the holiest of sacrifices is about to be prepared. Constituting an oblique avenue toward that "preparation", Gabriel predicts the birth of John the Baptist. The conversation also portrays the "authority" of Gabriel. He stands **in the presence of God**, and is **sent to speak to you and to tell you this good news** [Luke 1:19].

The miraculous birth is reminiscent of Abraham and Sarah who sired and birthed Isaac [Genesis 17:19 etc.] in their old age.

Into this wonderful, miraculous, sacred environment Mary is introduced to the reader. Luke's intention is to answer questions about what the environment around Jesus was like prior to his Baptism by John. It was holy. He begins with the Annunciation to Mary, and proceeds to the boy Jesus teaching the Jerusalem Priests.

Mary, in addition to Zechariah, is also visited by Gabriel. First, note the radical nature of the meeting. Not only does the Angel rarely speak to any human; in this case Gabriel speaks to *a woman!* One must point out that women in those ages were supposed to be obedient. Her obedience is not amazing until one realizes the peril she accepted. Unwed and expectant women were stoned to death, just as in some countries today. I suppose she could have said "no", but the example of Zechariah is already in front of us. Even so, her acceptance is remarkable.

Her soon-to-be husband has Davidic lineage [Luke 1:27]. How that is important is a mystery, since he is not the biological sire. Luke presented the lineage of Jesus as in Joseph's line **so it was thought** [Luke 3:23-38]. One reason for this lineage is that Jesus was to be born in Bethlehem. Another reason is that the lineage ends with **Adam, the son of God**. And that was Luke's point. All the details in between Adam and Joseph are not relevant; only that Jesus is also **the Son of God**.

Mary's first act was quickly to leave town for a quarter-year; from Elizabeth's sixth to ninth month. Elizabeth lived in a village in the **hill country of Judea** [Luke 1:39], which included Jerusalem and Bethlehem. What is important to note is that it was not Nazareth or Jerusalem. They were both areas of serious danger to her. And then, of course, miracles continue. John greeted Mary (and Jesus) from his mother's womb.

Along with the poetic prophecy by Simeon, [Luke 2:29-32] Luke included two lengthy poems, one by Mary [Luke 1:46-55], and one by Zechariah [Luke 1:67-79]. It stretches the imagination to believe that these poems were recorded and remembered for the seventy years before they were put to papyrus. They must, instead, have a more important literary function. They all claim the fulfillment of the prophetic tradition. Mary claims a kind of Divine Justice [He has brought down rulers from their thrones but has lifted up the humble. He has filled the hungry with good things but has sent the rich away empty. Luke 1:52-53], and Zechariah, inspired by the Holy Spirit, prophesied, [Praise be to the Lord, the God of Israel, because he has come to his people and redeemed them. He has raised up a horn [a strong king] of salvation for us in the house of his servant David (as he said through his holy prophets of long ago), salvation from our enemies… Luke 1:67-71], and Simeon's poem is a prayer of thanksgiving for prophetic fulfillment.

When Elizabeth's delivery approached, Mary returned to Nazareth. There she, of necessity, confronted Joseph with her soon-to-be-apparent condition. But we should note that this conversation, and Joseph's decision, is not recorded by Luke, only in Matthew. The first we hear of Joseph is **So Joseph also went up from the town of Nazareth in Galilee to Judea, to Bethlehem the town of David, because he belonged to the house and line of David** [Luke 2:4].

Some will ask: When was that? We have several clues. First, Luke said that it was "in the time of Herod" [Luke 1:5]. Only Herod the Great qualifies as possible, and he died in 4 B.C. Then he mentioned Caesar Augustus, who lived until 27 A.D. And also, Quirinius governor of Syria [Luke 2:2]. Quirinius had posed a problem for historians, because his term of office didn't begin until 6 A.D. which is too late. However, recent discoveries have shown that he had the actual authority over Syria while he was Governor of Crete and Cyrenaica [beginning in 14 B.C.]. So, the possible range of years for the birth of our Savior is from 14 B.C. to 4 B.C. Please note that our calendar was adopted many centuries later, and our dating is now more accurate. We also have the information from Matthew's Gospel, which helps us arrive at the year 7 B.C. and which makes Jesus about thirty-five in 29 A.D. We date the beginning of his ministry in that year, and note that thirty-five was the traditional age at which a Jewish man was felt qualified for a public position.

Everyone knows the story of The Nativity. Jesus was born in Bethlehem, the City of David, and the Shepherds were confronted by, first one Angel, and then *the whole* [GK: pléthó (to be full or plentiful); in Luke 1:10 the same word is translated "whole"] of the "Heavenly Host" [Luke 2:13]! If one Angel was "terrifying" [Luke 2:9], imagine what the entire Heavenly Corps of Angels must have looked like!

Recent studies have revealed details previously ignored. For instance, Jesus wasn't born the first day or night his parents were in the city. **While they were there** [Luke 2:6], she gave birth. Please note that Howard Johnson Inns had not yet been invented. Tribal members simply took refuge in the home of one of their relatives. Even today the authorities translate the necessity for a manger as "guest-room" or "lodging place". However, archeologists have revealed that the word translated "inn" indicates the living area of a house; the living space, the "living room". Many of the houses in Bethlehem included a space for animals and another for humans. Because Bethlehem was a "tribal" center, Joseph had many relatives, and thus could crowd into the living space most of the time. But one doesn't usually have a baby on the dining room table. The women of the house took Mary to the place which offered the greatest privacy, and assisted her in her birthing.

So, the Shepherds obeyed the Angel and went to Bethlehem, and found Mary, and Joseph, and Jesus, and related what they had seen. That is mentioned as a fulfillment of the prophetic track of Hebrew history. And, the next verse shows that the Law of Moses was also fulfilled [Luke 2:21]: **On the eighth day, when it was time to circumcise the child, he was named Jesus** [Yeshua; the same name as the man who followed Moses and is called by us Joshua; meaning "Savior".]**, the name the Angel had given him before he was conceived** [Luke 2:22]. Also, they made an offering at the Temple to "cleanse" Mary. Jerusalem is five miles north of Bethlehem, and in, those days, considered a short walk. This in accordance with the Law [Leviticus 12:8; And if she cannot afford a lamb, then she shall take two turtledoves or two young pigeons, one for a burnt offering and the other for a sin offering; and the priest shall make atonement for her, and she shall be clean."]. Luke presents yet another picture of the fulfillment of the prophetic, the Holy Spirit tradition. The prophecy of Simeon looks both back and forward. He thanked God for the fulfillment of the "Promised Salvation" [Luke 2:25-32], and prophesied that Jesus was to be the cause of **the falling and rising of many in Israel** [Luke 2:34]. Mary was saddled with the prediction that He would cause a piercing of her soul, or "psyche" [Luke 2: 35]. Mary's poem must be placed alongside that of Miriam [Exodus 15:21ff] the sister of Moses. Both are poems of exultation. Mary is linked to Jesus as Miriam was linked to Moses; and thus, Jesus and Moses are indirectly linked.

Simeon was followed by Anna who predicted that Jesus would be the "redemption of Jerusalem" [Luke 2:38].

The care Luke took to notate Mary's experiences; for instance, the pierced psyche and that she **treasured all these things in her heart** [Luke 2:51], suggests but does not prove, that she was one of his historical sources. That is not only amazing, it is readily plausible.

Chapter three begins with dating material related to the Baptism of Jesus by his cousin, John the Baptist. The dates are limited by the reign of Tiberius Caesar [14BC – 37AD]—when Pontius Pilate was governor of Judea [26 – 36AD], Herod tetrarch of Galilee [6 - 39AD], his brother Philip Tetrarch of Iturea and Traconitis, and Lysanias was Tetrarch of Abilene [26 -34AD]. We are able to limit this event to between twenty-six and thirty-four Anno Domini. As noted earlier, if Jesus was born in seven B.C., and was *about* **thirty-years-old when he began his ministry** [Luke 3:23], the Baptism must have been between the years twenty-three and twenty-nine. Most scholars date this event in twenty-nine, when Jesus was thirty-five.

The presentation of John begins with yet another poem; this one a quotation from Isaiah [Isaiah 40:3-6]. This linkage is very important. **A voice of one calling in the wilderness, 'Prepare the way for the Lord, make straight paths for him. Every valley shall be filled in, every mountain and hill made low. The crooked roads shall become straight, the rough ways smooth. And all people will see God's salvation.'** Isaiah's Chapter Forty begins the script of a dialogue between Isaiah, Israel, God, and the Messiah. By placing this poem at the inauguration of Jesus's ministry, Luke claimed for

Jesus, not only the title "Messiah", but a whole series of predictions about the Messiah, made during the sixth century B.C. Among them: that He would be a **Light to the nations** [Isaiah 49:6], the "suffering servant" [Isaiah 53], and this prediction: **Therefore I will allot him a portion with the great, and he shall divide the spoil with the strong; because he poured out himself to death, and was numbered with the transgressors; yet he bore the sin of many, and made intercession for the transgressors** [Isaiah 53:12].

John told the crowd that history had come to its fulcrum. From that moment onward, everything would be different. God was about to Judge the world. The Priests and Pharisees have no place in the Kingdom of God. Their righteousness is outward, while God requires inward repentance and the "fruit" of righteousness [Luke 3:7]. The contrast between outward obedience to the Law of Moses, and the renewal of one's inward nature is bold.

Into this convention stepped Jesus. But Luke skips the conversation between John and Jesus, instead focusing on the more important accolade from the Heavenly Holy Spirit: **You are my Son, whom I love; with you I am well pleased** [Luke 3:22; note, only Jesus hears the Voice, in contrast see Luke 9:35].

Jesus's lineage, going back to Adam, the son of God, has already been mentioned. However a note might be appropriate. While there are some similarities, Matthew and Luke differ greatly. Unlike Matthew, no women are mentioned. Liberal scholars claim that both lists, in Matthew and Luke, are inventions, intended to support the claim of Divine Messiah. We just don't know.

Jesus was "tested" [Luke 4:2] after His Baptism. The tests he faced are both unique to Him, and in some degree common to us. He was tempted by hunger for bread [Luke 4:3]. He was tempted by the desire for fame and authority [Luke 4:5]. He was tempted to use His authority for improper ends [Luke 4:9]. His response in each case was to quote scripture, specifically Deuteronomy six, verses thirteen and sixteen, and chapter eight verse three.

Many sermons have been aired about the temptation and how Jesus affirmed His role as Messiah and Son of God. My interest is in how His temptations are like ours. How early and often do we feel the need for financial security; for bread in the larder? Jesus tells us that our life is more than our finances. Most surely, the other parts of our "life" are more important than our bank balance. How often would we like some authority: "Just because I said so...!" Or, wouldn't a bit of fame be nice? Jesus tells us that our relationship to God is of much greater importance than ego satisfaction. Wouldn't it be nice to be sure beyond any possible doubt that God is Real and will protect us no matter what? Jesus simply affirms what Moses knew: Don't test God.

Having "passed the test", Jesus experienced a "rush" of spiritual power [Luke 4:14]. This, too, is something people experience today. People who have felt the "Baptism of the Holy Spirit" report an exuberance, and a feeling of unlimited strength. They profess a lasting and exquisite joy. Jesus undoubtedly felt these things, having decided, committed, and confirmed His Vocation.

Many years ago, I preached my "first sermon". In my case, it was awful. Jesus went home and announced that He was Messiah, that He was "anointed by God" [Luke 4:18-19], by reading from Isaiah [Isaiah 58:6 and 61:1-2] and claiming its prophetic completion. It did not go well. They knew Him as a boy. They knew Him as a teen. They knew Him as a young man. How could He be Messiah? It seemed blasphemous to them. They righteously wanted to kill Him, but the let Him walk away. What did they not understand when He proclaimed **the year of the Lord's favor** [Luke 4:19]? He was certainly correct in saying that prophets are not accepted by their familiars.

Unlike the people of His home-town and home-synagogue, the demons knew Him [Luke 4:31-37], and the people of the Capernaum Synagogue were amazed by His Teaching. He did not quote the earlier theological authorities. He simply stated as fact, and demonstrated Power by "casting out" the demon [There is a difference between exorcism, which relies on the authority of Church Ritual, and "Casting Out" by prayerful invocation of the Power of the Holy Spirit.]

Luke gave us details about the relationship between Jesus and Peter, prior to the calling of the Apostle. For instance, Peter was a member of the Capernaum Synagogue where Jesus had been teaching [Luke 4:31-37]. Jesus had relieved Peter's mother of a high fever [Luke 4:38]. His ministry expanded. People brought their ill to be healed. And, apparently, Jesus spoke at other synagogues [Luke 4:43] though Capernaum continued to be His "base".

So, Peter was not unaware of Jesus' spiritual prowess when people were crowding Jesus on the shore of Lake Galilee. Jesus needed a more appropriate "pulpit" and asked Peter to place his boat a few yards off shore [Luke 5:1-3]. Luke shares a simple act of generosity and kindness between Jesus and the businessman/fisherman Peter [Luke 5:4-7]. Peter had worked for Jesus, providing that watery pulpit, and Jesus paid for the service by providing a catch of fish that threatened to tear the nets. One might ask, however, what was caught in that net; fish or fishermen? Peter, James, John and Zebedee all enlisted in the Lord's Ministry [Luke 5:8-11].

Luke presented a series of events to illustrate or prove that Jesus is Messiah. They are full of insights.

The first of these event reports is the healing of a leper. The ill man said, **Lord, if you are willing, you can make me clean** [Luke 5:12]. Jesus "chose" to heal a leper [Luke 5:13; NRSV]. Is this a matter about which there might be a question? Of course not. Other translations have the clause: **I am willing: be cleansed** [e.g. NIV]. If one is willing to be cleansed, Jesus is willing to cleanse. This is a major spiritual dynamic. Often, in pastoral counsel, the major obstacle to healing or cleansing or forgiveness, is the parishioner's unwillingness. We hide our unwillingness in a myriad of ways; excuses, denial, avoidance; but all are simply a mask. Amazingly, we often prefer our "leprosy" to the fearful reality of cleansing.

The result of this miracle of cleansing, was that the "word" about Jesus spread rapidly [Luke 5:15]. That noun, "word", is a major obstacle to clarity of understanding. The Early Church always understood "word", when the Greek is "logos", to mean more than simply a sound or printing that communicates meaning. They always understood the connection between a word and the Spirit carried in that utterance. One must understand this verse as meaning "the Holy Spirit message about Jesus spread rapidly".

The second event is one of the favorite lessons in the children's department. The paralytic lowered through a hole in the roof [Luke 5:17-26]. We like to point out that support from friends is often needed for healing. And, of course, the Pharisees are portrayed as uncaring and aloof from the realities of hard life. They focused on the statement of Jesus: **Friend, your sins are forgiven** [Luke 5:20]. To them, blasphemy was of more significance than the wholeness of the paralytic. But the meaning of this event is not just the healing of the man, but of who it was through whom healing was extended. The Pharisees correctly stated: **Only God can forgive sins** [Luke 5:21], and they were correct. The inescapable implication is that God spoke through Jesus. And as the pericope ends: **We have seen some remarkable things today** [Luke 5:23]. Remarkable indeed.

If Matthew ever read Luke's Gospel, he must have had pleasure in the description of his first meeting with Jesus [Luke 5:27-32]. This, along with the following verses, present to us both a picture of Jesus at a party, and two expressions of the conditions for which the Messiah was sent. First, the righteousness-healing of sinners, and second, that all the conditions of blessedness are changing. It is self-aware sinners who will be saved, and like old wine verses new, many will prefer the old. **No one having drunk the old desires the new wine, for he says "the old is better"** [Luke 5:39]. The Pharisees preferred the law to the restoration of sinners to the grace of God.

And the next pericope is like a poetic "slam" [Luke 6:1-5]. On a Sabbath, the Disciples gathered grain heads into their hands and ate, thus violating the prohibition of labor on the Holy Day. In response to the complaint of the Pharisees, Jesus maintained that **The Son of Man is Lord of the Sabbath** [Luke 6:5]. Scholars continue to debate angels on the head of a pin, while the association of the meaning is absolutely clear. Luke connected Jesus to ancient Spiritual traditions. **As I watched in the night visions, I saw one like a son of man coming with the clouds of heaven** [Read here: "the entire Army of Angels]. **And he came to the Ancient One and was presented before him. To him was given dominion and glory and kingship, that all peoples, nations, and languages should serve him** [Daniel 7:13-14]. Other associations in Ezekiel are equally pertinent. The Prophet used the term "son of man" ninety-three times. His consistent definition is, a human possessed by, or under a dominating influence of the Spirit of God.

In other words, Jesus, as a Spirit Man, and as the Author of the Sabbath Command, is present. He stands above human legalities. His Presence indicates that the old age (old wine) is complete, and the new age (new wine and wineskins) is precipitously and urgently impending.

Evidence of this grand change was presented to the Pharisees in the Synagogue. Jesus had a man whose hand was paralyzed, stand in front of the congregation while the Lord asked: **I ask you, which is lawful on the Sabbath: to do good or to do evil, to save life or to destroy it** [Luke 6:9]? This is not the question posed by the Pharisees. They asked: "is it work or not". By re-focusing the conversation, Jesus was able to heal the man's hand. Embarrassed, the Pharisees began plotting how to destroy Jesus [Luke 6:11].

II

According to Luke's chronology, the number of disciples must have increased to the point that Jesus felt the need for organization. He, therefore, chose twelve leaders and styled them: Apostles [Luke 6:12-16]. Luke's narrative changes fundamentally. From demonstrations of power, Luke changes to the subject of Jesus's teachings. And he began with the Beatitudes.

The Kingdom of God belongs to the poor, the hungry, the sorrowing, the hated, and the excluded; not to the rich, the sated, the happy, the powerful/popular, or the elite [Luke 6:20-26]. As Luke presents it (different from Matthew), the Beatitudes are a statement of judgment, offensive to the Jerusalem Establishment.

Instead of the commonly accepted (today as well as then) moral view, a follower of Jesus is expected to love the enemy [Luke 6:37], and give rather than get [Luke 6:38]. Instead of the usual morality, Jesus called them (and us) to do good without expectation of reward: **Then your reward will be great, and you will be children of the Most High, because he is kind to the ungrateful and wicked. Be merciful, just as your Father is merciful** [Luke 6:35-36]. Only by forgiving are we to be forgiven and blessed [Luke 6:37-38]. We are to not take an interest in the sins of others, but deal with our own sinfulness [Luke 6:41-42], because only then will we be able to be a help to others. Veterans in the battle against their own sins might have better advice to those who still struggle than the self-judged righteous. Again, we have comments that apply to the Pharisees and to the Mosaic culture they represented.

The final "slam" against the Pharisaic way of life is the assertion that the old way has brought forth only "bad fruit" [Luke 6:43-45], because it failed to deal with the basic causes. One must deal with the inner-person rather than with outward behavior [Luke 6:43-45].

The people saw an obvious example of the righteousness Jesus proclaimed. It was Jesus Himself. To this He replied that those who set the Law of Moses as their foundation are foolish house-builders. Their sandy foundation will fail. His followers, establishing their faith on the hard foundation of Jesus' teaching will survive the tests of nature [Luke 6:46-49].

Luke relates an event which I think is wonderful. The subject is "authority" with the understood implication that Jesus has Authority from God. More interesting (to me) is the source of the request for healing: a Centurion who **loves our nation and has built our synagogue** [in Capernaum; Luke 7:1-9].

There were not very many Centurions in Judea who loved the Nation and built synagogues. Without proof, I believe this to be the man who commanded the platoon tasked with the Crucifixion [Matthew 27:54], and the same man who was Baptized by Saint Peter in Joppa [Acts Chapter ten esp. verse 22: **The men replied, "We have come from Cornelius the centurion. He is a righteous and God-fearing man, who is respected by all the Jewish people**.]. The latter, Cornelius, is named by Luke. To an historian, his name indicates an important place in the fellowship of the Church. It may be too much to include the crucifixion, because that would surely have been noted in the account of his Baptism. However, that he was "respected by all the Jewish people" and had already built a synagogue in Capernaum suggests a man who was very open to both the monotheism of Judaism and the Incarnation of Deity. Of course, that is not the point of the teaching. Rather, Luke pointed out: **tell you, I have not found such great faith even in Israel** [Luke 7:9]. By that "great faith", Jesus intended us to understand that "Cornelius" accepted that His [Jesus'] Authority derived from a Greater Source; from the Highest Source. The Centurion understood that his authority was derived from the authority of Caesar. And, Jesus' Authority came to Him from God.

Pastors, and others, who have experienced the Miracle Power of the Gospel, more than understand that the Power and Authority does not lie within the person through whom the miracle is called forth. The Truth of the Centurion stands today: If one is in the line of authority, the Will of the Highest and His Power are available. One may say: **'Go,' and he goes; and that one, 'Come,' and he comes. I say to my servant, 'Do this,' and he does it** [Luke 7:8]. Also, the Power expressed in Jesus does not flow from ritual or law. It is the direct act of the Spirit of God, working through a human being. That is what the Centurion saw in Jesus, and so may we.

That Authority in Jesus extends to life and death. Even before the Resurrection, Jesus has power over the boundaries of life. Biblical scholars point to the power exemplified over the centuries. For instance, Elijah resurrected the son of the Zarephath Widow [1 Kings 17], and Elisha resurrected the son of the Woman of Shunem [2 Kings 4:8ff]. And yet again, Jesus called Lazarus from the tomb [John 11]. Does that Power continue to flow today? Some say that it does, but it is seen only through the eyes of faith.

John the Baptist requested confirmation of that very Authority. He had Baptized Jesus, and had heard accounts of the Miracles. Now he wanted confirmation of the Messiah. It must have been a matter of great importance to the Baptizer. To make such an effort from Herod's prison indicates the seriousness of the question. It was the "legacy question" from one facing martyrdom. And Jesus affirmed the Truth by noting prophetic fulfillment: **The blind receive sight, the lame walk, those who have leprosy are cleansed, the deaf hear, the dead are raised, and the poor** *are* **Gospelized** [Luke 7:22 Ital: literal Gk.]. If the ministry of Jesus is expressed through Miracle Power, then His Authority must come from God. Those who are not offended by Him as Messiah, Savior, are blessed [Luke 7:23].

Affirming the calling of John, Jesus pointed to the last prophetic book of what at that time was "the Bible": Malachi. John, according to Jesus was the one who was sent ahead of the representative of God who is a refiner [Malachi 3:2], a purifier [Malachi 3:3]; who will come to the Temple "suddenly" [Malachi 3:1]; One who will enter into Judgment [Malachi 3:5] against sinners who **do not fear me, says the Lord of hosts** [Malachi 3:5]. John's ministry was to prepare the ground for the Savior. And yet, great Prophet that he was, he was the last of those whose ministry preceded the New Age: the Age of the Savior/Messiah. Any who accept Jesus as Messiah/Savior are greater than John, because they are in the new "greater" age [Luke 7:28].

And who are they? **All the people, even the tax collectors, when they heard Jesus' words, acknowledged that God's way was right, because they had been baptized by John. But the Pharisees and the experts in the law** [scribes] **rejected God's purpose for themselves, because they had not been baptized by John** [Luke 7:29]. It was they who, responding to John's exhortations, repented of their sins and amended their lives who are of the New Age. The Pharisees have modern day counterparts who feel righteous enough to deserve eternal life, but Jesus implied that without an act of repentance and amendment of life, (that is without accepting Jesus as Messiah/Savior), they will be disappointed. They are people who, like the Pharisees, find reasons to avoid the confrontation between the Righteous Savior and their own sinful nature [Luke 7:33-34 John the Baptist came neither eating bread nor drinking wine, and you say, 'He has a demon.' The Son of Man came eating and drinking, and you say, 'Here is a glutton and a drunkard, a friend of tax collectors and sinners.'].

Further proof of the division between sinner saved by grace, and sinners who refuse the acknowledge the Savior was provided by a "sinful woman". Our cultural unhealthy pre-occupation with sex has led many to speculate that the woman who anointed Jesus in the house of Simon was a prostituted woman. The Greek word *"hamartalos"* does not support the idea. It is used to identify all sinners, for instance tax collectors [Matthew 11:19, Mark 2:15,16, Luke 5:30] and even Saint Peter [Luke 5:8; When Jesus called him from his fishing for fish.]. Those who feel self-righteous are probably persons of pretty good behavior and thus feel little need of forgiveness. They feel they have only a "small debt", while those whose sins urge discomfort know they have a large debt to be forgiven.

Luke separated these teachings from the parables. He clearly wanted to delineate these sections. He shared some remarkable historic details. For instance, that Joanna the wife of Chuza, who was the manager of Herod's "Household", provided financial support for Jesus and the Twelve. Also, that Mary Magdalene had been cured of evil spirits or diseases [Luke 8:1-3]. Again, the preoccupation of our immature society has brought suspicion on Mary's former morality. Again, the Greek does not support those who speculate about her. She may have had a severe case of acne, but that would have been called leprosy. She might have had migraine headaches, and that would have been seen as possible demonic possession. She might have been a gossip, and that too would have been seen as demonic (and it certainly is today, whether seen that way or not). Moral charges are mere speculation.

The first of the parables is about the harvest of the farmer who sowed seed.

The first thing one must notice about all the parables of Jesus, is that they are offensive. If the listener is not offended, the parable has not been understood. On the surface, what could be offensive about a farmer spreading seed? And what is offensive about gaining a harvest of an hundred-fold [Luke 8:8]? The solution is to be found in "personification". Clearly, Jesus intends us to understand that the farmer is God, and that the several kinds of ground suggest the receptiveness of different people. To illustrate the technique of interpretation, which may be applied to other parables, Jesus informs the Disciples about its meaning [Luke 8:11-15].

Jesus told the Disciples that the seed on the path represents those who simply don't understand the Gospel makes them susceptible to demonic distraction [Luke 8:12]. I suspect these are folks who seek the Kingdom for personal gain. For instance, there are those who's assumed "spiritual superiority" is the opposite of the servanthood model put forward by Jesus [Matthew 20:28; The Son of Man came not to be served, but to serve.] Among this group (forgive me for "judging" in order to illustrate) might be some famous pastors whose life-style most certainly does not reflect servanthood. Among the laity, one might point to judgmental Christians who would refuse to help those who are "morally deficient" and "unworthy".

The Disciples were informed that the seed that fell on rocky ground are those who's courage fails in the time of testing [Luke 8:13]. This is especially poignant since Luke wrote his Gospel during the time of Paul's imprisonment in Rome. Many Christians today face the same deadly menace.

Then the seed that fell among the thorns represents those Christians who are concerned with things other than the Kingdom [Luke 8:14]. "I will believe and serve if things go my way". I recall a dear woman who left the church when the court awarded custody of her daughter to her ex-husband. She said, "I won't believe in a God who takes my daughter away from me". Tragically, her resentment of God led her daughter away also.

But finally, the seed also fell on good soil, and the Kingdom Harvest was grand [Luke 8:15].

Who are the offended? Many of those who listened eagerly to Jesus's sermons, eagerly witnessed the healings, and then simply turned away. To them, the fault lay with Jesus. He demands too much. He doesn't understand my needs. He didn't answer my prayer the way I wanted. The Kingdom just costs too much.

This technique of interpretation applies to the next parable also [Luke 8:16-18]. Almost everyone understands the outer meaning of the "lamp on the lampstand". So, who is offended? One might consider theologians who interpret the Faith as if miracles and spiritual power are "un-scientific nonsense", or those who suggest that Jesus was simply a fine moral teacher (rather than the Incarnation of God). Or, those who hide their faith because it might interfere with business. Or, those who say their faith is a "private affair". One might include persons who "believe" but don't worship publicly.

The consequence of hiding one's faith is that it will be "taken away", while they who demonstrate their faith will find additional spiritual strength [Luke 8:18]. Take this seriously. There are terrible consequences to hiding one's faith.

Hearing these parables, Mary and the "brothers of Jesus" [including James?] came to "see him". Mark tells us that they wanted to "take him home" [Mark 3:21; When his family heard it, they went out to restrain him, for people were saying, "He has gone out of his mind."]; they thought he was crazy. Rather than respond to them, Jesus took the opportunity to teach. Saint Paul affirmed what Jesus said, and enlarged the idea. Paul wrote that believers are **adopted into the Family of God** [E.g., Ephesians 1:5]. **Jesus asked, who are my (family)? Only they who hear God's word and put it into practice** [Luke 8:21]. He, thus, added Himself to the parable of the lamp on the lampstand. One may not, if He knows Himself to be the Son of God, "go home" and refuse to "shine One's Light".

Indeed, shining One's Light might mean taking the Good News to the Gentiles who lived across the Sea of Galilee. Is that not the next step of "putting it into practice"? So, Luke presented the account of Jesus calming the storm on the Sea [Luke 8:22-25]. Is this not another instance of the Light shining in the darkness? The Disciples are protected from the harms of nature. Jesus not only calmed the storm and waves; He calmed the fears of His Disciples.

While among the Gerasenes [We don't know how to spell this name, other manuscripts have: *Gadarenes* or *Gergesenes*.], Jesus healed a demoniac. "Legion" shows the symptoms of very serious schizophrenia. I have experienced some success in the treatment of schizoaffective disorder [schizophrenia and depression] through the prayer of "casting out". I have not felt the same confidence in other cases. And, I do not recommend this course unless requested by the parishioner/patient. The rule of thumb is "first, do no harm". Jesus, of course, has Authority over the demonic, is able to detect and call out the demonic. In this case, He sent the unclean spirits into the unclean swine, and destroyed both in the sea.

Interestingly, the citizens of that area begged Jesus, out of fear, to leave. Legion begged to accompany Jesus, but was told to remain. Apparently, Legion's witness [Luke 8:39] affected their attitude toward Jesus, because the next time He appeared in their area, they welcomed Him and brought their sick to Him for healing [Mark 6:53-56].

Upon His return to Capernaum, Jesus was hailed by Jairus [Luke 8:40-56; See also Mark 5:22ff], one of the leaders of the synagogue. That he is named suggests that he became a member of the new Christian Community. And that he witnessed the resurrection of his daughter at the touch of Jesus would be high motivation to do so.

Enclosed within this account, Jesus was touched by a woman who suffered many years from an uninterrupted menstrual flow. When she touched the hem of Jesus' robe, He felt Power go out from Him [Luke 8:46]. Luke included this account for three reasons. First to identify that the cleansing and healing Power flows outward from Jesus. And second, to illustrate the new principle that "clean cleanses unclean". That is the opposite of the Jewish practice for a thousand years. Third, a woman touching an unrelated man was taboo. But Jesus was not offended. Instead, He healed her.

Possibly, that healing Power is the main subject, rather than the specifics of the woman or of Jairus' daughter. Luke immediately informs his readers that this "miracle power" was now "given" to the Disciples [Luke 9:1]! This is a key to the full theme of Luke Acts. Luke intended to emphasize the historic movement of the Spiritual Power of God from Judea to the Gentile world.

The command to **Take nothing for the journey—no staff, no bag, no bread, no money, no extra shirt** [Luke 9:3], indicates that the followers of Jesus are to rely only on Spiritual Power. God will supply all their needs. There are, of course, many in this world who would not, will not, and do not, greet the followers of Jesus with charitable grace [Luke 9:5]. Jesus advised: "Pick yourself up, dust yourself off, and start all over again" [Jerome Kern, 1936].

Herod the Tetrarch's interest in the expanding ministry of Jesus, and his assumption that it was related to John the Baptist, suggests the beginning of opposition to the Gospel [Luke 9:7-9]. (Note that it was the Tetrarch, not Herod the Great, who executed John.) In other words, Luke has presented a new tension between the Spiritual Authority of Jesus and the temporal authorities (both civil and religious).

And, Jesus withdrew from public ministry for a time. He took his Disciples to the far northern town of Bethsaida, but His fame was such that they could not remain anonymous. He resumed His preaching and healing ministry [Luke 9:11]. And the crowd was too large and eager. They stayed past the time for a meal. Again, the subject is the miracle power of Jesus. I interpret the feeding of the five thousand more as a parable than as a miracle, though a miracle it is. The fish and bread became, by the time of Luke, primary symbols of the Christian Movement. As a parable, the meaning is that when Christians meet the world with spiritual power, miracles happen and many are fed (spiritually).

Luke's parable of power leads directly into the confession of Peter that Jesus is **God's Messiah** [Luke 9:20]. However, Luke's personal experience, as well as that of the Christian Community, has always been that the Presence of the Messiah always evokes danger. Thus, Jesus warns His Disciples of His approaching death and resurrection [Luke 9:22]. Surely the Christian Community understood their peril to be similar and in unity with their Lord. Jesus warned them that if they were to be His Disciples, they must resign everything worldly, but that if they did so, they would not taste death before entering the Kingdom [Luke 9:27].

Not only will we not taste death, as Saint Paul put it, **we will certainly also be united with him in a resurrection like his** [Romans 6:5]. Why this observation? First Luke learned his theology from Paul. And second, the next passage is an image of that resurrected life! It is the Transfiguration of Christ [Luke 9:28-36].

The obvious message is that Jesus, as Messiah, is the fulfillment of both the Law of Moses, and the Prophetic Power of the Spirit of God. He stood between Moses and Elijah. His face was changed. It shone brightly, just as did Moses when he returned from the top of Mount Sinai [Deuteronomy 34:29-35]. The brightness of his face was, and is in Jesus, the Shekinah Glory of God. In other words, the evidence of the Powerful and complete Presence of the Holy Spirit. That is the evidence that Jesus is the Divine Incarnation. It is also a vision of our future, and a prediction of Pentecost [See Acts 2].

A voice came from the cloud, saying, "This is my Son, whom I have chosen; listen to him" [Luke 9:35] asserts the Authority of Jesus, and is an echo of the Voice at His Baptism. But notice; unlike the Voice at His Baptism, others are able to hear it. In the first instance, the announcement was to Jesus. In the second, it is to His soon-to-be Apostles.   One may understand why the men **kept this to themselves** [Luke 9:36]. They had not yet been filled with the Holy Spirit, and thus were without the boldness and assurance that accompanies the Spirit. They had seen Jesus accused of insanity. They did not wish to be hustled off and "cared for".

There are four "high points" in the ministry-life of Jesus: Baptism, Transformation, Crucifixion, and Resurrection. Often many meanings in the Transfiguration Experience are missed. One might ask, what did the experience mean to Jesus?

First, these experiences don't *just happen*. Jesus often spent time in prayer away from others. And this was one of them [Luke 9:28].

Just as the Voice at His Baptism was His "Confirmation for the Ministry of Messiah", the Transfiguration was His "Confirmation for the Cross". Confirmation, in this sense, means a strengthening or an inward (spiritual) acceptance and agreement. Just as, at the Baptism, Jesus the man knew that God was with Him in the great enterprise unfolding before Him, so now the Voice and Shekinah Power provided the courage and resolve to complete the "Sacrifice for sins" [Hebrews 10:12].

One might ask, why Peter, James and John were the three He took along with Him. Did those three need a special experience to prepare them for their own ministry? These three were the first whom Jesus called to follow Him [Matthew 4:12, Mark 1:19, Luke 5:10], and Paul said they were "the pillars" of the Church [Galatians 2:9]. James was John's brother, and would be the first of the Apostles to be martyred [By Herod Agrippa in 44 AD]. The three accompanied Jesus to the Garden of Gethsemane [Matthew 26:37, Mark 14:32]. Peter would later be told that he would walk the path to a cross as did Jesus [John 21:18-19], and John would understand more about the Holy Spirit than any other Apostle. John's Gospel is the Gospel of the Holy Spirit.

Immediately after witnessing the Transfiguration, they failed Jesus. The account of the healing of a convulsive boy is not about healing power. It is about the lack of confidence among the Disciples. **"You unbelieving and perverse generation,"** Jesus replied, **"how long shall I stay with you and put up with you** [Luke 9:41]**?** While the three had witnessed the Transfiguration and the healing ministry of Jesus, the Disciples failed to heal the diseased lad. There are two reasons. First, they had not yet been filled with the Holy Spirit. But the second is just as important. They lacked spiritual confidence. And Jesus was disgusted. After healing the boy, he said **Let these words sink into your ears: The Son of Man is going to be betrayed into human hands** [Luke 9:44]. They were perverse, lacked confidence, and would be cowardly. And they were all Jesus had for the proclamation of His Good News.

But also take note that spiritual dynamics are again on display. Spiritual weakness always follows directly after a great spiritual event. Luke shares several events of spiritual confusion in the days following the Transfiguration.

First, they asked themselves **"who is the greatest in the Kingdom"** [Luke 9:46-48]? Is this an echo of the Temptations of Christ [Matthew 4:1-11, Luke 4:1-12]? Jesus responded with the example of a child, demanding that His Apostles follow Him with innocent faith [Luke 9:46-48]. Then, though they had failed in their own attempts at healing, and wanted to condemn a man who was successful, Jesus told them to not discourage anyone who was on His side [Luke 9:49-50]. And then, because they were on their way to Jerusalem and some Samaritans refused them the hospitality of their town, the Disciples wanted to call down God's wrath. Jesus "rebuked" His Apostles and simply **went on to another town** [Luke 9:55-56; The NRSV has a footnote which beautifully illuminates: Other ancient authorities read *rebuked them, and said, "You do not know what spirit you are of; for the Son of Man has not come to destroy the lives of human beings but to save them."*].

Luke had seen the persecution of the Apostles, Paul, for instance, at Philippi [Acts 16:22ff]. He knew that Peter and Paul were imprisoned in Rome. But more, countless Christians had faced beatings, imprisonment, and death. Luke was incensed. He compared the lot of Christian evangelists to that of Christ. It was not an easy message he related to his fellow believers. The life of a disciple (then and now) must not be the easy way. There will be (then and now) very serious opposition.

Luke's conclusion was that while Jesus had no place to rest His head [Luke 9:58], there is no excuse to delay following Him: **No one who puts a hand to the plow and looks back is fit for the kingdom of God** [Luke 9:62]. And that is also true of His Disciples -both then and now.

Jesus sent out seventy-two Disciples [Luke 10:1; text does not include "Disciples"]. There is a lot of meaning in this account. First, seventy-two is twelve times twelve. Twelve is the minimum number of Jewish men required to found a synagogue. The numerology suggests "an unlimited number of evangelist/church planters". **The harvest is plentiful, but the workers are few** [Luke 10:2].

But sometimes the message is not welcome and evangelists will not always be welcomed [Luke 10:5-16]. The evangelist is to simply wipe the dust of his feet [Luke 10:11]. That town or household will face disaster in the time of judgment. They will end up in the "place of the dead", "Hades" [Luke 10:13-14]. **Whoever listens to you listens to me; whoever rejects you rejects me; but whoever rejects me rejects him who sent me** [Luke 10:16].

The seventy-two were enthralled: **Lord, even the demons submit to us in your name** [Luke 10:17]. How many of today's disciples of Jesus even think of battling demons, much less causing them to submit in His Name? This is both encouragement and evidence of both Spiritual Power and of Ultimate victory. "Hang on Brothers, Jesus will reward us if we remain faithful!" **Rejoice that your names are written in heaven** [Luke 10:18]. To those who remained committed during that time of persecution, Luke wrote, **Blessed are the eyes that see what you see. For I tell you that many prophets and kings wanted to see what you see but did not see it, and to hear what you hear but did not hear it** [Luke 10:23-24].

With that, Luke and Jesus returned to the definition of Christian Way [Luke 10:25-37]. Jesus shared the parable of the Good Samaritan. The offense is, of course, the comparison between the most visible practitioners of the Law of Moses and a socially unacceptable Samaritan. Today one might point to the good works of a Communist Community Organizer in Chicago as the Samaritan, or a good deed by an illegal immigrant. Would that offend some of today's church-goer. What is of greater importance, the good done or the social class of the person performing the good? He argues that the Christian Way is to treat everyone as deserving of good, and implies that the Law of Moses (as practiced) intends good only to Jews.

Mercy, in this parable, has a deeper and more offensive meaning; at least to the Jews of that day. Should God have mercy on the Samaritan? Should God have mercy on Gentiles? Should God have mercy on Christians with communist political views? Should God have mercy on Christians who sin? It is the Disciples (then and today) who are instructed to **Go and do likewise** [Luke 10:37]! What must that mean to us when we are tempted to be judgmental? Christ's parables continue to have bite even to this day.

And even the story about Martha and Mary has bite for us today [Luke 10:38-41]. Taken as a teaching parable, as well as an actual event, one can see special meaning. What is the **better part**? Is it not "sitting at the feet of Jesus"? We can be so very busy with our hospitality ministries that we are blinded to the need for secluded time with the Lord. Disciples (then and now) are instructed to **sit at His feet**, *and only then* engage in ministry. Too often our ministries are pursued as "humanitarian" rather than Christian Mission.

What is sitting "at His feet"? It is the life of prayer. His Disciples could see that His prayer life was far superior to theirs. And so, **one of his disciples said to him, 'Lord, teach us to pray'** [Luke 11:1]. As discipleship is impossible without prayer, Jesus taught them the Lord's Prayer. Sometimes we fail to see that the prayer is in the plural. It is the prayer of "us"; not of "me". And we often miss the rest of the teaching. The Lord's prayer is the doorway to a deeper prayer life. Since true disciples will engage the opposition of the demonic, they will need the strength of that deeper prayer life. To **pray in this way** [Matthew 6-9; introduction to the Lord's Prayer] does not establish a ritual. It is rather an example. And, of even greater importance, corporate prayer is only part of a more extensive prayer life Jesus urged us to undertake.

Jesus used yet another parable to illustrate that life. He pointed to a "friend" who at midnight is asked for a loaf of bread [Luke 11:5]. Who is the "friend"? It is of course, God. Do we suppose that God would find a request "inconvenient"? Of course not! **Because of your shameless audacity** [or: to preserve His Good Name] **he will surely get up and give you as much as you need.** As much as you need? What is it "you need"? A Christian will recognize that the subject is whatever is needful for the ministry of mercy [Luke 10:36], or a ministry toward those who are counted as unacceptable. Indeed, Jesus said: **I have given you authority to trample on snakes and scorpions and to overcome all the power of the enemy; nothing will harm you** [Luke 10:19-20]. Who are the snakes and scorpions? They are the demonic opposition.

Will the effort cost much? Again, the answer is affirmative. See what it cost Jesus. See what it cost the Apostles. See what it continues to cost! But Jesus had already given His answer to the cost. In the parable of the Good Samaritan, He said, **When I return, I will reimburse you for any extra expense you may have** [Luke 10:35]. That expense is not simply a matter of cash.

Today's Disciple will engage the enemy, the snakes and scorpions. The fierce battle will be costly, but out of mercy to those who have not yet been freed from sin and death, the Disciple perseveres. And the Lord will reimburse for the effort.

So, the Disciple is expected to make "brazen requests" of God, not doubting that God will provide whatever is needful in this ministry. **Ask and it will be given to you; seek and you will find; knock and the door will be opened to you. For everyone who asks receives; the one who seeks finds; and to the one who knocks, the door will be opened** [Luke 11:9-10]. This promise is a brazen invitation, from Jesus. He said: **Test Me and see if I will not open the floodgates of Heaven** [Malachi 3:10]. God is not an uncaring parent. Luke saw the pun in the question of Jesus: **Which of you fathers, if your son asks for a fish, will give him a snake instead** [Luke 11:11]? If you ask for the Holy Spirit [Luke 11:13], will God give you a demon?

Today, our "House is divided" and is in trouble. Jesus was accused of driving a demon out by the power of the devil [Luke 11:14-20]. Today we don't even try to drive out demons. The demonic is political or social, so we think; a matter of policy, behavior or attitude. But Jesus tells us that the demonic is real and spiritual. Today's disciple ought to take the threat of the demonic as serious and real. Jesus cautioned His followers: **When a strong man, fully armed, guards his own house, his possessions are safe. But when someone stronger attacks and overpowers him, he takes**

away the armor in which the man trusted and divides up his plunder [Luke 11:21-22]. Unfortunately, today the house is not guarded, and the armor has been plundered [Ephesians 3:6-10]! We must call for a Stronger Guard if we are to have a "House" at all!

Possibly, from the experience of someone he knew, Luke shared a spiritual dynamic about the demonic [Luke 11:24-26]. Unless one's inner being is filled with the Holy Spirit, casting out a demon will do more harm than good. Perhaps he'd seen someone who'd been cleansed through prayer, fall to a worse condition during the "period of temptation" which almost automatically follows a great spiritual blessing. According to Luke, the demon wandered about until, seeing an opening in the cleansed Christian, returned with seven friends. Tragically, many Spirit-filled pastors can point to one or more examples.

Continuing with his instructional theme for Christians, Luke included a condemnation, by Jesus, of "the current generation" [Luke 11:29-35]. It stands for this generation too. Jesus already knew that a majority would reject His message. He noted earlier generations, of sordid reputation, as able to condemn the present, because **One who is greater is here** [Luke 11:32].

An awful lot of present-day Christians gloss over this text. We have been taught tolerance. The idea that a majority of our neighbors aren't going to "make it" is just un-American. But the One who sees the secrets of the heart says that **Nineveh will stand up at the judgment with this generation and condemn it, for they repented at the preaching of Jonah; and now something greater than Jonah is here** [Luke 11:32]. Do we suppose that Jesus meant only those who rejected Him in the flesh? Is He not "here", even now? We may leave to Him the knowledge of who will and will not succeed. That is not our business; it is un-Christian judgementalism. But every Christian ought to be aware that true faith is not something that will make us popular.

Many think that they are on good terms with the Almighty. They are fastidiously moral. They have wonderful political and social values. They truly live exemplary lives. -and they have hearts that are far from full of the "Love of God" [Luke 11:42]. Like the Pharisees, they are far from the Kingdom. Jesus reserved His most expressive condemnation for them: "unmarked graves". People are made unclean by contact with them [Luke 11:44].

Thinking that public morality and participation in worship makes them clean [Luke 11:39; Ritual cleansing of hands and outside of dishes], they exhibit pride in their social status within the congregation.

In the following paragraphs, our translators have failed us. What they term "Lawyers" does not correspond to modern practitioners before the bar. A better translation, and one that fits the group of people to whom Jesus was speaking and who were Luke's antagonists in the Gentile/Jew antagonism, is "legalists" [see: Luke 11:45 and 52]. They are the same persons whom Luke called "Pharisees and Scribes". It is they who "practice" the Law of Moses.

This better translation is also more accurate for today's application. There are "legalists" among the Christian Churches. They are those who would not permit a lesbian to enter the sanctuary. They are those who blame the poor for making "poor choices" [See James 2:]. They are those who feel no kindred to other Christians whose worship differs from their own ritual or style. **Woe to you legalists** [My translation]**! For you have taken away the key of knowledge; you did not enter yourselves, and you hindered those who were entering** [Luke 11:52]. -

According to Luke, this was the "point of no return". The Establishment now actively will set traps for Jesus [Luke 11:53-54].

Jesus shared some clear advice for His followers: **Be on your guard against the yeast of the Pharisees, which is hypocrisy. There is nothing concealed that will not be disclosed, or hidden that will not be made known. What you have said in the dark will be heard in the daylight, and what you have whispered in the ear in the inner rooms will be proclaimed from the roofs** [Luke 12:1-3]. They were to live as if "Big Brother" or the KGB had wire-tapped their very thoughts.

As a pastor, good advice is to think in such a manner that "what you see is what you get". One's inner life ought to be consistent with one's outer life. But as a faithful follower of Jesus, one ought to be prepared to pay a heavy price. Persecution is the promise, rather than safety and comfort. Luke took note of the problematic opponents of his day: the legalists of the synagogue, and the governmental authorities [Luke 12:11]. If one has followed the advice of the Lord (to be outwardly consistent with the inward reality), one will have no fear when one is tried. One will either be ready to speak, or ready to pay the price. The reality of the Holy Spirit will prepare one's testimony [Luke 12:12]. The Lord God knows the number of hairs on your head [Luke 12:7]. Don't you suppose He will reward your faithful witness?

That Luke took such pains to point out that one ought to fear Him who, after they kill you, may send you to Hell [Luke 12:5], suggests that a number of his fellow believers had been unable to overcome their fears. Jesus said that He would praise, before God, anyone who praised Him while being tried. But whoever spoke ill of the Holy Spirit would not be forgiven [Luke 12:8-10].

This is one of the only two "unforgivable sins". It was born out of the failure of some to stand firm for the faith in a time of persecution. If it were applied to people who faced an angry crowd with stones in their hands, how much more ought we to suppose it would be applied by God toward today's Christians who without much "duress" disavow their Savior?

Luke continued this long address of advice for Christians. He wanted us to know that our faith was of greater worth than all our possessions. The parable of the man who built new barns to store his goods and then died [Luke 12:13-21], is offensive both toward some of the Christians of Luke's time, as well as of our time. One who is poor must rely on His Lord for his daily bread. The rich, while worrying about the future of the stock exchange, rely on themselves. This is the great problem of our day: "How much is enough? How much shall I give to the Lord?"

Addressing this subject as a Christian who donated one-hundred percent of his salary for three years, and discovered that God was able to feed, clothe, and care for him and his family, I sometimes long for that utter dependency on God. The words of Jesus were bright and true: **Consider the ravens: They do not sow or reap, they have no storeroom or barn; yet God feeds them. And how much more valuable you are than birds! Who of you by worrying can add a single hour to your life? Since you cannot do this very little thing, why do you worry about the rest** [Luke 12:24-26]**?**

Why, then, does the secure Christian not give it all away? Jesus said, **But seek his kingdom, and these things will be given to you as well** [Luke 12:31]. He has blessed.

A wealthy man was being interviewed, prior to approval for ordination. He was asked, "Are you and your spouse prepared to make the financial sacrifices which may be required of you as a pastor?" He answered, "You do not understand my position. My challenge is to determine the proper uses for what the Lord has already given into my stewardship".

For middle- and upper-class American Christians, Jesus put the issue as: **where your treasure is, there your heart will be also** [Luke 12:34]. One *must* examine his/her conscience to answer the question.

 The Gospel is miraculous in the way Jesus anticipated our present-day needs. He went on to the parable of the wedding banquet. We are to have our lamps trimmed. We are to be properly dressed. We are to wait on the instruction of the Lord. When He arrives, we are to respond appropriately and immediately [Luke 12:35-39]. And, when Saint Peter asked, **Is this for the world, or for us** [Luke 12:41]? Jesus replied, **Who then is the faithful and wise manager, whom the master puts in charge of his servants to give them their food allowance at the proper time? It will be good for that servant whom the master finds doing so when he returns** [Luke 12:42-43]. Indeed, we are to be eagerly awaiting His Return. We are to be looking for Him: **It will be good for those servants whose master finds them watching when he comes** [Luke 12:37].

We can find several meanings in this text. In our daily life, should we be actively looking for opportunities to serve? Should we be regularly asking the Holy Spirit to point out ways we can do something, as Mother Teresa said, "something beautiful for God"?

Also, if we are not "the poor" we are managers of the Lord's Estate. Surely some will try to find meaning for "climate change". But that is not the gist of this text. Christians are to be looking for the things of the Kingdom. These are not things we create ourselves. We may only respond to the things God is doing. It is them for which we are to be alert.

Again, St Luke provided a glimpse into the problem of persecution. He included a threat: **You also must be ready, because the Son of Man will come at an hour when you do not expect him** [Luke 12:40, see also 12:46]. Jesus said that He would cause division [Luke 14:49-53]. Luke could see that for himself. He was writing at the time when the Christian Community was dividing along theological lines. The Pauline side favored salvation by grace through faith. The other side additionally demanded obedience to the Law of Moses. Luke provided a hint about the depth and ferocity of the debate. **I have come to bring fire on the earth, and how I wish it were already kindled** [Luke 12:49]! And: **As you are going with your adversary to the magistrate, try hard to be reconciled on the way, or your adversary may drag you off to the judge, and the judge turn you over to the officer, and the officer throw you into prison** [Luke 12:58].

Luke's attention to what we consider history, continued with a nod toward the execution of a number of followers of "the Galilean". We have insufficient information to identify who that was, but Luke made another reference toward them at Acts 5:39. The issue is whether they suffered divine judgment. Jesus denies that they did. It was simply another act of political violence...just another day in the life of the world.

However, Israel *is* under Divine judgment. God had previously punished the nation [Babylonian Exile]. Now she was under judgment again. The fig tree [Luke 13:6-9] is always a metaphor for Israel. Israel has been "unfruitful". Luke acknowledges that God has not, as yet, applied destructive force against the nation, but hints that time is limited before such a disaster falls upon the Jewish people. If we accept that Luke was written between 59 and 62 A.D., we may conclude that Luke saw it coming, the Roman Army was on the verge of its destructive war against Judea.

The meaning for Christians today is very different from what it might have been for the Jewish Christians of his day. For us, the text appears as a warning. God has been patient and graceful toward us, but the day is coming when grace will be replaced by violent judgment. The date of the Second Coming is today as unknown as it was to the Christians of Luke's time. We have only this time in which to be "fruitful" [Luke 13:9].

The next section of the Gospel identifies what "fruitful" means.

A woman with Kyphosis [an abnormally rounded upper back], was at the synagogue on the Sabbath. The physician Luke tells us that she'd had the condition for eighteen years, and identified the cause as demonic [Luke 13:10-13]. There are other examples of Jesus performing healings on the Sabbath [see Matthew 12 and Mark 3; a man with a shriveled hand]. This event has two purposes. First, just as with the healing of the man with the shriveled hand, Jesus demonstrated the difference between the inner Godly meaning and the outward Pharisaic expression of the Law of Moses. But as instruction to the followers of Christ, this event illustrates a new definition of Spiritual Worship.

We are never to deny requested healing to anyone, anywhere. But even more, healing is (or ought to be) part of the purpose of Sabbath, even the gatherings for worship.

This might shock some contemporary Christians. But, do we not acknowledge the remission of guilt at Communion? Do we not encourage emotional renewal? Are not many sermons intended to overcome unrighteous hatred, racism, co-dependency, and a host of other psychological ills? Only in the twentieth century has medical profession gained such ascendancy that physical healing has been all but banned from corporate worship. Yet, the practice continues among Pentecostal and Charismatic Christians. It is much more common in Africa and Asia, than in Europe and North America.

Physicians will readily admit that many illnesses have their source in the "emotional life" of the patient. If one is to deal adequately with those "dis-eases", one must deal with the root cause. Often that requires the healing of one's memory. The patient must allow the Holy Spirit to "reinterpret" one's identity and experience. The Spirit of God is able to accomplish much more than the modern church believes. We ought to ask ourselves, on behalf of those who suffer, **Should not this woman, a daughter of Abraham, whom Satan has kept bound for eighteen long years, be set free on the Sabbath day from what bound her** [Luke 13:16]?

Continuing with instructions for the church, Jesus spoke of His followers as yeast and mustard seeds [Luke 13:18-20]. His definition of the term "Kingdom" always included His followers. So, when He described the Kingdom as mustard seed, He intended His followers to understand that they are to be as pernicious and invasive as dandelions spreading unchecked across a lawn. Mustard seed is tiny, and once on the wind, will settle everywhere. It is almost impossible to defeat. It becomes a large shrub. His followers secretly spread throughout a culture changing everything, just as yeast changes a bowl of flour into bread dough.

Again, one must ask, are Christians changing culture today, or are the "cultural icons" changing the Church? In response, I can hear a discouraged Christians saying, **Lord, are only a few people going to be saved** [Luke 13:23]? To that person I can also hear the Lord say, "Keep trying hard. Don't let the world discourage you. The day will come when God will shut the door to Heaven. Just make sure you are on the inside, because if you aren't God will disclaim any knowledge of you. **Make every** effort to enter through the narrow door, because many, I tell you, will try to enter and will not be able to [Luke 13:24].

The Gentile loving Apostle gives us an interesting twist on the "first and the last". We are commonly taught that the "last" means the poor and those who serve, while the "first" means those who are served. If we note that Jesus was speaking to a Jewish audience, we can hear differently. Jesus said that, **People will come from east and west and north and south, and will take their places at the feast in the kingdom of God. Indeed there are those who are last who will be first, and first who will be last** [Luke 13:29-30]. The Jews were the first to hear the Good News! Gentiles are the last. Indeed, according to Luke, Gentiles will be more eager to enter the Kingdom than many of the Jews to whom Jesus was speaking. In fact, Herod was, according to a listener, seeking to kill Jesus. To that, Jesus conflated Herod and Jerusalem. He said that He would continue His work until He would die in Jerusalem [Luke 13:31-35]. "Jerusalem", meaning the Pharisaic Religious Establishment, would be the last to enter the Kingdom.

Our Bible editors have divided the Gospel into chapters, but there is no change in subject. Chapter fourteen begins with Jesus at a Pharisee's house on the Sabbath. The Lord healed a man with an abnormal swelling of his feet [Luke 14:2; Gk: hydrōpikos: dropsy, edema]. He then asked whether the Pharisee would pull his donkey or his child out of a well on the Sabbath, rather than let him drown [Luke 14:5]. Is not God like a Father who would ignore the Law of Moses to do what is obviously right and good? And, are not the Gentiles beyond salvation according to that Law? Breaking the Law of the Sabbath is equal and consistent with the extension of Salvation to the "Last" -the Gentiles.

Addressing the Pharisee as a representative of Judaism, and referring to the Great Heavenly Banquet of Salvation; Luke, through the voice of Jesus, implores "humility". Taking the place of pride, as if it is owned, the Jewish Establishment risks being "humiliated" [Luke 14:7-11, especially vs. 9]. Taking a secondary place at the Banquet will allow God to call the Jewish People to the place of honor. The Jewish People have been more than humiliated. They have been horribly abused. Perhaps they will be exalted in the future [See Romans 11:26]. Today, it is the Christian who requires humility.

To the Jews, Jesus said, invite the undeserving to the Banquet [Luke 14:12-14] and restitution will be made at the **resurrection of the righteous** [Luke 14:14]. Today He might say to us the same.

This conversation is taking a different direction than what we have been taught. Before the Great Banquet, the host (Jesus) sent out invitations to many. But one by one, they excused themselves. Each had an "earthly concern": property, newly married, etc. So the host (Jesus) sent out His Servants to invite others. Those others are common folk; the people found in the **streets and alleys of the town**, along with **the poor, the crippled, the blind and the lame** [Luke 14:21]. That is, not the Establishment but the common folk. Yet there was additional room at the Banquet. And so, the man (Jesus) commanded that the Servants (His followers) invite travelers and foreigners along the **roads and country lanes** [Luke 14:23]. I believe Luke intended us to think these are Gentiles; they are not local folks. The legalistic Establishment people will never be allowed at the Banquet [Luke 14:24]!

There are four characteristics of the persons who follow Jesus. They have left their families to the point of leaving this earthly life behind [Luke 14:26]. Note that when our translators say that we must "hate" our parents and family, they use the Greek word: "miseó" [μισέω], which means to put in *lesser estimation, to renounce, to love less than* (in this case) Christ Jesus and His Kingdom. Jesus does not require "hatred" in the sense of detestation or revulsion. The followers "carry their cross" [Luke 14:27] in the sense that each new day they re-dedicate themselves to the Lord and His Gospel [See also: Luke 9:23]. This re-dedication is a complete denial of one's own interests, replacing them with Kingdom interests. That is consistent with the definition of "miseó". The followers have counted the cost of the Kingdom [Luke 9:28-29]. It is very high, but the Kingdom is beyond earthly value. The followers have calculated and decided that the Kingdom is too powerful to resist [Luke 14:30-33].

Remember that Jesus was speaking about the Jerusalem Establishment, as different from the crowds of commonfolk who gathered around Jesus and His message. The parable of the salt losing its flavor makes sense only if it is applied to the Jerusalem Establishment. And that, updated to our contemporaries, is a judgement against the legalists who resist the merciful grace of the Good News. Contemporary Pharisaical Christianity is as deadly as the Pharisees of Luke's day.

The Parable of the Lost Sheep [Luke 15:3-7] was taught to me as a toddler by my parents. The meaning communicated was that Jesus loves little children. And that is surely true. But it is not the meaning of the parable.

The interpretation of any parable must demonstrate its offensive nature. In this instance, Jesus rebuked the Pharisees. If the impression we have, of the pharisaic culture, is correct, there was much to criticize. Morally upright, they detested the unclean, including the poor and the sick. They happily excluded from the fellowship of righteousness any who did not measure up. But Jesus clearly taught that God is like a foolish shepherd who would leave all the righteous sheep, those who remained in the flock, to find one wayward and lost little lamb. Jesus implied that His effort was to rescue the lost sheep: those whom the Pharisees counted as unworthy.

Jesus followed His parable with another, from the other side. Suppose a woman has ten days-worth of wages, but loses one [Luke 15:8-10]. Will she not search for it, a full day's wage? The offense to the Pharisees is that God rejoices in her recovery more than over a Pharisee who remains properly righteous. God rejoices when a lost sinner is found and restored to "the purse".

The offense, contained in the so-called Parable of the Prodigal Son, was cause for the loss of an entire family to one of the congregations I served. I pointed out that there are three personages in the parable [Luke 15:11-31]. The most obvious is that the Father is "Father God". The second and third are those who are properly a part of the "inheritance". They are the two sons. One remained "on the farm", or within the boundaries of the Law of Moses. He labored hard to maintain his place in the affection of the Father. The other, the younger, spurned his inheritance, and engaged himself in the pursuit of worldly pleasures. But when he "came to his senses" [Luke 15:17] returned to beg admittance to his Father's employ. The offense is deep, especially from the point of view of the Pharisees. It was, in Luke's time, even more pertinent to the increasing number of Gentiles gathering around the Gospel Community. The Father rushes out to meet him and them, giving the Jewish son and the Gentiles his full trust [A ring on his finger is equivalent to giving the son an unlimited credit card]. Thus far, everyone agreed. But then I had to preach that the offense was that the Church failed to welcome the beloved son back into the fold. Indeed, the older son refused to take part with the Father in the feast. He refused the opportunity of Love. He dwelt in his own, foreign land of resentment.

A family transferred to another church because, while they welcomed the "Gospel of the Second Chance", they still had a long list of people whom they would not welcome into the congregation. They were in the same spiritual state as the Pharisees.

I really like the way Eugene Peterson translated the "Parable of the Crooked Manager" [Luke 16:1-9; *The Message*, Eugene Peterson, NavPress, Colorado Springs, 1993]. The manager fraudulently reduced the debts owed to the master, in order that he might have friends when he was fired.

The affront the Pharisees felt, and which we too ought to feel, is made much clearer by Peterson. **Streetwise people are smarter [in this regard] than law-abiding citizens. They are on constant alert, looking for angles, surviving by their wits. I want you to be smart in the same way—but for what is *right*—using every adversity to stimulate you to creative survival, to concentrate your attention on the bare essentials, so you'll live, really live, and not complacently just get by on good behavior** [Luke 16:8-9].

The Pharisees depended on good behavior to please God. And so, do many contemporary Christians. And Jesus tells us "it won't work"! We need to do everything we can to make a God our friend.

Peterson continued: **Jesus went on to make these comments:**

If you're honest in small things,
  you'll be honest in big things;
If you're a crook in small things,
  you'll be a crook in big things.
If you're not honest in small jobs,
  who will put you in charge of the store?
No worker can serve two bosses:
  He'll either hate the first and love the second
Or adore the first and despise the second.
  You can't serve both God and the Bank.

When the Pharisees, a money-obsessed bunch, heard him say these things, they rolled their eyes, dismissing him as hopelessly out of touch. So Jesus spoke to them: "You are masters at making yourselves look good in front of others, but God knows what's behind the appearance" [Luke 16:10-17].

Too many cannot understand the next verse because they take it as a simple statement of the Law of Moses: **Anyone who divorces his wife and marries another woman commits adultery, and the man who marries a divorced woman commits adultery** [Luke 16:18]. It is not that. It is a condemnation of the complexity of the Law of Moses. The Pharisees had found exemption after exemption from the law of marriage and divorce. But Jesus simply related it to the hardness of their heart [Mark 10:4-6], and the lust they countenanced. The reality Jesus perceived is that in the Law of God, matrimony cannot be undone, any more than one could divide a child between father and mother. Jesus condemned them for believing that, in their own interest, they could amend that greater Law. So, it is not a statement of fact as much as it is yet another condemnation of the Pharisees and Legalists.

So, what is the offense in the story about "Lazarus and the Rich Man" [Luke 16:19-31]? The story has three separate themes. The first is about God's justice. Pernicious selfishness here leads to a fiery damnation. We ought to care for others. But who are the others? They are the ones who, in this life are excluded from the feasting, the rich living, the ones whom the Pharisees (and today's legalists) consider to be outside the boundary of righteousness. That attitude is the "gulf" between Abraham and the Rich Man.

The second theme reflected the contemporary dispute in the Early Church. Abraham was the founder of the Covenant of Salvation by Faith! The Pharisees insisted on a different Covenant: The Law of Moses. The error was that Moses was organizing a community, and the Pharisees had made it into the test of admission to Heaven. Luke learned this from his mentor, St. Paul. Luke believed that we are saved by grace through faith.

The third theme is the incredulity of many concerning the Resurrection. The Rich Man pleaded with Abraham to send him to his brothers in order that they might avoid his fate. But Abraham responded that, if they can't figure it out with what they already have, they will not be convinced by someone from beyond death...that is by the Resurrected Jesus [Luke 16:31]. It is a cold fact that many of the legalist party did, in fact, reject the Resurrection, and suffered the fate of the destruction of Jerusalem *and* their supposed pathway to heaven.

These teachings continue with the hardest curse of the Lord: **Woe to you who cause one of my little ones to stumble**. It is directed toward the Church. The wrath of God is reserved for anyone who causes a stumble [Luke 17:1-4, see also: Mathew 18:6-7]. There are stumbling blocks that occur because "this is the world". There is woe to the world because of them [Matthew 18:7]. That is not what Jesus pointed at. Rather, the greatest sin is the failure of the Church to forgive and restore a repentant member [Luke 17:4]. We are to caution each other, and upon repentance we must forgive [even seven times seventy times; see Matthew 18:22]. To fail is to cause the loss of one for whom Jesus sacrificed Himself. Matthew adds to this teaching, "If your hand sins, cut it off" [Mathew 18:8]. Failure to restore a repentant Christian to the fulness of the fellowship is apparently the worst of sins.

As Jesus approached the climax of His life, He must have been discouraged by the continuing faults of His followers. When they asked that He increase their faith, He said that faith, the size of a mustard seed, that is, almost invisible, one could move a Mulberry Tree into the ocean [Luke 17:5-6]; but that is not the point. The point is that we are worthless servants, even if we do all that we are commanded to accomplish [Luke 17:7-10]. He likened us to "bond-servants" who do not even deserve thanks. We are to serve, even when we are tired.

His disappointment in His followers continues to be displayed in the account of the ten lepers [Luke 17:11-19]. One may well interpret the event as a parable. Ten lepers were healed, but only one, a Samaritan, returned to give thanks. The account is included as an obvious lesson, but to whom? In all the previous lessons, Jesus spoke to, and of, His followers. Luke thinks God is like the mother who worked all day to prepare a feast, and to whom no one said "thanks". And worse, at this point in the Gospel, only Jesus is aware of what lies in His future.

If we are to get the full value of this parable, we ought to "self-evaluate" our individual response to our Lord. Are we thankful? Is our commitment complete? Sent on our way, will we return to give thanks, or are we like the nine lepers who did what was required but did not love Him enough to return?

And as for **your faith has made you well** [Luke 17:19], Jesus' next remark to the Pharisees has a cutting edge for the followers. When asked, by the Pharisees, **When will the Kingdom come** [Luke 17:20], His response was that it is, if at all present, **inside you** [Luke 17:21: Gk; ἐντὸς (entos); inside or within, as inside of a bottle]. Was the Kingdom within the heart of the nine lepers? Is it such a powerful love for God that it demands a complete response?

All these teachings are summed up for the follower in the rest of Chapter seventeen. Jesus observed that we followers will long for the Day of the Lord. We will look here and there, but will not find it. However, the Day of the Lord, a day of judgment, will arrive suddenly, and one *believer* will be taken while another is left behind [Luke 17:22-37]. The descriptions associated with the full arrival of the Kingdom are singularly violent. They include Noah's Flood and Lot's departure from Sodom. The day will be simply another day, and we will not know that the time of Judgment has arrived.

Are we to despair? As we self-evaluate, do we hear: "Not so well done, lukewarm servant"? Is there hope for us?

Luke relieves us with the parable of the widow and the unjust judge [Luke 18:1-8]. **Then Jesus told them a parable about their need to pray always and not to lose heart** [Luke 18:1]. We must continually beg for our salvation! On the Day of the Lord, **I tell you, he will quickly grant justice to them** [Luke 18:8]. The issue is clear to this Apostle of Pauline inclinations: **when the Son of Man comes, will he find faith on earth"** [Luke 18:8]?

One sees Luke's definition of faith as a *complete* devotion of one's entire being to the service of Jesus, the Disciple's Master and Owner. Like the widow, the Disciple never ceases to strive for God's Justice [Note: God's Justice is very different from human justice.]

The parable of the Tax Collector and Pharisee is perhaps second only to the parable of the Little Lost Lamb. We all think of ourselves as the Lamb, and of the Publican. We avoid the offense. Since we are followers, we think of ourselves as the subject of God's Favor. Instead, we are, more or less, the Pharisee, or one of the sheep left behind while the Lord searches for the lost. Our self-righteousness calls out to God, but not often enough "for mercy". **For all who exalt themselves will be humbled, but all who humble themselves will be exalted** [Luke 18:14]. Indeed, we ought to approach God as a child [Luke 18:15-17], that is, with trust, without guile and without reliance on our own righteousness.

If we have nothing with which to commend ourselves to God, how can we be saved? That is the question of the Rich Young Ruler [Luke 18-18-25; we should note that he was not young.]. He had kept all the commandments since his youth; that was not enough. Jesus told him to sell all that he had, give it to the poor ["The Poor" was, in Luke's time, a synonym for the Church], and become a follower, a disciple. He was unable to sacrifice his power in the community. He was unable to sacrifice his wealth. And so, he refused. And that provided the reason for the question: **who can be saved?** [Luke 18:26]? And the answer from the Lord is that those who sacrifice *all* in this life, those who withdraw from wealth, family, and illusions of righteousness, will be blessed. **Truly I tell you, there is no one who has left house or wife or brothers or parents or children, for the sake of the kingdom of God, who will not get back very much more in this age, and in the age to come eternal life** [Luke 18:29-30]. In this age? We are, perhaps, to think of this as a reference to the practice of the Early Jerusalem Church, having sold all assets and donated one's total net worth to the Community.

Luke's grammatical method uses asides from Jesus about what would happen to Him in Jerusalem as dividers. We have previously heard what will happen. Jesus repeats Himself [Luke 17:31-34; see also 9:22ff]. The literary purpose indicates that one long teaching section, on the character and requirements of a follower, has ended, and another subject is about to examined.

After setting the standards for becoming a Disciple, Jesus began announcing the most important event of all history. He entered Jericho, where Zacchaeus lived. How did He know Zacchaeus? Matthew accompanied Jesus. It is not beyond belief that two tax collectors might know each other. And so, possibly Matthew pointed out the short man in the sycamore tree, Jesus invited Himself to dinner, and announced: **Today salvation has come to this house, because he too is a son of Abraham. For the Son of Man came to seek out and to save the lost** [Luke 19:9-10]. But, was it only the house of Zacchaeus to which salvation had come? Not at all. Jesus implied that salvation had come to all "the sons of Abraham". Was it coincidence that Jesus made this announcement in Jericho? Perhaps not. That city was, after all, the place where the other Biblical Yeshua (Joshua) entered "the Promised Land". The Holy People were "invading", and dividing the population between God's Chosen One's and the those who were to be cast out [As they were in 70 AD].

In response to Zacchaeus' repentance and compensation of his victims, Jesus shared the ominous parable of the ten slaves [Luke 19:11-27]. **He summoned ten of his slaves, and gave them ten minas** [about thirty months wages]**, and said to them, 'Do business with these until I come back.' But the citizens of his country hated him and sent a delegation after him, saying, 'We do not want this man to rule over us'** [Luke 19:13-14]. Some scholars associate this parable with a delegation of Jews who went to Caesar Augustus with exactly the complaint in the parable against Herod. And they suffered the same result when they returned to Judah: the king had them murdered.

But to people like Zacchaeus, who responded to the great invitation, **Salvation has come to this house** [Luke 19:9]. Clearly, the "house" is the "House of Abraham", or the "House of the Faithful"; those who are found doing the work of the king. To them, the King will say: **Well done, good slave! Because you have been trustworthy in a very small thing, take charge of ten cities** [Luke 19:17].

Clearly, the announcement is intended for more than Jericho. Luke immediately announced that Jesus went on to Jerusalem [Luke 19:28], and that He wept over the city [Luke 19:41]. Of lesser importance within this theme, is the entry into Jerusalem (Palm Sunday), than the quotation announcing the arrival of the King: **Blessed is the king who comes in the name of the Lord** [Luke 19:38; see Psalm 118:26]! However, the announcement is not as celebratory as our contemporary Palm Sunday services. Instead, Luke paints the picture as one of judgment.

If you, even you, had only known on this day what would bring you peace—but now it is hidden from your eyes. The days will come upon you when your enemies will build an embankment against you and encircle you and hem you in on every side. They will dash you to the ground, you and the children within your walls. They will not leave one stone on another, because you did not recognize the time of God's coming to you" [Luke 19:42-44].

Liberal scholars will suggest that this passage proves that Luke was written after 70 AD. A different perspective is that, at whatever time it was written, it reflects the attitude of the persecuted sect of Jesus. It also reflects the Divine regret that the Hebrew/Jewish People, at least those of pharisaic convictions, rejected the Gospel of grace and mercy.

The condemnation is emphasized by Jesus, in the Temple, **'My house will be a house of prayer'; but you have made it 'a den of robbers** [Luke 19:46]. Robbers of what and whom? Most often this is connected with the money changers [Matthew 21:12, Mark 11:15, John 2:15], but in Luke it is reasonable to think that the loss is to God, and the Temple Establishment is the robber. The quotation is from Jeremiah [Jeremiah 7:9-11] **'Will you steal and murder, commit adultery and perjury, burn incense to Baal and follow other gods you have not known, and then come and stand before me in this house, which bears my Name, and say, "We are safe"—safe to do all these detestable things? Has this house, which bears my Name, become a den of robbers to you? But I have been watching! declares the Lord.**

The judgment cast by Jesus did not include the common **people (who) hung on his words** [Luke 19:48]. They could have easily answered the question posed by the Pharisees about the origin of John the Baptist: **Was it from heaven, or of human origin** [Luke 20:3]**?** They understood, at the least, that the "teachings of Jesus" had Divine Authority.

Jesus preached His Parable of the Evil Tenants [Luke 20:9-18]. When the tenants killed the son of the Vineyard's owner [Luke 20:16], the owner killed the tenants and gave the vineyard to others. The common people said, **God forbid!** The teachers of the Law, and the Priests plotted to have Jesus arrested [Luke 20:19]. Luke wrote that they did not do so immediately, because they **were afraid of the people**.

The authorities understood the parable. They were offended, which is the defining mark of a parable. They understood, as did Luke, that God was about to wrest the "promise" from the "chosen people" and give it to Gentiles. In their thinking there were only two kinds of people: Jews and Gentiles.

An interesting idea: Jesus must have been fully prepared for the question about His Authority. He had been tested before. It had been the basis for the Satanic Temptations after His Baptism [Luke 4]. It had been the subject of Demonic recognition of Him [Luke 4]. The members of the synagogue in Capernaum were amazed at His authoritative teaching [Luke 4]. He had been thinking about this for several years. He understood that, were His Authority denied, His whole ministry would collapse. And worse, He would know Himself to be a fraud. His entire personal integrity rested on this one point. He had Authority direct from God. Deny His Authority, and all else collapses. This parable may be the focal point of the entire Gospel. The Crucifixion and the Resurrection are simply the evidence of His Authority, and God's Judgment concerning the "Vineyard", Jerusalem and Judah.

Unfortunately, many innocents among the common people would be caught up in the Judgment. But some of them would be the foundation for the new "Chosen People". Jesus quoted Psalm 118:22;

**The stone the builders rejected
  has become the cornerstone?**

Cornerstone of what? Of a new Temple, not made with hands [Hebrews 9:11].

The "spies" [Luke 20:20] commissioned by the authorities to infiltrate the "Jesus movement" asked Him about paying taxes. The swift answer **Give to Caesar what belongs to Caesar** [Luke 20:20-26] is also part of Jesus' earlier meditations about Authority. They were unable to trap Jesus into a commitment, either to Caesar (an answer that would offend the people), or to the people who hated the Romans (the Romans were Gentiles). The "cornerstone" fits neither earthly group.

The Sadducees were a different cultural/religious group. Unlike the Pharisees, they denied any spiritual life, and thus any idea of a resurrection. They insisted Jewishness consisted in a singular obedience to the Law of Moses. Their question, about which of the seven brothers had marital rights after death [Luke 20:27-38] was intended to separate the followers of Jesus from the Pharisees. But the answer Jesus offered has meaning beyond the religious differences intrinsic to Judah. Seen as a parable, the resurrected individual relates to God as an individual, not as a Jew or a Gentile. The Sadducees were impressed that He had dodged their trap, and complimented Him. They heard Him say that God is not "God of the dead" [Luke 20:38]. Perhaps that was enough for them. It was not enough for Jesus.

Jesus had His own question. Whose son is the Messiah? Quoting Psalm 110:1, Jesus said that Messiah could not possibly be David's son, because the King had called Messiah his "Lord". This is a retort to the Sadducees. Obviously, Messiah must be older than David, but that is impossible unless Messiah is from the Spiritual realm.

The separation of Chapter Twenty from the first verses of Chapter Twenty-one camouflages the unity of these several teachings. The question they asked, and the retort, brought forth from Jesus a condemnation of the Sadducees at least as bad as any intended toward the Pharisees. They are scoundrels! They fake pride of status. They pray too long. They embezzle the estates of widows. They use the Mosaic Law for immoral purposes, and they will be **punished severely** [Luke 20:47].

Then Jesus saw one of the victims of the "Teachers of the Law", the Sadducees. A widow put two of the smallest coins into the Treasury. Her act of worship was of greater honor than all the pomp and erudition of the Sadducees, more than all the strictures of the Pharisees [Luke 21:1-4].

This brings an end to a section of Luke's Gospel. Just as Luke used Jesus' predictions of His Crucifixion and Resurrection as a "bookmark", so he also used apocalyptic predictions as dividers.

In this instance, a remark about the beauty of the Temple was the occasion of predictions about the end of the City. The most prescient statement was, **As for what you see here, the time will come when not one stone will be left on another; every one of them will be thrown down** [Luke 21:6]. The Lord, perhaps, intended to compare the Jerusalem Temple to the temple of the body [See John 2:21]. This is especially connected by His observation that harm would not come to His followers. **But make up your mind not to worry beforehand how you will defend yourselves. For I will give you words** [Gk: stoma, meaning mouth] **and wisdom that none of your adversaries will be able to resist or contradict. You will be betrayed even by parents, brothers and sisters, relatives and friends, and they will put some of you to death. Everyone will hate you because of me. But not a hair of your head will perish. Stand firm, and you will win life** [Luke 21:14-19].

Liberal scholars believe that either the passage was written after the events of 70 AD, or that He connected His own fate to the multiple predictions of the Old Testament prophets. Conservative scholars hold the view that as the Divine Presence, Jesus knew the entirety of the future.

This argument among scholars blinds us from the central truth; the instruction for the Followers. **Many will come in my name, saying, I am he,' and, 'The time is near.' Do not follow them. When** you hear of wars and uprisings, do not be frightened. These things must happen first, but the end will not come right away" [Luke 21:8-9].

That Jesus knew His presence and ministry had historic pretentions for the entire world must go without doubt. Parables are foundational to the search for historic veracity in the gospels.

He told them this parable: "Look at the fig tree and all the trees. When they sprout leaves, you can see for yourselves and know that summer is near. Even so, when you see these things happening, you know that the kingdom of God is near" [Luke 21:29-31].

The "fig tree" is the symbol for Judah, and "these things happening" may refer to both the fate of Jesus, and to the fate of Jerusalem. The truth in the parable, offensive to those near Jesus as He told it, is that the Jerusalem Temple will be destroyed along with the City. And, that will mean the end of the entire cult of sacrifice, the Priests, Sadducees, and to a lesser degree to the Pharisees [Note: the Pharisees contributed to the origins of modern Judaism.]. It also suggests Luke's anticipation of the Early Return of Christ.

The new section of the Gospel begins with the betrayal of Jesus by Judas

Judas went to the chief priests and the officers of the temple guard and discussed with them how he might betray Jesus. They were delighted and agreed to give him money. He consented, and watched for an opportunity to hand Jesus over to them when no crowd was present [Luke 22:4-6]. Apart from John's observation that Judas was angry that the perfume poured on Jesus at Bethany wasn't sold to provide for the poor, we have no historical evidence about his motivation. We only know that he sought a time when an arrest could be made without a commotion.

The date of the "Passover of Jesus" has been debated. Passover and Sabbath are not the same. Passover beginning on Thursday at sundown and ending on Friday at sundown leaves us with two possible years for the Crucifixion, 30 and 33 AD. Of these, I prefer April 3, 33 by out calendar. The Passover meal was celebrated on Thursday evening, after sunset. For other details of the Last Supper, one may look elsewhere. Here, the concern is toward what Jesus taught at the Supper. Specifically, we note what the contemporaries of Luke took as instructions from the Lord.

The poignant questions are: "Who is the greatest"? and, "Who will betray Him"?

In this regard, the betrayal question is both historic and, to Luke, contemporary; **Woe to that man who betrays him** [Luke 22:22]! Judas betrayed Him, and so did Peter. During the persecutions, others followed them. The admonition of Jesus echoes in Luke's ears.

And, who is the greatest among the Apostles and Followers? Again the question was contemporary to the Last Supper, and also to the time of Luke. While Matthew's reference to the greatness of the servant is part of a sermon [See Matthew 18], and is in opposition to those who would be "instructors" and was in reference to the Scribes, Pharisees and Sadducees, Luke suggests that those who serve the Lord are greater than all others. Their reward will be great. **But you are not to be like that. Instead, the greatest among you should be like the youngest, and the one who rules like the one who serves. For who is greater, the one who is at the table or the one who serves? Is it not the one who is at the table? But I am among you as one who serves. You are those who have stood by me in my trials. And I confer on you a kingdom, just as my Father conferred one on me, so that you may eat and drink at my table in my kingdom and sit on thrones, judging the twelve tribes of Israel** [Luke 22:26-30].

Luke undoubtedly knew Saint Peter. The account of his betrayal of the Lord [Luke 22: 31-34[most certainly is an accurate portrait. Peter's regret [Luke 22:62] must have been a potent vaccine against apostasy. Though he was assuredly "past" at the time of Luke's writing, his example to the Christians facing serious persecution must have heard "Don't deny our Lord...you will regret it". His experience in the courtyard of the High Priest [Luke 22:54-62] was duplicated regularly in Luke's time: **This man was with him** [Luke 22:56] and **You also are one of them** [Luke 22:58]. The lesson is reinforced by the lesson of the garden [Luke 22:39-53]. Jesus prayed, and the Apostles slept. The account is sprinkled with references to swords. No contemporary Christian would have considered violent resistance. That is undisputed historical fact. The sword is, instead, a symbol of the danger faced daily by the entire Christian Community. Jesus urges us to pray, and pray constantly. The world is violent, Christians must not be so. We must pray, in order to **"not fall into temptation"** [Luke 22:45]. Indeed, Jesus healed the ear of the injured servant [Luke 22:51]. This is not the era of Christian peace. Jesus spoke to the condemned, the soldiers and crowd, **This is your hour—when darkness reigns** [Luke 22:53[.

In contrast to the age of darkness, Luke's account of the Trial and Crucifixion emphasizes the innocence of Jesus.

The very first charge they laid against Him was that He opposed payment of taxes to Rome and by doing so, He was **subverting our nation** [Luke 23:2]. But Luke has just testified that Jesus had taught **Then give back to Caesar what is Caesar's, and to God what is God's** [Luke 20:25]. Discovering that the issue was doctrinal, Pontius Pilate sent Jesus to Herod [not the Great: Herod Antipas; 20-39 AD] who found no offense to Rome. Herod mocked Jesus and sent Him back to Pilate [Luke 23:8-12].

Pilate ruled that the charge of sedition against Rome was false, but sentenced Jesus to flogging [Luke 23:16; lit: "Having chastised Him, I will release Him of necessity"]. The Establishment would not have it. Pilate attempted a pardon, but that was refused by the crowd. The demanded the release of Barabbas [Luke 23:18].

Scholars have seldom noticed that the area in which Pilate sat for judgment could not have held a large portion of the population. The "crowd" must have consisted of those favorable to the Establishment. I see no reason in the text for a sudden reversal of **the people hung on His word** [Luke 19:48]. Likewise, the people who mocked the Lord on the Cross, probably did not reflect the view of many of the people.

Pilate decided to grant their demand. He released the man who had been thrown into prison for insurrection and murder, the one they asked for, and surrendered Jesus to their will [Luke 23:24-25]. Pilate had seen, and ruled, that Jesus was not guilty. His guilt consists of consciously permitting the execution of a man whom he knew to be innocent.

Some of the women of "the people" **mourned and wailed for him** [Luke 23:27] as He was led from the Praetorium to Golgotha. Luke, unique among the four gospels, included a remorseful condemnation from the Lord. **Daughters of Jerusalem, do not weep for me; weep for yourselves and for your children** [Luke 23:28]. The imagery is specific to the disaster of 70 AD. This is yet another "chapter-marker" separating the condemnation from the Crucifixion. The "daughters of Jerusalem" wept because of His innocence, but their daughters would pay the price of Jerusalem's rejection of the Innocent Lord. And the first words of the innocent Jesus on the Cross, according to Luke, were a futile prayer: **Father forgive them, for they know not what they are doing** [Luke 23:34].

Even one of the guilty thieves recognized the innocence of Jesus: **this man has done nothing wrong** [Luke 23:41[. Knowing and declaring the innocence of the Lord leads one to Paradise.

Again, a rabid portion of the population ridiculed Jesus. There are those who propose that this was a normative behavior of ancient oriental culture. They point to the contemporary blood-sport games, not only in Rome, but across the Empire. According to Luke: seeing how the Lord died, **the people who had gathered to witness this sight saw what took place, they beat their breasts and went away** [Luke 23:48]. Those who consider the actions of the crowd to be cultural, must then admit a deep change of opinion and heart.

And, even the Centurion saw the innocence of Jesus. He "glorified" God and said, **"Surely this man was righteous"** [Luke 23:47; lit. dikaios: righteous, innocent]. That the Centurion glorified God, leads me to believe that he became a Christian. Luke's description of the death of Jesus is too calm. **It was now about noon, and darkness came over the whole land until three in the afternoon, for the sun stopped shining. And the curtain of the temple was torn in two. Jesus called out with a loud voice, "Father, into your hands I commit my spirit"** [See Psalm 31:5]. **When he had said this, he breathed his last** [Luke 23:44-46].

The noteworthy details, from the Apostle's point of view, were symbols of Cosmic Judgment. Today they provide interesting historical details. There was a lunar eclipse on April 3, 33 AD. But it was at night. Luke and the other Gospel writers might well have taken the record of the eclipse elsewhere (and in the daytime) to be true of Jerusalem as well. Seismologists suggest that a place thirteen miles from Jerusalem was very active between 26 and 36 AD. They are unable to pin-point any particular day from their data. However, an earthquake as recorded by Luke and the other gospel writers was very possible. That Jesus **Called out with a loud voice**, and **breathed His last** [Luke 23:46], is consistent with medical evidence. In Jesus's last moments, when His diaphragm was seconds from paralysis, He emptied His lungs, and died of asphyxiation. He was probably dead within a few minutes.

Joseph of Arimathea is noted as being righteous and innocent [Luke 23:50; as in 23:47; lit. dikaios: righteous, innocent]. He must also have become a Christian, and thus was innocent along with all other followers of Jesus.

Luke's account of the Resurrection is pointedly different from the other gospels. The empty tomb is the occasion of the Divine message: **Remember how he told you, while he was still with you in Galilee: 'The Son of Man must be delivered over to the hands of sinners, be crucified and on the third day be raised again'** [Luke 24:6-7]. Yet Luke paid scant attention to the effect of the message on the Eleven, beyond that they believed the report to be **nonsense** [Luke 24:11].

Instead, Luke focused his attention on the two disciples walking to Emmaus [Luke 24:13-35]! Three things are noteworthy in his account. First, the Lord is present and conversant [Luke 24:17]. Second, the Lord helped the disciples re-interpret the Old Testament [Luke 24:27]. And third, the Lord is revealed in the "Breaking of Bread" [Luke 24:31]! These three were very important notions in the Early Church. They constitute the evidence of the Resurrection! At the time of Luke's composition, these evidences were of greater importance than the details of how the Eleven responded to the amazing message carried by the women.

More importantly even than that the Disciples were "witnesses", was the command and promise: **You are witnesses of these things. I am going to send you what my Father has promised; but stay** in the city until you have been *clothed with power from on high"* [Luke 24:48-49]. This is a hint of the subject of Acts, but more than that; it is the definition of what constitutes a Christian. In order to be an authentic Christian, one must be endowed with, or baptized in, or in-filled by the Holy Spirit.

It was only after the report from the Two Travelers that Jesus appeared among the Eleven. And, Jesus repeated what He had said the Two Travelers, after which He led them to Bethany and **was taken up into heaven** [Luke 24:51].

This is where Luke leaves the first half of his account. The second part of a unitary report is in the Book of The Acts of the Apostles.

JOHN'S GOSPEL

LESSON ONE

Why study John's Gospel? If I were able to bring only one book of the Bible with me to a remote island, it would be John. It is different from the others. Matthew, Mark and Luke are biographies of Jesus. John is a biography of the Holy Spirit in Jesus. John's book is the Gospel of the Holy Spirit. And so, to understand the entire three parts of the Holy Trinity, we must study John's Gospel. I recall, in seminary, being asked, "What is the difference between the synoptic Gospels and John?" I was unable to answer that question for many years. It was only after I discovered the Presence of the Holy Spirit in my life that I was able to open my eyes and "see".   It is the bridge between the way the Holy Spirit functioned in the Old Testament, and the new way in the New Testament. Prior to the Incarnation of Jesus, the Holy Spirit inspired a few individuals; David and Solomon for instance, and prophets like Ezekiel, Amos, Jeremiah and Isaiah, and Hosea. After Pentecost the Holy Spirit is made available to any and all who will believe in Jesus as the Word of God.

This Gospel can be confusing. Remember that St. John had been a resident of the Roman "gulag". He had been an enslaved prisoner. Is it, then, any surprise that he should use code-words to express his theology? He wrote in a code that the Romans simply could not de-encrypt. The words he used were ordinary but his meanings would have been seriously illegal and dangerous in his day. The Romans persecuted, as John had already experienced, those who expressed faith in a deity other than those in the Roman Pantheon.

We start at the beginning with the familiar but not-altogether-understood passage about the Word. The reason I say it is not well understood is that few of us study it in the Greek. But, more importantly, it involves us in an esoteric doctrine of the Early Church: that of the Pre-existent Christ. Christians have long held that the Word was present at the Creation of the Universe. That much is clear from Genesis Chapter One, verse two: I would like to denounce the liberal scholars who translated that verse (in the New Revised Standard Bible, at least they have a footnote) "a wind". The Hebrew word is Ruach, which means breath, wind, or SPIRIT. Very clearly, the Spirit of

God moved across the face of a formless deep. God had not yet created wind or breath. This is a clue to how John (a Jew after all), understood the passage, and how he used it in his Gospel. The Greek word he used as the equivalent of Ruach is Pneuma. And he clearly referenced Genesis: "All things came into being through Him, and nothing was made without Him" (1:3).

John pointed to the Spirit of God, present at the Creation and present in John's time in the person of Jesus. That is what makes Jesus (flesh) into the Christ (the Messiah).

Furthermore, John, having read his Jewish Scriptures, knew that it had happened before. When a being, looking like a man but with the power of God, visited Abram, to announce the coming birth of Isaac (according to John), it was Jesus that spoke to the Progenitor of our Faith. When Abraham argued with God about there being a righteous man in Sodom, it was Jesus who stood in front of him. From time to time, God has presented Himself enfleshed within this world. John's only distinction was that in this special instance, Jesus was the Messiah, the Savior, the Incarnation.

I find amusement in the Muslim so-called scripture, because the Koran states that Jesus was the Word of God. Part of my amusement derives from the fact that while Mohammad understood, some of our own scholars do not. They apparently cannot understand what a seventh-grade confirmation student can grasp, that this Gospel is about the Spirit of God inhabiting a man, **The Word became flesh, and dwelt among us, and we have seen His Glory, the Glory as of a Father's only Son, full of grace and truth** [1:14].

Here, now, is the key to understanding this Gospel: **To those who believe, He gives the power to become Children of God, who are not born of the flesh....but of the Will of God** [1:12] . That is: a person who believes in Jesus as the Incarnation of God, is granted a second nature. We'll visit this in Chapter Three. That nature is the indwelling of the Holy Pneuma (Spirit) of God.

John's book is not one of the Synoptic Gospels. Matthew, Mark, and Luke, tell the chronological life of Jesus, they are biographies. John's Gospel is not a biography of Jesus. It is the Gospel of the Holy Spirit.

That John concerned himself with the Holy Spirit gives more "light" (understanding) to verse in which the term translated "overcome" [1:5 NRSV] can mean either overcome (in the sense of extinguished), or "comprehend" (in the sense understanding). In the first meaning the Light (or Spirit of God) has not been overcome by our sin. In the second meaning, the sinful world had not understood God Who has arrived in human form in Jesus Christ.

And so, the first miracle of Jesus is at the wedding in Cana. At the end of the account, John tells us that **Jesus did this, the first of his signs, in Cana of Galilee, and revealed his glory; and his disciples believed in him** 2:11 NRSV.

Here the Light begins to shine so that those closest to Jesus may understand. But, what is it about this unique miracle that reveals the Glory of Jesus? Wine is a metaphor for the Holy Spirit. Jesus didn't just pour out wine. He poured out God's Spirit. And that illuminates verse 10: **Everyone serves the good wine first, and then the inferior wine after the guests have become drunk. But you have kept the good wine until now.** I can see St. John chuckling as he wrote the verse. It is a loving criticism of God; whose self-revelation previously was partial but now was full.

In John 3:5-6 we read, **Jesus answered, "Very truly, I tell you, no one can <u>enter</u> the kingdom of God without being born of water and Spirit. What is born of the flesh is flesh, and what is <u>born</u> of the Spirit is spirit.**

In this world many people think they are spiritual because they have feelings. John tells us that it just isn't so. One must be born of the Holy Spirit by way of a relationship with God through faith in Jesus as Messiah/Incarnation. Such people are called "worshipers". Those who do not accept Jesus as the Incarnation of God are cursed and remain in the darkness. **And this is the judgment, that the light has come into the world, and people loved darkness rather than light because their deeds were evil. For all who do evil hate the light and do not come to the light, so that their deeds may not be exposed** [3:19-20].

As an aside, multiple scriptures reference "Darkness" as the place of weeping and gnashing of teeth, that is the place of the damned. And that is how it is used here as well as throughout John's Gospel. At 8:7 Jesus tells us that whoever believes will never walk in darkness but will have (be accompanied or dwell in) the Light of Life. This is yet another way for Jesus to refer to the life of Spirit. And interestingly, the location of the Gehenna of Darkness is within view of the City of God. Lazarus was in the Dark and could see but not get to the Light where the poor man rested in the bosom of Abraham.

Then, at John 4:23-24, we are told; **But the hour is coming, and is now here, when the true worshipers will worship the Father in spirit and truth, for the Father seeks such as these to worship him. <u>God is spirit</u>, and those who worship him must worship in spirit and truth.**

One ought to do a serious study of "True Worshipers". Does it refer to the Christian Community as opposite the Jewish? Does he refer to the kind of Judaism which we witness today, or is it a reference to the recently destroyed Temple cult? Or, in our contemporary time, does the passage refer to false Christians and true Christians? I have, as yet, no opinion on this.

At any rate, it is those whose spirit is truthful in worship of God that are sought out by the Spirit God.

Chapter four is the account of the conversation with the Samaritan Woman at the well. Jesus offered her "living water"; again meaning the Holy Spirit, which flows out of Jesus, as the wine from the jars at Cana.

Chapter five is about judgment, authority, and "seeing" what God is doing. Clearly a pun; only those with eyes to see can understand the Incarnation. But we have an interesting verse (25), in which Jesus says that the hour has arrived when the dead will hear the voice of the Son of God. Who are the dead? They are the ones who exist but have not yet been born again.

All of us were once among them. Some of us have no idea when we passed over from the dead to the living, but it is only through our faith that we are able to hear and discern who it is that speaks to us.

Chapter six is perhaps the most complex of all scriptures. One of only two books that I could not read was the published doctoral thesis of one of my professors on the bread of life. It was written in English, French, Latin, German, Greek, and Hebrew, without translation footnotes. But as he taught us simple folk, the Bread of Life is the Holy Spirit. It is the food that does not perish, and which is given by Jesus. Jesus said that he was the **Living Bread that came down from Heaven** [6:51].

Whoever eats that bread (which He said was His flesh) would live forever and never die (never taste death). Later Jesus told His disciples that **the Spirit give Life, the flesh is useless** [6:63]. I think the references to eating His flesh refer to the Eucharist which had already become the standard form of worship liturgy by the time of John's Gospel.

John 7:37-39 includes yet another metaphor. John tells us of the visit to Jerusalem for the Festival of Booths. He wrote: **On the last day of the festival, the great day, while Jesus was standing there, he cried out, "Let anyone who is thirsty come to me, and let the one who believes in me drink. As the scripture has said, 'Out of the believer's heart shall flow rivers of living water.'" Now he said this about the Spirit, which** <u>believers in him were to receive</u>**; for as yet there was no Spirit, because Jesus was not yet glorified.**

The true sign of one's salvation is the river of Living Water. Have we demonstrated sufficiently that this river must be the flow of God's Spirit? Jesus told us that we should be known by our fruits. St. Paul wrote that the emblem of this river of Living Water is the Love of God [1 Corinthians 13].

Yet when Jesus spoke these words, the Holy Spirit had not yet made Its "general appearance". The long sweep of our Bible demonstrates that the Spirit interrupted our world here and there until Pentecost. After that, the Spirit is poured out on believers. Fifty or sixty years later, John put pen to scroll to express the Gospel of the Spirit.

Chapter eight includes the adulteress woman, but most scholars suggest that it has only a tangential relationship to what concerned John. It may well be yet another metaphor directed toward the Jews. You have not properly lived out your marriage to God. Stop sinning and judging (both the woman and her accusers), and live faithfully as God intended.

Instead, the subject of this chapter is the "Light of the World". This is yet another metaphor. The meaning of this term, which sets itself apart from earlier terms of Light, is that it is expansive. Jesus, as the Incarnated Spirit of God, is to be the Light of the World, not just the light of Israel.

Regarding the sinful woman, as a metaphor for Israel, the following passage makes sense. **Then Jesus said to the Jews who had believed in him, "If you continue in my word, you are truly my disciples; and you will know the truth, and the truth will make you free." They answered him, "We are descendants of Abraham and have never been slaves to anyone. What do you mean by saying, 'You will be made free'?" Jesus answered them, "Very truly, I tell you, everyone who commits sin is a slave to sin. The slave does not have a permanent place in the household; the son has a place there forever. So if the Son makes you free, you will be free indeed** [8:31-36].

Freedom is the same as salvation. The condition of freedom and salvation is that one continues in the "Word". As is almost always true in John's Gospel, the word "Word" (singular) is translated from the Greek: "Logon" or "Logos". Remember Chapter One. The Word is the Spirit of God that created everything, and the Spirit that was incarnated in Jesus. To continue in the Spirit is the means by which we are set free from simple existence and born into the Real (as opposed to the apparent). Jesus told the crowd [8:47] that persons who have been born again are enabled to hear the words [rhemata] of God. Rhemata is the Divine communication intended for a particular individual. It is not a general communication. It is unique and personal, the answer to a prayer for instance. In the Gospel, when the translators use "words" (plural) they always have this meaning. Jesus then said that if one is not able to hear these words from God, one is not "of" God.

We will pick this up, next week, with Chapter nine.

LESSON TWO

Chapter nine includes perhaps the funniest story in the entire Bible. It is about the healing of the man born blind. Few people see the humor in the story. I recall being asked in my first religion course at college about whether the Bible includes humor. I thought not. Since then, I have discovered my error. Many jokes, understatements, ironic and pun-filled asides fill the Bible. This is premier among them. It contrasts the blindness of one who cannot see to those who can, but refuse to, see.

The key to the passage is in verse five: *"While I am in the world, I am the light of the world".* At the Feast of Tabernacles, the courtyard in front of the Temple was lit at night by huge forty-five-foot-tall lamps with large flames. Jesus, pointed at them and said, "I (not they) am the Light of the World". The blind man, at the beginning of the account, cannot perceive light; either of the physical or spiritual variety. But note what happens. It illustrates several layers of perception.

After washing at the Pool of Siloam, the man can perceive physical light. In verse nine some of the people are confronted with a miracle of serious proportions: **Nobody has ever heard of opening the eyes of a man born blind** [9:32]. And yet they refuse to accept it. Some of them have a higher commitment to the Law of Moses than to the evidence of Christly Power: **This man is not from God, for he does not keep the Sabbath** [9:16]. And his parents demonstrate an understandable fear of the authorities: **He is of age; he will speak for himself** [9:21]. I can picture John, so completely aware of the Power of the Christ, snickering up his sleeve at these people who can't seem to grasp the Power of God standing in front of them.

So, the authorities call the formerly blind man and compel him to testify under oath, and when he says that Jesus is a prophet [9:17], they respond that Jesus is a sinner [9:24]. They say that they don't know where he comes from. He replied, **Whether he is a sinner or not, I don't know. One thing I do know. I was blind but now I see!" Then they asked him, "What did he do to you? How did he open your eyes?" He answered, "I have told you already and you did not listen. Why do you want to hear it again? Do you want to become his disciples too?" Then they hurled insults at him and said, "You are this fellow's disciple! We are disciples of Moses! We know that God spoke to Moses, but as for this fellow, we don't even know where he comes from."** His answer is steeped and brewed in sarcasm. Christians of the day would howl in laughter as John was read: **The man answered, "Now that is remarkable! You don't know where he comes from, yet he opened my eyes. We know that God does not listen to sinners. He listens to the godly person who does his will. Nobody has ever heard of opening the eyes of a man born blind. If this man were not from God, he could do nothing." To this they replied, "You were steeped in sin at birth; how dare you lecture us!" And they threw him out** [9:25-34]. The people who had experienced the persecution of the Romans could see what we would call a "keystone cops" performance.

And finally, the blind man understands that Jesus is Messiah, and worships Him [9:38]. At that, Jesus confirms what John intended to communicate: **For judgment I have come into this world, so that the blind will see and those who see will become blind** [9:39 The Greek suggests that this *event* came into the world for judgement. Understandably, the translators read that Jesus came into the world.] When the Light shines, the unbelief is plainly revealed.

In Chapter Ten, John employs the metaphor of the shepherd and the sheep. We must be careful, because the object of the metaphor in one verse is not necessarily the same in another verse. For instance, let us look at 10:2-7 (NIV): **The one who enters by the gate is the shepherd of the sheep. The gatekeeper opens the gate for him, and the sheep listen to his voice. He calls his own sheep by name and leads them out. When he has brought out all his own, he goes on ahead of them, and his sheep follow him because they know his voice. But they will never follow a stranger; in fact, they will run away from him because they do not recognize a stranger's voice." Jesus used this figure of speech, but the Pharisees did not understand what he was telling them. Therefore Jesus said again, "Very truly I tell you, I am the gate for the sheep.**

In verse 2, the Shepherd is Jesus, and God is the Gatekeeper, and (of course) the followers of Jesus are the sheep. But, then, in verse seven Jesus claimed the title of Gate. This might obscure, but might also direct our attention to the deeper meaning of the passage.

This chapter is a continuation of the discussion centered on the act of Jesus bringing sight to the blind man [chapters 7 to mid-chapter 10]. There are two groups; the ones who "see" and those who are blind. As we will see, either one is one of the Sheep of Jesus, and invited into the Sheepfold [Heaven] or one is outside the Sheepfold.

The Pharisees just don't get it. They have a strong attachment to the law. Jesus proclaims that his Disciples have a strong relationship to God, and "hear" a Voice: the Voice of the Shepherd. To clarify this: The Voice of the Holy Spirit is the same as the Voice of Jesus. It was the Incarnated Spirit of God that spoke through the human Jesus. It is the same Voice that continues to speak to the Disciples. And only those who actually hear that Voice are admitted into the Sheepfold.

Now this raises two more questions. First; what is that Voice like? How can we distinguish it from all other voices? And second: What is the Sheepfold? And a third question is even more important for us today: Did John mean for us to understand this "literally"? Are we not part of the Sheepfold if we do not hear His Voice?

To John, the task of discernment was easy. It was not as much of an issue for him, and for the little community of Christians, as it might be today. Simply put, it sounds like the Pharisees are the "hired hand, who cares not a whit for the sheep". **"I am the good shepherd. The good shepherd lays down his life for the sheep. 12 The hired hand is not the shepherd and does not own the sheep. So when he sees the wolf coming, he abandons the sheep and runs away. Then the wolf attacks the flock and scatters it. 13 The man runs away because he is a hired hand and cares nothing for the sheep** [10:11-13]. If it sounds like a caring shepherd, it is more likely the Voice of the Lord. If the sound of the voice does not express the Character of God revealed in Jesus, it is not the Voice of the Holy Spirit

Since John intended that the audience include Jews, he included verse 16. **I have other sheep that are not of this sheep pen. I must bring them also. They too will listen to my voice, and there shall be one flock and one shepherd** [10:16]. The other flock is the Gentile Christian Community. He promised that we too will hear the Voice. At the time of John, the divorce between Jew and Gentile in the Christ Community was continuing, but not complete. John, a Jew, hoped, even that late, that there would be one flock and one shepherd. And, indeed, there is but one Flock. Some Jews are members, and some are not. It is the same with Gentiles, even among the members of the Church. Jesus promised to those who believe and are born again: **I give them eternal life, and** they shall never perish; no one will snatch them out of my hand. My Father, who has given them to me, is greater than all; no one can snatch them out of my Father's hand. I and the Father are one [10:28-30].

The last part of the chapter ties the previous into the account of the healing. It was Hanukkah and Jesus caused a stir when he claimed that God and He were the same. The idea was to as offensive to the Pharisee as saying Jesus is greater than Muhammad to the Muslim. While they intended to murder Jesus for blasphemy, Jesus tied it to the healing. **I have shown you many good works from the Father. For which of these do you stone me** [10:32]? It was as if He had asked, why can't you see? If they could see, they would be brought from the dead into Life Eternal.

Chapter eleven is the account of the raising of Lazarus from the dead to apparent life. One of my favorite authors, Par Lagerkvist, wrote about the raising. He wondered what Lazarus thought of being plucked back out of Heaven to spend more time here. He concluded that Lazarus spent the rest of his earthly life waiting to die and go back to Heaven. He must have been totally uninterested in this life.

In verse four, Jesus seems to acknowledge that Lazarus was going to pay a price. He said that this rescue mission wasn't for Lazarus' good, but for the Glory of God. And, in verse thirty-five, we are told that **Jesus wept.** People have wondered ever since why this was so. I suggest that it is because Jesus was going to require this price from Lazarus. Lazarus was going to "hear the Word" and would be called back from Heaven to this earthly life.

The purpose of resurrection has come to the fore. According to John the Chief Priest, Caiaphas, prophesied that **Jesus would die for the Jewish nation, and not only for that nation but also for the scattered children of God, to bring them together and make them one** [11:51b-52]. Here again is the issue of one Flock and one Shepherd, including Jew and Gentile. [One could study the responses of Mary and Martha, but that is beyond the scope right now. Neither quite grasped the Power of the Christ.]

The main point of this chapter is found in the decoding of the word "life". **I am the resurrection and the life. The one who believes in me will live, even though they die; and whoever lives by believing in me will never die** [11:25-26]. In the context of the raising of Lazarus, what is meant by life and live? It is the previously noted difference between apparent life and real life. It is the difference between eternal life, which we will discover in chapter fourteen, is already present in the believer, and apparent life, which is temporal and temporary. Those who have the Life given through the Holy Spirit in Second Birth, are alive, while those who reject Jesus, even though they have apparent life, do not participate in real life. They are temporal and temporary.

At this point the subject has morphed into the preparation for the Crucifixion and Resurrection. The next chapter (12) is the dinner with Lazarus, at which Mary anointed the feet of Jesus with a pint of pure nard, thus preparing Him for burial.

LESSON THREE

Chapter twelve recounts what we call Palm Sunday; the procession of Jesus into Jerusalem. It is the halfway point of the Gospel. Prior to chapter twelve John recounts the miracle life of the Holy Spirit working in the person of Jesus. From here forward, John will show God's Demonstration Project. To give perspective to Palm Sunday, we must note two things. First, the King of Israel is to rise up from among the "brothers of Israel" just as David rose among his brothers. So, the new

King of Israel might ride a horse up from the Kidron Valley into the City of David. But Jesus *descends* from Bethany and the Mount of Olives. Plainly, this event was organized to demonstrate that Jesus is not a King from the brothers, but a King from Heaven. John records: **At first his disciples did not understand all this. Only after Jesus was glorified did they realize that these things had been written about him and that these things had been done to him** [12:16]. What was it they didn't understand, that became clear only after he had been Glorified? It was that the Christ had entered the City from Heaven.

When a Jew from Greece asked to see Jesus, he replied: **The hour has come for the Son of Man to be glorified. Very truly I tell you, unless a kernel of wheat falls to the ground and dies, it remains only a single seed. But if it dies, it produces many seeds. Anyone who loves their life will lose it, while anyone who hates their life in this world will keep it for eternal life. Whoever serves me must follow me; and where I am, my servant also will be. My Father will honor the one who serves me** [12:23-26].

And so, we must answer the question: how is Jesus Glorified? He tells us. Just as a seed must lose itself as a seed in order to be born again as a plant, so anyone who minimizes the value of their earthly life [that is: anyone who serves and follows Jesus], will find their glorified life where "He is", and will be honored by Father God. Glorified is an end, and death is the process. But death has two meanings. First, one must submerge his/her will into the Will of God. Second, one will be partially glorified in this life by the indwelling Holy Spirit. We may say that because earlier we noticed that the indwelling of the Spirit is the definition of Glory. One will be fully glorified, and will be honored by Father God only after death. Partially glorified in the death of one's earthly will, and fully glorified in the Heavenly Reward. Each glorification is gifted through the working of the Holy Spirit.

Jesus again identified the life of the disciple with the indwelling Holy Spirit at verses 35-36: **Then Jesus told them, "You are going to have the light just a little while longer. Walk while you have the light, before darkness overtakes you. Whoever walks in the dark does not know where they are going. Believe in the light while you have the light, so that you may become children of light."**

Remember that Light is synonymous with Spirit. At that historical moment, the Spirit was present to the disciples in Jesus. With His Crucifixion, that "light" would no longer be available. They would be in the "darkness". He wanted them to believe and become children of the Spirit.

One last note about this chapter. Why did John, at 12:37-38, include the references to the prophet Isaiah 53:1? **Even after Jesus had performed so many signs in their presence, they still would not believe in him. This was to fulfill the word of Isaiah the prophet:**

 "Lord, who has believed our message
  and to whom has the arm of the Lord been revealed?"

John gives a very human answer: **Isaiah said this because he saw Jesus' glory and spoke about him** [12:41]. Nether John nor Isaiah could understand how a person could be witness to the Presence of God and still not believe that God was, indeed, Present. It is yet another coded pointer toward the workings of the Holy Spirit. Without the denial of faith, there would not have been the final revelation of the Love of God: the Crucifixion and Resurrection of Jesus.

Chapter thirteen details the Last Supper. Unlike the Synoptic Gospels, John includes none of the sacramental instructions. Instead, Jesus focuses on Godly Love, servanthood and betrayal. Peter, the host of the dinner failed to wash the feet of the guests. We know he was the host, because he was the last to have his feet washed. That indicates Peter's location at the table. Jesus took Peter's role of the host of the supper. The host's place at the table was by custom between the guests and the doorway. By Jewish custom, the host was required to be the guarantor of the safety of the guests. But Jesus, in a much larger way, was and is the guarantor of our safety. His instruction should be reflected in our relationship to each other. **Now that I, your Lord and Teacher, have washed your feet, you also should wash one another's feet. I have set you an example that you should do as I have done for you. Very truly I tell you, no servant is greater than his master, nor is a messenger greater than the one who sent him. Now that you know these things, you will be blessed if you do them** [13:14-17].

Too often we do not understand this command. Surely it is to God-Love [13:34: Gk: agapete] each other. By doing so, and by serving each other's needs (within the Fellowship of the Christ Community) we "cleanse" or wash the other spiritually. But there is yet another side of the command. We are to be the messenger/servant. How is that possible? What does it entail? A "Spirit-filled Christian", a "Born-again Christian", might understand that we are to bring and be the Word of God to the other. Now we refer back to chapter one, in which the Word is the Spirit of God.

Serving the other is not simply providing a food bag, or fixing a widow's automobile. Those are worthy, but not on point. We are to speak the "Spirit Word" to each other. We are to be the Presence of God to the other Christian. One will be blessed if he/she does this.

We must see the foot washing in the light of previous verses. **Jesus replied, "Anyone who loves** [agapa] **me will obey my teaching** [Lit: will keep my Word, Gk: Logon]. **My Father will love** [agapesei] **them, and we will come to them and make our home with them. Anyone who does not love** [agapon] **me will not obey my teaching** [Lit: will keep my Word, Gk: Logon]. **These** <u>words</u> [logous] **you hear are not my own; they belong to the Father who sent me** [14:23-25].

These are extraordinary verses in the way the translators have delt with them. In verse 24 we have the only time in which the translators have rendered "logous" as "words". "Words" usually mean the personal communication between God and an individual Christian. It is true that logous is the plural of logon, and that it cannot mean "Holy Spirits". It is sort of halfway between Logon (meaning Holy Spirit), and rhemata (meaning personal communication). I think John meant something like "general Holy Spirit teachings", or something like, "What the Holy Spirit teaches the entire Church". Another way of saying this is that anyone who, filled with the Love of God, obeys the Holy Spirit teachings as exemplified in the servanthood personality of Jesus will find that the Father, Son, and Holy Spirit have indwelt that person.

Here is grace beyond belief. God will indwell a person who struggles with his earthiness. Jesus is fully aware of our earthy side. He knows that both Judas and Peter will betray Him. He knows that we will too, and do too often. Yet, as John relates, we may be reconciled after our multiple betrayals. And that brings us to perhaps the most famous verses in this Gospel: **Do not let your hearts be troubled. You believe in God; believe also in me. My Father's house has many rooms; if that were not so, would I have told you that I am going there to prepare a place for you? And if I go and prepare a place for you, I will come back and take you to be with me that you also may be where I am** [14:1-3].

Do not let your heart be troubled? Troubled after betrayal? Remember that the chapter and verse headings are not part of the original scripture. These verses are a continuation of the previous verses. Peter is told he will deny his Lord three times. Then Jesus said: "Do not let your heart be troubled. Believe in me!" What greater comfort could Jesus have given Peter. As if to say, "I already know you will betray me. I also know your heart. I know your Love for me. Don't worry. I am going on to prepare a place in Glory for you, Peter."

Now we go on to another instruction. This one is closely related to the command to God-Love and become servant messengers to and for each other. **Very truly I tell you, whoever believes in me will do the works I have been doing, and they will do even greater things than these, because I am going to the Father. And I will do whatever you ask in my name, so that the Father may be glorified in the Son. You may ask me for anything in my name, and I will do it** [14:12-14].

How are we to do greater works than Jesus? And, more pointedly, do we take this seriously or just gloss over it?

Let us ask, how did Jesus do His Works? Each of the miracles of healing (not to mention the transformation of the personality of Peter evidenced in future chapters) is a witness to the Present Working of the Holy Spirit. God's Holy Spirit healed through the human Jesus. When Jesus was no longer present on the Earth, the Holy Spirit was given to each Born-Again Christian. Same Spirit, same working. Do you believe that miracles are possible? Do you believe that your prayers change things? Millions of miracles occur every day. Prophecies, healings, Words of Knowledge, graces of forgiveness and reconciliation...and countless other miracles are hidden from common view.

The unbeliever taunts the Christian by his own ignorance: "Ask anything in my name and I will do it", really? Yes really. If the Holy Spirit moves one to ask, that Spirit will accomplish what is asked. The formula is not magic. It is rather an algorithm. Each part of the formula must be present and fulfilled for the solution. When it is, it works wonderfully. Millions of Christians testify to its efficaciousness.

The unbeliever, even if he/she is a member of a church cannot perform miracles, and cannot admit to their occurrence. Why? Because he/she has not received the Spirit. **This is the Spirit of truth, whom the world cannot receive, because it neither sees him nor knows him. You know him, because he abides with you, and <u>he will be in you</u>. But the Advocate, the Holy Spirit, whom the Father will send in my name, will <u>teach</u> you everything, and <u>remind</u> you of all that I have said to you** [14:17and 26].

So, where does this leave us? The whole meaning and reason for John's Gospel is found in verses sixteen and seventeen: **If you love [agape]me, keep my commands. And I will ask the Father, and he will give you another advocate** [Gk: Parakleton; lit: close beside helper advocate] **to help you and be with you forever— the Spirit of truth. The world cannot accept him, because it neither sees him nor knows him. But you know him, for he lives with you and will be in you** [14:15and 17].

LESSON FOUR

Chapter fifteen, one of my favorites, is the great vine and branches metaphor. We are drifting into a conversation about the meaning of "life". There are many people who are walking about but who do not have "life". "Life", as John uses the term means only the second birth. Life comes from

Heaven. Existence comes from earth (dirt). Unless one abides (lives) in the Vine (The Spirit of God) he/she is cut off from the root. **I am the true vine, and my Father is the gardener. He cuts off every branch in me that bears no fruit, while every branch that does bear fruit he prunes** [Gk: cleans] **so that it will be even more fruitful. No branch can bear fruit by itself; it must remain in the vine. Neither can you bear fruit unless you remain in me** [15:1-2, 4].

The translation of "fruit" is of serious importance. The Greek "Karpos" does exactly refer to a vegetable or fruit. However, it also means deed, action, result: *profit, gain.* One can see a clear reference here. Only those who are "profitable" to the Kingdom remain in the Vine. Also, one cannot be profitable to the Kingdom unless he/she is related to the Vine. In other words, only the Christian who is connected to the root will be fruitful: **I am the vine; you are the branches. If you remain in me and I in you, you will bear much fruit; apart from me you can do nothing." "If you remain in me and my words remain in you, ask whatever you wish, and it will be done for you"** [15:5, 7].

On the other side, Jesus tells us that **If you do not remain in me, you are like a branch that is thrown away and withers; such branches are picked up, thrown into the fire and burned** [15:6].

The most awful contemporary illustration is the United Methodist Church. In 1968 she was the largest Protestant denomination in America with nine million members. Today we are a mere four million [in the USA]. The problem? In the early 1960s our denomination moved from preaching the Gospel of Salvation by Faith through Grace, toward an intellectual evaluation of morality and political policy. Rather than a Gospel of Good News to the unsaved, it became a gospel of political good news to the poor and disenfranchised. Where the denomination remained strongest, the message remained faith in Christ.

Other contemporary examples, even more extreme, are the United Church of Christ, the Episcopal Church. Where the dominant message has been social change, rather than forgiveness of sins, the American populace has seen it as irrelevant.

Our denomination has peopled the Baptist, Evangelical, and Free Church movements to the tune of several million members, and has been unable to interest younger people who feel no need of our guidance in their morality or politics.

So, we are confronted by a very serious challenge from our Lord. If this is the most apparent dynamic in the text; what are the others. How may we take strength from the Truth laid out for us: **You are already clean because of the word I have spoken to you** [15:3]. Why is it important to be cleansed? Is that simply a sop tossed out to comfort the Jews who held tenaciously to the law of Moses? Or, is it a spiritual dynamic? What does John mean by "clean"?

In chapter thirteen [10 and 11] Jesus used the word twice; once referencing the disciples, and the other referring to the un-clean nature of Judas Iscariot. Jesus had washed the feet of the disciples, and had spoken to Peter suggesting that it was symbolic of an inner cleansing...a spiritual cleansing. But what does that mean?

It means that the Light has overcome the dark, that Truth has replaced ignorance, that inwardly the disciple has had a new birth as a spiritual being. That had already happened in the hearts of the eleven. Now Jesus promised a new thing. This is the thing that makes all the difference in the life of the Disciple, and in the effectiveness of the Gospel messenger (you and me). [Note: this is the difference between fruitful and unfruitful followers of Jesus]

Look to John 15:26. **When the Advocate comes, whom I will send to you from the Father, the Spirit of truth who comes from the Father, he will <u>testify on my behalf.</u>**

Here we have two promises. An Advocate [paraclete; close beside helper syn: lawyer] will be sent to the believer. That helper is the Spirit of Truth. I need to note that there are two kinds of truth: factual and/or Ultimate. Factual truth is not what is intended here. Ultimate Truth is more important than the multiplication tables. Ultimate Truth glimpses things like: There is only one God. God is Love. Jesus is the Incarnation of God. God Loves you. And so on. The Spirit of Truth will affirm that Jesus is the Son of God. See also 16:13: **When the Spirit of truth comes, he will <u>guide you into all the truth;</u> for he will not speak on his own, but will speak whatever he hears, and he will declare to you the things that are to come.**

Now we come to the pivotal point of this entire Gospel. John 20:22: **When he had said this, he breathed on** [Gk: emphusaó lit: breathed into related to Heb: ruah used in Genesis to indicate the Holy Spirit as it Created] **them and said to them, "<u>Receive the Holy Spirit</u>".**

This is perhaps the most important verse in the entire New Testament. Combined with the account of Pentecost, this verse requires us to acknowledge that True Christians are born again into the Spirit Life by the indwelling breath of God. If the Holy Spirit has not entered the Christian's heart, he or she is not yet saved.

So, what are the signs that one is born again, or Spirit filled? Later in the chapter Jesus tells us. **As the Father has loved me, so have I loved you. Now remain in my love. If you keep my commands, you will remain in my love, just as I have kept my Father's commands and remain in his love. I have told you this so that my joy may be in you and that your joy may be complete. My command is this: Love each other as I have loved you** [15:9-12].

In each instance, the Greek word for Love is Agape: God's Love. Just as **I am in the Father, and the Father is in Me** [14:11], and the fact that **God is Love** [1 John 4:8, again agape]; this is a statement about the Incarnation. Jesus is **God with us** [Matthew 1:23]. It is a clear statement of our relationship to the Father. If the Love of God animates our life, then we have assurance that the Holy Spirit has indwelled our heart...our life. And indeed, we have Life. As we have already seen, John uses the word "life" forty-one times in the Gospel. With one exception [8:11 I say to you (adulterous woman) **leave your life of sin.**] the definition is the same: Eternal, Born-Again, Spiritual and Spirit-filled or Spirit-Animated, Life. If the Love of God animates our life, then we know we are "saved".

One of the two most distinctive Wesleyan doctrines is that of "Assurance". **Now faith is confidence in what we hope for and assurance about what we do not see** [Hebrews 11:1]. Wesley said that the born-again Christian will feel a deep assurance that God Loves him (her), and that Christ had died for him (her). Wesley felt that at the moment of his Aldersgate Experience. That assurance continued throughout his life. There were moments when he experienced depression and doubt, but over his lifetime he continued in the assurance of salvation by grace through faith. His opinion was of such strength that he felt that those who lack assurance probably lack salvation. This is my analogy: If the vine feels no relationship to the branch, it probably hasn't got one.

Does that bring joy? Both the assurance, and the movement of Love within our heart, are the most meaningful and joy-bringing experiences of which a human being as capable.

There is, here, one caveat, one warning: **If you keep my commands** [15:10]. But what is His command? It is to have God's Love for each of the Christian brothers and sisters. Simple in the sentence. Sometimes difficult in the execution. Some of our brothers and sisters are difficult to get along with. But then, sometimes we are difficult for Jesus to get along with, aren't we? It is a practical dynamic of the Christian Life. To be alienated from other Christians is to be alienated from the Body of Christ. Some years ago, a member of our congregation left our fellowship because he was angry at other members of the congregation. He said, "I can't sit in the same pew as them". In concern for him, I said, "This is a serious matter. I want you to understand that it compromises your salvation. When you arrive at the Gate to the City of God, Jesus will greet you, with his arm around the shoulder of one of those others. You will be required to decide whether you want to go in, and worship God with them, so you might as well 'get over it' right now". I was unsuccessful, but I hope my words will have eventual impact on him.

The next paragraph of the chapter deals with our relationship to "the world". "The world" means, all who are not within the Body of Christ. One of the signs of our faith is that **If the world hates you, keep in mind that it hated me first. If you belonged to the world, it would love you as its own. As it is, you do not belong to the world, but I have chosen you out of the world. That is why the world hates you** [15:18-19].

This is a bit complicated because we still live among those who are fellow Christians. However, increasingly, there are among us who hate our Christ and hate Christians. Like so many others, they count us as responsible for all the terrible sins of the world. Around the world, it is not different. Christians are the most persecuted of people. According to Open Doors, 2020 World Watch List, 260 million Christians live in areas of intense persecution. That is one in eight Christians out of the 2,080,000,000 Christians in the latest world-wide count. And that count includes nominal Christians. The rate of persecution for spirit-filled Christians is likely higher. The Christian Faith has ever been and continues to be the most persecuted group in the world. Even in today's America, Christians are told to not wear Christian tee shirts to public schools, say public prayers in "the Name of Jesus", or attempt to apply the authority of our faith in debates about public matters. Churches continue to be burned, and the faithful intimidated. Indeed, unless we understand this dynamic, we fail to see the power of the Gospel. One of the most difficult of historic truths is: *The Church has grown on the blood of the martyrs.* Truth be told, we anticipate a greater reward in Heaven than "72 virgins". We anticipate a white robe and a place closer to the Lord [Revelation 6:9-11].

Finally, Jesus gives us one more task. Even though it will incur the wrath of others, and even though it is completely impractical from an earthly point of view, we must testify or give witness to the Truth of Christ. ***When the Advocate comes, whom I will send to you from the Father—the Spirit of truth who goes out from* the Father—he will testify about me. And you also must testify, for you have been with me from the beginning** [15:26-27].

And that brings us back to the beginning of the chapter. We cannot give testimony except the Holy Spirit speak and act through us. Testimony apart from the working of the Spirit of Christ is false and will detract from the strength of the Body of Christ. It is that intellectual philosophy espoused by so many, a gospel of politics and morality rather than of second birth and regeneration.

Chapter sixteen leads us through an encounter with Evil. We are acquainted with the warning of Jesus that terrible conflict will be the life of the Christian. He said that He was forewarning them before His own encounter, in order that they not fall away in fear: **the time is coming when anyone who kills you will think they are offering a service to God. They will do such things because they have not known the Father or me. I have told you this, so that when their time comes you will remember that I warned you about them. I did not tell you this from the beginning because I was with you, but now I am going to him who sent me** [16:2-5]. We can all understand; but what does Jesus say He will do about this problem? He promises the Holy Spirit: **Unless I go away, the Advocate will not come to you; but if I go, I will send him to you** [16:7]. Not only that, **the Prince of this world now stands condemned** [16:11]. What He (Jesus), and by extension they, will experience has Cosmic implications. With that judgment comes also the guidance of the Holy Spirit. What the Spirit says to believers is Ultimate Truth. The disciples will have confidence in the words [rhemata] of the Spirit because they have already experienced that Truth in Jesus. **When he, the Spirit of Truth, comes, he will guide you into all the Truth. He will not speak on his own; he will speak only what he hears, and he will tell you what is yet to come. He will glorify me because it is from me that he will receive what he will make known to you** [16:13-14]. This is partly a defense of the Gospel, because John claims that all the things he has written are verified by the Spirit.

Here we have one of the spiritual dynamics of the Christian Life. How may one know whether the inward Voice is of God or not? The answer is, of course, that the Holy Spirit will say only that which is consistent with the Revelation of God in and through Jesus Christ.

Along with His warning of the coming persecution, Jesus shared a sweet little parable. **Very truly I tell you, you will weep and mourn while the world rejoices. You will grieve, but your grief will turn to joy. A woman giving birth to a child has pain because her time has come; but when her baby is born she forgets the anguish because of her joy that a child is born into the world. So with you: Now is your time of grief, but I will see you again and you will rejoice, and no one will take away your joy** [16:20-22]. Then He promised (a second time in the Gospel) that the Holy Spirit will be responsive to our every need. This, as I proposed earlier, is not a magic formula or a witches' incantation. Jesus intends for us to understand that with the guidance of the Holy Spirit we will have the Ear of God whose will for us is always Love. "In that day" means the day of our persecution. Ask for a Lexus all you want. If it isn't particularly a needful part of your discipleship, God won't magically get one for you. If, however, you are facing martyrdom, God will answer your prayer for the salvation of your spirit. **In that day you will ask in my name. I am not saying that I will ask the Father on your behalf. No, the Father himself loves you because you have loved me and have believed that I came from God. I came from the Father and entered the world; now I am leaving the world and going back to the Father** [16:26-28].

Chapter seventeen is the High Priestly Prayer. Most of us read it as a gloss. The language is stilted. Often Jesus seems to be speaking more to the disciples than He is to God. Here is, in list form, what John wanted us to "take away".

The time has come for Jesus to be "Glorified". Remember that means it is the time for Jesus to fully reveal the Character and Presence of God. Through belief in Him, the followers will be inducted into Eternal Life. Theologians debate whether the Glorification is on the Cross, in the

Resurrection, both or in the Revelation of the Eternal Christ. **And now, Father, glorify me in your presence with the glory I had with you before the world began** [17:5]. I say "Who cares!" The Lord Jesus is Glorious!

After asking that the final act be accomplished, Jesus presented His disciples to the Father: **For I gave them the words** [rhemata] **you gave me and they accepted them** [17:8]. What has this to do with the Glorification of Jesus? The key is in the word "words". The Greek is "rhemata". I remind you that it is the individual, personally directed communication of God to the Disciple via the Holy Spirit. That the Disciple has "accepted the words" equates to accepting the Spirit who speaks directly.

Jesus astonishes us today with the next statement: **All I have is yours, and all you have is mine. And glory has come to me through them** [17:10]. In the Greek "them" is a little more complicated. It isn't just you and me. Rather, Jesus is glorified in all the Things of God, which includes us, but is not limited to us.

He commends the Disciples to the Father in as much as He will no longer be able to stand between the Disciples and the "world". "World" also must be defined. It is that part of our natural reality which stands apart from the Divine. That is, the world is ungodly, demonic, and in some parts Satanic. The power of the world is such that without the protection of God by way of the Holy Spirit, the followers of Christ would be utterly destroyed. This is what happens in many parts of the world. Christians are the most persecuted minority. Daily Christians are being murdered for their faith. The Protection of the Lord God must be of an eternal nature, rather than temporal. **Holy Father, protect them by the power of** [Gk: keep them faithful to or by the power of your Name] **them your name, the name you gave me, so that they may be one as we are one.** What is the characteristic of "as we are one"? It is that: **they may have the full measure of my joy within them** [17:14].

We now come to the gist of this prayer: [17:14-19] **I have given them your word** [logon] **and the world** [kosmos] **has hated them, for they are not of the world** [kosmos] **any more than I am of the world** [kosmos]. **My prayer is not that you take them out of the world but that you protect them *from the evil one*. They are not of the world, even as I am not of it. Sanctify** [Gk: hagiason; en-Spirit] **them by** [Gk: keep them faithful to] **the truth; your word** [logos] **is truth. As you sent me into the world, I have sent them into the world. For them I sanctify myself, that they too may be truly sanctified.**

Again, we have words that require definition. Word is Logon, or the Holy Spirit. World is literally Cosmos or the natural world. Sanctify means to en-Spirit (as in "born again"), or to separate the Spiritual and Holy from the profane and natural. We are no longer part of the natural world only. We are here, but not of here. In the same way, Jesus is here, but not of here. Christians are given in inner radio with one station: the Holy Spirit. But more than that, we are actual parts of the Divine Communications System. We are set aside from the Cosmos for God's Purpose in the same way that Jesus (the man) was separated from the world of nature.

That Unity is emphasized. It is not unimportant. It is the fundamental reality of our Salvation. **Father, just as you are in me and I am in you. May they also be in us so that the world may believe that you have sent me. 22 I have given them the glory that you gave me, that they may be one as we are one— 23 I in them and you in me—so that they may be brought to complete unity** [Gk: teleioó (tel-i-o'-o), to complete or perfect]. **Then the world will know that you sent me and have loved them even as you have loved me** [17:21-23].

The "Glory" that the Father gave to Resurrected Jesus is identical to the Glory that the Father will give to us. Glory has become synonymous with God's Love (agape). The Beloved Son and the Beloved Believer are set aside for Mystic Eternal Unity with the Father God.

Chapter eighteen is a description of the arrest in the Garden at Gethsemane. Our translators have failed us in its most important statement. The NIV, following the example of other translations has verses four through six: (Jesus asked the Temple Guards,) **"Who is it you want?" "Jesus of Nazareth," they replied. "I am he," Jesus said. (And Judas the traitor was standing there with them.) When Jesus said, "I am he," they drew back and fell to the ground.** This appears to be simple nonsense. Why would anyone be knocked to their knees by "That's me"? The answer is, or course nobody. That's because that isn't what He said. When they named Him as Jesus of Nazareth, his response was the four-letter sacred tetragrammaton: The Name of God revealed to Moses. That Name was so Holy that no Jew would ever dare to speak it. And in this instance, Jesus correctly identified Himself as God. Jesus should be translated as saying "I AM" or "I Am God".

This "I Am" is the contrast to St. Peter's trinitarian **I am not** [18:17 and 25]. Recall that Peter denied knowing Jesus three times. Well, in addition to Peter's shameful denial of his Master, he spoke honestly. He did not know Jesus as God in the flesh. That would not come to him until after the Resurrection, when he met Jesus in the Upper Room.

There is a bit of irrelevancy in the account about the use of swords. Did Peter, or anyone else, think that cutting off the ear of a servant would free Judea from Rome? What I find intriguing about that passage is a possible Prophetic statement about Islam. Is it possible to think of Jesus establishing a coercive empire by the use of violence? And that is compared to the demonic Mohammad who took to the sword only weeks into his so-called prophetic revelation of God's Will. Christians have only one sword; the sword of the Spirit [Ephesians 6:17].

Along this line, we have one other comparison to the non-violent nature of Christian evangelism. One of the officers of the Temple guards slapped Jesus, perhaps hard enough to break the cheek-bone of our Lord [18:22]. The slapped Him, He did not respond in anger.

Then, finally, Pilate demanded that Jesus declare Himself a king, to which Jesus responded: **You say that I am a king. In fact, the reason I was born and came into the world is to testify to the truth. Everyone on the side of truth listens to me** [18:37]. Again, we have a response that makes no sense until we define Truth. "Truth" is a code-word for the Holy Spirit! Another word mis-translated is "kingdom". In the Greek "basileia" means king; but it also means "sovereignty" or "heart-influence". Let us substitute that and repeat the conversation: **"What is it you have done?" Jesus said, "My sovereignty is not of this world. If it were, my servants would fight to prevent my arrest by the Jewish leaders. But now my sovereignty is from another place." "You are a king, then!" said Pilate. Jesus answered, "You say that I am a king. In fact, the reason I was born and came into the world is to testify to the Holy Spirit. Everyone on the side of Holy Spirit listens to me." "What is this Holy Spirit (nonsense)?" retorted Pilate. With this he went out again to the Jews gathered there and said, "I find no basis for a charge against him** [18:35-38].

One last note on this chapter. We have pitted against each other, Barabbas and Jesus who is called Christ. Jesus is called the Son of God, or the Son of man. Barabbas is literally son of a father.

Chapter nineteen is the account of the Crucifixion. For basic information about the event, check the synoptic Gospels. They give all the historical data needful for a believer. John's Gospel is notable in only a few historical regards.

As you scan the chapter, look at verse 24: **This happened that the scripture might be fulfilled.**

John connected the Crucifixion to the Spirit inspired prophetic ministry. Then note verses 26 and 27: **When Jesus saw his mother there, and the disciple whom he loved standing nearby, he said to her, "Woman, here is your son," and to the disciple, "Here is your mother." From that time on, this disciple took her into his home.** Some scholars point to an Early Church tradition, along with several scriptural references to infer that John was a cousin of Jesus. His mother, Salome was at the Cross along with her supposed sister, St. Mary. And it was for that reason that Jesus commended his mother to John [John 19:26-27]. The basis for the authority of John in the Early Church is that he, among all the eleven, was chosen by the Lord to care for Mary.

The same is true for John's account of the empty tomb. [19:3 So Peter and the other disciple started for the tomb.] If "the other disciple" [20:3,4,8] is John, we have an eye-witness account. It is especially important because it is embarrassing to John. He believed but did not yet know the Biblical/prophetic references [20:9]. Perhaps more important is the word Mary Magdalene used as she greeted her Lord. The risen Christ touchingly spoke her name, and in recognition she responded with "Rabboni". Grammatically, that is the emphatic form of rabbi or teacher. In the common usage of the day, Rabboni referred only to the highest religious leader in Jerusalem. It is as if an Italian Roman Catholic referred to her local priest as "Papa" -the term for the Pope. Yet another meaning of the term is: "my teacher" or "my highest religious leader". The term is loaded with high emotion and vision.

Pastor W.C. pointed out that the error of Saint Thomas, is not that he doubted, but that he withdrew from the fellowship of believers [John 20:24]. He was not with the others when Jesus appeared to them [John 20:19]. Pastor pointed out that "things happen within the fellowship that don't happen when we are alone!" Lone Ranger Christians are not as effective as Fellowship Christians.

We now turn to the highest and perhaps most telling verses of the entire Gospel. **Jesus said, "Peace be with you! As the Father has sent me, I am sending you." And with that he breathed on them and said, "Receive the Holy Spirit. If you forgive anyone's sins, their sins are forgiven; if you do not forgive them, they are not forgiven"** [20:21-23]. John meant this literally. Jesus breathed His Holy Spirit into the Apostles.

These verses are critical because they place on the Disciples, and because He included us in His High Priestly Prayer [17:20 I am praying not only for them, but for those who will believe in me through their message.] both authority and responsibility.

The authority of God is placed on you and on me through the indwelling Holy Spirit. When Jesus "breathed" on the Apostles, He mimicked the Creative act of the Holy Spirit in Genesis. The word used for Spirit in Genesis 1:2 (Ruach) also means breath or wind. His breath echoes John's third chapter about being born again. Literally, the Risen Christ breathed/created within the Apostles, and by implication you and me, a new being, an eternal being. That is our Authority. It is the Holy within.

The responsibility is given in verse 23: **If you forgive anyone's sins, their sins are forgiven; if you do not forgive them, they are not forgiven.** We have been accustomed to thinking this is an act of graciousness on our part. But that is the secondary meaning. If "sin" is defined as "separation and alienation from God", then, unless we do something to assist a person toward that moment of surrender to the Lord, they remain separated/alienated from their Loving Creator. This is the evangelistic responsibility. It is placed on every Spirit-endowed Christian.

A student asked: "Does this mean that, if I do not forgive someone a wrong done me, that I am condemning that person to Hell?" Absolutely not. Matthew made the point that if you do not forgive the sins of others, God cannot forgive *your* sins [6:14-15]. That is not John's point of view. John intended that we understand this as a command for evangelism. If we do not live expressing the Love of God, if we do not express the invitation for others to come to Christ, they remain alienated from God and apart from salvation. It is evangelism that is commanded, not our "getting over" some moral or emotional slight.

God expects each Christian to be the doorway to Heaven. We are to be Christ to our neighbor. We are to be a Banner of Invitation to each soul we meet. I am terribly frustrated by the weakness of the witness made by the Body of Christ in America. We have made our faith a matter of "I feel okay", rather than a pathway of reflecting the Glory, the Spirit of Jesus Christ. Thousands of Christians, perhaps millions, face possible martyrdom today, and we think that, as long as I feel okay, all is well in the world.

LESSON SIX

Chapter 21, the final chapter of the Gospel, seems personally intimate to John. He begins with the account of the great netful of fish. He continues with the Revelation of the Risen Lord and the restoration of Peter. He concludes with a linked instruction for Peter and a defense of John's long life. Let us take them in order.

The Great Draft of fish suggests that the subject is evangelism. The not-very-hidden meaning is that evangelism apart from the direct command of Jesus is unsuccessful, unfruitful. Only when the net is cast according to the verbal (that is an important word) instruction of the Lord will there be success. And then the success will be enormous.

That word "verbal" is my reference back to the Greek word "rhemata". Unless the Christian is guided by the direct communication of the Holy Spirit, efforts at evangelism will be useless. Clever advertising techniques will not avail. Social pressure may result in church-participation, but not in conversion. Where such an act of conversion takes place, very often it fails over time. Then, shall we not invite people to church? That is not my intended message. Church services are among what John Wesley called "the means of grace". The un-converted at church is more likely to hear the invitation of the Holy Spirit than the un-converted at the golf course (though I have heard theological language on the golf course). Also, there are times when an invitation to participation is more likely to be successful than others. When is person is struggling, or lonely, or seriously questioning for instance. But those are times when a Christian might very well hear the call of the Spirit to invite the person.

The second part of the miraculous catch is the sense of unworthiness felt first by Peter, and then by all the Eleven. Peter had turned his back on his friend and mentor, Jesus. Later he discovered the

Presence of the Risen Lord. Indeed, Jesus had breathed the Holy Spirit into Peter. But Peter had no idea what to do next. He was a pastor without a church, a shepherd without a flock; called to what he did not understand.

The Greek version of the account opens a very interesting window of questions.

When they had finished eating, Jesus said to Simon Peter, "Simon son of John, do you love [agape] me more than these?"

"Yes, Lord," he said, "you know that I love [phileo] you." Jesus said, "Feed my lambs." Again Jesus said, "Simon son of John, do you love [agape] me?" He answered, "Yes, Lord, you know that I love [phileo] you." Jesus said, "Take care of my sheep." The third time he said to him, "Simon son of John, do you love [phileo] me?" Peter was hurt because Jesus asked him the third time, "Do you love [phileo] me?" He said, "Lord, you know all things; you know that I love [phileo] you." Jesus said, "Feed my sheep [John 21:15-17].

Scholars have pointed out that Peter denied Jesus three times, and in this three-fold questioning, Jesus forgave Peter three times. However true this interpretation is, I find it totally unsatisfying.

Why did Jesus twice ask Peter if he "God-Loved" his Lord? And, on the third iteration, why did Jesus give in to the brother/friend love term Peter used and replace "God-Love" with "family-love"? After reading the commentaries, I have found none that have the slightest idea. Mostly they assume that the two terms are synonymous. John's Gospel is much too beautifully written for me to accept such a sophomoric solution. But then, few scholars have understood this Gospel as singularly pertaining to the Holy Spirit. So, please know that I am stepping out on a limb of unknown strength as I share my personal interpretation.

First notice that Peter announced his return to his former occupation of fishing. The others followed him. Peter was leading the Apostles away from their calling. It was a public pronouncement that "these past years have been interesting, but they are over and done". He was also headed away from his own calling. I take this meaning from the otherwise irrelevant passage about Peter's old age. Here is an imaginary paraphrase: "Now (right now) Peter, you are in denial of your calling as an Apostle (God's Ambassador church planter). This is what must be overcome right now, right here."

Jesus asked, "Peter, do you God-Love me more than you love your brethren?' (This has two meanings: 1. Do you Love Me more than you love them? And 2. Do you Love Me more than they do? To this Peter responded: "Yes Lord You know that I family love you." Jesus responded by instructing Peter to "Feed my Lambs". Most scholars think this refers to the Church, but I say to you that Jesus intended that Peter feed the Apostles (lambs are intimates of the Good Shepherd, closer than sheep because they are utterly dependent on Him). But with what shall he feed them? Financially as owner of a fishing boat? Or with faith, grace, an understanding of forgiveness, a humility unmatched by others? A second time Jesus asked Peter, "Do you God-Love me", but this time using Peter's given name (Simon), not his faith name. Peter is in need of restoration to that name which means "Rock". This is clearly a reference to the denial in the courtyard of the Priest. Again, Peter responded with the term for family love. And Jesus instructed Peter to feed the Sheep; the Church. In the final test, Jesus asked Peter if the Apostle family-loved his Lord. And that broke Peter's heart because he had already twice said that he did. And in the final answer Peter acknowledged the deity of Jesus, "You know everything". The scholars are correct in assuming that this is the point of restoration to leadership of the Missionary Apostles, but they have missed the distinction Peter made, and Jesus accepted. Peter could love Jesus with all the fervor and depth one has for his dearest brother, but he could not achieve the love of Jesus measured by the Love of God. The Love of God surpasses all human ability. Peter's response was both spiritually and emotionally correct. And Jesus accepted Peter as he was. Remember that this was prior to Pentecost, and the outpouring of the Holy Spirit. And, just so, Jesus accepts us just as we are.

So, with his new-found depth and affection for his Lord, Peter is invited to "Follow Me!" **Very truly I tell you, when you were younger you dressed yourself and went where you wanted; but when you are old you will stretch out your hands, and someone else will dress you and lead you where you do not want to go." Jesus said this to indicate the kind of death by which Peter would glorify God. Then he said to him, "Follow me** [21:18-19]**!"**

The Greek meaning of "follow" is that Peter is to "walk the same road" as Jesus. Therefore, this is to indicate that Peter's death would be like that of his Lord.

And the chapter concludes with the question about John. If Peter is to walk the road of Jesus toward the Cross, what about John; the Apostle that Jesus loved [agape]. And John's answer, these many years after Peter's death was, "If it is the Lord's will that (John) should live until the second coming, that should have no effect on Peter's calling and destiny.

Conclusions about the Gospel of John

Review meaning of terms: John's Gospel is the "Gospel of the Holy Spirit". That is why it is so very different from the synoptic gospels. John wrote his Gospel during a time of persecution. He, therefore, used code words to make his Gospel less obnoxious to outsiders. His code words included: Word (meaning Holy Spirit), words (meaning the direct communication of God to the believer via the indwelling Holy Spirit), Light (meaning the Holy Spirit), Truth (meaning ultimate Truth as different from ordinary/facts), wine (meaning Holy Spirit), water (meaning life), salt (meaning influence), Glory (meaning the revelation of God's Character), Life (meaning Eternal/Spiritual Life as different from temporal life), blind (meaning those who have sight but reject the Truth as presented in, by, and through Jesus Christ), see (meaning understanding the Truth of the Character of God in Christ Jesus)

The way to determine whether our interpretation of John's Gospel is correct, is to turn to his letters. I say that now, and trust you to do that on your own. A few relevant quotations from the letters will be included in this lesson.

What did John desire to be the outcome of his effort? He wrote **But these are written that you may believe** [Gk: continue to believe] **that Jesus is the Messiah, the Son of God, and that by believing you may have life in his name** [20:31]. Having "Life in His Name" means participation in the Spirit-reality for Eternal Life and Glory. But what does "Glory" mean? Glory is the revelation of God (particularly God's Character).

John uses the term in two distinct ways. In the first, he relates the term to Jesus. For instance; **We have seen his glory, the glory of the one and only Son, who came from the Father, full of grace and truth** [1:14]. And: **Isaiah said this because he saw Jesus' glory and spoke about him** [12:41].

There are too many references in Isaiah for specificity. However, his usage is identical to our definition: "Glory is the evidence or revelation of the Character of God".

Another: **I have brought you glory on earth by finishing the work you gave me to do** [17:4].

Jesus says that an impartial person ought to be able to see the Character and Presence of God in His preaching, and especially in His miracles. **Do not believe me unless I do the works of my Father. But if I do them, even though you do not believe me, believe the works, that you may know and understand that the Father is in me, and I in the Father** [10:37-38].

Beginning with the first miracle, turning the water into wine at Cana, John tells us: **What Jesus did, here in Cana of Galilee, was the first of the signs through which he revealed his glory; and his disciples believed in him** [2:11]. What was the miracle? Changing the nature of a natural substance? More likely John intended that they saw the Presence of God in Jesus. They saw the generous nature of God.

In chapter eight Jesus tells us, **If I glorify myself, my glory means nothing. My Father, whom you claim as your God, is the one who glorifies me** [8:54].

We might cite 5:41 [I do not accept glory from human beings] and 11:4 [When he heard this, Jesus said, "This sickness will not end in death. No, it is for God's glory so that God's Son may be glorified through it.], but at 11:40 Jesus tells the man born blind, the one whom He had healed: **Did I not tell you that if you believe, you will see the glory of God?** And that is the major point for John. It isn't so much that the Glory of God, the revelation of God, was found in Jesus, but rather that we too might "see" it. Indeed, seeing is not enough. Others must see it in us.

So, John also used the word "Glory" in a manner that references the follower of Jesus.

This is to my Father's glory, that you bear much fruit, showing yourselves to be my disciples [15:8]. The fruit to which He referred is the Glory of God. Living in Glory results in fruit. Or, the fruit of a Christian's life demonstrates Glory (reveals the Character of God). We can go to St. Paul for a definition of fruit: **But the fruit of the Spirit is love** [agape]**, joy, peace, forbearance** [patience, humility]**, kindness, goodness, faithfulness, gentleness and self-control. Against such things there is no law** [Galatians 5:22-23].

But it would be better to take John's definition. Most theologians teach that God's Justice was satisfied in the Cross, and has been replaced by God's Love. And so, John wrote **Dear friends, let us love** [all in this verse: agape] **one another, for love comes from God. Everyone who loves has been born of God and knows God. Whoever does not love does not know God, because God is love. This is how God showed his love among us: He sent his one and only Son into the world that we might live through him** [1 John 4:7-9]. These few words are the best summary of John's Gospel. For those who are "born again" the Love [agape] of God has been made apparent in the life, teaching, miracles, crucifixion, death, and resurrection of Jesus. That Godly Presence is now made apparent in the Love [agape] between and among the Christians. That is the evidence of the True Life...the Eternal Life.

How is this possible? I will be blunt. It is not possible by human means. It happens only when the Spirit of God has in-filled a Christian...that is what being "born-again" means. But that is not simply an event in the life of a fourteen-year-old at church camp. It must be continual/constant. The

Spirit does not come and go. We may listen more or less, but once we have been filled by the Spirit of God it will not go away unless we send it away.

There are things we may do to reduce the times of our indifference, our deafness to the Word. The "Means of Grace" are God's gymnasium for the exercise of the Spirit. One's life as a disciple really depends on our regularly exercising these disciplines.

The Gospel climax might not be the crucifixion and resurrection, especially since John kept writing after his account of that. I suggest that the climax of the Gospel is in what is called Jesus' "High Priestly Prayer. [John 17:10-20] **All I have is yours, and all you have is mine. And glory has come to me through them. I will remain in the world no longer, but they are still in the world, and I am coming to you. Holy Father, protect them by the power of** [or: Oh Father, keep them faithful to] **your name, the name you gave me, so that they may be one as we are one. While I was with them, I protected them and kept them safe by** [or: kept them faithful to] **that name you gave me. None has been lost except the one doomed to destruction so that Scripture would be fulfilled. "I am coming to you now, but I say these things while I am still in the world, so that they may have the full measure of my joy within them. I have given them your word and the world has hated them, for they are not of the world any more than I am of the world. My prayer is not that you take them out of the world but that you protect them from the evil one. They are not of the world, even as I am not of it. Sanctify them by** [or: live in accordance with] **the truth; your word is truth. As you sent me into the world, I have sent them into the world. For them I sanctify myself, that they too may be truly sanctified. "My prayer is not for them alone. I pray also for those who will believe in me through their message.**

Walk in Glory (Spirit)!!!

Notes on Phileo in John:

5:20 The Father family-loves the Son. John 11:3. 11:36, 12:25 **Anyone who loves** [phileo] **their life** [psyche] **will lose it, while anyone who hates their life** [psyche] **in this world will keep it for eternal life** [zoan, from zoe =life]. 15:19 **if you were of this world the world would family love you.** 16:27 **"The Father family loves you" because you have believed in Me.** 20:2 **the disciple whom Jesus loved like a brother** 21:15 **"You know that I love you like a brother"**

THE ACTS OF THE APOSTLES

This book might properly be titled: Transitions. There are transitions from law to grace, from law to Holy Spirit, from Jew to Gentile, from Jerusalem to Rome, Peter to Paul, the Apostles to the second generation of leaders, and so on. It seems these transitions are the greater theme.

The first verse of Acts illuminates a very important viewpoint. **I wrote about all that Jesus *began* to do and to teach** [Acts 1:1]! Clearly, Jesus was not finished when He ascended into Heaven. Jesus continues to work. In **Luke's** time and in ours, the Spirit of the Risen Lord continues in ministry. Acts is the accounting of the foundational work of that Spirit. Acts is the story of the founding of the Community of the Risen Lord. It is descriptive of all the dynamics of the interface between the Spirit and the Christian. Always, the work of the Spirit in the life of one, is (as Saint Paul will have it) an "in-order-that". The Spirit of God never treats an individual Christian as one might view the winner of a lottery. Instead, the Spirit ever and always calls and equips the Christian for the benefit of the Community; the Kingdom of God. **On one occasion, while he was eating with them, he gave them this command: "Do not leave Jerusalem, but wait for the gift my Father promised, which you have heard me speak about. For John baptized with** [or "in"] **water, but in a few days you will be baptized with** [or "in"] **the Holy Spirit"** [Acts 1:4-5].

The Apostles thought He meant the re-establishment of the Kingdom of Israel, but Jesus intended the "Spirit Kingdom". **"Lord, are you at this time going to restore the kingdom to Israel"** [Acts 1:6]**?** His answer demonstrates the wide gulf between His intention and their colloquial interests. He set out the theme of the entire book: **"It is not for you to know the times or dates the Father has set** by his own authority. **But you will receive power when the Holy Spirit comes on you; and you will be my witnesses in Jerusalem, and in all Judea and Samaria, and to the ends of the earth"** [Acts 1:7-8]. The Apostles are to become witnesses and advocates *empowered* by the Holy Spirit, to bring the "Good News" to **"the ends of the earth"**. A promise was also given, at the Ascension, that He would return in the same way as He departed [Acts 1:11]; a promise of the "Second Coming".

The Ascension took place forty days after the Resurrection [Acts 1:3]. After the Ascension, the "Church" was gathered in Jerusalem. Luke shared a noteworthy event. Mary and the brothers of Jesus were participants. This is a dramatic change from when they thought He was crazy [Mark 3:21].

They were conscious that something ought to be organized. They based their plan on the rules for the foundation of a synagogue. The law required twelve Hebrew men. They had only eleven. So they chose **Matthias; (and) he was added to the eleven apostles** [Acts 1:26]. Matthias was never heard of again. The organization was a "man-driven" effort with no real result. Christians today ought to take note of this grand spiritual dynamic: **Unless the Lord builds the house, the builders labor in vain** [Psalm 127:1].

Over my ministry of five decades, I read many "how to" books by successful pastors and social scientists. Pastors who have tried to follow the insights of those authors have, without exception, failed to achieve similar results. The reason is simple: unless the Holy Spirit is at work in a congregation, any growth is simply of no importance. Sociological or business growth has little or nothing to do with the growth of the Kingdom of God.

Instead, the Holy Spirit brought forth God's Plan for the creation of the Church. The Holy Spirit baptized the Apostles on the Day of Pentecost [Acts 2:1]. The characteristics of the "Spirit Baptized" Apostle include a fearless devotion to Jesus as the Resurrected Son of God [Acts 2:32], a revised understanding of the Scriptures [Acts 2:16], and a courageous desire to save others from the on-coming judgement [Acts 2:40].

One wonders what happened during the forty days between the Resurrection and Pentecost. The Apostles must have spent long hours studying the Torah and the Prophets. The new understanding of the Covenant was apparent from the first [Acts 2:16-17].

No, this is what was spoken by the prophet Joel:

"'In the last days, God says,
 I will pour out my Spirit on all people.
Your sons and daughters will prophesy,
  your young men will see visions,
  your old men will dream dreams.

Yet that cannot explain the radical change in character and courage. One must have had a deep, spirit-changing experience to suddenly do what Peter (later, along with John) did and said.

Pentecost is the most important day in the history of the Church. Intellectual belief in the Crucifixion and Resurrection will not change the character of a believer. Only the "fiery" touch [Acts 2:3; think Shekinah glory] of God's Spirit is capable of instantaneously reforming the character of a man or woman. While the Crucifixion teaches us the depth and breadth of God's Love, and the Resurrection teaches us the Power of God and the grandeur of our hope; only the Pentecost experience reshapes the human character in the image of the Master.

Saint Peter clearly stated the expectation: **"Repent and be baptized, every one of you, in the name of Jesus Christ for the forgiveness of your sins. And you will receive the gift of the Holy Spirit. The promise is for you and your children and for all who are far off—for all whom the Lord our God will call"** [Acts 2:38-39]. Two things are required, and one thing is promised. Repentance and baptism in the Name of Jesus Christ will bring forgiveness of sin, AND the in-filling of the Holy Spirit. The Early Church expected and experienced this. The sign of salvation is the Active Presence of the Holy Spirit. That Presence had evidence: the **many wonders and signs performed by the apostles** [Acts 2:43]. "Signs and wonders" is a secondary theme of the entire book. If one is to understand Luke's writing, one must grasp the necessary active Presence of the Holy Spirit.

There is a small bit of interest to the theme of the book at verse twenty-three: **This man was handed over to you by God's deliberate plan and foreknowledge; and you, with the help of wicked men, put him to death by nailing him to the cross.** "Wicked men" [NIV Bible] is a translation of "anomos". The word means men without law, lawless men, wicked men, and possibly "godless men".

There are a number of plausible implications in this word. Peter could have meant that the Priests were "godless" and/or wicked. But "godless" can also refer to Gentiles; and the theme of this book is "the extension of salvation to the Gentiles".

Where the Holy Spirit is active in a fellowship, amazing things happen. Priorities are changed. One's expectations of life and death are altered. One values "things" only as a means to express one's Love. And the Church grows rapidly.

All the believers were together and had everything in common. They sold property and possessions to give to anyone who had need. Every day they continued to meet together in the temple courts. They broke bread in their homes and ate together with glad and sincere hearts, praising God and enjoying the favor of all the people. And the Lord added to their number daily those who were being saved [Acts 2:44-47].

Peter's sermon is evidence of a radical new understanding of scripture. The healing of a man's feet is only a pretext or excuse to preach this new and powerful Gospel. In ignorance of this Gospel, Jesus was crucified [Acts 3:17]. But that is exactly what God had predicted in the prophets [Acts 3:18]. Beginning with the Promise to Abram that all nations would be blessed through his offspring [Genesis 22:18; 26:4], and embedded in the Law of Moses [Deut. 18:15,18,19], God had planned what happened to Jesus. As a result, the time had come for all Peter's hearers to **"turn from your wicked** [Gk: ponéria (pon-ay-ree'-ah); painful and criminal iniquity] **ways"** [Acts 3:26]! The Resurrection is the evidence that God had sent Jesus first to the Jews [Acts 3:26: When God raised up his servant, he sent him first to you to bless you...], but that is the first step because God had said to Abraham, **'Through your offspring all peoples on earth will be blessed** [Gen. 22:18; 26:4].

This, of course, provoked a response from the authorities. Peter and John were arrested and appeared before the Sanhedrin. They were not questioned about their "teaching", but rather about the healing of the beggar's feet. The authorities wanted to know by what authority they had performed the healing. It is as if one were jailed for saving the life of someone by CPR without a proper medical license. They could not punish because the man had, obviously, been healed. And so, they instructed the Apostles to no longer teach about Jesus [Acts 4:18]. According to them, Jesus was not the proper authority [Acts 4:26; GK: chrió -anointed] by which to perform miracles.

The opposition from Pilate, the "gentiles" and the Jewish authorities did not inspire fear. Instead, it led the community to prayer and a profound strengthening [Acts 4:27-31]. This ought to be a lesson to the Church today. Opposition strengthens. Our problem today is not opposition, but indifference. However, the day of opposition is quickly dawning.

This early in the account, Luke introduced Barnabas, a Levite from Cyprus [Acts 4:36]. Barnabas will call Paul into missionary work.

The sad account of Ananias and Sapphira [Acts 5:1-10] was, perhaps, an object lesson for the Early Church. One must do what one has set out to perform, even in a day of persecution. One of Luke's secondary themes is loyalty to Christ at whatever cost. If one must die, it is better to die faithfully.

The Apostles were arrested by the authorities [Acts 5:17-26]. Miraculously, the next morning they were in the Temple precincts teaching, as usual. Gamaliel provided the standard of truth which is applicable universally. **If their purpose or activity is of human origin, it will fail. But if it is from God, you will not be able to stop these men; you will only find yourselves fighting against God"** [Acts 5:38-39]. Let us give those men the benefit of our doubt. They sincerely thought they served God. Gamaliel was the teacher of Saul [Acts 22:3].

The choosing of the seven deacons is one of the important developments of church history. Seven Hellenist men of blameless character were chosen to properly divide the food servings so that Jews and the "semi-gentile" Hellenists would be treated equally [Acts 6:1-5]. It illustrates that the original community of Christ had its internal issues; just as is the Church of today. It is a step toward the inclusive community of Jews and Gentiles. And, it is the occasion for the introduction of Stephen.

The story of Stephen [Acts 6:8-7:60] is yet another call to loyalty in the face of deadly opposition. As a deacon, Stephen is declared "blameless". His sermon provided Luke with the opportunity to enlarge his re-interpretation of scripture. And his death is a promise of glory for those who hold true to their faith [Acts 7:54-56].

The re-interpretation of scripture was perfectly acceptable to his hearers until Stephen denounced, not just their ancestors but also those present: **"You stiff-necked people! Your hearts and ears are still uncircumcised. You are just like your ancestors: You always resist the Holy Spirit! Was there ever a prophet your ancestors did not persecute? They even killed those who predicted the coming of the Righteous One. And now you have betrayed and murdered him— you who have received the law that was given through angels but have not obeyed it"** [Acts 7:51-53]. Any preacher, worthy of his salt, must point to the similarity between those listeners and all of us today.

Luke was a master story-teller. That each event flows directly from the previous, however, is not just good editing. Luke intends that his reader should understand that each event in our own lives is the precursor to another of the unfolding of God's Redemptive Love.

In this case, Saul was present to hear Stephen's sermon, and to see the grace in the Deacon's death: **"Hold not this sin** [Acts 7:60; Gk: hamartia (ham-ar-tee'-ah), ethical failure] **against them"**. Saul approved [Gk: suneudokeó

(soon-yoo-dok-eh'-o); joined in] of Stephen's death [Acts 8:1]. He thought it appropriate.

Stephen's sermon seems to have inspired a rabid hatred of this new community, such that many fled the city [Acts 8:2], again providing the way forward. Not only does this early diaspora account for the communities in which Saul would find refuge, it is also the means by which the Faith was spread. For surely, the Apostles were not the only missionaries. **Those who had been scattered preached the word wherever they went** [Acts 8:4]. Saul/Paul accounts for the main theme of Acts, but Philip casts out demons in Samaria. Each dispersed Christian became the seed of a new community. The more the Church was hated, the more it grew.

The difference between believers and Spirit-filled Disciples is apparent even today. Philip was successful in gaining believers, but the Power of the Spirit had not been spread among the congregation. And so, Peter and John were sent to Samaria to empower the Spirit among the people of the community [Acts 8:15-17]. The distinction is overlooked in a majority of American Christian churches, but is essential to a growing Body of Christ.

The story of Simon the magician illustrates the truth that the Holy Spirit is a "free" gift. It cannot be bought or manipulated, and is different from magic [Acts 8:20]. Moreover, no pastor with motives other than simply serving Christ will receive the Baptism. Simon's request seems laudable, but Peter saw personal ambition rather than humble service [Acts 8:19].

Philip is the patron saint of the Ethiopian Coptic Christians. It was he who enlightened the eunuch of the Queen Mother [Acts 8:27; "Kandrake" or in other translations "Candace" is a title, not a name.], and through the eunuch comes that entire branch of Christian Faith.

II

The calling of Saint Paul is, historically, pivotal. As the author of most of the New Testament, a mentor of Luke, a colleague of Peter and John, and with a troubled relationship to a very young Saint Mark, his experiences must be taken very seriously.

The dramatic experience on the road near Damascus suggests a man with a troubled conscience and a confused mind. Dozens of authors have psychoanalyzed him. Some of their work is convincing. However, I want to take only what I find in scripture. The confusion is demonstrated in the words, **"Who are you Lord"** [Acts 9:5]? Paul was on a mission to arrest those who believed in Jesus as the Son of God. Why this question? The deeper question might be stated, "Lord, are you Jesus?" And, of course, the answer is **"I am Jesus, whom you are persecuting"** [Acts 9:6].

In any call, there is a command and an acceptance or rejection. In Saul's case it was simple: go into Damascus and wait; and in the meantime, you will be blind. If you believe that God is able to heal the blind, there should be no trouble with the idea that God could make a man blind. But that is not the issue. Saul had to be "disarmed" in order to be approachable by any Christian. And even blinded, Saul presented a fearful possibility. One might suppose that the real hero of this account is Ananias [Acts 9:10-17]. He was an example for the benefit of other Christians. In the face of possible arrest and execution, he obeyed what he considered a direct command from God. Without him, Gentile Christianity might not have been born.

Again Paul's mentor, Barnabas, appears in the account [Acts 9:19-30]. Possibly he was living, at that time, in Damascus. He could also have been a resident of Jerusalem. He clearly had contacts in both cities. And, it was only through his efforts that Paul was accepted by the Jerusalem community. He is much more important to the growth of the Early Church than is often extended to him. However, the most important historical note is that the Jerusalem Community sent Paul to his home town [Acts 21:39, 22:3], Tarsus [Acts 9:30] after he provoked a difficulty with the Hellenistic Jews.

No data exists, but it would be interesting to know the basis for their wrath [Acts 9:29]. The wanted to kill him. As a missionary to the Gentiles, one wonders what he might have learned from that experience. It certainly shows him as a fearless debater.

Peter's ministry prepares the way for Paul. Paul said that he spent fifteen years in Arabia. Tarsus is not exactly Arabia. During those fifteen years, the "Way" grew in size and geography.

Luke noted the healings performed by Peter, including Aeneas [Acts 9:32-35], and Dorcas (Tabitha) [Acts 9:36-41]. Two things are important about these healings. First, they added to Peter's position of leadership. And second, the brought him to Joppa. It was there that the next step of Church growth took place. These two events were critical to the development of the new Church.

The first is that Peter stayed at the home of Simon the Tanner [Acts 9:43]. Simon, according to Jewish law, was unclean. A tanner necessarily touches carcasses every day, and thus is unclean until he washes in the evening [Leviticus 11:39]. Peter must have learned from the Lord [Matthew 15:17-19; Mark 7:20-22] that it is our thoughts rather than contact with a carcass that makes one unclean. Do not underestimate how radical a departure from his earlier orthodoxy this must have been for Peter.

The second development is that Peter visited Cornelius [All of Acts 10]. This visit must be akin to President Nixon (a staunch conservative) visiting Premier Zhou Enlai of China, and opening direct relations between the USA and the People's Republic of China.

Cornelius was a Centurion (Commander of One Hundred) of the Italian Cohort. He was a "God-Fearer", that is, a Gentile who worshipped the Jewish God. He lived in Caesarea. With an Angelic Vision, he was instructed to ask for a visit from Peter. How did he know of Peter? I speculate that Cornelius and his regiment were brought to Jerusalem every Passover to assist in peace-keeping. While there, it was perhaps his soldiers who Crucified Jesus. If so, Cornelius was a witness, and was (again, perhaps) the Centurion who said, **"Truly this was the Son** [Matthew 27:54; Gk: huios, (hwee-os'): either "the" or "a" son, often "the", also Mark 15:39. Unfortunately, Luke 23:47; Gk: dikaios, righteous, approved of, innocent] **of God!"** If this is the case, Cornelius must have had an urgent need to learn about Him, and since Peter was one of the leading Apostles, sought him out.

In the case, living in the home of Simon the Tanner, when the messengers requested that Peter travel to Caesarea and to the home of a Roman, Peter responded. When he arrived, he stated that it was unlawful for a Jew to enter the home of a Gentile, **"But God has shown me that I should not call anyone impure or unclean"** [Acts 10:28].

Luke's grammatic usage, as he presented the words of Peter, "you" is a personal pronoun, singular, and familiar (thou). He spoke directly and with intimacy to Cornelius; **You know what has happened throughout the province of Judea, beginning in Galilee after the baptism that John preached— how God anointed Jesus of Nazareth with the Holy Spirit and power, and how he went around doing good and healing all who were under the power of the devil, because God was with him.**

"We are witnesses of everything he did in the country of the Jews and in Jerusalem. They killed him by hanging him on a cross, but God raised him from the dead on the third day and caused him to be seen. He was not seen by all the people, but by witnesses whom God had already chosen—by us who ate and drank with him after he rose from the dead [Acts 10:37-41]. That Cornelius "knew" is possible evidence that Cornelius was a witness to the Crucifixion.

Expressing his faith, the Holy Spirit was gifted to Cornelius. He received the gift of tongues as evidence of the Spirit's Presence. And, Peter could see no reason to withhold baptism into the Christian Community [Acts 10:45-47]. He and his family are the first Gentile Christians.

The Gospel took another step forward after the martyrdom of Stephen. Congregants spread in every direction. Some arrived at Syrian Antioch on the Orontes River. Antioch was the third-largest city in the empire, and comprised a rich diversity of cultures. There, after an unspecified time, the Jerusalem Council sent Barnabas to oversee the fellowship [Acts 11:22]. The "unspecified time" must have been quite a few years, since Paul wrote to the Colossians that he **went away into Arabia; and again (he)returned to Damascus. Then after three years (he) went up to Jerusalem to visit Cephas, and remained with him fifteen days. Then (he) went into the regions of Syria and Cili'cia** [Colossians 1:17-18 and 21]. The time involved may have been three to fifteen years.

During that time, Paul studied the scriptures. He discovered the prophecies, and developed his theology of salvation by grace through faith.

We underestimate the importance of Barnabas. He called and tutored Paul. Without Barnabas, there would have been no Paul. He found Paul at Tarsus [Acts 11:25] and brought him to Antioch.

A NOTE: In the Early Church period, there were three significant and different theological centers (Jerusalem was destroyed in 70 AD and is not one of the three.): Rome, Alexandria, and Antioch. Each developed a complete theology which differed from the other two.

The Holy Spirit predicted a deep famine across the empire, which Luke affirms, took place during the reign of Claudius (41-54 AD). What is important about this is that it became the occasion of the first general church offering for the relief of the Church in Jerusalem. Paul would collect another, during his "Third Missionary Journey" [Galatians 2:10]. Barnabas and Saul were chosen to carry the money gift to Jerusalem [Acts 11:30].

Chapter twelve is a wonderful story. Peter was arrested by Herod, and experienced a miraculous escape from prison. James, the brother of John was executed. John Mark was taken, by Barnabas and Paul, to Antioch for training [Acts 12:25]. Mark was the cousin of Barnabas [Colossians 4:10], and may well have been related to Peter. Peter called him, **"my son"** [1 Peter 5:13], though that may have been an honorific. He was the author of the Gospel of Mark [See Mark 14:51-52]. Mark and Luke knew each other well [Colossians 4:10-14, 2 Timothy 4:11, and Philemon verse 24]. Historians tell us that he [Mark] was the first Bishop of Alexandria. Only this last verse of the chapter has importance to the growth of the Church, though the Angelic Escape would have been a moral lesson for persecuted Christians.

Thus begins the missionary work of Saint Paul. **While they were worshiping the Lord and fasting, the Holy Spirit said, "Set apart for me Barnabas and Saul for the work to which I have called them." So, after they had fasted and prayed, they placed their hands on them and sent them off** [Acts 13:2-3].

Barnabas was the leader, Saul/Paul the associate, and Mark the assistant. They went to Cyprus where Paul cursed a magician with blindness "for a time" [Acts 13:1], resulting in the conversion of the Proconsul [Acts 13:12].

Mark's return to Jerusalem as soon as they reached the coast of Asia Minor was noted [Acts 13:13]. This had important ramifications later. It resulted in the "contentious" separation of Barnabas and Paul [Acts 15:37-39].

Paul traveled to Pisidian Antioch near the center of Asia Minor, where he was invited to speak a word of exhortation at the synagogue on the Sabbath [Acts 13:15]. There is a great sermon in one of his remarks. He said that **'I have found David son of Jesse, a man after my own heart; he will do everything I want him to do'** [Acts 13:22]. Not a word about David's sins and faults. Only that in the event of God's need, David obeyed. Today many Christians fail to see their place in the grace of God. Too aware of sins, failures and faults, they also fail to hear and obey when God wants something done.

Interestingly, Luke noted that Paul spoke not only to Jews, but to God-fearing Gentiles [Acts 13:16,26]. "God-Fearers" were Gentiles who converted to Judaism. Was it Providential that Paul had found an inclusive synagogue? That Gentiles were present before Paul spoke suggests that, in the Diaspora, Jews may have been more tolerant of Gentile monotheists. This may suggest that the Holy Spirit preceded Paul, paving the way for him. Did Paul have prior knowledge of their presence -even before he began his journey? There is no evidence, except that Luke noted their presence. Paul urged them to continue **"in the grace of God"** [Acts 13:43]. We hear the beginning of the doctrine of salvation by grace through faith.

The next Sabbath, Luke carefully pointed out "the whole city" attended to hear Paul [Acts 13:44]. It seems implausible. What may have happened? Paul may have spoken at the amphitheater. Luke also noted the beginning of Jewish resistance to the Gospel. Was the divide over the doctrine of salvation by grace through faith? Quite possibly Paul had already fully worked out his theology. Luke also noted the unity of the missionary team. This, however, is the first time Paul is given priority. Given what we know about Barnabas, it is probable that his gentleness would not have permitted such a harsh response to the "abuse".

Then Paul and Barnabas answered them boldly: "We had to speak the word of God to you first. Since you reject it and do not consider yourselves worthy of eternal life, we now turn to the Gentiles. For this is what the Lord has commanded us:

"'I have made you a light for the Gentiles,
    that you may bring salvation to the ends of the earth.'[Isaiah 49:6]*"* [Acts 13:46-47].

The quotation from Isaiah is a word of God to Messiah, and the word "you" is singular. It means that Messiah is a **"light for the Gentiles"**, rather than the Jewish People a whole.

The opposition seemed to have won the day. Paul and Barnabas were expelled from the city. They returned to Iconium. But the victory was Paul's. The new **disciples were filled with joy and with the Holy Spirit** [Acts 13:52].

The lesson or spiritual dynamic from these verses is that opposition promotes growth. Every time the Apostles were forced to flee, the Gospel was proclaimed in yet another location. At Iconium the Apostles worked for an extended period, but a plot was discovered and they fled to Lystra and Derbe [Acts 14:1-7]. The accumulated opponents gathered in Lystra, and, after the Apostles had been mistaken for pagan gods, had Paul stoned [Acts 14:8-19]. The work was so successful that prior to their return to Pisidian Antioch, **Paul and Barnabas appointed elders for them in each church and, with prayer and fasting, committed them to the Lord, in whom they had put their trust** [Acts 14:23]. It may have been the serious lesson they had already learned: **"We must go through many hardships to enter the kingdom of God," they said** [Acts 14:22]. On their return to Antioch, they reported that God had **opened the door to Gentiles** [Acts 14:27]. Luke noted that: **"they had been committed to the** grace of God for the work they had now completed" [Acts 14:26]. Considering the persecution, the two had experienced, we may have yet another spiritual dynamic. One of my Preacher's Proverbs is that "one never gets in trouble unless he is trying to be helpful".

Discussion of what I call "The Great Divorce" (between Gentile Christians and Jewish Christians) is the subject of the next section of Acts. It begins with: **Certain people came down from Judea to Antioch and were teaching the believers: "Unless you are circumcised, according to the custom taught by Moses, you cannot be saved." This brought Paul and Barnabas into sharp dispute and debate with them. So Paul and Barnabas were appointed, along with some other believers, to go up to Jerusalem to see the apostles and elders about this question** [Acts 15:1-2].

The decision was made when Peter recounted his experience with Cornelius [Acts 15:7-10, Cf: Acts 10], and testified about **the signs and wonders God had done among the Gentiles through them** [Acts 15:12]; but it was not "certified" until James (the brother of Jesus) announced his decision [Acts 15:19]. James was the primary official in the new organization.

Of critical importance is their short list of requirements. These duties for Gentile Christians seem designed to limit the irritation between Jew and Gentile. **It seemed good to the Holy Spirit and to us not to burden you with anything beyond the following requirements: You are to abstain from food sacrificed to idols, from blood, from the meat of strangled animals and from sexual immorality. You will do well to avoid these things** [Acts 15:28-29].

The humanity and personality differences of the Apostles shows through in the separation of Barnabas and Paul. **Barnabas wanted to take John, also called Mark, with them, but Paul did not think it wise to take him, because he had deserted them in Pamphylia and had not continued with them in the work. They had such a sharp disagreement that they parted company. Barnabas took Mark and sailed for Cyprus, but Paul chose Silas and left, commended by the believers to the grace of the Lord. He went through Syria and Cilicia, strengthening the churches** [Acts 15:38-41]. One may see the gentleness of Barnabas toward Mark. Barnabas could see the potential in the young man, whereas Paul could only see Mark's failure to stand up to the rigors of the missionary life.

There is a sermon here. It seems that Luke is making a case for the new, younger, set of leaders: himself, Mark, Timothy, and Silas. From this point onward, Luke is careful to note when and where each of these younger men are sent, and by whom. One might suppose that, with the failure of the doctrine of an Early Return, and with the execution of most of the Apostles during the reign of Nero [AD 54-68], the Church experienced a "leadership vacuum". Acts doesn't chronical only the transition from Jew to Gentile, and Jerusalem to Rome; it also notes the transition from Peter and Paul to Luke and Mark [Gospel writers].

I do not understand Paul's decision to circumcise Timothy [Acts 16:2]. Luke related that it was because the Jews knew Timothy's father was Greek. Paul must have experienced some resistance among other Gentiles. He wrote to the Corinthians that **Circumcision is nothing and uncircumcision is nothing. Keeping God's commands is what counts** [I Corinthians 7:19]. In view of his attitude toward the Law of Moses, he must have regretted the compromise.

The story of their arrest, beating, and release from jail [Acts 16:16-40] seems to have little purpose beside relating that "the jailer" was converted. That Luke fails to name the man leaves the account a bit suspect, from the point of view of an historian. Lydia is named, and is the patroness of the church at Philippi, but the jailer is not. It does illustrate the violent nature of the opposition to the Gospel. And, Silas is mentioned as experiencing the same treatment as Paul [Acts 16:19, 22, 25, 29, 36]. Is one of the marks of a true Apostle the necessity of experiencing violent opposition?

The geography of their travel is of grand importance. The Provence of Asia [Acts 16:6] into which they were unable to move, is western Turkey. Unable to go there, they moved north. Then, seeking the Will of God, Paul was informed by the Holy Spirit that he ought not go into Bithynia, which is the northern coast of Turkey [The coast of the Black Sea]. Instead, the Apostle dreamed that Macedonia was in need, and open to his ministry [Acts 16:9-10]. Crossing the Aegean Sea, the group passed several cities, intent on Philippi [Acts 16:11-12]. This is the transition of the Christian Faith from "oriental" to "European" and "multi-cultural".

There is a second transition. In Thessalonica, clearly the leaders are Paul and Silas [Acts 17:4]. That is true in Berea also. However, due to the danger of persecution, Paul was "sent to the coast" while Silas and Timothy remain as the leadership team. Was Timothy an Apostle? That depends on the definition of the term. If, "Called of God to found churches" is appropriate, then Silas, Timothy and others are Apostles. If "Having met Jesus in the body, and having been called to found churches" is the definition, clearly something else is happening here. As had been true in all the previous churches founded by Paul, a second generation is left in charge. Apostolic Succession? Something like it. With or without the legalist's strictures, the Faith is entrusted to new hands.

As a recipient of Apostolic Succession (through John Wesley), I have felt the authority of that status. There really is something more than tradition in the words, "Take thou authority to…". It lacks power in those who do not have an authentic calling. Many begin, but few finish. And yet I have seen those whose spiritual power is undeniable, greater than my own, who have not experienced the laying on of hands by those who have had hands laid upon them. The Spirit is at work, selecting the leaders of the Community of Faith. Paul and Barnabas were keen observers of the work of the Spirit in the hearts of young men whom they invited into the ministry.

In this instance, Paul left Silas and Timothy in Berea, while he went to Athens (alone?) [Acts 17:14]. Though Luke included a summary of Paul's sermon at the Areopagus [Acts 17:16-31], and notes the curiosity of the stoics and epicureans [Acts 17:18], and names the couple who must have been left with responsibility for the new fellowship [Acts 17:34; Dionysius, a member of the Areopagus, also a woman named Damaris.], Paul seems to have had little success in the city. Luke's excuse is: **All the Athenians and the foreigners who lived there spent their time doing nothing but talking about and listening to the latest ideas** [Acts 17:21]. People of philosophical bent often have trouble distinguishing between intellectual ascent and a complete spiritual devotion.

We have yet another transition. Damaris is only the second woman to be named and left in a leadership position. The first was, of course, Lydia [Acts 16:14; in Thyatira]. That this is a major turning point is evident in a constant increase in the role of women. Beginning with Acts 1:14 **They all joined together constantly in prayer, along with the women and Mary the mother of Jesus, and with his brothers,** the women were simply present and joining in prayer. But even this is remarkable. In orthodox Judaism, women sat separately as an audience, but did not participate in formal worship. At 2:18 Luke quoted Saint Peter's Pentecost speech as he quoted the Prophet Joel [Joel 2:28-32]: **Even on my servants, both men and women, I will pour out my Spirit in those days, and they will prophesy.** Then at Acts 5:14: **Nevertheless, more and more men and women believed in the Lord and were added to their number.** And at Acts 8:3 and 9:2, Luke noted that women were included in the victims of Saul's persecution. **But Saul began to destroy the church. Going from house to house, he dragged off both men and women and put them in prison.** And next women were baptized **"in the name of Jesus Christ"** [Acts 8:12]. By the time Paul had reached Philippi, his evangelistic method actually began with women. **On the Sabbath we went outside the city gate to the river, where we expected to find a place of prayer. We sat down and began to speak to the women who had gathered there** [Acts 16:13]. And by the time Paul reached Athens, women seemed to be his means of access to Greek men [Acts 17:4, 12]. Luke used the term "prominent" to lift the status of those women. **As a result, many of them believed, as did also a number of prominent Greek women and many Greek men** [Acts 17:12]. Note that "women" are listed first; not as a secondary thought. And finally, her husband Dionysius and Damaris are left in Athens as the leaders [Acts 17:34].

At Corinth the major transition took place. **But when they** [Jewish leaders] **opposed Paul and became abusive, he shook out his clothes in protest and said to them, "Your blood be on your own heads! I am innocent of it. From now on I will go to the Gentiles** [Acts 18:6]**".** Paul's letters reveal an intensive effort to prevent the divorce of Jewish Christian and Gentile Christian. Here, it seems, his anger at his abuse from the Jewish leaders has led to a change in evangelistic technique. Since Paul later worshipped at the Temple in Jerusalem, it seems clear that he did not relinquish his own Jewish heritage.

Paul met and worked alongside Aquila and Priscilla, tentmakers who had been expelled (with all other Jews) from Rome by Claudius [AD 41-54]. Because they had been expelled from Rome, we know they were Jews. Again we have the makings of a leadership team. Paul wrote of them in a letter to the churches in "Asia" (Turkey). **Aquila and Priscilla greet you warmly in the Lord, and so does the church that meets at their house** [1 Corinthians 6:19].

Apparently, Paul had convinced quite a number of salvation by grace through faith. Crispus, the head of the synagogue, joined Paul, with his family, when Paul started separate meetings in the home of Titus Justice (a Gentile) [Acts 18:7-8]. We can date this, because Gallio was Proconsul of Achaia [Acts 18:12] in 53 AD. Gallio was the brother of Seneca (the philosopher). In a bit of noteworthy irony, Luke recorded that when Gallio rejected the suit of those remaining in the synagogue, the members turned on Sosthenes, who had succeeded Crispus, and beat him in front of the Proconsul. Paul took this, and a Divine vision, to mean that he was safe in Corinth. He remained there for a year and a half [Acts 18:9-10].

For the rest of Chapter 18 Paul seems to be the secondary character. He traveled with Aquila and Priscilla to Cenchreae [Acts 18:18], where he shaved his head after a rite of purification. He left Aquila and Priscilla in Ephesus where they became the head of the church [Acts 18:19-24]. Their ministry included sessions of instruction for Apollos [Acts 18:26]. He was a speaker of great spiritual vitality [Acts 18:25]. Later Apollos was sent to Corinth where he became head of the church.

Apollos was part of the dissention at Corinth. Some of the people followed the teachings of Apollos, while others held Paul to be superior, and others considered Peter to be the final authority. Paul wrote to them **What, after all, is Apollos? And what is Paul? Only servants, through whom you came to believe—as the Lord has assigned to each his task. I planted the seed, Apollos watered it, but God has been making it grow. So neither the one who plants nor the one who waters is anything, but only God, who makes things grow. The one who plants and the one who waters have one purpose, and they will each be rewarded according to** their own labor. **For we are co-workers in God's service; you are God's field, God's building** [I Corinthians 3:5-9]. Here we have an instance in which the second generation is training others.

In one of the more interesting notes in Chapter eighteen, Luke noted that Paul supported himself in the absence of Silas and Timothy. After they rejoined him, **Paul devoted himself exclusively to preaching** [Acts 18:5]. Does this mean that Silas and Timothy worked to support Paul? Or, did they bring funds for their mutual support?

When Paul began his third mission, he traveled through the middle of Asia (Turkey) rejoining the "front-line-troops" at Ephesus. Apparently, reception of the Holy Spirit had become an issue [Acts 19:1-2]. People must have been accepted into the fellowship on the basis of intellectual agreement, rather than the evidence of the Spirit's Presence. Indeed, some disciples at Ephesus had not even **"heard that there is a Holy Spirit"** [Acts 19:2]. We have a subtle distinction here. Baptism of repentance faces the past. Baptism in the Holy Spirit faces the future. The one is about guilt, and the other about discipleship. The Baptism of John [Act 19:4; (the Baptist)] was intended to make ready for the One who was to come. Baptism by the Holy Spirit was understood to be the Baptism of the One who already had come.

That is a major issue in the church today. When parents receive their children into the fellowship of believers, often the Baptism of the Holy Spirit is not even questioned, much less taught. Here is clear Biblical evidence that the Baptism of the Spirit was an expectation of Saint Paul. Intellectual agreement does not equip for spiritual battle or spiritual ministry. Only the In-filling Spirit has the capacity to enable Christian Discipleship.

Paul stayed at Ephesus even longer than he had at Corinth [Acts 19:10; two years, only one and a half at Corinth (Acts 18:11)]. He performed many ministries of the Spirit, and his fame spread across Asia. So much fame accrued to him that others began mimicking his style of "casting out" demons, but with ill effect [Acts 19:8-16]. That may have been part of his motivation to return to Jerusalem [Acts 19;21; **After all this had happened, Paul decided (in the Spirit) to go to Jerusalem...**]. From Luke's perspective, that had consequence, but so did: **He sent two of his helpers, Timothy and Erastus, to Macedonia** [Philippi, Thessalonica, etc.], **while he stayed in the province of Asia** [Ephesus] **a little longer** [Acts 19:22]. This is yet another mission team of the second generation.

Perhaps the greatest transition of all has been taking place, and now became very apparent at Ephesus. The contest is no longer between Christian and Jew, as it was between Christian and Pagan. The devotes of Artemis [Acts 19:28; she is the sister of Apollo, and the Greek counterpart of Diana (the huntress)]. Demetrius, an idol maker, heard Paul and started a riot because, as Paul had said, **"gods made by human hands are no gods at all"** [Acts 19:26]. The City Clerk refused to enter an indictment [Acts 19:35-41], but Paul considered it warning-enough and departed for the Holy City [Acts 20:1].

His travels, through Macedonia, around to Athens and back again, are of little importance. Rather, Luke took that opportunity to mention the names of yet more young men and future leaders of the Church. Among them were: **Sopater son of Pyrrhus from Berea, Aristarchus and Secundus from Thessalonica, Gaius from Derbe, Timothy also, and Tychicus and Trophimus from the province of Asia** [Acts 20:4]. In his farewell speech, Paul identified the role these, and others were to assume. **Keep watch over yourselves and all the flock of which the Holy Spirit has made you** *overseers* [Acts 20:28; Gk: episkopous: bishop].

A conference with the elders of Ephesus is the turning point between Paul's outreach, and the beginning of Paul's martyrdom. He said to them: **"And now, compelled by the Spirit, I am going to Jerusalem, not knowing what will happen to me there. I only know that in every city the Holy Spirit warns me that prison and hardships are facing me. However, I consider my life worth nothing to me; my only aim is to finish the race and complete the task the Lord Jesus has given me—the task of testifying to the good news of God's grace. Now I know that none of you among whom I have gone about preaching the kingdom will ever see me again"** [Acts 20:22-25].

Whether it was Paul, or Luke's addition makes no difference. The leaders, listening to Paul, were warned: **"I know that after I leave, savage wolves will come in among you and will not spare the flock. Even from your own number men will arise and distort the truth in order to draw away disciples after them"** [Acts 20:29-30]. Acts reflects the passionate theological debate which flourished at least until the beginning of the fifth century. The Early Church debated whether Jesus was. or was not, fully God and/or fully human. They debated the nature of Baptism, whether it cleansed all or only past sins. They debated the Trinity. They constructed the Bible. And so on.

There is, in Paul's words, a beginning clarity of that theology: **"Now I commit you to God and to the word of his grace, which can build you up and give you an inheritance among all those who are sanctified"** [Acts 20:32]. As per usual, the word "word" is the translation of "logos", which much of the world has defined as the Bible. But the Bible did not exist at the time Paul spoke. Instead its meaning has always been "the Holy Spirit"; and thus: **"I commit you to God, and to the Spirit of His Grace, which can build you up and give you an inheritance among all those who are *sanctified*** [Gk: hagiazó (hag-ee-ad'-zo); to purify the of soul of a person: Joh 17:17, 19; by the indwelling of Truth (a code word for Holy Spirit) John 8:32, 1 Thessalonians 5:23, 1 Corinthians 1:2; and Romans 15:16): imbued with the Holy Spirit).

With those words, Paul and Luke boarded ship for the journey to Judah. They landed at Tyre and spent a week with the Disciples there. Luke's account gives one the possible idea that Paul's martyrdom in Rome was not God-ordained or predestined. **Through the Spirit they** [the disciples] **urged Paul not to go on to Jerusalem** [Acts 21:4]. We are so conditioned by events to consider it God's Will, when in fact, it might have been Paul's error.

After a stop-over at Ptolemais (the shore on the northern side of the Jezreel Valley), they landed at Caesarea, and stayed at the home of Phillip the Evangelist (not Phillip the Apostle). Continuing Luke's emphasis on the indwelling Spirit, he noted that Phillip had four unmarried daughters with the gift of prophecy [Acts 21:9]. This is a continuing affirmation of the transition from a strict (Jewish) patriarchy to a congregational form in which women may participate fully.

And yet another warning was given via the Holy Spirit. Agabus, a prophet, told Paul that if he went to Jerusalem, the "Jewish leaders" would hand him over to the Romans, bound hand and foot [Acts 21:11].

The stubborn and fearless Apostle insisted on his continuing to Jerusalem where he met with James and the elders [Acts 21:18; "Elders": Gk: presbuteros (pres-boo'-ter-os)]. The sentence should have been translated "Presbyters", meaning: "those who preside".

The Jerusalem Establishment of the Christian Community had continued its faithfulness to the Law of Moses, and counted thousands who had come to Christ. They condemned what they thought Paul taught European Jews. Paul's permission to preach salvation by grace through faith to Gentiles, along with freedom from the Law, did not, according to the Presbyters and James, extend to Jewish Christians [Acts 21:20-25]. Paul was required to ritually purify himself in order to prove his loyalty to the Law.

The rest of Chapter Twenty-one is an account of Paul's arrest after a riot caused by his old Jewish opponents from Asia, possibly from Ephesus [Acts 21:29].

Of most interest to me is the Providential provision of Paul with Roman Citizenship [Acts 22:27]. It was the means by which the spiritual dynamic was applied: Opposition always leads to greater opportunities for the Gospel. In this case, Paul was enabled to witness to the Chief Priests and the Sanhedrin [Acts 22:30]. The Commander who rescued and arrested Paul [Acts 23:26; Claudius Lysias] **wanted to find out exactly why Paul was being accused by the Jews. So the next day he released him and ordered the chief priests and all the members of the Sanhedrin to assemble. Then he brought Paul and had him stand before them** [Acts 22:30].

After Paul stated that his life was blameless, the high priest Ananias ordered that he be struck on the mouth (for blasphemy?). Paul cursed him, saying that he would be struck by God [Acts 23:2], which happened, but only after the publication of Luke's work. He was, however, charged with crime and sent to Rome for trial in 52 AD. He was acquitted by Claudius. He was murdered at the beginning of the Jewish Revolt in 66 AD. His troubles were co-instant to the possible publication of Acts.

Paul exploited the differences between the Sadducees [Acts 23:6; the Sadducees did not accept the doctrine of the resurrection] and Pharisees, starting a riot. At the end of the First Jewish War (70 AD), the Sadducees disappeared, the Pharisees founded Rabbinic Judaism when Rabbi Yohanan ben Zakkai founded a school at Yavneh (near the center of Israel) [wikipedia.org First Jewish–Roman War]. The Commander rescued Paul and held him in the Legion Barracks [Acts 23:10].

While there, Paul experienced the Presence of the Lord who encouraged the Apostle and predicted his testimony in Rome [Acts 23:11].

This is a transition point. God used the opposition to extend Paul's ministry to Rome, thus bringing the Gospel to the center of the Empire. If my assumption that the Holy Spirit had tried to warn Paul away from Jerusalem is correct, then we see a wonderful spiritual dynamic. If a Christian errs in what he/she understands as obedience, God will use our mistakes to fulfill His great purpose.

"The son of Paul's sister" [Acts 23:16]; how often we ignore really important information. Paul had family living in Jerusalem. Astonishing? Not at all. Recall that Paul was educated by Gamaliel [Acts 5:34, 22:3]. The base of his persecutions was Jerusalem. We may add the presumption of Paul's marriage and widowerhood [I Corinthians 7:8; GK: agamos (ag'-am-os), unmarried whether formerly married or not], to see the life of a very normal man, called into Apostleship at an early age. We may attribute normal feelings, fears, joys and hopes. His earthly desires have all been subsumed in his desire to serve his Lord. I wonder how his sister felt about him. Yet, was he normal? One woman wrote: "I have to wonder what shape their relationship was in. He did, also, go about methodically killing people who didn't think his way prior to this...... also it is clear he was a man of his times.... she was nothing but a WOMAN... I have a definite love/hate relationship with Paul" [Deborah Rose Kneen].

Tribune Claudius Lysias sent Paul to Caesarea under very heavy guard when Paul's nephew warned him of a plot to assonate the Apostle. There Paul witnessed to Felix. The implied legal charge against Paul was that he tried to desecrate the Temple [Acts 24:6]. Felix must have known how emotionally potent was their assertion. On the outside, they appealed to his concern for peace and order. They claimed that Paul was stirring up trouble all over the empire [Acts 23:5]. They were not very wrong. Their charge demonstrates the radical concept of the Incarnation, and its revolutionary potential for socio-political change. As a point of fact, the practical application of the implications of the Gospel have not yet been fully realized. Some of them have made progress. For instance, the unity of humanity, the sacredness of human life, and the "way of Godly Love".

Paul's defense is a revelation. He said that he continued to believe in (and observe) the obligations of the Law of Moses [Acts 24:14-16], but of greater importance: **I came to Jerusalem to bring my people gifts for the poor and to present offerings** [Acts 23:17[. This statement confirms Galatians 2:10. Paul's purpose in his journey to Jerusalem was not simple.

Some theologians believe that Paul's motivation was to complete a prophecy and "trigger" the Return of the Lord. He might have thought that bringing to the Temple, the offerings from Gentile congregations may have been the beginning of the fulfillment of Isaiah Chapter Sixty. Also not very clear is the meaning of "the poor". Because of the origins of the offering among the Gentile congregations, one must think that it means the Christian Community in Jerusalem. Here, Paul may have fudged his definition for the sake of emphasis. He may have intended for Felix (and Ananias) to think he had a gift for any and all the poor of Jerusalem.

Felix had a Jewish wife [Acts 24:24; Drucilla], and was at least interested in learning the doctrines of the Nazarene sect. So, Paul spent quite some time as a prisoner with the freedom of the palace. His approach to Felix seems to have been about the Second Coming and the Judgement [Acts 24:25; As Paul talked about righteousness, self-control and the judgment to come], which frightened Felix [according to Luke]. But, after two years, Felix was succeeded by Porcius Festus [Acts 24:27], which meant that the process was re-started at the beginning.

The result of a request to have Paul transferred to a Jewish Court in Jerusalem was Paul's appeal to Caesar [Acts 25:11]. That would have been to Nero, and not such a good idea. But it was better than the kangaroo court in Jerusalem with a predicable outcome. In between two bad ideas, Paul made the choice which permitted greater ministry.

Festus gave Paul the opportunity to witness to Agrippa and his wife Bernice, because he couldn't find an indictment to place against Paul when sending the Apostle to Rome [Acts 25:13-27].

Chapter twenty-six and twenty-seven are a summary of Paul's witness. We may assume that he used the same outline often. And, ironically, both Agrippa and Festus agree that his religious views do not constitute a violation of any Roman Law.

The trip to Rome, reads like a dime novel, leading modern scholars to doubt its facticity. But the account is in the first person, and there is no reason to doubt Luke's veracity. One may only wonder at the power of Paul's personality. By the end of the account, he is virtually in command of the ship. The crew intend to escape in the lifeboat, and the soldiers, on Paul's command, cut the rope letting the boat "drift away" [Acts 27:29-32]. He insists that all two hundred seventy-six people eat, which they do [Acts 27:32-38]. And it is the Centurion, perhaps thankful for the calm authority of Paul, and "wanting to save" him, who gives the "abandon ship" order Acts 27:42-44].

This is not the only storm at sea in the Bible. Consider Noah, and Jesus on the Sea of Galilee. In each, God's purpose was salvation. And in this instance, not only did everyone survive, the storm extended the Gospel to Malta [Acts 28:1-10]. Paul had yet another opportunity to speak to Jewish leadership, and again without much success [Acts 28:24-25].

As a final statement about the Jewish/Gentile cleavage, Luke quotes Isaiah [Isaiah 6:9-10]

"'Go to this people and say,
"You will be ever hearing but never understanding;
**   you will be ever seeing but never perceiving."**
For this people's heart has become calloused;
**   they hardly hear with their ears,**
**   and they have closed their eyes.**
Otherwise they might see with their eyes,
**   hear with their ears,**
**   understand with their hearts**
and turn, and I would heal them' [Acts 28:26-27].

After this, Paul was able to rent a home and freely teach any and all who would listen to his good news, presumably Gentiles.

The quotation from Isaiah represents the end-point of the "transitions". From Jerusalem to Rome, from Jew to Gentile, and from first to second generation, and from "Jewish Sect" to independent faith.

ROMANS

LESSON ONE

INTRODUCTION

St Paul had spent fifteen years after the Damascus Road experience, somewhere in Syria or Jordan, studying and researching the meaning of his conversation with the Risen Jesus. That was before Barnabas contacted him about becoming part of a "Mission Team". He spent the next several years in the first three of his mission journeys, starting congregations, writing, re-visiting, etc. His third journey concluded with an offering of money from the Gentile congregations to the Jewish congregation in Jerusalem. It was perhaps on his journey to Jerusalem, or during the two-year imprisonment there, that he wrote to the Roman congregation. It was certainly before he "appealed to Caesar" that the letter was written.

His intention was to introduce himself, and his theology, to the mixed congregation of Jews and Gentiles. As was true in Asia Minor (Turkey) and Greece, a tension existed between those who insisted on obedience to the Law of Moses for salvation, and those who countered that the Law did not apply to Gentiles.

Because of the importance of Martin Luther's discovery of Romans 5:1ff, and his application of salvation by grace through faith to the corrupted theology of the Roman Church in 1517, we tend to read Luther's interpretation back into St. Paul in +/- 55 AD. By doing so, we miss much of what he has to say to us. Luther was correct, but his opponent was the Roman Church, not the Jewish/Gentile tension in Rome. The real meaning of the Letter relates to the coming divorce, which St Paul wanted to avoid, between Jew and Gentile.

So, where should we begin? I suggest we begin with an understanding of what Paul discovered while he studied theology during those formative fifteen years.

ABRAHAM AND MOSES

Paul re-read his Old Testament. He asked, why and for what purpose did Jesus live, die, and resurrect? In order to answer that question *as a Jew*, Paul had to take a much larger view than did the majority of his contemporary rabbis.

He asked himself, What was the purpose of the call of God to Abraham? Was it the salvation or selection of the Hebrews as God's Chosen People? Well, yes and no. Abraham was not a Jew. He was a Hebrew...or perhaps even the FORE-father to the Hebrews. How was Abraham saved? He was saved by two things: 1) He believed in God. 2) He obeyed God as far as he understood God. Moses was five hundred years in the future. Later Paul asked what Moses contributed to the process of salvation, but for now we need to focus on how Paul understood Abraham.

Abraham wasn't just the father of Israel; he was father of many nations. God's purpose must be found within that larger definition of Abraham.

What was the purpose of God in calling Abram? To answer that, we must understand how Paul pictured God. God, to him, was the Supreme Judge of what is appropriate. The Creator applies the standard of His intention against what is today's reality. Salvation History is the process by which God has communicated dissatisfaction with today's reality. Our reality is shot through with sin. God did not, and does not, intend that it should be so.

To Paul, the calling of Abram was the first step by the Judge to *redeem* the world from sin. I remind you that the book of Isaiah, from chapter forty onward, is an account of a trial in which Israel argues that God is unjust because they are in exile. God responds that the exile is the appropriate judgment against a people who disobeyed and broke the Covenant, and that furthermore, He was about to restore Jerusalem, and even yet further, God had selected Messiah who would bring salvation to "all the nations". **God has become my strength— He says, "It is too light a thing that you should be My servant to raise up the tribes of Jacob and to restore the survivors of Israel; I will give you as a light to the nations, that My salvation may reach to the end of the earth." Thus says the Lord, the Redeemer of Israel and his Holy One, to one deeply despised, abhorred by the nations, the slave of rulers, "Kings shall see and stand up, princes, and they shall prostrate themselves, because of the Lord, who is faithful, the Holy One of Israel, who has chosen you"** [Isaiah 49.5-7].

So, St. Paul understood God to be primarily, the Supreme Judge. Yet God is not a malicious Judge. The character of God is "hesed" -what we now call God's Love and is translated in the NT as agape. Any condemnation by God always has the purpose of bringing the condemned closer to salvation.

One of the reasons I, along with John Wesley, have serious trouble with the idea of Predestination (as interpreted by John Calvin and today's Evangelicals), is that it implies God creates a few persons for election and a lot of people for eternal torture. Paul would have had nothing to do with that. It denies the foundation of the loving nature of God. God is, rather, a righteous Judge whose decisions are always redemptive. God judged Israel as broken, not for the sake of wrath, but "in order that" God's Mercy might be demonstrated. Let me put that in another way: God is like a Judge whose only son has been rightly accused of a crime. The Judge struggles to find a "way out", a way to excuse as well as correct his son. It is not enough to excuse, and it is not enough to punish. Any punishment must lead to both release and to better behavior. Just so, God condemned Israel to exile *in order that* Israel might also experience a second Exodus (a return to Jerusalem and the correct relationship between God and the Chosen People.

Paul devoted the first four chapters to this foundational understanding of God. God called Abram from and for the salvation of the entire world...not just the Jews. God provided the Law of Moses to educate/illustrate how far humanity is from obedience to God's Righteous Love. God judged Israel and Judah for their inappropriate disobedience to the Covenant, and condemned them to a sort of prison term in exile; but only as preparation of His further judgment of pardon or parole.

The Law of Moses was also the "set-up" if you will, for the Saving Sacrifice of Christ. That Sacrifice was not just for the Jews, but for the entire world, just as was the call of Abram not just for the Jews but rather for the entire world.

This calls to the fore, our understanding of the relationship between the Jews of today and God. We will deal with this in a later lesson. For now, let us simply state, with Paul, that a calling is not subject to revocation. God called the Jews, and they are still called. They may have fulfilled their function as the People from whom Jesus was born; but they are still the Chosen Ones.

This is going to be very important later in Paul's letter to Rome. God, according to Isaiah, sent the Messiah in order that the nations should come to the Light, but also to restore the survivors of Israel.

Have you ever been troubled by the idea of God as Righteous Judge? American theology begins with a sermon by Cotton Mather, titled "Sinners in the Hands of a Wrathful Judge". It was the first Billy Graham revival sermon in the history of the Church. He pictured his congregation as hanging by the most slender thread of Grace over the depths and horrors of Hell. He urged them to get right with God before the thread snapped...before it was too late. It spawned the Great Awakening, and through George Whitfield to Wesley, our own church.

There are other places in the Bible to find support for God as Righteous Judge, but not Romans. Paul had a different idea of the nature of God as Judge. It is fully grounded in the Old Testament.

Leviticus 16 sets forth the rubrics for the sacrifice of redemption. This was to happen once each year; the day of atonement. The Priest slaughters a bull, and brings the collected blood of the animal to what the Hebrews called the Mercy Seat, e.g., the place where God will meet with the Priest to annul the sins for which the animal was sacrificed.

Long ago I learned to characterize the Fall from Grace at Eden. I would say, God's curse is always a blessing. God condemned women to painful childbirth. Yet what gives more satisfaction and meaning to a woman than childbirth? God condemned men to labor; but what gives men more satisfaction than a job well done?

In the same way God has dealt with human sin, according to Romans. We are accustomed to hearing that the cost of human sin was the blood of Christ. God required the excruciating sacrifice of Christ before humans could be reconciled to God. But Paul, basing his understanding on the Old Testament, thought of the Christ Event as the Mercy Seat. On the Cross, God reveals Himself, the lengths and depths to which God will go to redeem sinful humanity. After all, it is not humanity that makes the sacrifice: It is God Himself, in the Person of the Son who sacrificed Himself for our redemption.

Now we have another word which we think we understand but which St. Paul used differently: redemption. For the Apostle, again based on his study of the Old Testament, redemption refers to a price paid to purchase the freedom of another from slavery. Later in Romans, Paul will write about how humanity, this is you and I, are or have been "slaves to sin". The Blood of Christ is the price God paid to redeem us from that slavery...that (perhaps voluntary) involuntary servitude. But it is colored by what we find in Hosea. That man bought a prostituted slave, Gomer, and made her his wife. Later she returned, voluntarily, to prostitution. Again he bought her freedom and made her his wife, but only after he had paid her salary during the second period of *voluntary* slavery.

God supports our existence, blesses us with much, much, good while we are slaves to sin. Yet God is waiting for a time and opportunity to redeem us, to justify us, through an individual act of faith in the Christ Event. Strange way of saying: God Loves us while we are sinners, and yearns for the moment when our eyes will open and we will understand the Love of God as expressed in the Free Self-Sacrifice of Jesus on our behalf (or if you will "in order that").

At another time we can discuss whether the "indwelling" of Christ's Spirit actually frees us from all sin. That is a very big lesson. The answer depends upon one's definition of sin. The answer, surprisingly, will lead us to Wesley's doctrine of Perfection.

For now, let us look at the word "Justify". Our redemption depends on justification. Look to chapter three. Most people take a nap trying to read it. The argument seems esoteric. Paul, the former Pharisee, asks about the advantage before God of being a Jew. He has already made the case that no one is able to perfectly keep the law of Moses. The result is a condition of "faithlessness" or "unfaithfulness". Therefore, there is no advantage to being a Jew. Both Jew and Gentile are un-clean, un-righteous. Does that mean that God is unfaithful, because of the promise God made in the Covenant? Not according to Paul. God is not unfaithful; God has taken step one in His "in order that". Paul quotes Jewish writings extensively to demonstrate that Jewish theologians agree about the unrighteous condition of the Jew. In verse 20, Paul finally makes his point: **"through the law comes knowledge of sin"!** The ministry of Moses, if you will, was to establish, in obedience to God, a religious/legal system which God already knew would be impossible for them to keep.

This, by the way, is where the Methodist doctrine of Predestination derives from Paul's theology. Predestination simply means "God's Plan". God planned that by the failure of the Old Covenant, God would be able to demonstrate just how far short of obedience and righteousness falls every human person (both Jew and Gentile). This, again, is an "in order that". The next step is found in verses 20 to 25: **For "no human being will be justified in His sight" by deeds prescribed by the law, for through the law comes the knowledge of sin. But now, apart from law, the righteousness of God has been disclosed, and is attested by the law and the prophets, the righteousness of God through faith in Jesus Christ for all who believe. For there is no distinction, since all have sinned and fall short of the glory of God; they are now justified by His grace as a gift, through the redemption that is in Christ Jesus, whom God put forward as a sacrifice of atonement by his blood, effective through faith** [Romans 3:20-25].

Here Paul shows how the Gentile is dependent on the Jew. The Jew understood the system of substitutionary sacrifice. Just as, under the Law of Moses, the sinner was redeemed, that is, freed from the penalty appropriate to a sin, because he sacrificed a goat or lamb or bullock, so now both Jew and Gentile are freed from the penalty of sin by the Sacrifice of Christ. The big difference here, and one Paul glosses over, is that whereas in the Temple it is the sinner who owns and provides the sacrifice, in this case it is the Ultimate Judge who provided the one and only perfect sacrifice. God paid the penalty and meets us at the "Mercy Seat".

LESSON TWO

Previously, we reviewed the first three chapters of Paul's Letter to the Romans. Perhaps more than any other book of the New Testament, it is the foundation of our faith. Let me remind you of the points he makes in those three chapters:

- Abraham was pre-Jewish. He was saved because he obeyed God as well as he could without a Bible. That is, he was saved by faith.

- Moses, 500 years later, founded Judaism with the Law. God is the Judge of those who practice the Law of Moses.

  - But God is a Righteous Judge, one who seeks to excuse and justify...although always with an "in order that" one's faith might be strengthened, and one's behavior improved.

  - God instituted the system of "substitutionary sacrifice"...a goat for one's sin.

  - That system was a "set-up" for the time when all would understand that salvation by morality, salvation by obedience to a written law, doesn't work.

- God always has an "in order that" the next thing happen. The covenant of Abraham is a covenant of faith, and the Covenant of Moses is one of Law. Both were designed to prepare the way for the Covenant of Christ, which is one of justification by faith through the grace (forbearance) of the Righteous Judge.

- God provides our sustenance while we continue in sin (Hosea). Christ sets us free from sin, by means of our faith.

Paul finishes Chapter three with the triumphant statement that God is God of both Jew and Gentile, and that God's faithfulness is such that both (or either) Jew and Gentile are justified by faith. Abraham was justified by faith, and so are each of us. So then: Justification means that one is considered to have perfectly kept the Law of Moses, perfectly kept the intention of God. One is in perfect relationship to and with God.

The righteousness Paul mentions is the righteousness of God, *imputed* to the one who understands that God, Himself, has offered the sin-sacrifice on our behalf. It is as if a rich man provided the animal for the sacrifice of a poor man. God has provided a sacrifice on our behalf, in order that you and I might understand the height and depth of God's Love for each of us. Justification is that condition of having God's righteousness attributed (or imputed) to you or me.

Chapter four is Paul's argument that "faith" is reckoned as righteousness [Romans 4:4]. What is more, faith is considered righteousness prior to any action on the part of the believer. Abraham was justified prior to circumcision. There was no law of Moses at the time. Abraham was not even a Jew, being prior to Judaism. He never kept the law, because the law did not exist. He was obedient to God as far as he understood God. And that obedience constituted the expression of his "faith".

The final verses of Chapter Four [Romans 4:22-25]: **Therefore his faith "was reckoned to him as righteousness." Now the words, "it was reckoned to him," were written not for his sake alone, but for ours also. It will be reckoned to us who believe in him who raised Jesus our Lord from the dead, who was handed over to death for our trespasses and was raised for our justification.** This is the source of the doctrine of *imputed righteousness.*

Again I invite you to read Romans Chapters one through four. St. Paul lays out the foundation for his theology of salvation by grace through faith. That foundation is of vital importance if we are to understand the rest of the letter.

We're going to look at Chapter five; "the Lutheran Chapter".

According to Luther, the Roman Church had established a system of salvation that was as complicated and unhelpful as was the Old Covenant. Just as in Jerusalem, the Priest offered an animal sacrifice on behalf of a sin, so in the Eucharist the Priest re-creates on the altar the crucifixion of Jesus. In so doing the Church (that is, those ecclesiastics [clerics] who are in perfect agreement with the Pope) gains merit which then may be distributed among the members of the Church by their participation as witnesses to the mass.

Again, according to Luther, Paul would have had nothing to do with such a perverse idea. Behind that idea is a definition of God as Judge that would have enraged Paul. Here is an idea that God is an angry, vicious, eager to condemn, Judge. Paul understood God to be kind, slow to anger and abounding in Hesed (steadfast Love). Paul believed that God's Love was redemptive, not condemnative! Paul would certainly have agreed with St. Barnabas (whom I believe wrote Hebrews) when he said: **For it was fitting that we should have such a high priest, holy, blameless, undefiled, separated from sinners, and exalted above the heavens. Unlike the other high priests, he has no need to offer sacrifices day after day, first for his own sins, and then for those of the people; this he did _once and for all_ when he offered himself** [Hebrews 7:26].

A little aside here: There are no more priests. Ministers have no advantage over laity. We only occupy one of the offices within the church, just as do each one of you. No sacrifice on the altar, no priest; only a ritual of remembrance which becomes affective by the faith of the participants. And what should we remember? That, because of God's revelation of God's Love in the once and for all sacrifice of Jesus, we may have peace with God. If, indeed, like Luther before he read Romans, one has an idea of God as a punitive judge, St. Paul writes that because of Jesus, we have peace with God...have gained access to this grace in which we stand...and have hope of sharing the Glory of God. Later we're going to have to define what sharing the Glory of God means. A clue comes from St. John. In his Gospel, the word Glory is a synonym for the Holy Spirit.

I'm taking pains to say that Romans 5:1 was not the point of the letter to Rome. However, it is one of the main sub-points. Here, then, is the key to understand Paul's real intention. His word was "parakaleo", and is translated as "Therefore". It means, "to come alongside, to urge onward". It is, as Paul used it, an imperative; whereas and whereas, therefore.

In every letter, even today, there is a well understood format. We begin with an address: Dear whatever your name is. That is followed by one or two baloney paragraphs: Greetings from your oldest customers. Then we get one or more "whereas" paragraphs: We've always had great service from your company. This last batch of widgets was unacceptable. Then we get a "Therefore": Unless you send us a new batch of widgets which are up to our high standards, we will sue your pants off! And then closing baloney paragraphs: How's the wife and kids? We're going on vacation next week. And a closing salutation: Ever your most satisfied customer....

Paul's letters, unless they were edited (as is the case with Corinthians) follow a format. The sub-points and the main point are all indicated with the word "therefore", but not all of them are parakaleo.

Now, back to Romans 5:1. Notice the word "we". Ask, to whom does "we" refer? Is it the Jews? Is it the Gentiles? Is it the sinner? It is not Paul himself. It is all of the above. Jew and Gentile, sinner and saint. Each and all MAY have peace with God by believing/trusting in the Christ-Event (as theologians like to call it). That is because Christ didn't die for the Jews. He didn't die for the Gentiles. He died for the un-godly!

What did that prove? It proves or demonstrates God's Love! God is revealed not as punitive but loving! And, God's Love is superior to any and all human love. Our love is imperfect; God's is Perfect. While one of us might be willing to risk death, or even choose death to save someone of great value, God's Son died for those who have a negative value...a lower than zero value. That is to say, Christ died for you and me. We are included in the "we" of verse one, if we have faith in Christ.

Note how this undoes any claim the Jew or the Gentile has on God. The Jew cannot claim that because he/she is a child of Abraham, a follower of Moses, descended from Israel, that he/she has a leg up in the salvation game. There is no advantage to the Jew. Only that Jesus was a Jew. However, just as must the Gentile, a Jew must approach God with faith. An unbelieving Jew is in exactly the same state as an unbelieving Gentile.

I'm going to introduce the subject of the next lesson. Let me read this: **Much more surely then, now that we have been justified by his blood, will we be saved through him from the wrath of God. For if while we were enemies, we were reconciled to God through the death of his Son, much more surely, having been reconciled, will we be saved by his life** [Romans 5:9-10].

What does Paul mean by being saved by Christ's *Life*? It means that reconciliation means more than that God ignores our unrighteous behavior and attitudes [the doctrine of imputed righteousness]. It must have something to do with the present-time Life of Jesus. It must mean the Resurrected Life of Jesus.

So, reconciled sinners must have some means of actual participation in the present-time Life of Jesus. There is a verse in 1 Corinthians which the translators haven't been able to adequately present. They put a footnote at the bottom of the page to indicate a meaning that they personally don't quite understand. The verse is 15:49: **Just as we have borne the image of the man of dust, we will also bear the image of the man of heaven.** The footnote tells us that Paul meant to say "Let us right now bear the image of the Man of Heaven (Jesus). Reconciliation means that the sinner has been transformed [The doctrine of imparted righteousness], that the resurrection life that is in Jesus is also within the now saved believer. You and I have already had our resurrection.

Luther understood it to mean that when you and I enter Heaven, we get to put on a disguise. The Judge who sits at the Gate doesn't see a sinner. God sees Jesus. Like those old Nixon Halloween masks, we get to sneak into Heaven wearing a Jesus mask. Here is where I depart from Luther.

However, a very careful reading of Romans shows that the word Spirit is used on connection with Jesus only after the Resurrection. It is as if, according to Paul, the preexistent Messiah became flesh in a man named Jesus, and only post-resurrection is that man and that Spirit united in a way that is accessible to you and me. Only theologians need to worry about that one.

Here is how it works out for you and me. Ever since the Resurrection, the Holy Spirit, the Spirit of God, and the Spirit of Jesus are united in one entity: the Trinity. That Spirit, which was made flesh and dwelt among us in a fully human is now able to enter and indwell other human beings.

That it does so both among Jews and Gentiles, is Paul's basic evidence for everything he asserts: that there is no advantage to a Jew, that God has enacted his next "in order that", and that his understanding of the nature of God is correct.

So, bottom line, the doctrine of Salvation by Grace through faith has a far greater impact than just your salvation. It is the game-changer of all time.

Still, it is the main point of Paul's Gospel, it isn't what he was writing to the Romans about.

LESSON THREE

INTRODUCTION

One of the most important and original contributions of St. Paul, and especially in the letter to the Romans, is his idea of the Holy Spirit. His huge contribution is absolutely foundational to our faith. And, while he doesn't use the term, the ideas in this letter are the first written record of the forming idea of the Trinity. Only in Matthew, which was written at least ten years later (and *possibly* twenty or more), does one find the Trinity expressed fully.

Paul distinguishes the idea of the Holy Spirit from the Old Testament idea of the Spirit of God, in so far as he identifies the Holy Spirit with Jesus. He also attributes several functions to the Holy Spirit which are not notable in the Old Scriptures. That is what we are going to share today.

THE OLD TESTAMENT

The Prophets were influenced by the Spirit of God when they performed oracular miracles. The Judges and Kings might be more or less obedient to the Will of God as presented in, for instance, the Levitical Law, or the announcement of a Prophet. However, in the Torah and in the Prophets, there is no comparable "in-dwelling" of the Spirit. The Spirit operates from outside the person; as one might whisper to another, or might take one by the hand. That is very different from what the Apostle means.

The Spirit of God is a creative power, as for instance, when God speaks the Word of Creation the Spirit of God moves forward over the Deep to bring forth Light. It was this idea that was manifested in John's Gospel; that the Spirit of God, the Word, became flesh and dwelt among us "full of grace and truth". There is, prior to Pentecost, no Scriptural witness of any outpouring of the Spirit of God on any group of individuals. Pentecost is the pivotal point of the New Testament. It is the fulcrum upon which history tips toward an obedient and saved people (the Body of Christ)

THE IDEA OF THE HOLY SPIRIT IN JESUS

When I was a teen, and later as a young man, I heard pastors speak of spirit; comparing the excitement one experiences at a football rally to the Divine Presence. Today, I am ashamed and embarrassed that any Methodist Pastor should utter such sublime stupidity.

Paul saw the Presence of the Spirit of God in Jesus as something quite original and unprecedented. Paul does not refer to Jesus as "the Spirit of God". Rather he saw the Spirit of God *in* Jesus. **His**

Son, who was descended from David according to the flesh and was declared to be Son of God with power according to the spirit of holiness by resurrection from the dead, Jesus Christ our Lord [Romans 1:3-4 NRSV].

By the Presence of the Spirit of God within Jesus, God was working out the reconciliation between the believer and God, revealing Himself to humanity, and putting the seal of divinity upon the human Jesus. Paul called Jesus the first-born of all creation. Jesus, the man, was the first of the "sons of Adam" into which the Spirit of God was "infused", or, in whom the Spirit of God dwelt.

Only after the Resurrection, does Paul use the term "Spirit of Jesus", and relate that Spirit to the Spirit of God. It is the Resurrected Savior who is God, within the Trinitarian formula. And it is, only as the Resurrected Savior that the Spirit of Jesus is able to in-dwell the Christian believer. Clearly, to St. Paul, the Resurrection made a difference. It was the Resurrected Jesus, after all, who spoke to Paul on the road to Damascus.

THE IDEA OF THE HOLY SPIRIT IN THE BELIEVER

The Resurrection is the fulcrum over which God is fulfilling God's intention for the entire Creation. Paul said that the entire Creation is hopping about on tip-toe to see the New Creation, i.e., you and me. In this letter, Paul presents a bunch of functions of the Holy Spirit within the Believer. Let's list them.

First and foremost (5:1ff) It is the Resurrected Jesus who gives us access to the Righteous and Merciful God Judge. The Holy Spirit of Jesus justifies the Believer and brings about peace between the Believer and God. That is to say, by faith in the Resurrected Jesus, the Believer is the recipient of God's Love poured out and into the Believer. This Love brings with it hope and a host of other blessings. It is not available to those who think of Jesus as simply a "wise teacher".

Justification as a word only approximates the change in relationship between God and the Believer. Justification means "made righteous or holy". The means by which the Believer is made holy is, in fact, the in-dwelling of the Holy Spirit, the Spirit of Jesus, the Spirit of God's Holy Love. In other words, we are joined together in and as the Body of Christ.

If sin equals separation and alienation from God, the in-dwelling Spirit is the reconciliation. The distant and alienated God has come, and by the permission of our faith, in-filled our being. Where that has happened, sin no longer reigns. Rather, God's Love is supreme. Please note that sin is not understood (here) as untoward behavior. The Law has been eliminated (8:2). Elsewhere (I Corinthians 6:12) Paul wrote: "All things are lawful for me, but not all things are helpful". We will get back to Paul's ethics in a later lesson. Here, we are at pains to say that the Holy Spirit creates an intimacy between God and the Believer and that is how we are freed from all sin.

Secondary to this reconciliation, the Holy Spirit brings gifts. In Galatians 5:22 we find the quotable summary: **The fruits of the Spirit are God's Love, joy, peace, patience, kindness, goodness, faithfulness, gentleness and self-control. Against these there is no law.** Paul is not quite so organized in Romans, but the meanings are all here.

15:13 = energizer (May the God of hope fill you with all joy and peace in believing, so that you may abound in hope by the power of the Holy Spirit). 14:17 =joy peace and hope (For the kingdom of God is not food and drink but righteousness and peace and joy in the Holy Spirit). 8:14 = adoption as children of God (For all who are led by the Spirit of God are children of God). 8:26 strength through intimacy = (Likewise the Spirit helps us in our weakness; for we do not know how to pray as we ought, but that very Spirit intercedes with sighs too deep for words). Paul witnesses that only by the power of the Holy Spirit had he been able to perform "signs and wonders".

One of the un-noticed implications comes from his description of the "members of the Body". While one is called to be apostle, another is called to teach, and another is called to perform miracles. These are also "gifts of the Spirit".

What I'm aiming at here is that, by means of the Holy Spirit indwelling the saint, God is reconciling the entire Creation to His intention. The Holy Spirit within the saint (that is: you) working within the Body of Christ is the New Creation, a reality within which the intimate relationship between God and the Creation is continuously enacted.

I've been reading a book about the Reformation. One of the lessons the Body learned five hundred years ago is that the over-emphasis on the indwelling Spirit leads to some really bad experiences. Even today, especially among Pentecostals, some persons claiming to be under the influence of the Spirit do really dumb things. I've had personal experience with some of those folks. It is really important to identify, apart from the Bible, what we have learned. The indwelling Spirit does not bring infallibility, perfect health, financial success, perfect wisdom, nor the right to judge the behavior of one's neighbor. It also does not mean that one's actions are always godly. Any and every Christian, into whom God has sent His holiness, must judge himself by the highest of standards, not because of the fear of wrath, but rather because, as one of my Bishop's used to translate Paul, "Because of you guys, God is getting a bad reputation". **(The name of God is blasphemed among the Gentiles because of you** [Romans 2:24].

I have developed this test which any Christian may use: 1. Is my action, attitude, idea, belief, affirmed by other wise Christians, and 2. compatible to the Character of God as revealed in the person of Jesus, and 3. Biblically sound?

Having said that, St. Paul was accurate and correct. And it makes all the difference. The Spirit of God does indwell individuals, and it is an ultimately transformative experience.

LESSON FOUR

INTRODUCTION

According to St. Paul, there is no wrath of God which must be feared by believers. Wrath is contrary to the nature of God revealed in Christ Jesus: 1 John 4:8: God is Agape.

This is what St. Paul understood. He was a great sinner; in his words: chief among sinners. Yet, on the Road to Damascus, the God of Agape appeared to him in the resurrected person of Jesus. The experience was so totally life-changing that it took Paul fifteen years of careful study to understand its meaning in full.

Someone gave me some gentle push-back. The valid point was made: "we see a lot about God's wrath in the New Testament".

If we look at Romans, both singly and in context with Ephesians and Thessalonians, we will, indeed, see much about wrath. **By your hard and impenitent heart you are storing up wrath for yourself on the day of wrath, when God's righteous judgment will be revealed** [Romans 2:5]. **For those who**

are self-seeking and who obey not the truth but wickedness, there will be wrath and fury [Romans 2:8].

Within the outline of Paul's letter, this is addressed toward those who continue to insist on the requirements of the Law of Moses. They are his theological opponents. Today we may gloss over theological differences, say between Presbyterian and Methodist, or Calvinist Baptist and Methodist; however, Paul was defining the nature of Christian belief. He was the first writer of Christian Theology. To get it wrong would have made the entire edifice of the Body of Christ untenable.

We are, at last bumping up against the real reason Paul wrote this letter. He called himself an "Apostle to the Gentiles". In Chapter 15, during his summing up, Paul is effusive about the grace extended to him; the power of the Spirit of God, performance of signs and wonders, his Gospel proclaimed by word and deed from Jerusalem throughout Illyricum. It is this Gospel of "Escape from wrath and law by faith in Jesus" to which he refers: **For the law brings wrath; but where there is no law, neither is there violation** [Romans 4:15].

And yet, as someone pointed out, we must take up this issue of wrath: What is it, and to whom is it directed? How does "wrath" relate to Paul's Good News?

Paul first directs his attention to what later theologians have called "the Judaizers": those who insisted that the Law of Moses, in every detail, applied to Gentiles who wished to become members of the "Sect of Jesus". (Much as Islamists today would and do insist that sharia customs are obligatory on non-Muslims.) Indeed, they (the Judaizers) saw the Christian Fellowship as, and only as, a sect within the greater House of David. Paul reasoned, that since Abram was saved by faith, Gentiles are saved by faith, and Jesus died for more than the House of David. He died for all of us. To resist this larger boundary of Christ, was to make little of the sacrifice of Christ. If Jesus died only for Jews, then His sacrifice was a small thing. If Jesus died for all humanity, then it was a very large event. Reluctance to come to terms with this larger dimension is and was the same as denying faith in Christ Jesus. (As long as I have mentioned the Muslims, I might as well say that their denial of salvation by grace through faith puts them in the same category as the Judaizers.)

Now, in my terms: God's wrath is, in this case, the "impassible gulf" fixed by the legalists and those who have correctly understood Paul's Good News of salvation by grace through faith. God didn't put it there; the legalists have done it themselves. Since they cannot or will not accept the gift of God, they put themselves outside the boundary of God's Love. While that seems like wrath, it is a self-inflicted wound.

Interestingly, in the predestination chapter [Romans 9], Paul turns the argument of the pharisaic legalists against themselves. Yes, God hardened the heart of Pharaoh, *in order that* the Hebrews might be freed. Now, wrote Paul, He hardens the heart of the Judaizers against God's historic act of freeing the Gentiles from slavery to sin. Paul asks. "Who are you (Judaizer) to question God?" And he concludes that only a remnant of Israel will find salvation, and the Judaizers are not part of that remnant, unless they come round to the Truth of Salvation by grace through faith.

In Chapter eleven, Paul changes his focus to the Gentile Christians. Don't you dare, he says, look down on Israel. The Jews are the vessel through which God has brought salvation to the Gentiles. They are not funny, nor quaint. Their zeal for God is the reason you, Gentile, are able to know anything important about God.

It is true that we Gentiles need not obey the Law of Moses. However, we have a debt of gratitude toward God (not to mention Israel and St. Paul). We therefore must not continue to sin. What did he mean by sin? I thought we were done with sin. Paul wrote that we must obey ruling authorities. **Therefore** (he wrote) **one must be subject** *(to governmental authorities)*, **not only because of wrath but also because of conscience** [Romans 13:5]. This is confusing. Done with one law, but subject to another. Does our obedience to governmental law amount to sin?

Well, in I Corinthians Paul discusses the morality of a Gentile Christian. If the Gentile can eat meat offered to idols, or pork for that matter in Greece, one must ask how that affects his fellow worshiper (both Gentile and Jew). My freedom must not become the cause of the downfall of another. I owe a debt of God's Love to them. And to act in a manner other than what corresponds to the full Love of God toward them, constitutes the same sin as the Judaizer: opposing the Will of God. It places the Gentile believer outside the boundary of God's Love. Unless we show grace to each other, God is unable to show grace to us. Jesus said that if we fail to forgive, God cannot forgive us. Jesus also said that to deny the witness of the Holy Spirit (that is the Presence of God) our denial cannot be overcome. If you won't accept God's Love, no amount of God Loving you will overcome your stubborn resistance. It is the same self-inflicted wound. Stand outside the feast, like the elder brother, and refuse to come in. Stand outside the Gate of Heaven, and refuse to enter. God will not put you in an arm-lock and march you into the City of Heaven.

The second argument Paul made with the Gentile Christians had to do with the "unhelpful" things of life. We are to put away, shuck off, run away from, the old life of self-gratification. That is because of our debt to Jesus. We are to discipline ourselves. We are to support each other. We are to gently correct each other, lest God be embarrassed by our attitudes and practices. Self-gratification means, here, more than a sensual life. It means living according to our own will, our own wisdom. We are to take on, by the Grace of God, the power of the Holy Spirit. We are to apply God's Love within our God-rejecting world.

If you, as do I, fail in some aspect of morality or attitude, that doesn't undo our salvation. It does de-sensitize our spirit. Thus, certain aspects of Old Testament morality apply to us, not as law, but as guidepost. The teachings and example of Christ are likewise guides to the wise Christian. We need not fear God. At least not until we (figuratively) take up arms against the Body of Christ.

To fail, from time to time, or even daily, need not jeopardize salvation. It is a matter of the heart. At the bottom of all, do you love God and wish you could serve Him fully and perfectly? In Wesley's terminology, "are you earnestly striving for perfection?" Thus to fail is simply to err. The penalty is not one of guilt, but of loss. I have lost the opportunity and/or the ability to serve as well as I might have done.

Paul witnessed to his own struggles: **Who will release me from this body of death** [Romans 7:24]**? The thing I do not want to do is the thing I do** [Romans 7:15]. Yet, Paul did not fear judgment on that account.

The third focus would be on wrath as it applies to "the world". To St. Paul, "the world" and "the flesh" are approximately the same. To focus on the world, or on the flesh, leads one to death. To focus on the things of the spirit, that is to focus on the Presence of the Holy Spirit within the practicing saint, leads to Life. The world is guilty of the same sin as the Judaizers. I suspect Paul would put Gentile Christians who deny the working of the Holy Spirit into this category. All are guilty of opposing the Will or Plan of God to reconcile the Creation and humanity to Himself.

The Community of Christians, both Jew and Gentile, are personally and corporately the New Creation; a new reality within the old. The second fruits, Jesus being the first [1 Corinthians 15:20].

They shall know that we are Christians by our God-Love for each other. Our morality must not be adherence to a written code, but one of obedience to the Holy Spirit. Not a negative: thou shalt not, but rather a positive, thou shalt.

The Body of Christ, according to the Apostle, is the community of the last days. There will be a judgment, but not of the sort so often portrayed by modern media. It will, for most (if not all) of us come in two parts. The second is when human life on Earth comes to an end. The first also comes in two parts; when we are confronted by the need to accept salvation by grace through faith, and the second when this mortal life ends (and with it the opportunity to accept salvation by grace through faith). I have coined a phrase. I call it, "my immanent personal eschaton". As far as I am concerned, the world ends the moment I die. Either I die and it ends, or it ends and I die. Makes no difference to me.

At that moment, my choice is fixed. Either I will accept Grace and Salvation, or I will stand afar off and resent the gulf I have placed between me and those who dwell in the warmth of God's Love. Again, God has not placed the gulf between us and Him. We do so ourselves. God has created us with the freedom to do that. Like the little child who won't take the candy bar because it isn't the one he wanted, we are free to stay away from the Loving embrace of our Savior. Perhaps we dislike someone who is sitting on His lap like a little child. Perhaps we cannot surrender our own rationality. Perhaps we resent the outward inequality of this life. Perhaps we feel so unworthy that we make little of the Christ Event: "I cannot forgive myself, I am unworthy". Perhaps we are fearful. Paul would say that there is no person whose sins are so awful that God has stopped Loving him or her. All the negativity comes from us, not from God.

God's plan is, and has been from the beginning, to reveal Himself as Love within the entire human community. Can't do it as hate. Can't to it as aggression. Can't do it as lust or greed or power or control. Can only do it as sacrifice, like Jesus. And it is to that life-style that Paul calls us. As such, we are the sign of the coming Kingdom of God- an eschatological people along with the Jews.

Therefore do not let sin reign in your mortal body so that you obey its lusts, and do not go on presenting the members of your body to sin as instruments of unrighteousness; but present yourselves to God as those alive from the dead, and your members as instruments of righteousness to God [Romans 6:12-13].

LESSON FIVE

INTRODUCTION

The lesson last week begged the question: What about the Jews; are they blessed or cursed? St Paul was in a quandary. Beginning in Chapter nine, he wrote that only a remnant of Israel will be saved [Romans 9:27]. He spent time trying to distinguish between the Jews who had accepted Jesus as Savior/Messiah, and the Judaizers. He had made the case that only those who hold the Promise, that is those who have accepted Jesus as Messiah/Son of God, are the true descendants of Abraham. In other words; those Jews and Gentiles who claim salvation by grace through faith are children of Abraham.

Theologians have figured out that Paul had two different definitions for the word "Israel". One was the ethnic group, and the other a spiritual group. It is very clear that the Spiritual Israel corresponds to the "elect from every tribe and nation". That group consists of the Gentile Christians as well as those Jews who have found the truth of salvation by grace through faith in Jesus. But what of the Ethnic Israel? Are they elect or not? Are they blessed or not?

Well, here in chapters nine through eleven we have an answer. Paul can't abide a negative answer. He must find a formula within the Old Testament by which Ethnic Israel is saved, because **to them belongs the sonship, the glory, the covenants, the worship, and the promises** [Romans 9:4]. Paul knew that a calling is not subject to revocation. God called the Jews, and they are still called. They may have fulfilled their function as the People from whom Jesus was born; but they are still the Chosen Ones.

Now, what I have to say next depends on technical aspects of Greek grammar. Also, there are a few words which can be translated in a couple of different ways. And, theologians differ about all of this. I am going to share what makes sense to me.

The Revised Standard Version has a great deal of Calvinist influence. They are the ones whose frame of reference is Predestination as a personal matter rather than as a historical matter. In their interpretation, God elects certain persons for salvation and damns the rest. In a different frame of reference one can suggest that God has chosen certain groups, led by certain persons, to forward God's Plan of Salvation. We Methodists, and I personally, find the latter more persuasive than the former.

I need for you to look at Chapter eleven, verse eight, to see how the Titanic can turn on a single wave. The RSV has it: **God gave them a spirit of stupor, eyes that should not see, and ears that should not hear, down to this very day.** However, other theologians translate it: **God granted them a spirit of stupor, eyes that would not see, and ears that would not hear, to this day.** God granted them the freedom and the right to "not see or hear".

And in Verse ten, as per the RSV: **David says "...let their eyes be darkened so that they cannot see forever".** But it can also be translated: **"let their eyes be darkened so that they cannot see continually".**

Note how by changing those few words, the meaning changes: from an angry God causing the People of Israel to stumble and fall; to God of Love who grants freedom to people. They themselves choose to have eyes that see or not, and ears to hear or not. And, the choice is not final. Individually, they can change their mind to accept the Love of God apart from obedience to the Law of Moses. Individually they may open their eyes to a Loving and Redemptive God, One who loves not only Jews but also Gentiles. "Continually" rather than "forever" allows for a redemptive change. Continually...but for how long?

It all depends on God. Just as Pharaoh had hardened his heart, and the Hebrews prior to the Exile had hard and impenitent hearts, so in Paul's day many of the Jews blindly rejected and crucified Jesus. In 11:15 Paul uses extreme irony. He wrote that inclusion of the Jews who had rejected the Lord would be like resurrection; "life from the dead" [Romans 11:15 **For if their rejection is the reconciliation of the world, what will their acceptance be but life from the dead!**]. Paul implies that Pharaoh was granted mercy, and so would the Jews. Romans 11:25-27 **I want you to understand this mystery: a hardening has come upon part of Israel, until the full number of the Gentiles has come in. And so <u>all Israel will be saved</u>; as it is written, "Out of Zion will come the Deliverer; he will banish ungodliness from Jacob." "And this is my covenant with them, <u>when I take away their sins</u>."**

For us, Christ is, of course, the Deliverer who comes out of Zion to take away sins. However, "With them" is indefinite. It can refer either to Jacob, or to those who are delivered, that is the Gentile Christians, or it can refer to them both. And so, the Covenant to take away sins is not fully defined.

This is really revolutionary stuff. God's Plan continues. God, on His own, can and (according to Paul) will take away the sins of persons who forward His plan. Some think God forgives even those who resist it. Note that we are talking about Ethnic Israel here, and not Spiritual Israel. Spiritual Israel is already saved by grace through faith. Ethnic Israel will discover salvation *only after* the full number of Gentiles have received salvation. Theologians can't agree on whether Ethnic Israel is fully inclusive of those who are genetically descendants of Jacob, or limited to those Jews who are faithful to the Covenant of Moses.

I don't fully understand God's Plan, and perhaps Paul didn't fully grasp the implications of what he wrote. There seem to be four steps. First the Hebrew people experience both judgment and grace as they live under the Law of Moses. Second, the Jews receive the Messiah and then reject Him. Third, a portion of the Jews accept Jesus as the Son of God, while the rest continue in denial. Finally, God steps in, perhaps at the Second Coming, and the sins of the Jews are "taken away" by the mercy of God. They receive mercy rather than grace. Again, we are uncertain as to whether Paul meant all Jews or only those who worship.

Many theologians agree with this interpretation: The so-called "Jesus Movement" is for Gentiles and those Jews who accept Jesus as the Messiah. But the New Covenant does not abrogate the Old Covenant. It still holds force. And as Holy Writ says: God **will have mercy on whom** (God) **will have mercy** [Romans 9:15, Exodus 33:19].

Look carefully at the passage concerning the Olive Tree [Romans 11:17ff]. The Olive Tree has long been a symbol of Israel. We Gentiles are a wild olive branch, grafted into the Olive Tree. We are not a tree, but only a branch. We should not look too adoringly on ourselves. We are attached to the Tree only by Grace. Ethnic Israel has a different place. According to Paul, Ethnic Israel has been lopped off, in order that we might take its place. Many have taken that as an excuse to denigrate Israel and the Jews. But look closely: our place is temporary or transitional. We are dependent on the Tree and on the Gardener. They have a Covenant with One who cannot be dishonest. **And even those of Israel, if they do not persist in unbelief, will be grafted in, for God has the power to graft them in again** [Romans 11:23 grammatically parsed], indicates that the Jews will/may come to belief and will be re-grafted; this time to the Spiritual Israel. We, on the other hand, may stay in the Tree only so long as we continue in the Kindness of God. I suggest that "the Kindness of God" really means "faithful to the indwelling Holy Spirit".

So, we end without only a partial answer. Israel will be saved. Whether that means the totality of Ethnic Israel or only Spiritual Israel remains to be seen. How ever that turns out, what is evident is that God is not finished with Israel.

As I worked through this, I realized that a paradigm shift was taking place in my own thinking. I have, as I suspect most of you too, thought of the Christian Church as the mainstay of God's activity in the world. I now realize that Israel was, and continues to be, the main focus of God within the Plan of Salvation. We should cultivate humility toward Israel, and toward God. In any case is that not a part of grace?

LESSON SIX

We finally get to the point of this entire lesson series: What did Paul mean his readers to understand?

For this we need to look again at the form of a letter. I'm going to remind you that before the advent of e-mail and tweets, a letter began with a formal introduction: who it is from, to whom it is intended, and perhaps a word about the occasion for which it is written. This is followed by several paragraphs of blarney: what a great product you have produced for us...your service has always been exemplary, etc. This is followed by at least one "whereas" and in many cases by several. Then one gets to the point, a "therefore". You've always sent us good widgets, but this last was unacceptably bad. Therefore, we're not paying for them...and furthermore we expect full replacement before we sue your pants off! A letter then concludes with more polite blarney; "hoping business is good for you, greet the wife and kids" etc.

Ancient letters had some variations on this format, but the rule still follows. We've even followed that kind of outline in our lesson series. Starting with definitions, we have had a series of whereases, and now we get to the therefore. Paul usually set off his therefore with the Greek word "parakaleo". If you want to look for the meaning of any of his letters, look to the "therefores". I almost guarantee that you will be discouraged. They tend to be prosaic. "Don't be discouraged," or "Behave better toward one another," or "Don't make me come over there!"

In Romans, Paul has a very important series of "Therefores"! They are found in chapter twelve through chapter fifteen, verse thirteen. I will list them here, and then develop each.

- Spirit guided Christian life (both Jew and Gentile) must be and is worship

- The stronger among us must make allowance for the weaker

- All are welcome: both Gentile and Jew.

Martin Luther was correct to focus on the whereas, because the definitions Paul uses to define the Christian in relationship to God are so very different from what went before. Even more importantly, he was right because even today we desperately want to use our own definitions; they help us avoid confronting our own spiritual poverty. Luther's last words were: "We are beggars, indeed".

These "therefore(s)" were of critical importance to Paul. The Gentile Christians and the Jews were still together in one fellowship, but the tensions between the groups threatened a divorce. Paul wanted to avoid that. There are two possible reasons, besides the obvious inward one (that Paul was Jewish but called to save Gentiles). The first possibility is that Paul anticipated the immediate return of Christ, and saw his ministry in apocalyptic terms. He said that he would magnify (enlarge or brag about) his ministry in order to make ever more of his fellows Jews jealous of the grace they saw applied to Gentiles, as well as of the power of the Gentiles to perform signs and wonders. That jealousy was an "in order that" more and more Jews would join the Jesus sect, before Christ's immanent return.

The second possibility is that Paul understood that Christ would return on God's time scale, and that Paul's message was prophetic; intended for many generations to understand. In this case, Paul was laying out his hope for the relationship between the Jewish community and the Church. The divorce did, in fact, take place, in and after the destruction of Jerusalem in 70 AD.

We need to take note that one possibility is that Paul thought the Return of Christ was immanent, and God knew that his message was prophetic rather a news bulletin.

So, to the first point: Spirit guided Christian life (both Jew and Gentile) must be and is worship.

The tension within the Body of Christ, at the time of his letter, was between Law-obedient Jews, and Law-exempt Gentiles. His really revolutionary idea was that correct worship does not consist of ritual, but rather of right-living (Spirit filled and Spirit directed). One may be Jewish or Gentile, and God (the Righteous and Merciful Judge) will approve. If one believes that right living consists of obedience to the Law of Moses, one must keep the entire Law. If one believes that right living consists of conforming to the Spirit of God found in Jesus the man, and is now the Spirit of Jesus as well, one will be guided by the Holy Spirit from within. The Law is the guide from outside, the Spirit is the guide from within.

You will remember my oft repeated condition: an act or attitude is appropriate only if it is consistent with the will of God revealed in the Bible; only if it is consistent with the Character of God revealed in Christ Jesus; and only if it can be approved by other (mature) Spirit-filled Christians.

There are two sides of this: one is to do what the Holy Spirit affirms, and the other is to cease doing those things the Holy Spirit abhors. Paul, using the example of Jesus, expects our every moment to be filled with prayer, that is: an awareness of the Presence of God's Spirit, and to approach each moment with a worshipful thanksgiving. I am certain that each of you can fill in the appropriate scriptural references.

Today many Christians have substituted a new law for the Law of Moses. It consists of an abridged form of the moral teachings they glean from the New Testament. Abridged, I say, because they ignore the moral teachings of Jesus that are the most inconvenient. Some "Bible-thumpers" can be really hateful people: for instance, that congregation that holds rallies at the funerals of soldiers. On the other side, some of the Charismatic/Pentecostalists substitute their own psyche for the Spirit of God. They wind up following their own desires, rather than the Spirit of God. As a Charismatic, I sometimes find myself tempted to excuse my own "less than loving" desires as permitted by the Holy Spirit. I might be tired and want to avoid some act of discipleship which God thinks is urgent. I might look down my ample nose at a multi-colored human pin-cushion thinking that God really condemns such a self-negating culture, rather than look at the person as God's child. Sometimes I just don't want to look at a person the way Jesus would have done. God's Spirit, to be brief, is the Spirit of God's Love as revealed in the life and Character of Jesus. Any deviation from that Spirit is not the Life-Worship intended by St. Paul.

So, to the second point: The stronger among us must make allowance for the weaker. Here I must make a very big distinction. The moral life guided by the Holy Spirit is for mature Christians. As I write this, I am listening to my grand-daughter cry "he started it...." Clearly, moral development from childhood to adult maturity requires that the younger among us learn rules and live under a form of moral law. For a child "all things are lawful, but not everything is helpful" does not apply. One of the serious problems of our society is that we ascribe moral thinking to children much earlier than they are developmentally ready. Not even an eighteen-year-old has a fully developed frontal lobe, where moral reasoning take place. Yet our legislatures and academic moral guides have demanded that we allow sixteen-year-old children decide whether to have intercourse. Their moral guidance is simply, if it feels good, do it; if it feels really good, do it often. As evidence I present Spring Break, a phenomenon which did not occur in my college years. Moral thinking does not apply, and far too many adults approve. They call it a "moral sabbatical". The moral notion of these self-proclaimed moral experts is that since kids want to have sex, it is OK if they do so.

How different are Paul's expectations! Using (from Ephesians) marriage as an example about which Paul wrote more than once: We husbands are to surrender our lives for the benefit and welfare of our wife. Wives are asked to respect their husbands, and out of reverence for Christ treat him as the head of the family. Such a relationship is possible only when Christ is the Head of the Family, and His Spirit has in-dwelt both the husband and the wife. Yet that is what he expected. The Christian to sacrifice his/her welfare for the sake of the other. One makes this sacrifice because we love the other as Christ has loved us and gave himself up for us.

If wine will lead my companion to debauchery, I cannot defend my own indulgence. If sharp words will lead my companion to use the Name of God in an unworthy or even casual way, I will abstain from sharp words. If the purchase of a luxury would lead others to greed and a denial of God's intention that we be generous; then I will abstain from luxury. How far one can take this, is often a measure of his or her spiritual maturity.

And finally; Both Jew and Gentile are welcome at God's Table. We are not gifted with the power to judge the hearts of others. In the first place, you may not compare me to others. Only I may judge whether I am better than I would have been had I not met Christ. And beyond that, I do not know myself. Only God can see the fulness of my heart. A parishioner in Northern Ireland once asked me whether I thought the Catholic Church is the Anti-Christ. Now, I cannot believe a good bit of what the Catholic Church teaches. Yet, I have Catholic friends who demonstrate daily that they are led by the Spirit of God. One can say the same about Jews, Hindus, Muslims and others. We cannot see their heart. What Paul taught, about the difference between Ethnic Israel and Spiritual Israel can be made to apply to others. Please note that I am not endorsing any other religious faith, and most certainly am not saying that it makes no difference (all paths lead to Heaven?). Absolutely not. What I am saying is that God is willing to receive one whose heart is right. Wesley, in his *Open Letter to the Catholics of Ireland*, wrote: "If your heart is like unto my heart, give me your hand, we are brothers". Paul would approve.

And so, these three come out of the same source. If the Spirit of God indwells a person, then one's life becomes worship, one's morals spring from the Love of God poured out on and through us, and one is no longer able to judge another. One becomes a living image of the sacrificial Love of God revealed in the Person of Jesus.

LESSON SEVEN

INTRODUCTION

What is the reason for Salvation by Faith through Grace? It is that you and I may have our minds transformed by the indwelling Holy Spirit for the Glory of God.

I remind you that this life is only transitional and temporary, a fleeting moment. What the Scouts say about camping is true for most of us: "we leave no trace". So, what is God's purpose for your life according to St. Paul? There are only a very few original thinkers about this sort of thing. Buddha, Jesus, and Paul. Most others think of religion as "how to live now". These three taught how to live, hereafter. There are lots of people who, after these three, have expressed many of the implications, but have not been "original" in their thinking.

Paul wanted us to live this life as an "in-order-that". He wanted us to keep our eye on the doughnut and not on the hole. Life is for the Glory of God. Life is intended to enlarge and enhance the Body of Christ. As I mentioned in an earlier lesson, each one of us is gifted, before we are born, with abilities, disabilities, interests and disinterests. Each one is formed by God for a particular ministry within the Body. Paul had several lists. Here is the one from Romans: **12:4 For as in one body we have many members, and not all the members have the same function, 5 so we, who are many, are one body in Christ, and individually we are members one of another. 6 We have gifts that differ according to the grace given to us: prophecy, in proportion to faith; 7 ministry, in ministering; the teacher, in teaching; 8 the exhorter, in exhortation; the giver, in generosity; the leader, in diligence; the compassionate, in cheerfulness. 9 Let God's Love be genuine; hate what is evil, hold fast to what is good; 10 love one another with mutual affection; outdo one another in showing honor. 11 Do not lag in zeal, be ardent in spirit, serve the Lord.**

I've mentioned Paul's reasoning seems always to include or indicate an "in order that". The truth of these gifts is that they are each an "in order that". In Corinthians he was explicit. Your gifts were given to you, not for your own sake, but "in order that" Christ may be glorified in and through the Body. And thus the preacher at a mega church may not look down on the pastor of a small ethnic inner-city congregation. One wise man once suggested to me that the pastor of the mega church cannot even imagine the burdens carried by the other pastor.

When I started out, I had ambition to be the pastor of a mega congregation. However, I was gifted as a teacher and preacher, and called by God to serve problem churches. I had to take a hard look at myself, when I was almost forty. God very clearly communicated to me that I was mistaken about my calling, and that I should find real happiness in doing what God had created me to do. I found, in the next three decades that God was right, and I had been wrong. Imagine that.

I would like to take a short detour, for just a moment. We rarely find time to talk about this, and this is my big chance. And, by the way, I am not about to ask you to do anything I have not already done myself.

In Paul's list we find:12:7 **"he who gives, with liberality".** I have already witnessed the liberality of members of this class. So, this is not by way of concern or criticism. Recently one of my friends died. He was a mufti-millionaire. He left nothing to the church in his will. I regret his oversight. His heirs are already wealthy and have no need of his estate. Biblically, we have a financial responsibility to our parents, not to our children. Our obligation to our children is to lead them in the right paths; paths from which they should not wander. Sue and I have told our kids that they will get whatever they get, while we are alive. They should not look for much after we're gone. A few weeks ago, Sue and I walked through an estate sale. We were very disappointed to see included in the sale the wedding pictures of Mom and Dad. What possible value could anyone other than family attach to those pictures. And so it is with much of what we treasure. Things are meant to be used. If a child of mine really wants something, he or she can have it. But mostly they don't need or want most of my stuff. And, in my case, that stuff can be better used to help the Body of Christ. So, I challenge you, if you have not done so, speak to a lawyer and put Emmanuel in your will.

Now back to our text. Paul's challenge is this: 6: 19 **For just as you once presented your members as slaves to impurity and to greater and greater iniquity, so now present your members as slaves to righteousness for sanctification.** Paul promised that the indwelling Holy Spirit would _impart_ righteousness to the believer,

As we live the Christian life, guided by the Indwelling Holy Spirit, that way of life becomes more and more a part our our inner being. Just as, having lived with Sue for these many decades, parts of her personality have become part of mine. Her goals have become my goals; and visa-versa. Living with God helps one grow more godly.

Now a word of caution. I recently saw in Prevention magazine, a "spiritual" meditation. The gist of the page was: when you have a crisis, trust your inner voice. The author thought that her inner voice was trustworthy and had guided her for many years. Let me say, categorically, one who follows his or her inner voice is a fool, and possibly neurotic. It was the inner voice, after all that got the individual into the crisis in the first place. Narcissists love to follow their inner voice, but then, they already know that they are god.

No, according to St. Paul, we are to follow God's Spirit, not our spirit. And Paul affirms the inner communication of God's Spirit with our spirit. God's Spirit intercedes with sighs too deep for words; in other words, wordlessly. It will come as a surprise to men, but not to most women, feelings can be a stronger guide than words.

So: how do you know that God has imparted His Righteousness and guidance through the indwelling Holy Spirit? That was the basic question behind Wesley's search for entire sanctification, or what we have called "going on to perfection". The marks of the sanctified Christian are Godly Love, joy, peace, patience, kindness, (here we go again) generosity, faithfulness, gentleness, and self-control (Gal. 5:22). Whenever an attitude or action is proposed, one must ask whether it is characteristic of the Holy Spirit. It is consistent with the will of God revealed in the Bible? Is it consistent with the Character of God revealed in the person of Jesus? Is the action or attitude confirmed by other mature Christians? Even then, we are liable to err. God's Grace is sufficient for those errors.

And so we come to the end of the seven lessons about Romans. Paul's intention in writing to them, was 1. to avoid a split between the two factions of the Body of Christ: the Jew and the Gentile. 2. To establish his Gospel of salvation by grace through faith, as the fundamental reality for both Jew and Gentile. And 3. To establish this new ethic: God's will effective in the life of the Spirit-filled Christian.

FIRST CORINTHIANS

The whole of the Corinthian correspondence must be viewed under the lens of St. Paul's understanding of agapē. Agapē is the Greek word for God's Love. It wasn't always defined as does the Christian Church. The love of the gods for humanity was unreliable and fickle. St. Paul redefined the word. He inserted into that word, the Character of God revealed in the ministry, teachings, life, death and resurrection of Jesus Christ. Now, it can have no other meaning. It is distinctly different than philia (most often defined as brotherly love. The Greeks had other words for love: Storge [say: store-jay"] is family love. Philia is more properly understood as deep friendship. Philautia is self-love; akin to narcissism. Eros is creative love. Today, secular society has tried to expropriate the word Agapē, defining it as "universal affection", as in charity. Paul would have none of that.

Most scholars, though certainly not all, think there were at least four letters from Paul to the Church at Corinth. Confusing jumps of logic are explained by the action of an editor who merged the three of the four into two. The earliest letter has been lost.

The Apostle identified his concern at the very beginning. The congregation was dividing into factions, each following one of the "second-generation" leaders. Apollos [see Acts 18 and 19], and Cephas [St. Peter] were thought by some to have contrasting (or different) understandings of the Gospel than Paul. Others held Paul to be superior to all others. Paul would not allow it. Christ Jesus is the point.

Apparently, the basis for some of the factionalism was related to who had been baptized by whom. **Christ did not send me to baptize but to proclaim the gospel, and not with eloquent wisdom, so that the cross of Christ might not be emptied of its power** [I Corinthians 1:17]. The first question to ask of the Corinthian letters is: What is that Power?

It is not "wisdom", and it is not "signs". **For Jews demand signs and Greeks desire wisdom, but we proclaim Christ crucified, a stumbling block to Jews and foolishness to Gentiles** [1 Corinthians 1:22]. Signs and wonders have their followers today also. Fascinated by miracles of healing, they miss the point. The Gospel is not about performing magic. It is about service as the expression of God's Love. And "wisdom" [Gk: Sophia; I suspect "wisdom" is a code word for the Sophists], is not the purpose of the Gospel. It is about Salvation and the Christ Jesus **who became for us wisdom from God, and righteousness and sanctification and redemption** [1 Corinthians 1:30].

If "wisdom" is a reference to the philosophical school of sophistry, then Paul's reference to his preaching the Gospel in "weakness", not using clever words [1 Corinthians 2:1; **lofty words or wisdom**], makes sense. And he concluded that faith must not rest on clever logic [ala sophistry] but (again) on **the power of God** [1 Corinthians 2:5].

My message and my preaching were not with wise and persuasive words, but with a demonstration of the Spirit's power, so that your faith might not rest on human wisdom, but on God's power [1Corinthians 2:4-5; "wise and persuasive words" ought to read "sophisticated spirit", and "demonstration" ought to read "manifestation".].

The Sophists were proud of their ability to use the rules of logic in such a way that they could prove anything and everything to be moral. They are the source of our term "sophistication", which is the ascendant current school of thought. The most influential moral philosophers of the second half of the twentieth century were Hugh Hefner, and Helen Gurly Brown (Playboy and Cosmopolitan respectively). For they taught a sophisticated ethic: whatever "feels good" to the individual is good. St. Paul would not sit in the same room as them.

Instead of the **wisdom of this age** [1 Corinthians 2:6], St. Paul claimed a different and ancient wisdom, God's plan for the **glory** [1 Corinthians 2:7] of the saints; **those who love him** [1 Corinthians 2:9]. That plan was "revealed" to Paul and others, not by philosophy or sophistry, but rather **through the Spirit** [1 Corinthians 2:10]. **The person without the Spirit does not accept the things that come from the Spirit of God but considers them foolishness, and cannot understand them because they are discerned only through the Spirit** [1 Corinthians 2:14].

Clearly, the Power which we seek to define, has its reality within the Holy Spirit.

When Paul addressed the issue of divisiveness, he did not rebuke Apollos. He commended his successor. **I planted the seed, Apollos watered it, but God has been making it grow. For we are co-workers in God's service; you are God's field, God's building** [1 Corinthians 3:6 and 9].

What is it that Paul had worked to lay as a foundation [1 Corinthians 3:10], and God, through Apollos, was building? **You yourselves are God's temple and that God's Spirit dwells in your midst** [1 Corinthians 3:16]. Now we see how Paul is preparing the way for him to speak about the Holy Spirit. The "group" of people who comprise the Church are God's Temple. This may seem rudimentary, but it is Paul's "foundation". A nd so, each person is to seek God's Wisdom, rather than worldly insights. We are to think "from God's point of view". **For the wisdom of this world is foolishness in God's sight** [1Corinthians 3:19].

When Paul wrote about judging the works of each leader, his intention was that the Church limit itself to **what is written** [1 Corinthians 4:6], rather than extend the Gospel into conclusions unsupported by the Holy Spirit, and thus undermine the work of one or another leader. **Therefore** [Gk: hóste (hoce'-teh), simple conjunction meaning "so then"] **judge nothing before the appointed time; wait until the Lord comes** [1 Corinthians 4:5]. A little humility is required of those of us who have received the Gospel. **What do you have that you did not receive? And if you did receive it, why do you boast as though you did not** [1 Corinthians 4: 7]**?** That is a very important restriction for latter day theologians! Even direct inspiration of the Holy Spirit is subject to this rule. The inspired rhema [Romans 10:17: "So *faith* proceeds from (spiritual) hearing; moreover, this hearing (is consummated) through a *rhema-word, see Bible Hub.com]* of the Holy Spirit will never conflict with what has been given us by the Apostles!

Verses eight through thirteen of Chapter Four, are rich in sarcasm. **You are rich** [1 Corinthians 4:8], we apostles are **fools for Christ...We are weak, but you are strong** [1 Corinthians 4:10]**!**

This letter of warning concludes with an appeal to **imitate me** [1 Corinthians 4:16] as he claimed the role of father to them [1 Corinthians 4:15]. And there we have it. Paul re-interpreted the existing Jewish Scriptures under the guidance of the Holy Spirit. That is, he was taught by God. What has been written down is Holy Spirit Truth. Don't mess with it.

II

A second letter to the Corinthians begins with Chapter Five. The subject is entirely different from that of the first four chapters. There is a greater subject and a painful explicit subject. The greater subject is the effect of the behavior of Christians on others. The painful subject is sexual immorality. **It is actually reported that there is sexual immorality among you, and of a kind that even pagans do not tolerate: A man is sleeping with his father's wife** [1 Corinthians 5:1].

One may speculate that the man's father was dead, though that is not apparent. Some suggest that the woman was not the mother of the Christian. One may guess that he thought that the Gospel of salvation by grace through faith gave him permission to follow his desires.

Paul referenced a letter no longer in existence [1 Corinthians 5:9] in which he had expressed his concern that the Christians were associating with sexually immoral people. They must have sent a letter back asking how in the world that might be possible. Corinth was a seaport city, full of sailors whose sexual appetites were satisfied by a large contingent of the willing. It was, apparently, one of the major economic engines of the city state economy.

So, Paul's letter was a response to a non-extant letter from the congregation. He wanted to clarify his position. Christian brothers or sisters who engaged in an immoral life-style should be expelled [1 Corinthians 5:9]. To avoid association with sexually immoral non-Christians would have required the entire withdrawal from the world [1 Corinthians 5:10]. There is no place one can go without associating with sexually immoral people. It is part of the human condition. Expulsion from the fellowship must always have a constructive purpose. It is a caution to others within the fellowship, and it will, hopefully, bring the wrong-doer to repentance and re-admittance. Paul always thought about what will "build up" [1 Corinthians 8:1. 14:12] the Body. It was his preeminent concern.

His concern was that **a little yeast leavens the whole lump** [1 Corinthians 5:6]. He wanted to prevent the immoral from affecting the entire group [1 Corinthians 5:7]. Is it uncharitable to note that Jesus wanted His followers to be yeast in the body public [Matthew 13:33], for instance]? On the other hand, the Church of today may well be more tolerant of sexual misbehavior than is wise. Paul was in a quandary, and so are we. How may we express disapproval without obviating the doctrine of grace?

Paul's answer is that a private meeting is the first step. One most certainly ought never bring suit against a Christian in a government court [1 Corinthians 6:1-6]. That we do so, along with our ancient brothers and sisters, means that our fellowship has **already been completely defeated** [1 Corinthians 6:7]! Paul would rather that the Christian suffer abuse without response than that we should be judged by those **being despised by the Church** [1 Corinthians 6:4]. Instead, find someone in the Church who is qualified to decide these sensitive matters [1 Corinthians 6:5].

The issues which seem to exclude one from the Kingdom of God are not limited to sexual matters. They include a long list of offenses. While the list includes the verbally abusive, swindlers, thieves, the greedy, and drunks [1 Corinthians 6:9-10], it is very difficult to suggest that homosexual behavior is "not prohibited in scripture", as some liberals aver. **Neither the sexually immoral nor idolaters nor adulterers nor** *men* [GK: malakos (mal-ak-os'), an effeminate man] *who have sex with men* [GK: arsenokoite (ar-sen-ok-oy'-tace), a sodomite, a man who has sex with other men] **... will inherit the kingdom of God** [1 Corinthians 6:9-10].

But then, Paul argues the opposite! **Such were some of you. And this is what some of you used to be. But you were washed, you were sanctified, you were justified in the name of the Lord Jesus Christ and in the Spirit of our God** [1

Corinthians 6:11]. This is one of the most astonishing claims of the entire New Testament! So called sinners of the worst stripes are not prevented from participation in the Kingdom, or from adoption as children of God!

I recall seeing the wonderful joy emanating from a woman on the verge of her execution for a murder she admitted she had committed some twenty years previously. Since then, she had met her Lord, been washed in His Blood, and was saved by grace through faith! In other words, these *behaviors* are regrettable and violate one's intimacy with God, but they are not beyond His ability to forgive. To believe otherwise is to make the Sacrifice of Christ a limited and small thing: "He died for me, but not for thee".

While **All things are lawful for me, but not all things are beneficial** [1 Corinthians 6:12]**,** it is also true **that your body is a temple of the Holy Spirit within you** [1 Corinthians 6:19]. Sin may be defined as "alienation from God". When a person lives for him (or her) self, they limit the space set aside within their spirit for intimacy with God. That is at the root of all these various sins. They are all examples of persons living for their own gratification. While freedom from legalistic morals is an absolute requirement of the doctrine of salvation by grace through faith, the freedom to give God a cold-shoulder is inescapable.

Paul wants us to know that the cost of our salvation by grace is the crucifixion of Jesus. **You were bought with a price; therefore** [Gk: de, a simple conjunction] **glorify God in your body** [1 Corinthians 6:20]. And there is one more reason: **Do you not know that your bodies are members of Christ** [1 Corinthians 6:15]. Would you have Jesus accompany you in these sins? Would you have Jesus join in intimate relations with a prostitute? Would you have Jesus do what you experience shame in doing?

This letter was a response to more than one question. On the one side, Paul is concerned about sexual immorality, and on the other side, he is concerned about sexual asceticism. They had written, **"It is well for a man not to touch a woman."** Paul did not agree. This asceticism might be an early part of a movement within the church, or it might be part of the beginnings of the Gnostic heresy [Gnostics believed that Jesus was never really flesh, that spirit is good and flesh is evil]. As a Jewish man, and as a Pharisee, one cannot imagine Paul as a never-married man. It was his duty as a Pharisee to marry and produce children.

Instead, he wrote that if a man experiences too much sexual stimulation, it would be better to be married. To the unmarried [1 Corinthians 7:8; Gk: agamos (ag'-am-os), presently unmarried, never married, divorced, or widowed]. and to the widows he wrote, **It is well for them to remain unmarried as I am.** Possibly he was widowed. In any condition, however, Paul cautioned that the demands of the flesh [Gk: sark, flesh life, the opposite of spiritual life] will diminish one's sensitivity to the Holy Spirit.

Apart from that dichotomy, Paul provided serious wisdom about marital relationships. Marital sexual relations must be based on meeting the needs of the other, not the self: **For the wife does not have authority over her own body, but the husband does; likewise the husband does not have authority over his own body, but the wife does** [1 Corinthians 7:4]. Mutuality of affection is the minimum standard of Christian Matrimony, **so that Satan may not tempt you because of your lack of self-control** [1 Corinthians 7:5].

Paul was troubled by his notion that "the two become one flesh" means that two spirits mingle. Spiritual influence between husband and wife is enormous. He believed that divorce doesn't exist in reality apart from legal fictions. When the two become one, and the spirits inter-mingle, no act of divorce can separate that which God has joined together. Thus, remarriage amounts to adultery.

So, if one is married to an unbeliever, one ought to stay in hope that the other will come to faith [1 Corinthians 7:12-14, 16]. But if the unbeliever wants to divorce, the Christian will not be accounted for the fault [1 Corinthians 7:15]. He wanted as little disturbance as possible in each believer's life.

His morality was based on the notion of an early return of Christ. Basically, he didn't favor any change of status. New marriages, divorces, improper sexual relations, even emancipation from slavery [1 Corinthians 7:21-23], meant "troubles" [1 Corinthians 7:28] and new concerns that demanded attention. That meant a loss of focus on what was, to Paul, the most important concern: looking to Christ. **What I mean, brothers and sisters, is that the time is short. From now on those who have wives should live as if they do not; those who mourn, as if they did not; those who are happy, as if they were not; those who buy something, as if it were not theirs to keep; those who use the things of the world, as if not engrossed in them. For this world in its present form is passing away** [1 Corinthians 7:29-31].

How would Saint Paul address the Church today? Our culture and world are not more, and certainly not less sinful than Corinth in the first century. The human condition has not changed. The chapter has an overall meaning. *Pay attention to the things of the Spirit.* The flesh (our obsession with the things of the world) is of no worth, compared to the blessings that await us in the Presence of God. Immorality is, simply, something that gets in the way of our spiritual relationship with God through Christ's Spirit. We Christians are free from slavery to law (moral codes), but that does not mean we should engage in immoral activities or attitudes. Instead, we are to focus our entire lives and energy on serving Christ. Blatant immorality in the Church must not be tolerated. We are to confront one another as a help in self-discipline.

I would like you to be free from concern. An unmarried man is concerned about the Lord's affairs—how he can please the Lord. But a married man is concerned about the affairs of this world—how he can please his wife— and his interests are divided. An unmarried woman or virgin is concerned about the Lord's affairs: Her aim is to be devoted to the Lord in both body and spirit. But a married woman is concerned about the affairs of this world—how she can please her husband. I am saying this for your own good, not to restrict you, but that you may live in a right way in *undivided devotion to the Lord* [1 Corinthians 7:31-35].

The next chapter (eight) is Paul's continuing response to the query of the Corinthian Church. The subject changes, but the same ethical or spiritual rule is applied; just from a different perspective.

All the meat sold in the Corinth marketplace had been part of ritual sacrifices in pagan temples. The same would have been true in Jerusalem, except that the sacrifice there would have been in the Jewish Temple. Paul extended the moral perspective he had already established. This time he focused on one's life as witness and its influence on others.

Some people are still so accustomed to idols that when they eat sacrificial food they think of it as having been sacrificed to a god, and since their conscience is weak, it is defiled. But food does not bring us near to God; we are no worse if we do not eat, and no better if we do [1 Corinthians 8:7-8]. Participation or abstinence is of little meaning to our own salvation. Abstinence does not mean holiness. That focus misses the real point: **God's love builds up** [1 Corinthians 8:1; agape] the other. It does not harm the other. How that Love is applied is what counts. If I have freedom to eat meat, but that would cause someone (Christian or not is of no importance) to think that the idol has reality as a god, then I do harm to the other [1 Corinthians 8:10-11].

My ordination vows included abstinence from "any indulgence which may tend to harm my influence, including alcohol and tobacco". I promised to abstain. Did that bring me spiritual importance? Not at all. It was, instead, a real-world application of Paul's principle: **If what I eat causes my brother or sister to fall into sin, I will never eat meat again, so that I will not cause them to fall** [1 Corinthians 8:13]. Whether ordained or not, every Christian is called by the Apostle to the same standard of morality: Exercise God's Love that we build up each other in the things of the Spirit.

An interesting note: **Those who think they know something do not yet know as they ought to know** [1 Corinthians 8:2], might be a reference to incipient Gnostics. The root of the word Paul used for "know" is "gno", from which gnosis is a derivative.

One wonders what the problem was that required Paul to devote a page to his right to not-get-paid for his labors in the Gospel [1 Corinthians 9:1-18]. Only once in my life-time as a pastor did I experience an objection to my refusing a raise. Perhaps it is Providential. The work of a pastor is stressful enough without having to work elsewhere for his keep. Not only that, a part-time pastor may well be subject to pressures from his employer. If one, for instance, wanted to preach that "keeping the Sabbath holy" means keeping the store closed, would his employer be upset? The effect of Paul's demand that he not be required to accept financial support, is that other pastors can point to scripture for their own support.

Paul might have seen pressure put on an Apostle to say or do something *because* he was salaried. That happens quite often. The churches have committees to evaluate whether the pastor is "earning his keep". But Paul sets a different standard: He was free to "run his race", not for a salary-prize, but rather for the sake and glory of Christ: **I do all this for the sake of the gospel, that I may share in its blessings** [1 Corinthians 9:23].

Perhaps Paul used this entire argument as an illustration of the ethic he proposed in earlier, and applied in later verses: that of "building up" [1 Corinthians 8:1]. Building up requires spiritual strength gained through regular exercise; self-discipline. **I do not fight like a boxer beating the air. No, I strike a blow to my body and make it my slave so that after I have preached to others, I myself will not be disqualified for the prize** [1 Corinthians 9:26-27].

I can hear myself muttering, "But, Paul, the temptation is so constant and powerful". And then I read: **No temptation has overtaken you except what is common to mankind. And God is faithful; he will not let you be tempted beyond what you can bear. But when you are tempted, he will also provide a way out so that you can endure it** [1 Corinthians 10: 13]. When he wrote **flee from idolatry** [1 Corinthians 10:14], I think he used the term "idolatry" to mean the deification of all those earthy temptations he has been considering. To do so is to give our earthy parts divine power. He, apparently, had found his self-discipline in the Spirit strong enough to defeat them. Later he will write that the Lord had given him a thorn in the flesh [2 Corinthians 12:7], and so one must temper these claims by observing his sometimes failure to keep his own standard. Of course, we would not have the doctrine of grace without his full expression of the human condition. This "civil war" within us is not new, but our spiritual welfare depends on our waging it.

The theme of a Christian ethic continues in Chapter eleven. One ought to not-use his/her liberty at the expense of another. We hear an echo of Jesus; **if your right hand causes you to stumble, cut it off and throw it away** [Matthew 5:30]. The difference is that Jesus referred to a sin causing the self to fall, while Paul addressed the fall of a brother or sister through one's action.

There must have been a discussion in the Corinthian congregation about the rubrics of worship. Some thought it improper for a man to pray without covering his head. And, certainly, a woman ought to cover her head. But doesn't that conflict with one's liberty from the law?

Saint Paul retained enough of his Pharisaic training to insist that a woman ought to cover her hair, and a man ought not [1 Corinthians 11:3-12]. His reasoning seems ridiculous to the modern mind. Yet, it may be that he has inadvertently revealed his own weakness. He wrote that the reason women ought to cover their hair while at worship is because their beauty distracts angels from their worship duty [1 Corinthians 11:10]. It is more likely that a beautiful woman would distract the men...and Paul from their worship duty. I read this in the light of all that has been considered by him previously in this letter; matters of temptation and sexual morality.

It is, after all, the worship experience that is most important to him [1 Corinthians 10:1-22]. The sanctity of worship is the all-important issue. If her hair distracts a brother from his prayers, ought she not cover her hair? And if a man, following Jewish tradition, covers his head and offends a Gentile brother, ought he not forgo the practice?

If we take these as literal instructions, I think we miss the deeper meaning; a meaning that has been the theme of the letter. Unless the participants are able to worship without distraction, something is amiss with the sacrament.

And so, Paul addresses the conditions of the Lord's Supper. This passage is the earliest written tradition and the most authentic. It is the source of all modern traditions. It is, for instance, the source for the Protestant assertion that the sacrament is one of "remembrance" (an invocation of His Presence), rather than a "re-enactment of the crucifixion" (as per the Roman Catholic Mass). It is, also, a public proclamation by participation that one expects the Lord to return in the final Judgment.

For I received from the Lord what I also passed on to you: The Lord Jesus, on the night he was betrayed, took bread, and when he had given thanks, he broke it and said, "This is my body, which is for you; do this in remembrance of me." In the same way, after supper he took the cup, saying, "This cup is the new covenant in my blood; do this, whenever you drink it, in remembrance of me." For whenever you eat this bread and drink this cup, you proclaim the Lord's death until he comes [1 Corinthians 11: 23-26].

The intended focus of this definition of the Sacrament is not on "magic" or rubrics. Paul continues his discourse on ethics.

So then, whoever eats the bread or drinks the cup of the Lord in an unworthy manner will be guilty of sinning against the body and blood of the Lord. Everyone ought to examine themselves before they eat of the bread and drink from the cup. For those who eat and drink without discerning the body of Christ eat and drink judgment on themselves [1 Corinthians 11:27-29].

Implicitly and explicitly, Paul cautioned his fellow Christians who arrived early and ate all the "good stuff" leaving only the remnants for fellow Christians whose jobs or slavery kept them from early attendance [1 Corinthians 11:17-22]. In "discerning the body" one must ask, "where is the body"? Roman Catholics focus their attention on the elements of bread and wine. Protestants insist, I think along with Paul, that the Body is within the members of the congregation. One must translate his admonition: "if you don't acknowledge the Body of Christ in your fellow Christians, you won't find it on the table either". "If you are thinking about someone's hair, you have missed the Body". If you have caused a brother or sister to stumble by the application of your moral freedom, you have "missed the Body". **If we were more discerning with regard to ourselves, we would not come under such judgment** [1 Corinthians 11:31].

Please note: it is not an individual who comes "under such judgment"! It is the entire fellowship! Paul seems to have connected the failure of an "early return of Christ" to a lack of unity and *agape fellowship* within the churches. That makes the matter of hair, or dining habits truly important.

And so, the Apostle turned his attention to "Gifts of the Spirit", literally: pneumatikos [pnyoo-mat-ik-os'], or "spirituals".

The Body of Christ is gifted with a number of "manifestations" [1 Corinthians 12:7] of the Holy Spirit. But they are not the same in each individual. And there is a reason for that. The "spirituals" are distributed "in-order-that" the entire Body be strengthened. It is **given for the common good** [1 Corinthians 12:7]. One manifestation is not inferior or superior to another. **All these are the work of one and the same Spirit, and he distributes them to each one, just as he determines** [1 Corinthians 12:11]. All earthly distinctions are silly. We were Baptized in the Holy Spirit [If we are authentic Christians], and so we are a new creation [2 Corinthians 5:7].

The "silliness" of human distinctions is demonstrated in the allegory of the foot and the body [1 Corinthians 12:15]. Indeed, I have seen a poor widow whose prayers were literally of more important to the congregation than the gifts of the richest members. Her prayers were more powerful, and affected more situations than the totality of my pastoral counsel. Her prayers protected me from dangers, inspired my courage, assisted my discernment. I have seen another poor widow whose distribution of cookies was a far more effective expression of God's Love than our most extensive evangelistic program. They were more important to the Body than was their pastor. Their ministry continued when he was transferred. In human eyes, the clergy are the most honorable and important persons in a church. And God has arranged affairs to support the **less honorable** [with] **special honor. And the parts that are unpresentable are treated with special modesty, while our presentable parts need no special treatment. But God has put the body together, giving greater honor to the parts that lacked it, so that there should be no division in the body, but that its parts should have equal concern for each other** [1 Corinthians 12:23-25].

What seems to be a hierarchy is instead a "business plan". God first sent **apostles, second prophets, third teachers, then miracles** [miracle workers], **then gifts of healing, of helping, of guidance, and of different kinds of tongues** [1 Corinthians 12:28]. Seeing them as a business plan will further Paul's assertion of equality in the Body. The Apostle is not superior to one who helps out. They are different callings, with different gifts of abilities and disabilities.

I recall a member who always said, "yes" when asked to do a task. However, he almost always did the job poorly. During an intensive study of scripture, we discovered that his gift was "helper". From then on, when we needed something done, we would assign responsibility to one person and say, "and x will be your helper". His contributions to the work of the Body increased significantly. His standing in the fellowship grew. Christ was glorified! That is the way it is supposed to work!

So, first the Apostle planted the congregation, then the prophet spoke God's rhema to the fellowship, then teachers searched and explained the scriptures, then miracles began to happen, healings occurred, assistance provided, wise counsel occurred [the church was guided wisely], and then members began speaking rhema with the tongue of glossolalia. And each served God equally to those who came before. Each was needful for the full growth of the congregation.

And then the greatest miracle of all! God showed human beings how to Love each other [1 Corinthians 13; the entire chapter!]! **The more excellent way** [1 Corinthians 12:30] is about God's Love, not human love. The word used to translate love is unique. It is AGAPE. Saint Paul redefined the term. It no longer meant the love of the Greek pagan gods for a human being. It meant the self-giving Love of God demonstrated in the birth, life, teachings, death and resurrection of Jesus, now the Christ, the Messiah, the Son of God! **God's Love is patient, God's love is kind. God's Love does not envy, God's Love does not boast, God's Love is not proud. God's Love does not dishonor others, God's Love is not self-seeking, God's Love is not easily angered, God's Love keeps no record of wrongs. God's Love does not delight in evil but rejoices with the truth. God's Love always protects, always trusts, always hopes, always perseveres. God's Love never fails** [1 Corinthians 13:4-8]. As for human gifts, **they will pass away** [1 Corinthians 13:8b]. Prophecy has no meaning when all is complete. One need not speak in tongues when God speaks directly to us. What we have now is a faint expression of the unspeakably wonderful gifts that await the faithful Christian. **When completeness comes, what is in part disappears** [1 Corinthians 13:10], and we **shall see face to face. Now I know in part; then [we] shall know fully, even as [we are] fully known** [1 Corinthians 13:12; my edit for grammatic clarification].

When God's Love is active, the ethic Paul has labored over is irrelevant! And, in those places where God's Love animates a congregation, nothing on Earth can prevent it from growing!

If that Love is present, it follows that one desires more and more conversation with God. Again, we have a badly translated verse. Instead of **eagerly desire gifts of the Spirit, especially prophecy** [1 Corinthians 14:1, NIV], the verse ought to read **now earnestly desire the spirituals, especially now that you might prophecy.** Paul assumed that the new Christians had been "baptized in the Holy Spirit" and would express the gifts [abilities] of the Holy Spirit. And prophecy is a matter of listening to, and repeating, what the Holy Spirit says. And every Spirit-filled Christian is potentially a prophet, that is someone who can speak God's rhema.

Today the definition of prophecy has been diluted. Now it often means that one relates his/her own views about so-called justice issues. Seldom do such outbursts reflect Agape. One ought to remember my three-fold rule: The Holy Spirit's words [rhema] are always consistent with scripture, always reflect the Character of God as revealed in Christ Jesus, and always may be confirmed by several mature Christians.

Prophecy is superior, as a Spirit Gift, to glossolalia because speaking in tongues is speaking to God [1 Corinthians 14:2], while prophecy is God speaking to the Church, providing edification, encouragement, and consolation [1 Corinthians 14:3]. Tongues edify the praying person, but prophecy edifies the Church. **Since you are eager for gifts of the Spirit, try to excel in those that build up the church** [1 Corinthians

[14:12]. Paul prayed often "in the Spirit", but he said that he'd prefer **to speak five intelligible words to instruct others than ten thousand words in a tongue** [1 Corinthians 14:19].

After quoting Isaiah 28:11,12: **"With other tongues and through the lips of foreigners I will speak to this people, but even then they will not listen to me, says the Lord"**, Paul insisted that tongues are for believers, but unbelievers will think Christians are insane [1 Corinthians 14:22-23]. And, isn't that true today?

So, speaking in tongues actually benefits the believer, but it is not one of the better gifts for the "building up" of the Church. So, Paul instructed the congregation to regulate their worship. **Everything must be done so that the church may be built up** [1 Corinthians 14:26b]. Christian worship was intended to be "participatory". Parishioners come not to see a show but to contribute from their "spirituals": **each of you has a hymn, or a word of instruction, a revelation, a tongue or an interpretation** [1 Corinthians 14:26a].

During one of my pastorates, with the help of a woman [who later became a United Methodist pastor], I organized a Saturday evening worship service on this basis. Participation was never "wide', but it was "deep". It became a strongly bonded fellowship of people who were in need of, and deeply committed to, the guidance of the Holy Spirit. Our commitment was such that as the Spirit revealed a particular issue, the whole worship would be turned toward that issue. We would not end the service until the Holy Spirit ministered in some way to the brother or sister whose need had been identified. The fellowship was comprised of bi-polars, schizophrenics, alcoholics, persons with PTSD, legal or marital troubles, etc. It was serious business, and helpful. Each person was extended the respect and honor of presenting a word, a song, an inspiration, or an insight into scripture. We all prayed.

From today's perspective, Paul's view of women in worship is unfortunate. I think his motivation and his heritage as a Pharisee are in evidence. May a woman be denied the opportunity to contribute a hymn, word of instruction, revelation, or even interpret a word given in a tongue? To him, a woman's voice was intrusive. He wrote that **everything should be done in a fitting and orderly way** [1 Corinthians 14:40]. To Paul, a woman's voice at worship upset the "natural order" of creation. I think we probably ought to extend to Paul a bit of the grace he taught us to anticipate from the Lord, and which we are to extend to each other.

III

The remainder of the book is part of the first letter which ended at the end of Chapter four. He continues his reiteration of his calling as an Apostle [1 Corinthians 15:3-10]. His teaching authority rested on that calling. The word must be defined if it is to be understood. "Apostle" is listed in Strong's Concordance [consulted for all the Greek definitions in his book]. It comes from the Greek word: Apostolos (ap-os'-tol-os), and it mean: a messenger, an ambassador [2 Corinthians 5:20], one sent to represent a leader or a kingdom; and in this case one who has met Jesus personally [1 Corinthians 15:3-7; note: "abnormally born" (NIV) ought to be translated "untimely born" as one overdue].

His doctrine of salvation by grace through faith is on display. **For I am the least of the apostles and do not even deserve to be called an apostle, because I persecuted the church of God. But by the grace of God I am what I am** [1 Corinthians 15:9-10].

Even then, the resurrection seemed a wild claim, as it does today among some "intellectual Christians", and so Paul was required, on his authority as an Apostle, to state again that Jesus rose from the dead. But that didn't end the matter for him. Much hung on its reality. **If Christ has not been raised, our preaching is useless and so is your faith** [1 Corinthians 15:14]. And because of rampant persecution (which has not ceased to this day) **we are of all people most to be pitied** [1 Corinthians 15:19]. Paul has, after all, suffered severe persecution.

However, we are "not to be pitied" because: Christ has been raised from the dead [1 Corinthians 15:20], and as He is the first-fruits [1 Corinthians 15:23], so in due order shall those who believe in Him [1 Corinthians 15:23], and then shall be "the end" of time when He hands over the Kingdom to God [1 Corinthians 15:24], and God will be all in all [1 Corinthians 15:28].

Scoffers asked: **With what kind of body will they come** [1 Corinthians 15:35]? His answer is one of the blessed notions of the Christian Church: **The body that is sown is perishable, it is raised imperishable; it is sown in dishonor, it is raised in glory; it is sown in weakness, it is raised in power; it is sown a natural body, it is raised a spiritual body** [1 Corinthians 15:42-44].

My favorite mis-translation is understandable from the point of view of an intellectual Christian who has never experienced the in-filling of the Holy Spirit. **And just as we have borne the image of the earthly man, so shall we bear the image of the heavenly man** [1 Corinthians 15:49]. The Greek word "phoreó" [for-eh'-o] is problematic for the intellectual. He thinks we cannot possibly have already been given the **image of the Heavenly Man**. So, in spite of his clear understanding that the word means "to *constantly* wear", he translated "we *will* wear"!

Yet that is what Paul wrote: Just as we have worn the image of (Adam), the earthly [meaning: of the dirt] man, *so we constantly wear* the image of (Jesus) the Heavenly Man! Our resurrection is in the past! When we accepted Jesus as our Lord and Savior, when we surrendered entirely to the will of God for our life, when the Holy Spirit entered into our being, when we were "born again" [John 3:5; no one can enter the kingdom of God unless they are born of water and the Spirit.]; that was the moment of our resurrection! One ought to ask of these men and women: **"You are Israel's teacher,"** said Jesus, **"and do you not understand these things** [John 3:10]?

Though Paul doesn't write this out, his letter implies an answer to this question: What is your proof? The proof of the resurrection of the Christian is that he/she embodies God's Love. Can there be any other? Is that not why the Lord will say to the goats: **'Depart from me, you who are cursed, into the eternal fire prepared for the devil and his angels. For I was hungry and you gave me nothing to eat, I was thirsty and you gave me nothing to drink, I was a stranger and you did not invite me in, I needed clothes and you did not clothe me, I was sick and in prison and you did not look after me'** [Matthew 25:41-43]. And the Apostle John wrote that Jesus assured some in the room with Him that **"Those who love me will keep my word, and my Father will love them, and we will come to them and *make our home with them*** [John 14:23]. John also wrote: **Before long, the world will not see me anymore, but you will see me. Because I live, you also will live. On that day you will realize that I am in my Father, and you are in me, and I am in you** [John 14:19-20]. How may He live within us, if we do not wear His Image?

Indeed, **flesh and blood cannot inherit the kingdom of God** [1 Corinthians 15:50]. Our "perishable nature" will die. But our "imperishable nature" will continue. Paul shared **a mystery: We will not all sleep, but we will all be changed— in a flash, in the twinkling of an eye, at the last trumpet. For the trumpet will sound, the dead will be raised imperishable, and we will be changed. For the perishable must clothe itself with the imperishable, and the mortal with immortality. When the** perishable has been clothed with the imperishable, and the mortal with immortality, then the saying that is written will come true: "Death has been swallowed up in victory" [1 Corinthians 15:51-54]! His logical conclusion, in the face of determined persecution: **Therefore** [Gk: hóste (hoce'-teh), wherefore], **my dear brothers and sisters, stand firm. Let nothing move you. Always give yourselves fully to the work of the Lord, because you know that your labor in the Lord is not in vain** [1 Corinthians 15:58].

The final chapter of First Corinthians must not be from his initial letter. The offering to which he referred was taken up later in his ministry, and was the reason for his final return to Jerusalem. The chapter includes much biographical detail that church historians have used to piece together the wanderings of the Apostle and his assistants, especially Timothy and Apollos.

SECOND CORINTHIANS

Paul's Second Letter to the Corinthian Church addresses the same problem expressed in the early chapters of Genesis: If God is good, why are we in such a mess? If God is Love, why was Paul suffering? And to make short-shift of the issue, his first statement is both question and answer. **Praise be to the God and Father of our Lord Jesus Christ, the Father of compassion and the God of all comfort, who comforts us in all our troubles, so that we can comfort those in any trouble with the comfort we ourselves receive from God** [2 Corinthians 1:3-4].

Not that we want trouble, and not that God causes us trouble. Troubles, pains, losses, illnesses, sorrows all have their own origin. Even so, there is a "silver lining" to our troubles. Who can understand the night-terrors of a veteran of combat, better than another veteran of combat? Empathy is a hard-won treasure. Along with it, a Christian armed with God's Love can make a real difference. Spiritual healing often precedes physical or emotional healing.

Paul didn't identify his suffering beyond a euphemism: **We were under great pressure, far beyond our ability to endure, so that we despaired of life itself. Indeed, we felt we had received the sentence of death** [2 Corinthians 1:8-9]. He might well have wanted to address the possible persecution of his friends in Corinth, and referenced the devastating persecution he endured in his earlier missionary journey [2 Corinthians 1:8; We do not want you to be uninformed, brothers and sisters, about the troubles we experienced in the province of Asia.]. His troubles at Ephesus, from which this letter was sent, came after his previous correspondence.

The Apostle identifies a great "spiritual dynamic". **If we are distressed, it is for your comfort and salvation; if we are comforted, it is for your comfort, which produces in you patient endurance of the same sufferings we suffer. And our hope for you is firm, because we know that just as you share in our sufferings, so also you share in our comfort** [2 Corinthians 1:6-7].

Is this relevant to Christians who live in a society that prides itself on the embrace of diversity [one ought to note the hypocrisy of those who embrace all diversity except Christianity]? The answer is, partly, that it isn't necessarily for Christians who are not suffering. Partly, his letter is a preparation for future suffering. Partly it may be anticipatory, for few people do not suffer. And partly it can inspire prayerful consideration of our fellow Christians who suffer from aggressive persecution. In our Love for them, we share in their sufferings. Perhaps by prayer we may help them avoid trouble. **On him we have set our hope that he will continue to deliver us, as you help us by your prayers. Then many will give thanks on our behalf for the gracious favor granted us in answer to the prayers of many** [2 Corinthians 1:10-11].

The occasion for this letter is a broken commitment. Paul wanted to visit the Corinthian Church during their troubles. His other two letters, contained in First Corinthians, addressed the issues. Paul probably felt a responsibility toward them, as former pastors often do. Somehow the commitment had been made, and not fulfilled. Both he and they felt keen disappointment. **I call God as my witness—and I stake my life on it—that it was in order to spare you that I did not return to Corinth. Not that we lord it over your faith, but we work with you for your joy, because it is by faith you stand firm** [2 Corinthians 1:23-24].

But what was "spared"? Most likely it was related to the expulsion of the man who was living with his father's wife [1 Corinthians 5:1]. More unlikely it may have been their embarrassment over the factional loyalties that were splintering the congregation [1 Corinthians 1:12]. That would have been a meeting of grief, both his and theirs [2 Corinthians 2:1-2]. Most probably critical return visits by founding pastors are unhelpful. They tend to wound rather than "build up" the church.

The Apostle of Grace now delivered the second part of his judgment against the man who was living with his father's wife. **The punishment inflicted on him by the majority is sufficient. Now instead, you ought to forgive and comfort him, so that he will not be overwhelmed by excessive sorrow. I urge you, therefore, to reaffirm your love [agapē] for him** [2 Corinthians 2:6-8].

As a retired pastor his "testing the obedience" of his former flock is troubling. However, they passed the test and, apparently had expelled the errant member. Over the years, and as I reflect on my own behavior as a pastor, I find Paul's attitude a bit self-righteous. Did he plan in advance to write a letter demanding the expulsion, so that later he could write another demanding his readmittance? I give Paul credit for a genius, but doubt he would have done that well. He was, after all, didactic and strict. I believe that he demanded the expulsion in a time of righteous indignation, and after sending that letter realized his own inner conflict between morality and grace. This may well have been a "learning experience" for Paul. If we see it as that, the correspondence opens to us a wonderful introduction to how we too may "grow in grace" [2 Peter 3:18; Colossians 1:6].

The following paragraphs of his letter sound defensive. He tried to explain, without directly addressing the issue of his own sensitivities, how and why he should be understood. And within his discussion of his "qualifications" as an Apostle, he offered: **Not that we are competent in** ourselves to claim anything for ourselves, but our competence comes from God. He has made us competent as ministers of a new covenant—not of the letter but of the Spirit; for the letter kills, but the Spirit gives life [2 Corinthians 3:5-6]. "Not of the letter but of the Spirit"! Paraphrase that, "Not according to moral law or tradition, but rather under the continuing edification of the Spirit of God's Love".

His "defense" gives us a wonderful insight into God's long-term unveiling of His Love [2 Corinthians 3:7-11]. God showed His Love in the Covenant of Moses. When Moses came down from the Mount Sinai, his face glowed with shekinah glory. That is; when we enter God's Presence the glory [Gk: doxa, from which we derive doxology: to attribute glory], the Power of God's Love produces a shinning glow. That glow is termed shekinah. It is found throughout scripture, including the Mount of Transfiguration [Matthew 17:2; Mark 9:3]. Moses was required to wear a veil so as to not frighten the people [Exodus 34:33-35].

Paul's literary skill is evident as he reverses the meaning of Moses' veil, from a demonstration of glory to a covering hiding the truth of Christ [2 Corinthians 3:14]. Thus, his Gospel is immeasurably superior to that of Moses' commandments and law [2 Corinthians 3:7-11]. His Gospel is the proclamation of *the ministry of* the Holy Spirit [2 Corinthians 3:8].

Now the Lord is the Spirit, and where the Spirit of the Lord is, there is freedom. And we all, who with [now] unveiled faces contemplate [Gk: katoptrizó (kat-op-trid'-zom-ahee) see a reflection as in a mirror] **the Lord's glory, are being transformed into his image with ever-increasing glory, which comes from the Lord, who is the Spirit** [2 Corinthians 3:17-18].

This increasing shekinah glory, this Loving Presence, in the believer provides freedom. That freedom is emancipation from a slavish obedience to the Law of Moses. **Therefore** [Gk: dia; meaning because]**, since through God's mercy we have this ministry, we do not lose heart** [2 Corinthians 4:1]. He had already stated that a veil had been placed over their [the Hebrews/Jews] heart [2 Corinthians 3:15]. In other words, what the Jews can't understand because of their devotion to law, is that the Spirit of God administers God's Love and mercy [Even to the man who was living with his father's wife].

We have an unfortunate translation again. **By setting forth the truth** [should read: "**By manifestations of the Truth**"...] **plainly we commend ourselves to everyone's conscience in the sight of God** [2 Corinthians 4:2 NIV]**,** obscures the spiritual meaning of the verse. The original states that Paul commended himself, and his Gospel by "manifestations" of the Spirit. That is to say, he didn't commend himself by means of logic or sophistry. Rather, by demonstrating the Power of the Holy Spirit (healings, etc.) and by actions that demonstrate the Love of God, Paul shows himself and his Gospel to be True.

That had the effect that: **The god of this age has blinded the minds of unbelievers, so that they cannot see the light of the gospel that displays the glory of Christ, who is the image of God** [2 Corinthians 4:4]. Let me explicate the next verse: **For God, who said, "Let light shine out of darkness,"** [Genesis 1:3] **made his light** [Hebrew: shekinah, Gk: doxa] **shine in our hearts to give us the light** [Gk: phótismos (fo-tis-mos'); illumination, radiance] **of the knowledge of God's glory displayed in the face of Christ** [2 Corinthians 4:6]. The glory displayed in the face of Christ was seen at the Transfiguration. Only believers saw it, and only believers experience it afresh in the ministries of the Holy Spirit.

When Paul wrote that: **We have this treasure in jars of clay to show that this all-surpassing power is from God and not from us. We are hard pressed on every side, but not crushed; perplexed, but not in despair; persecuted, but not abandoned; struck down, but not destroyed** [2 Corinthians 4:7-9], he spoke of himself, but included the persecuted Corinthians too. "Jars of clay" refers to our humanness. That humanness even includes an occasional error initiated with good intentions, as for instance demanding that one be expelled from the fellowship. (Were there no other means to discipline the man?) Paul admits his fault by writing: **So then, death is at work in us, but life is at work in you** [2 Corinthians 4:12]. That "death", that frailty or limitation of "clay jars" is intended (so Paul thinks) to denote the difference between us and the Spirit. And thus, his error and his correction are both for their benefit, so that the grace that is reaching more and more people may cause thanksgiving to overflow to the glory [In this instance, the meaning is related more to "praise" than to manifestations of the Spirit] of God [2 Corinthians 4:15].

I really like how Paul suggests that this life is temporary and Heavenly Life is permanent, or ultimate reality. I like to use temporary and permanent to describe our situation as born-again, Spirit in-filled Christians. **So we fix our eyes not on what is seen, but on what is unseen, since what is seen is temporary, but what is unseen is eternal** [2 Corinthians 4:18].

Let us address that dichotomy. Paul is the source of Christian notions of what eternal life is like. **We know that if the earthly tent we live in is destroyed, we have a building from God, a house not made with hands, eternal in the heavens** [2 Corinthians 5:1].

If indeed, when we have taken it off [unclear] **we will not be found naked** [2 Corinthians 5:3], is unclear. The Greek is a negative: **if we having been clothed not naked will be found.** I suppose our translators can see logic in either taking off the Temporary, or being clothed in the Permanent. The word "not" can be attached in either direction: not-naked, or not-clothed. Of central importance is: **God... has given us the Spirit as a guarantee** [2 Corinthians 5:5]. It is uncharitable to suggest that those who have not experienced the indwelling Holy Spirit do not have the guarantee, and will perhaps not be clothed with the Permanent body.

Indeed, that is not what he meant. His message is astonishing, and few of us have understood it.

While We walk by faith, not by sight [2 Corinthians 5:7], **all of us must appear before the judgment seat of Christ, so that each may receive recompense for what has been done in the body, whether good or evil.** [2 Corinthians 5:10]. There will be, for each of us, a moment of judgment. And so, aware that he, himself, will face that judgment, Paul presented himself to the Corinthians. He said, that his "manifestation" was not for his pride, but so that they could have the insight necessary to confront those who took pride in their earthly status [2 Corinthians 5:12]. Did he mean the Christian who takes pride in his salvation? It appears so. That he used the Greek word for manifestation suggests that he intended an association with his previous employment of the term [2 Corinthians 4:2]. "Manifestations" has Holy Spirit implications. He commended himself not by argument, but by demonstrations of Holy Spirit Power [1 Corinthians 2:4; My speech and my proclamation were not with plausible words of wisdom, but with a demonstration of the Spirit and of power. "Demonstration" ought to read "manifestation", words of wisdom ought to read "sophisticated spirit".].

His fundamental Truth is that Christ has died for *all* [2 Corinthians 5:14], and that *all* should Live for Him [2 Corinthians 5:15]. "Live" has "pun-power". It can have eternal life painted on its face while it also points to our daily existence. All of humanity ought to live for Christ. Of course, that was not, and is not, the case. And so, the Love [agape] of Christ thrusts him onward [2 Corinthians 5:14]. Paul no longer lived for himself, but for Christ. He was entirely devoted to Christ, come what may. **Whether drunk or sober** [2 Corinthians 5:13] he must serve Christ.

He could no longer see a person in the guise of their earthly condition: "saved" or "unsaved". He could only see them as *in Christ.* This is astonishing! **We regard *no one* from a human point of view** [Gk: sarka, meaning sinful flesh]. That is, Paul could no longer see any person as sinful flesh, alienated from God. He admitted that earlier in his life he saw Jesus as sinful flesh. Instead, we must see *all others* as a New Creation. Those who have accepted Christ as Lord and Savior, those who have been "born again" and baptized in the Holy Spirit now are *aware* of the New Creation [2 Corinthians 5:17]. Those who have not accepted Christ are that new creation, but are not aware of it. He, therefore, considered himself an Ambassador for Christ, "therefore" [Gk: parakaleó; an imperative therefore] that each one be reconciled to God [2 Corinthians 5:20]. Note that Paul had already written that all of us must appear before the judgment seat of Christ, so that each may receive recompense for what has been done in the body, whether good or evil [2 Corinthians 5:10]. **In Christ God was reconciling the *world* to himself, not counting their trespasses against them, and entrusting *the message* of reconciliation to us** [2 Corinthians 5:19]. Christ, he wrote, **God had made sin in order that we who are sin might become, through Him, the righteousness of God**]2 Corinthians 5:21]! The definition of the word we render as "sin" is of great importance. It means to "not have a part in". It means alienation, separation, cursed, disinherited. Jesus was separated, cursed, disinherited by God, *in order that* our disinheritance, our alienation, our cursedness might be overcome. Paul argues that it has been overcome, but some of us don't know it yet.

Paul "therefores" [Gk: parakaleó; an imperative therefore] his readers to work with him in order that we not accept the grace of God in vain [2 Corinthians 6:1]. How can we accept the grace of God in vain? By not working with Paul **to put no obstacle in anyone's way, so that no fault may be found with our ministry** [2 Corinthians 6:3]. We are to follow the example of Paul who **commended [himself] in every way: through great endurance, hardships, calamities, beatings, imprisonments, riots, labors, sleepless nights, hunger; by purity, knowledge, patience, kindness, holiness of spirit, genuine love, truthful speech, and the power of God; with the weapons of righteousness for the right hand and for the left; in honor and dishonor, in ill repute and good repute. We are treated as impostors, and yet are true; as unknown, and yet are well known; as dying, and see—we are alive; as punished, and yet not killed; as sorrowful, yet always rejoicing; as poor, yet making many rich; as having nothing, and yet possessing everything** [2 Corinthians 6:4-10]. It was his *expectation* that we would join him in suffering through aggressive persecution.

There seems to be an implication of which perhaps he was unaware. Our attitude toward others is more often an obstacle placed in front of others. Sociologists tell us that the major reason many of the younger generations of our day make the Church irrelevant along with the faith she proposes, is exactly what they think is our attitude toward them. Unless they adopt identical cultural values as ours, they feel we will make them unwelcome. That is certainly true for those who are not heterosexual. Racial and economic differences are also important. Political viewpoints separate continually. But Paul said, place no obstacles in anyone's way. Have we accepted the grace of God in vain?

We have spoken frankly to you Corinthians; our heart is wide open to you. There is no restriction in our affections, but only in yours. In return—I speak as to children—open wide your hearts also. Do not be mismatched with unbelievers. For what partnership is there between righteousness and lawlessness [2 Corinthians 6:11-14]? Who are the lawless unbelievers? They are the legalists, those who insist on obedience to the Law of Moses. We err if we assume he meant gentile sinners. We are to open our hearts wide to them, but cease to mingle with judgementalists. The are open only to those who live as they do. But Christ has opened the door to any who would enter. That is a definition of grace. God's Love is real. There are those who do and will oppose accepting it. We are called by Paul to NOT BE a cause of that opposition.

And so then, because we are Loved by God and understand the promises, we ought to cleanse ourselves of every defilement of flesh [Gk: sarkos] **and spirit** [Gk: pneumatos] **accomplishing righteousness in the fear of God** [2 Corinthians 7:1 my translation]. What are those defilements? Possibly he meant by flesh, things like cultural or ethnic status, economic status, or moral status. Possibly, spiritual defilements are things like pride in our saved status, or of our spiritual attainments, or of our loyalty to the Law of Moses. All of these things will stand between a Christian and others.

And what is righteousness? Righteousness is simply entering into a Love relationship with God and others. I would be remiss if I did not bring to mind a Wesleyan definition of perfection; God's Love filling the Christian to the exclusion of all else: perfect Love for God, Perfect Love for self, and Perfect Love for *all* others.

That Paul had erred, by insisting on the expulsion of a man who was living with his father's wife, is evidenced in these words: **Even if I caused you sorrow by my letter, I do not regret it. Though I did regret it** [2 Corinthians 7:8].... He had hurt them by his harsh demand. Yet Paul felt he was, in some way, justified in his demand, because your sorrow led you to repentance. Well, repentance for accepting a sin is one thing, harsh judgement is another.

By way of "full disclosure" I should note that while in college, I was a member of a fraternity. The fellowship was decent; a fellowship of young men bound together to help each other toward graduation. One of our members returning late in an evening, found the President of our House beating another member with his belt. The fellowship expelled its President. Almost a year later, we re-admitted him, feeling assured that such an event would not happen again. I approved of both actions. I should, and do, give Paul the benefit of doubt. He may have been right and aware of the pain and the hope of reconciliation his actions could cause.

What is the lesson we may glean from this unfortunate event? At least me may find a spiritual dynamic at work. **For godly grief produces a repentance that leads to salvation and brings no regret, but worldly grief produces death. For see what earnestness this godly grief has produced in you, what eagerness to clear yourselves, what indignation, what alarm, what longing, what zeal, what punishment! At every point you have proved yourselves guiltless in the matter** [2 Corinthians 7:10-11].

Paul closed the matter by stating, **I have complete confidence in you** [2 Corinthians 7:16].

Either turning to a different subject, or sending yet another letter; Paul appeals for a generous offering.

We may learn much about stewardship from this letter. And, I think it wise to begin with a disclaimer. Stewardship is not God testing the Christian, as Paul was testing the Corinthians against the generosity of other communities [2 Corinthians 8:8]. There is a wide difference between faithful stewardship and "fund raising". Probably, the distinction hadn't occurred to the Apostle, but we are very much aware of it now. It is a relief that the Apostle chose to note his lack of authority in the matter. He would not and could not "command". And so, he wrote: **I am giving my advice** [2 Corinthians 8:10]. He undoubtedly knew that our generosity is rooted in what we know: **the grace of our**

Lord Jesus Christ, that though he was rich, yet for your sakes he became poor, so that by his poverty you might become rich [2 Corinthians 8:9]. Giving begins in and through the gift of God's grace, demonstrated in the Lord Jesus. The Lord looks on the desire of our heart; if the eagerness is there, the gift is acceptable according to what one has—not according to what one does not have [2 Corinthians 8:12].

As a normal Christian (if there is such a thing), I learned that "eagerness" is part of one's spiritual growth. When I was young and poor, I had no eagerness. It was only as I matured in the generosity of His grace, that I began to "want" to give. Then, even though my gifts were small as compared to others, I began to discover happiness in giving.

This offering was intended to support the Christians in Jerusalem. They had begun an experiment in, what today would be called, socialism. The pooled their assets in anticipation of an early return of the Christ. Now they, lacking any means of earning or gaining assets, experienced extreme poverty. Thus Paul, in return for the Jerusalem Council granting him authority to bring the Gospel to the gentiles [Galatians 2:10] was obliged to perform this ministry.

The worldly wisdom of the early churches provides us with a glimpse of reality. Paul assured the congregation that he would not "administer" the offering by himself. Titus, whom they knew very well, would accompany Paul to Jerusalem [2 Corinthians 8:16-19]. And that, in itself, is a great lesson to the churches. While we owe each other trust, "it is not enough to avoid doing wrong, we must avoid the appearance of doing wrong" [I'm quoting my mother, though I'm sure the words were not original with her]. Yet other Apostles would accompany Paul and Titus [2 Corinthians 8:23-24]. It must have been a big offering to require such a delegation.

Another serious lesson: careful organization and time are required. **But I am sending the brothers in order that our boasting about you may not prove to have been empty in this case, so that you may be ready, as I said you would be; otherwise, if some Macedonians come with me and find that you are not ready, we would be humiliated—to say nothing of you—in this undertaking** [2 Corinthians 9:3-4]. When this rule is ignored, or when careful organization results in a negative response and the authorities ignore the reluctance of the people, "humiliation" is the inevitable result. The "authorities" may propose an offering, but it is the people who decide whether or not the purpose is worthy of their "eagerness".

The point is this: **the one who sows sparingly will also reap sparingly, and the one who sows bountifully will also reap bountifully. Each of you must give as you have made up your mind, not reluctantly or under compulsion, for God loves a cheerful giver** [2 Corinthians 9:6-7]. This is a theological certitude. It goes both ways. A reluctant giver may very well express the opinion of the Lord, that the purpose for the offering is not appropriate.

He who supplies seed to the sower and bread for food will supply and multiply your seed for sowing and increase the harvest of your righteousness [2 Corinthians 9:10]. Please note, it is "righteousness that is increased. Too often charlatan evangelists and errant pastors have suggested that God will provide a return of lucre rather than the spiritual reward of having done something "beautiful for God" [Mother Theresa].

I suppose that often times a special offering is "a test of a ministry" [2 Corinthians 9:13]. The congregation may well present the Lord with a vote of "confidence", or "no confidence". In that way, it is a very useful tool and can be used to gage whether the congregation is supportive. Paul thought so too.

After describing the power of his ministry, Paul presented the only evidence a congregation requires. **For the weapons of our warfare are not merely human,** [Gk: sarkos; sinful flesh] **but they have divine power to destroy strongholds. We destroy arguments and every proud obstacle raised up against the knowledge of God, and we take every thought captive to obey Christ** [2 Corinthians 10:4-5]. Those "weapons" were employed within the experience of the Corinthians. **Look at what is before your eyes. If you are confident that you belong to Christ, remind yourself of this, that just as you belong to Christ, so also do we. Now, even if I boast a little too much of our authority, which the Lord gave for building you up and not for tearing you down, I will not be ashamed of it** [2 Corinthians 10:7-8].

(Just a reminder: the subject has not changed. Paul is still making his appeal for a substantial offering.) In a reference to an earlier problem, that of divisions within the congregation, Paul addressed those in opposition. There are always persons in opposition. What other kind of humanity might we find to people a congregation. Opposition is needed for wisdom. Christians, in spite of our Lord's wonderful parables, are not sheep. Christians are gifted with the Holy Spirit just as are their leaders. And the discussion within the congregation will determine whether the Spirit is heard or not.

Paul needed to confront the opposition. He did so by reminding them that they had come to the Lord under his ministry. He was the first to arrive in Corinth with the Good News [2 Corinthians 10:14]. Was this fair? It certainly was fair. It was his demonstrations of the Power of the Holy Spirit that led them to the Cross. His insights from the Lord guided them. And now, as he spoke on behalf of that same Spirit, he hoped they would respond; so that we may proclaim the good news in lands beyond you, without boasting of work already done in someone else's sphere of action. **Let the one who boasts, boast in the Lord. For it is not those who commend themselves that are approved, but those whom the Lord commends** [2 Corinthians 10:16-18]. This offering for the Church in Jerusalem was most certainly a preparation for the next step in his missionary wanderings. The approbation of his congregation, he felt, was necessary for that next step. This offering was a measure of that approval.

IV

Chapter eleven deserves to be considered separately. It may be part of a different letter than that of the offering. The subject is "demonic clergy" [2 Corinthians 11:14]. If they preyed on the Church in his time, they are surely present in ours as well.

In his time, they were the False Apostles who proclaimed Jesus but insisted on obedience to the Law of Moses. They were masters of preaching [2 Corinthians 11:6], administered corporal punishment for violations of law [2 Corinthians 11:20], demands a salary [2 Corinthians 11:7-10; I imagine the salaries were substantial], and claimed a status superior to that of Paul [2 Corinthians 11:5; super-apostles]. They preached a different gospel than Paul's. A "spirit-filled" Christian would be able to detect a different spirit behind the words. That spirit was one of enslavement: many boast according to human standards [2 Corinthians 11:18; Gk: sarka, meaning of the flesh]. Instead, Paul would boast of suffering.

Of what did they boast? They were sons of Abraham (Jews) [2 Corinthians 11:22]. They considered themselves "deacons" of Christ [2 Corinthians 11:22]. They were proud of their accomplishments. But

Paul pointed to his sufferings [2 Corinthians 11:23-27]. Of historical note: he received lashing five times. The consisted of "forty lashes minus one" [2 Corinthians 11:24]. We know that if one died after forty lashes, those responsible were punished. Only a Roman soldier could administer the entire forty without fear. The list included many incidents for which we have no historical record beyond these verses. However, in view of his veracity in everything else, we ought to accept him as he presents himself. If he were untruthful, he would certainly have been exposed as a fraud.

They were, instead, servants of themselves while Paul cared about the churches [2 Corinthians 11:28].

We have an unfortunate editing issue. Chapters and verses were added to the Greek Bible in 1551, and to the English Bible in 1557. In this case, they separate verses that belong together.

Paul noted his escape from the authorities at Damascus [2 Corinthians 11:32] as introduction to his account of his spiritual experience. He felt it would be blasphemy to claim the experience for himself, but his readers knew of whom he wrote [2 Corinthians 12:2; I know a person in Christ]. He was knocked from his horse, and heard the voice calling "Saul, Saul, why do you persecute me [Acts 22:7]? According to this account, he was caught up to the third heaven [2 Corinthians 12:2]!

One may ask why "the third heaven"? And the answer is astonishing. It was inaccessible until very recent decades. The answer is found in "string theory". Astrophysicists posit ten dimensions. In Christian terms, they extend from a dot (from hence the Big Bang), to the singular Place of God. We are in the fourth dimension (characterized by height, depth, length and time). There two dimensions between the fourth and the seventh. The fifth dimension is the place in which we shall be able to "see" our entire life in detail. We will compare it to what it could have been, by God's intention, in the sixth dimension. Those two dimensions are the judgment we will inevitably experience. The seventh dimension (Paul's "Third Heaven": three above our fourth dimension) is Paradise. It is the place described by Saint John in Revelations. There we shall dwell in glory and awe. There we shall see the Christ. And there, Saul saw Him and heard Him ask, "Why do you persecute me"?

The result of his unmatched [except by Saint John] revelations, **a thorn was given me in the flesh, a messenger of Satan to torment me, to keep me from being too elated** [2 Corinthians 12:7]. Scholars have speculated over the nature of his "thorn". To some it was epileptic seizures. To others it was sexual. To others it was "existential doubt". Still others thought it was a desire to cease his labors for Christ, and to live in peaceful security. The truth must evade us, because he never willingly gave us a clue. Any speculation must be speculative.

What he does say, and this is hugely important, is a comfort to all who experience a thorn of any kind: **He said to me, "My grace is sufficient for you, for power is made perfect in weakness."** Paul's word for "power" is "dunamis". Scholars agree that his usage suggests spiritual power. That is; what Paul has been able to accomplish for Christ was due to Christ's Power *AND* Paul's weakness. Moreover, the context indicates that the weakness *includes* the thorn.

It is only those who know sin that may reach out to sinners on behalf of Christ. Possibly one of my best and most effective sermons was titled: But I am a Broken Man. Throughout this Epistle Paul presented himself as weak and broken, a contrast to the "super apostles". **I will boast all the more gladly of my weaknesses, so that the power of Christ may dwell in me. Therefore I am content with weaknesses, insults, hardships, persecutions, and calamities for the sake of Christ; for whenever I am weak, then I am strong** [2 Corinthians 12:9-10].

Returning to his subject; **The signs of a true apostle were performed among you with utmost patience, signs and wonders and mighty works** [2 Corinthians 12:12].

Like Paul, every authentic pastor hopes for the perfection [see Wesley] of his parishioners. Yet it is not to them he must give an account. They are not even the means by which he is scored. His Love [agape] and his faithfulness are evaluated in the Court of God's Love and Grace. And so, Paul concluded his letter:

Have you been thinking all along that we have been defending ourselves before you? We are speaking in Christ before God. Everything we do, beloved, is for the sake of building you up. For I fear that when I come, I may find you not as I wish, and that you may find me not as you wish; I fear that there may perhaps be quarreling, jealousy, anger, selfishness, slander, gossip, conceit, and disorder. I fear that when I come again, my God may humble me before you, and that I may have to mourn over many who previously sinned and have not repented of the impurity, sexual immorality, and licentiousness that they have practiced [2 Corinthians 12:19-21].

He threatened the congregation. If he did not see purity of faith and behavior, along with belief in grace, he would speak harshly and act with spiritual authority: **If I come again, I will not be lenient** [2 Corinthians 13:2]. The integrity of the Body of Christ was at stake. **Therefore: Examine yourselves to see whether you are living in the faith** [2 Corinthians 13:5].

Often the last word is the most important word to understand the intention. So, Paul explained in his last words why he wrote this epistle. The words sound angry, but are hopeful, judgmental, but are instead a "tough grace". Here is the mark! Please meet God's expectations. Grace toward all, and righteous holiness in the disciple.

I write these things while I am away from you, so that when I come, I may not have to be severe in using the authority that the Lord has given me for building up and not for tearing down [2 Corinthians 13:10].

GALATIANS

Galatia was a Roman province in what is now central Turkey. The cities Paul visited in Galatia, on his first journey were: Antioch (near) Pisidia (not to be confused with the Antioch where he had lived with Barnabas), Iconium, Lystra, and Derbe. Timothy lived in Derbe with his parents. His mother was Jewish, and his father a Greek. By Jewish tradition that made Timothy a Jew, though he had not been circumcised. Paul circumcised him, though I think he later regretted doing so, because it violated his principle of salvation by grace through faith.

Arriving at Derbe, Paul began, I believe, by preaching to the Jews. That was his custom, and it makes good sense. As a Jew, Paul would be able to make contacts within the Diaspora Jewish community. Later, Paul would begin to invite Gentiles with whom he had contact in the city and who were interested in his Gospel.

It seems to me that the letter to the Community in Galatia may only be fully understood as if it were directed toward a mixed community which had been introduced to the freedom of Gentile Christians, but were slipping back toward the legalism of the Jewish Law.

Like just about everything Biblical, the letter's date has been hotly debated, as well as the church(es) to which it is intended. The best dates seem to be around 48-49AD. Textual problems aside, the later date seems excluded by the idea that, **you are so quickly deserting the one who called you to live in the grace of Christ, and are turning to a different gospel** [1:6].

The other textual problem, according to the experts, is the illness with which Paul was afflicted when he arrived at the church to which the letter is addressed [4:13-14]. The first subject Paul addressed, in this letter, was his history of attacking and persecuting Christians to the death [1:13 For you have heard of my previous way of life in Judaism, how intensely I persecuted the church of God and tried to destroy it.]. Some have suggested that Paul suffered from serious depression and guilt. Anyone familiar with such PTSD afflictions can quickly understand. Paul felt he was called by Christ while still in his mother's womb [1:15 But when God, who set me apart from my mother's womb and called me by his grace...]. And now he carried within his spirit a deep guilt that, in spite of his Gospel of "salvation by grace through faith", he sometimes felt that he, himself, was beyond redemption. Some among us today, persons who are aware they are saved by grace through faith, continue to carry a sense of regret and guilt over previous offenses. St Paul was not immune to such mental afflictions.

Here we have one of the deepest and most profound of all the spiritual dynamics of the Christian Faith. Forgiveness and salvation do not depend upon the believer. I can share a personal example from pastoral counselling. I recall a tangential associate of one of the congregations I served. He had led a vile life. His life experience was well beyond what can be discussed in polite society. Suffice to say that he had paid a high price physically. His body was at the point of death. In fact, he had died and gone to Hell. He had been resuscitated but knew that he had two weeks before he died again...and this time permanently. I have never known a person so well motivated to get a pardon from God. He knew he deserved Hell, but after his experience there, he was desperate to not return.

When I said to him that, at the point of death, all he need do is to call out "Lord Jesus, save me by Your grace and mercy!" He could not believe that Jesus would be that generous and kind. He knew he deserved Hell. Well, he did indeed. All of us deserve Hell. It is only by the grace of Christ that we are delivered from that fate, hard as that is for us to believe.

Something of the sort may well have been working in the heart of Paul.

Thus, since the people of Galatia already had a dramatic example of the healing that comes from the Gospel of salvation by grace through faith, Paul was doubly dumbfounded that they should be so quickly falling back into a gospel of salvation by obedience to the Jewish Law.

Allow me this diversion for another spiritual dynamic. Each and every Christian is called to a vocation before they are born. Strong defines the Greek word for "set aside" [aphorizó]: "-to mark off by boundaries from, set apart". We have a principle I have never seen happily defied: God creates each person with unique abilities and disabilities, interests and disinterests, in-order-that the Church may be built up for the work of ministry [Ephesians 4:11-13]. Again, counselling experiences come to mind. My elder brother was set aside and called to be a minister. He did not want to be a preacher. He wanted to be rich and that seemed antithetical to his calling. He decided he wanted to be a rich architect. God said "No, Jon, you are going to be a poor preacher". Jon said, "I'll make a deal with you. I'll be a rich church-architect". God said, "No, Jon, you are going to be a poor preacher". Jon flunked out of three colleges before he accepted his calling. And afterward, he never regretted his calling. He was poor in money and rich in happiness. Deeply challenged, but more effective than just about any pastor I ever met. And another example, a young man who suffers from Dyslexia, ADHD, short-term memory difficulties, and a school history of being treated as if he were (his word) "stupid". Told that God gives us troubles and disabilities in-order-that we be prepared for a good future as a blessing to others, began to see himself in an entirely new light.

This was Paul's experience. God prepared him to be "zealous" [1:14 I was...extremely zealous for the traditions of my fathers.]. knowing that after his conversion he would need a unique degree of fortitude as the great missionary. God intended that even the sacrifice of un-named Christians was an in-order-that Paul might be able to endure the tests he would face in so many places, including Rome. This is often a difficult and hard-hearted insight into the workings of history. And one is reluctant to even put words to it. When in a discussion about this dynamic, one person responded "How can you say that the death of someone is part of God's working out the salvation of the world?" My response was yet another hard dynamic: "Apparently, God is not very much concerned about the boundary between temporal life and eternal life". Martyrs have always been required to advance the Gospel. That is not as much a requirement of God as it is a requirement of human nature.

And so, Chapter One is an announcement of the problem: that the people who had been taught salvation by grace through faith, had been falling back into salvation by works of the law. Paul quickly transitioned into an autobiographical description of God's preparation of him as an Apostle of Truth for the Gentiles.

Chapter two continues his autobiography. Note that he spent three years in "Arabia" after his conversion. After that, he lived in Damascus. He visited St Peter in Jerusalem for fifteen days, and met St James. Then he spent fourteen years re-studying what we know as the Old Testament. He felt he had to re-interpret all that he had learned at the hands of the rabbis. We should note that it was Barnabas who "invited" Paul into the company of leadership in the Church. Paul required additional educational time in preparation for his work as a missionary, and Barnabas was his mentor. Too often we gloss over the time and effort Paul invested in his faith-understanding before he was ready to undertake what God had intended since before his birth.

After I graduated from seminary, laypersons and wise pastors mentored me for seven years before I was prepared to be an effective pastor. And even now I continue to be in need of the guidance of others. Each of us ought to be aware of how we contribute to the effectiveness of those around us.

It was only after several years in Antioch, with Barnabas, that Paul had a "revelation" [2:2]. In other words, the Holy Spirit instructed him, and went to Jerusalem to seek the approval of the high leaders of the Christian Community there. He met with James, the brother of Jesus, with Peter, and with John. (Just a note here. When you find the name Cephas in this letter, it is yet another form of Peter's name.)

Apparently, the discussion was extended and difficult. Paul was the radical in the room. The leaders of the Christ Community were asked to give up more than a thousand years of faith tradition. They were asked to accept in a few hours what took Paul fifteen years to learn. Not everyone agreed. However, James, Peter and John gave their approval to his Gospel of Salvation by grace through faith. I suspect that agreement was reached because the leaders of the Community had gone through their own re-evaluation of Holy Scripture. In the months and years after the Resurrection, the Community studied Scripture together. They discovered new meanings in Isaiah, and other prophets. They had begun the difficult task of defining what had happened in the Crucifixion and Resurrection. That process wasn't completed for hundreds of years. And here we have a glimpse of the origins of our Faith.

Some-time after that, some emissaries came from James, who, at the time was the Head of the Church in Jerusalem (the first Pope). Peter had been meeting with the entire congregation. When the emissaries arrived, Peter withdrew to meet only with the Jews. Paul called Peter an "hypocrite". What is of note is the power and inward security Paul had gained in his ability to stand up for his Gospel and correct even St. Peter

Peter began his time there mingling with Gentile members of the little fellowship. But when representatives of James arrived, Peter pulled back into the segregationist position of the more conservative, "Mosaic Christians". He thus deserved the epithet "hypocrite" from Paul. One of the best things about Peter is that whenever he was accused of a wrong, he was able to fearlessly assess himself. He, apparently, took the criticism and amended his behavior.

One more note about Chapter Two is needed. At Jerusalem, James requested that: **we should continue to remember the poor, the very thing I had been eager to do all along** [2;10]. This is interesting because it was the basis for the offering that Paul collected among the Gentile Churches and took to Jerusalem at the end of his third Missionary Journey. And it was because he brought along some Jews of Greek origin that a riot began and he was imprisoned. But that story is for another day.

Next time we will explore Paul's earliest thoughts about the relationship between the Mosaic Faith and the new Christian Faith.

LESSON TWO

The reason that Galatians is such a prominent book of the Bible is that, in it, we see exactly how St Paul re-interpreted the Hebrew Scriptures. Some will be shocked.

He looked at three covenants: The Covenant of Abraham, the Covenant of Moses, and the Covenant of Jesus. Of the three, he learned, the Covenant of Abraham and the Covenant of Jesus are the same: Salvation by grace through faith. The outlier, which he assigned a secondary role, is the Covenant of Moses.

I think Barnabas had much to do with the depth of Paul's insights. Or it may have been the other way around. At any rate, the Letter to the Hebrews, which I believe was authored by Barnabas, has wonderful insights into the Covenant of Faith. It begins with: **In the past God spoke to our ancestors through the prophets at many times and in various ways, but in these last days he has spoken to us by his Son** [Hebrews 1:1-2]. He announced that he intended to demonstrate how the Lord fulfilled all the hopes of the earliest Saints. And in Chapter Eleven, Barnabas listed by name, those who, according to Hebrew tradition, were justified within the Covenant of Faith. They included Abel, Enoch, Noah, Isaac, Jacob, Esau, Joseph and Sarah.

Without Paul, Barnabas may well have been willing to apply this stupendous insight to Jews only. Paul, in an astonishingly brilliant insight, applied the Covenant of Faith to the Gentile world! And Barnabas agreed. All those chapters in Hebrews were devoted to faithful people who lived before Christ, and were the pioneers before the Great Pioneer of our Faith [Hebrews 12:2; actually, the word translated "Pioneer" means "founder".].

The proof of the efficacy of the Covenant of Faith, according to Paul, is that Gentile Christians receive the Holy Spirit by faith in Christ Jesus [Galatians 3:2] **Did you receive the Spirit by the works of the law, or by believing what you heard? He compared them to Abraham:** [Galatians 3:6] **So also Abraham believed God, and it was credited to him as righteousness** [Ref: Genesis 15:6]. **This** is radical. This is revolutionary. This is exactly what cost Paul his life. It is this idea that resulted in his arrest in Jerusalem. No orthodox Jew would agree that God worked outside the Covenant of Moses. The idea that God would grant His Spirit to Gentiles, and credit them with righteousness equal to Abraham. was an intolerable insult to what they held to be holy truth. It seemed to them that Paul was ending, or subverting, their distinction as Chosen People. They might have asked, "How may we be chosen and unique if the Gentiles are chosen too?"

Paul felt this was God's Plan from the very beginning. [3:8] **Scripture foresaw that God would justify the Gentiles by faith, and announced the gospel in advance to Abraham: "All nations will be blessed through you"** [Ref: Gen. 12:3, 18:18, 22:18].

Righteousness before God, he asserted, could not be achieved by means of the Law of Moses. The Law itself states: Cursed is everyone who does not continue to do everything written in the Book of the Law [Deut. 27:26]. And then he reached to the other end of Jewish history, quoting the prophet Habakkuk [2:4]: the righteous will live by faith. So, in his view, from the beginning of the Hebrew Faith to the end of the prophetic era, God communicated that the Law was not the means to righteousness. Rather, the faith effort to comply with the law had salvatory effect.

This is reflected in his Letter to the Romans. He wrote, [Romans 3:20b] through the law we become conscious of our sin. He meant that when the law required obedience, no one was able to perfectly perform his or her duty toward the law. By violating the smallest part of the law, they began to understand that something else was required. According to Paul, that "something else" was faith.

Paul used this legal argument going both ways. He set forth the legal notion that once a covenant has been ratified, it remains a contractual obligation on both sides. Here, in Galatians [3:17], he argued, **What I mean is this: The law, introduced 430 years later, does not set aside the covenant previously established by God and thus do away with the promise. In other words, the Covenant of Abraham (the Covenant of salvation by faith) remained both obligatory and effective, even after the Covenant of Law was established through Moses.**

Wonderfully enough, in Romans he turned that around to claim "salvation by mercy" for Jews under the Law of Moses [Romans 11:28-32]: **As far as the gospel is concerned, they [the Jews] are enemies for your sake; but as far as election is concerned, they are loved on account of the patriarchs, for God's gifts and his call are irrevocable. Just as you who [Gentiles] were at one time disobedient to God have now received mercy as a result of their disobedience, so they too have now become disobedient in order that they too may now receive mercy as a result of God's mercy to you. For God has bound everyone over to disobedience so that he may have mercy on them all. In other words, the Jews who remain under the Law of Moses will be saved by mercy because God is compassionate.**

So the law was our [the Jews] guardian until Christ came that we might be justified by faith [3:24]. A guardian is one who is in charge of and guides the development of a minor, a person not quite legally responsible for his/her behavior. This means that now we have new "guardian" [3:26]: **So in Christ Jesus you are all [Jews and Gentiles] children of God through faith. Something extraordinary has happened. Since the Law has been superseded, we** (both Jew and Gentile)**, who are participants in this New Covenant of Salvation by Grace through Faith, are now children of God through faith** [3:26].

What did the Saint mean by calling each of us a "Child of God"?

The legal argument continued in chapter four. The first paragraph is extraordinary. To fully understand it, one must be aware of Paul's habitual form of thinking. He had an original idea of why things happen the way they do. Everything that God causes or allows to happen are an "in-order-that". So he (Paul) became zealous, "in-order-that" he might persecute Christians, "in-order-that" he might become an Apostle, "in-order-that" Gentiles might hear the Good News of salvation by grace through faith, "in-order-that" we might understand ourselves as children of God. Everything is connected to this process by which God is bringing Good News to the world.

His legal argument is that God intended that we understand the Law of Moses as rudimentary, fundamental, a guide [4:3]; **we were in slavery under the elemental spiritual forces of the world.** [Gk: Stoicheion (say stoi-ky-on); from Stoixea; meaning either fundamental philosophical ideas (axioms) or cosmic spiritual powers.]. That guide, or teacher of righteousness, was given to Moses "in-order-that" the stage be set for the Incarnation. The condition of the Hebrew People, as well as of the Gentile world was that of what later theologians began to call, "the natural man". We lived according to our natural or physical reality. We had little or no awareness of a God of Love; a Father God. **Formerly, when you did not know God, you were slaves to those who by nature are not gods** [4:8]. Here is the "in-order-that". **But when the set time had fully come, God sent his Son, born of a woman, born under the law, to redeem those under the law, that we might receive adoption to sonship. Because you are his sons, God sent the Spirit of his Son into our hearts, the Spirit who calls out, "Abba, Father"** [4:34-5].

Stop for just a moment. You think the idea of our relationship to our Creator as a Father-child relationship is a "well-duh"? Only Christians and Jews have that idea. And, Paul is the revolutionary source of this huge grace to us.

Having this new understanding, Paul couldn't fathom why anyone would want to give it up! A pauper, miserable and hungry, having been adopted by the richest man in the world, would want to go back to his hopeless, homeless, hunger-filled existence? How daft might one get? Going back to salvation by compliance with the Law of Moses is like giving up the estate of the richest man in the world! Did any of the slaves in America want to go back to involuntary slavery and misery after the Civil War? Not very likely. And yet, the Galatians were returning to the celebration of certain days as a legal requirement for salvation; [4:10 **You are observing special days and months and seasons and years!**].

We ought to make a serious point here: we celebrate holy days like Christmas and Easter, not because by doing so we gain salvation. Rather they are parties to which we are invited because we have our salvation by grace through faith in Christ. We are saved by faith in Him, not because we go to church on Easter.

At verse 21, Paul restates the argument with which he had originally converted them to Christ and the freedom of salvation by grace through faith. I can paraphrase his argument.

Abraham had two sons. The first was born of a slave, Ishmael. Since his mother was a slave, he was too. His second son, Isaac, was born to Sarah. Isaac was the son predicted and "promised" by God. Since she was his wife and free, so was Isaac. He said that they were metaphors for the covenants. His argument is bizarre to twenty-first century Americans. The metaphor is not logical. It takes leap after leap without constraint. Ishmael's mother Hagar is first Mount Sinai, then Jerusalem, and therefore the Jewish Law is a covenant of slavery. Isaac's mother is compared to the Heavenly Jerusalem, and therefore is the progenitor of freedom through the grace of promise. Make sense to you? Not to me either. But we must allow him his argument. Perhaps it was persuasive in the first century.

Perhaps verse 23 can help us. Let us delete the rest and follow this suggestion: **His son by the slave woman [Hagar and Ishmael] was born according to the flesh, but his son by the free woman [Sarah and Isaac] was born as the result of a divine promise. This is better for us. We know that God promised Abram (Abraham) a son. And we know that Abraham and Sarah got out ahead of the promise by requiring Hagar to bear a child for them. So, Ishmael is a product of the flesh**

rather than the promise of God. There we have the connection to the two covenants: slave and free.

Paul opined that the descendants of Ishmael (the Canaanites) persecuted the Hebrews, and that Mosaic Jews were persecuting Christians. Therefore (another leap of ill-logic), the Jews had become what the descendants of Ishmael were: the covenant of slavery. They were slaves under the Law, while Christians are free according to the Covenant of Promise.

We must leave it here. Next, we turn to the really good stuff. We'll see spiritual dynamics in abundance. If you want to understand how to make our Faith into a power working and joy giving reality, join me for lesson three.

LESSON THREE

Today we look into some of the greatest thoughts ever put to paper. St Paul presents to you and me a template of victory through faith in Christ. Last time I spoke of spiritual dynamics. They are the "in-order-that" of our faith. We are encouraged to do this "in-order-that" something else might also happen.

Too many Christians fall under the spell of what Paul condemned in the first four chapters of his Letter to the Galatian Church. We, like they, fail because we think that we are "pretty good" people. The notion that I'm okay because I don't swear much, pay most of my taxes, usually don't feel hatred toward others, and am kind to dogs, is Satanic non-sense. One isn't afforded salvation if one doesn't need it. But we, each and every one of us, need it. We need salvation because we are sinners.

What is sin? It isn't the guilt of a naughty child. Sin is separation and alienation from God. Jesus didn't die on the cross because you had angry words about that driver who cut you off. Jesus died because you and I believe that I am more important to me than is God to me. Jesus died because we try to find ways to save ourselves; like the Jews who tried to deserve salvation by compliance with the Law of Moses.

Paul addressed the issue with a declarative "in-order-that": [5:1] **It is for freedom that Christ has set us free. Stand firm, then, and do not let yourselves be burdened again by a yoke of slavery.** His statement begs a question. To what kind of freedom does he refer? Freedom from sin? Freedom from fear? Freedom from the Mosaic Law is apparent. But why is it so important?

Paul's answer is that, **You who are trying to be justified by the law have been alienated from Christ; you have fallen away from grace** [5:4]. He presented an either/or dynamic. Either we are saved by grace through faith, or, we are saved by a perfect completion of the entirety of the Law of Moses. The engagement of our faith in the grace of Christ equals freedom from the Law.

His example was circumcision. Here is the reason I believe he regretted circumcising Timothy. If one indulges in the game of trying to satisfy God by means of a ritual or a rite, the result will be failure.

He doesn't say this, but I will. The most ancient human religions are attempts to appease a goddess who was about as evil as she was good. The Goddess is chaotic, unpredictable, unfeeling, and unconcerned about us. Abraham's righteousness rejected that. He is the greatest man who ever lived; second only to Christ Jesus. He opened to humanity the idea that God does care, and does intervene in human affairs for the benefit of those whom He Loves.

If one attempts to gain that Love by means of circumcision, that is akin to going back to the pre-Abrahamic, pagan faith. It is a rejection of the God of Love. It is a rejection of the Christ who sacrificed Himself in-order-that we never again might require a sacrifice for sin.

That is the "Freedom" for which Christ has set us free [5:1].

The rest of the chapter is a comparison of light and dark. There is the way of the world: what he called "flesh" [sark; 5:13]. On the other side is "pneuma" -spirit. This is not a theoretical theological distinction.

It has very real and ultimate consequences. To see the consequences fully, one ought to look at the word translated as "value" in the NIV: [5:2] **I, Paul, tell you that if you let yourselves be circumcised, Christ will be of no value to you at all.**

The Greek word Paul used is ópheleó [Phonetic: (o-fel-eh'-o)]. It means value, benefit, usefulness, profit. I think we get an insight into Paul's message if we translate the verse with "profit": Christ will be of no profit to you at all. The "profit" here is like the "benefit" from an insurance policy. It is the recompense, the reward, for one's faith in Christ Jesus. In other words, if one tries to gain salvation by way of obedience to the Law of Moses, there is no benefit, no profit.

This is completely contrary to logic. Does it mean that if we try to obey the law of God, we fail? Does it mean that we simply let Christ live through us by faith, we have a reward?   Well, that is what Paul tells us. Do we want to take his word for it?

Listen; every one of us has been, is, and will be "naughty". We haven't outgrown self-interest. But the Holy Spirit enables a better way. First, being naughty is part and parcel the life of the flesh. But, by faith in Christ, we have been set free (here is the freedom of 5:1). When we live the life of spirit, we are literally free from naughtiness. The famous contrast is between "works of flesh" and "works of spirit". He used the word "works" because that refers to the Law.

The contrast, if I may use my own metaphor, is between being and performance. My brand-new little granddaughter (three weeks old at the time of writing) is incapable of performing righteousness. She is not loved because of what she able to do. She is loved because of her "being". She hasn't done anything to deserve the fascinated love of her father and mother. She gets it simply because they love her. They are willing to do the most extraordinary things (like going sleepless week after week) just because they love her. If she were a boy, and they circumcised her, would they love him more? So, circumcision is of no value: [5:6a] **For in Christ Jesus neither circumcision nor uncircumcision has any value. Ritual or legalistic salvation is the darkness.**

By contrast we have the light: **For through the Spirit we eagerly await by faith the righteousness for which we hope** [5:5]. And what is that righteousness? Paul stated it clearly: [5:6b] **The only thing that counts is faith expressing itself through Love** [agape].

Paul lifted up a very old concept that was also lifted up by the Lord. **For the entire law is fulfilled in keeping this one command: Love [agape] your neighbor as yourself** [5:14; ref: Leviticus 19:18; **Do not seek revenge or bear a grudge against anyone among your people, but love your neighbor as yourself. I am the Lord.**]. Unsaid is the great tragedy. On our own, none of us is able to love our neighbor to the degree that we love ourselves. St. Paul wrote about "daring to die" for a really good person [Romans 5:7]. He went on to show that Jesus died for the unrighteous! But more than that is brought to light in Galatians. In Galatians, Paul tells us that the ability to love our neighbor is within our reach. The Holy Spirit makes possible the fruits of the Spirit.

As a teenager, sometime before the dinosaurs, I listened to a preacher at church-camp. He said "Spirit" is like the feeling of exuberance you get at a football game". What non-Christian nonsense! What a vapid and useless idea. We are saved by the indwelling happiness we felt when our high school football team was winning? I need to point out that many people think they are "spiritual" because they have feelings. That is non-Biblical "nit-wittery"! We are spiritual only when the Spirit of God invades our being. When Paul wrote of the spiritual life, he intended us to understand that the Character of God intrudes our personhood.

The professor who taught me Systematic Theology was one of the authors of what is called "Boston Personalism". They insisted that the Reality of God must include "Person" if God is to relate to you and me. Personhood requires some limits. That I am thus and so, means that I am not this and that. If God is Love [1 John 4:8], God's Spirit cannot be the opposite of Love (indifference). Thus, we rightly call the Holy Spirit a "Person". And just so, Paul describes the realities of the Holy Spirit as He indwells a human person. They are, of course: **love, joy, peace, forbearance, kindness, goodness, faithfulness, gentleness and self-control** [5:22-23a]. These are the Character of God.

The life of spirit is enabled only through the indwelling Holy Spirit. Elsewhere Paul wrote: **I no longer live, but Christ lives in me. The life I now live in the body, I live by faith in the Son of God** [2:20]. To Paul, "Christ in me" is the same affirmation as "The Holy Spirit lives within me". The ability to Love your neighbor as yourself, is a gift of the Holy Spirit.

Here is the wonderful insight of Paul. Remember that, in verse three, he claimed that a life of obedience to the Law of Moses had no "profit"? Well, there is another word for profit. And Paul used it to introduce the life of the Spirit, and the life of the flesh. He used "Karpos", which means 'fruit', but also "profit" or 'gain".

In other words, the profit, the benefit on the life insurance policy is cashed out to us in this life! We needn't wait for "pie in the sky bye and bye". We get the benefit here and now, and it continues and improves as we continue eternally. **Love, joy peace, patience, kindness, goodness, faithfulness, gentleness and self-control are much better than** [5:19-20] **sexual immorality, impurity and debauchery; idolatry and witchcraft; hatred, discord, jealousy, fits of rage, selfish ambition, dissensions, factions and envy; drunkenness, orgies.**

Hollywood doesn't agree. But it is true. And since they don't agree, Paul added a stern warning: Do not be deceived: **God cannot be mocked. A man reaps what he sows. Whoever sows to please their flesh, from the flesh will reap destruction; whoever sows to please the Spirit, from the Spirit will reap eternal life** [6:7-8].

And then, he implores us to give aid to each other. If one of us is tempted to the life of the flesh, we are encouraged to remind him/her. We are to carry the burden of temptations for each other. If we do so, we will all (Jew and Gentile) reap the reward together.

GALATIANS, STUDY NOTES

CHAPTER ONE

Paul an apostle by/with authority Jesus to the Christians at Galatia

You are drifting away from the Gospel I preached. If anyone preaches differently than I, reject them. (Why do I write this?) Am I seeking human favor or God's favor? If I seek human favor, I lose the favor of God. (Because) My Gospel was not taught to me by any man. God taught me. (How?) You know that I persecuted the Church. I was a zealous Pharisee. (Yet) Vs 15: God had set me apart (to be an apostle) before I was born. Later God called me by name and through Grace [GK: charis: "the merciful kindness by which God, exerting his holy influence upon souls, turns them to Christ, keeps, strengthens, increases them in Christian faith, knowledge, affection, and kindles them to the exercise of the Christian virtues".] (Grace is what attracted me as opposed to the rigid law, and caused my spiritual crisis) Went to Arabia for three years; then to Jerusalem with Barnabas. I met Peter for 15 days; saw James (Head of the Council).

CHAPTER TWO

Then to Celicia near Antioch and Tarsus for 14 years. (Later Barnabas will call him [from Tarsus?] to come to Antioch where they form the Mission Team.) Then he went back to Jerusalem, taking Titus with him. Titus was Greek and uncircumcised. The Jewish Christian leaders did not require him to be circumcised. Paul had spent those years studying the OT Scriptures. Galatians tells us what he learned. Shared his Gospel with the Council and leaders of the sect. No objections. Then "False Brothers" (Christians who insisted on obedience to Law of Moses) came in to challenge him. He refused any attempt to modify his Gospel. The Council Decision: Paul will preach to Gentiles. Peter will preach to Jews. Peter's Gospel had the same spirit and content; see Acts and his preaching to Cornelius. Peter James and John shook hands with Paul as contractual agreement with Paul and Barnabas. Agreement required an offering for the Church in Jerusalem which had adopted a communal life-style and was going to run out of money. 2:11ff [Note this is early...well before the beginning of the Mission Trips]. Peter and Paul in Antioch. Merged community. Delegation arrives from Jerusalem. Peter, Barnabas, and Jews separated themselves from Gentile Christians. Made Paul mad. Q: If a Jew lives like a Gentile, how may that Jew require Gentiles to live like Jews? Explain: If Jews separate themselves from Gentiles, how will we be able to include Gentiles in the Community of Christ? Vs 15: Paul's Mission Gospel: Jews by birth are not "Gentile Sinners", i.e. not separated from God [definition of sin]. Jews know there is no salvation by works of the law. Jews in the Sect of Jesus know that Salvation is by faith in Jesus. Can Paul or Peter then claim that Jesus is an agent of sin? i.e., separating Gentiles from God? Indeed, if we restore salvation by works of the law, we become agents of sin...separating Gentiles from God. Vs 19: "I tore down the law, crucified with/in Christ. So now: Christ in me. I live by faith. If we live by the law, we nullify the Crucifixion."

CHAPTER THREE

Did the Galatian Christians (Jews and Gentiles together) receive the Holy Spirit by obedience to the law, or by hearing of faith in Jesus? Are miracles worked by faith or because of the law?

HERE COMES THE PAULINE GOSPEL:

Abraham was counted as righteous by faith. By faith we are "sons" of Abraham [vs 8: In you all nations shall be blessed]. All under the law are cursed [vs 10: Any who do not obey the whole law are cursed]. Vs 13; esoteric: "Christ became a curse for us". i.e., IN ORDER THAT: Abraham's Covenant be extended to Gentiles. Vs 15: Human example: Abraham's Will/Covenant was not to an unspecified group. It was to one individual: Christ. Offspring is singular not plural [Note: "Christ" is the Heavenly Being who became flesh temporarily]. A Will/Covenant may not be annulled or modified after the death of its owner. May not be superseded. The Covenant of Moses does not replace the Covenant of Abraham. Vs 19: Moses is a "temporary intermediary". Must be...can't have two conflicting wills. Vss. 21-22 If salvation by law were possible, then the law would have made all Jews righteous, Instead, law proves all to be guilty/unrighteous. IN ORDER THAT: Righteousness through faith! Vs 23: We Jews were under the law until the Christ [Heavenly Being] took flesh, IN ORDER THAT we [Jews] might be made righteous [justified] through faith. Now we [Jews] are no longer under the law [custodian/temporary covenant] because "you [Jews and Gentiles] are all Sons of God" [cf. Brothers of Israel]. vs 27: Baptized in Christ; put on Christ...[from which Luther] are endowed with righteousness.
Endowed is the same as put into Christ's Will and Testament. We become inheritors of righteousness. Vss. 28-29 There is no distinction between Jew and Gentile; after Baptism [Not male/female Jew/Greek/Slave/free]...all are a new creation: Sons of Abraham---Abraham's heir.

CHAPTER FOUR

We have not yet inherited: a child/owner has no more authority over the estate than a slave. There is a regent, guardian, trustee = Church? Jesus? Holy Spirit? Paul? While we were children, we were subject to "elemental spirits of the universe" [vs 3] i.e., we were held in bondage to the "basic principles or orders of nature". The sacrifice of Christ, as per 3:13 sets us free from that bondage and makes us eligible for adoption...no long a slave but a child of the owner. Father God placed His Son under the bondage of nature in order to set the Jew and Gentile free from that bondage and make us legally [cf. law] eligible for adoption. The evidence is that from our heart the Spirit helps us cry out Abba [Lit: Daddy] Father...i.e. The relationship had changed from creature to child. Therefore: we are heirs, Vs 8 Paul returns to the original problem: Having been a slave, and having been emancipated by the sacrifice of Christ, why do you want to go back from Heir to slave to beings that are natural and not gods? "The beggarly elemental spirits" [Vs 9]. How do they do this? They celebrate or observe special days, months, etc. As per astrology.Vs 13: When Paul arrived at Galatia, he suffered a serious illness. They [Jews] took him in and nursed him back to health. That gave him the opening to preach his new Gospel. Vs 14-18: Expressions of their love for him. Vs 19: How could one who received such love from them become their enemy...especially by speaking the truth?! Paul regrets that he must start over (from the beginning) with them.

Vs 20: GOSPEL RECAP: [see how Paul re-interprets OT] The law says that Abraham had two sons. One of slavery and one of promise. Interesting lineage: Flesh, Hagar; Ishmael, Arabs, separated from God...Sinai and law. Sarah: Isaac; promise, faith; freedom: Abraham got the promise on the mountain in Jerusalem: [Mt. Zion] present Jerusalem...future Jerusalem equals the heavenly city.

Quotes Isaiah 54:1-3

"Sing, O barren one, who did not bear;
   break forth into singing and cry aloud,
   you who have not been in travail!
For the children of the desolate one will be more
   than the children of her that is married, says the Lord.
Enlarge the place of your tent,
   and let the curtains of your habitations be stretched out;
hold not back, lengthen your cords
   and strengthen your stakes.
For you will spread abroad to the right and to the left,
   and your descendants will possess the nations
   and will people the desolate cities.

Vss 28-29 We are like Isaac...born into the Covenant of Abraham...which existed before Moses and continues to this day. This faith is persecuted just as Jews were persecuted. THEREFORE: Excommunicate the false teacher -the one who teaches that Christians must obey the law of Moses.

CHAPTER FIVE:

To the Jewish Christians: Stand fast for and in faith. Do not allow that the law has any claim on any part of you. If you do, you lose all that you gained. You go back to the covenant of Moses and lose the Covenant of Abraham. You lose the saving sacrifice of Christ. To the Gentiles: Any adult male who accepts circumcision loses the Covenant of Abraham and must keep the whole law of Moses [not just part]; and Jews know there is no salvation in works of the law.

ANTINOMIAN [Def. Relating to the view that Christians are released by grace from the obligation of observing the moral law.] PROBLEM: vs 6: the law is of no value; only faith working through God's Love. Reminder: a little yeast [false teaching] leavens [changes] the whole lump. Get rid of the bad yeast! "If Sons of Freedom are persecuted [as per Saul], "Why am I still persecuted [by the false teacher]? Excommunicate him. "I wish he would castrate himself [as per circumcision only more dramatic]. The whole law is summed up in God Love your neighbor as yourself. If the congregation is divided [free and slave] it will destroy itself. Instead: walk by the Spirit. Pneuma not sark. Sark = elemental spirits [see fruits of the flesh vs 19-21] Now the works of the flesh are plain: fornication, impurity, licentiousness, idolatry, sorcery, enmity, strife, jealousy, anger, selfishness, dissension, party spirit, envy, drunkenness, carousing, and the like. I warn you, as I warned you before, that those who do such things shall not inherit the kingdom of God.

Pneuma = fruits of Spirit: [see vs 22-23] God's Love, joy, peace, patience, kindness, goodness, faithfulness, gentleness, self-control.

Against these there is no law.

Vs 24 The free (Jew and Gentile) have freed themselves from the elemental spirits by faith in Christ. They have crucified themselves...cf a spiritual circumcision. The evidence of that freedom is that God's Love doesn't argue/provoke others.

CHAPTER SIX

If a member is trapped in sin (slavery to elemental spirits...devoted to Mosaic Law) the Spirit-filled should "restore with gentleness. Bear (endure) one another's burdens...care for one another. Fulfill the law of Christ ("that you love one another as I have loved you). Remember, pharisaic pride is nothing. Test your own works (not those of someone else) and do not boast in the works of anyone else. Everyone carries his own load (of sins?) vs 6 "If you understand the revised meanings of the OT, teach others [Salvation by grace through faith] Vss.11-18 Condensed summary of his argument; Circumcision counts for nothing. The pharisaic members only want the Gentile Christians to be circumcised in order to avoid criticism by other Jews. Paul has no pride except in Christ. World means nothing to him (free from elemental spirits). Those who accept Paul's Gospel constitute the new Israel of God. He bears the stigmata or lash scars to prove his devotion to Christ.

EPHESIANS

First, in order to fully understand Paul's Letter to the Christians at Ephesus, we must simplify Paul's run-on sentences. Then we will be able to explain what he really meant.

CHAPTER ONE:

Paul, an Apostle to God's People in Ephesus.

Praised be God who has blessed us in Christ. God chose Him to be holy and blameless. In Love [agape]He predestined us for adoption. Through Him (Jesus) He (God) has given us forgiveness through grace. He made known to us the mystery of His Will, that at the time of fulfillment He will bring all things into unity.

We were chosen [1:12, "in order that"] to put our hope in Christ for His Glory. And you were included when you heard the Word [logon] of the Gospel. When you believed, you were sealed with the Holy Spirit as a guarantee of our inheritance until the redemption of all who belong to God.

Ever since I heard about your faith, I have not stopped giving thanks in my prayers. I ask that God will give you the Spirit of Wisdom and revelation (in order that) you may know the hope of His calling and the riches of Glory in the inheritance of the Saints.

His great power was exerted when He raised Christ far above all other authority, not only now but in the future. God put everything under His feet, and appointed Him "Head over everything" for the Church.

CHAPTER TWO:

You were dead in sin. All of us lived among (the dead) once, gratifying our flesh[sarx]. Because of His Love [agape] He made us alive with Christ. By grace you are saved. He raised us [past tense] and seated us in Heavenly realms in order that He might show the riches of His grace in Christ Jesus. By grace you are saved through faith. This is the gift of God, not as a result of works. We are the workmanship of Christ Jesus for the good works God has prepared for our (walking in them).

Therefore [Gk: dio, not emphatic, meaning so-then] remember, Gentiles, that you were excluded from Israel without hope and without God [Gk: atheoi: athiesits]. But now you have been brought near by Christ's blood. He is our peace. He destroyed the hostile barrier. He annulled the Law (of Moses). His purpose was to create a new man in Himself (Jew and Gentile) reconciling both to God through the Cross. He preached peace to both, for through Him we both have access to the Father through the Spirit.

Through Him we both have access to the Father by the One Spirit [Gk: Pneumati]. You (Gentiles) are fellow citizens of the Saints [other gentile Christians?] and the Household of God [Jewish Christians], built on the foundation of Apostles and Prophets, Christ Jesus Himself the Cornerstone. In Him the whole building is being fitted together as a Holy Temple in the Lord. You are being built together for the Habitation of God in the Spirit [Pneumati].

CHAPTER THREE:

He made known to me the mystery. You may have my insights into the mystery of Christ. It was not revealed to earlier generations. But now it has been revealed that the Gentiles are joint-heirs and a joint-body [Gk: syssoma] and joint-partakers [Gk: symmetocha] of the promise in Christ. I was given to preach the unsearchable riches of Christ to Gentiles. So that now the rulers in Heaven may see God's Wisdom in the Church.

Therefore, don't lose heart at my tribulations. It is glory for you. I bow to the Father, that he might give you glory with the strength of the Spirit [Pneumati], that Christ may dwell in your hearts by faith in Love [agape] so that you may be fully able to comprehend the Love [agape] of Christ and be filled with all the fulness of God.

To the One able to do all things according to the power [dynamin] working in us, be glory in the Church [Gk: ekklesia] and in Christ Jesus to all generations. Amen.

CHAPTER FOUR:

Therefore [Parakaleo; THIS IS THE MAIN POINT OF THE LETTER], I exhort you to walk worthily according to your calling, with humility and gentleness (and) patience, bearing with one another in Love [agape]. Be diligent to keep unity of Spirit [Pneumatos] and peace: one Body [soma] and one Spirit [Pneumati] just as you have been called into one Hope [elpidi], one Lord, one faith, and one baptism, one God and Father who is over all, through all, and in all.

Each one has been given grace according to Christ's gift-measure. Therefore [Gk: dio] it says: having ascended, He led captive captivity, and gave gifts to men[anthropois]. Does that not also mean that He descended into the lower regions of Earth? The descended on is the same as the ascended one above all the Heavens so that He might fill everything. He gave some to be Apostles, some Prophets, some Evangelists, some shepherds and teachers toward the perfecting of the Saints for the work of ministry [diakonias] for the upbuilding of the Body of Christ until we may attain to unity of faith (and) knowledge of the Son of God, a man complete to the measure of Christ.

We might no longer be infants subject to the cunning of deceitful men. (Rather) speaking the Truth in Love [agape] we should grow up into Him in all things for the upbuilding of (the Body) in Love [agape].

This I say that you should no longer walk in the futile mind of Gentiles, alienated from God with hard hearts, given to sensuality, working impurity and greediness. This is not what you learned from Christ. The Truth is in Christ. You are to put off the former way of life with its corrupt desires. You are to be renewed in the spirit [pneumati] of your mind [noos]. To have put on the new humanity [antthropon] according to God; created in righteousness and holiness of truth.

Therefore, speak truthfully with your neighbor because we are fellow members of each other. Be angry but don't let the sun set on your anger. Give no opportunity to a slanderer [diabolo: a slanderer]. The thief shall no longer steal. Rather let him work good with his hands to impart to the needy. Do not allow an unwholesome Word [logos] to go forth from your mouth, rather what is good for edification and grace. Do not grieve the Holy Spirit in who you were sealed [see 1:13] for the day of redemption. Bitterness and rage, anger, clamor and blaspheming must be removed along with malice. Be tender-hearted and kind forgiving each other just as God in Christ forgave you.

CHAPTER FIVE:

Be imitators of God as beloved [agapeta] children. Walk in Love [agape] as Christ Loved [agapesen] us. Sexual immorality, impurity and covetousness unnamed among you Saints. Filthiness, foolish talk and crude jokes are not fitting. Rather thanksgiving. You know that no fornicator [pornos] or covetous person (an idolater) has an inheritance in the Kingdom of Christ and of God. Do not deceive with empty words [logois] because the wrath of God comes to the disobedient.

Once you were darkness. Now you are light; the Children of the Lord of light. The fruit of Light is in goodness, righteousness and truth. Do not have fellowship with unfruitful darkness, rather expose the things done secretly by them. Everything exposed to the light [becomes light]. Be careful how you live, redeeming the time for the days are evil [pornerai]. Don't be foolish, understand what the Lord's will is. Don't be drunk or debauched. Instead be filled with the Spirit [Pneumati]: giving thanks for everything in the Name of our Lord Jesus Christ to God and Father.

Submit yourselves to one another in reverence of Christ. The husband is head of the wife similar to Christ the Head of the Church [see 1:22]; Savior of the Body. As the Church is subject to Christ, so wives to their husbands in everything [see 1:22]. Husbands Love [agapate] the wives just as Christ Loved [agapesen] the Church and gave up Himself for her, so that He might sanctify [hagiase: make holy], having cleansed by washing of water and word [rhemati] so that He might present her to Himself in Glory, the Church having no spot or wrinkle, but is blameless. Just so, husbands (are) to Love [agapan] their wives as their own bodies. The one Loving [agapon] his wife himself Loves [agapa]. No one hates his flesh. One nourishes and cherishes it just as Christ the Church. We are members of the Body: the flesh and bones of Him. Because of this a man leaves his father and mother and be joined to the wife...and the two into one flesh will become. This great mystery is to speak of Christ and the Church. So let each man Love [agapato] his wife as himself, that the wife may respect the husband.

CHAPTER SIX:

Children: obey your parents-in-the-Lord, for this is right. Honor your father and mother. That is the first commandment with a promise: that it will be well with you and you will be long-lived upon the Earth.

Fathers: do not provoke your children. Bring them up in the discipline and admonition of the Lord. Slaves: obey the masters of your flesh in sincerity of your heart as if to Christ. Not as a man-pleaser but as servants of Christ doing God's Will from the heart. Know that (you) will receive good from the Lord whether slave or free. Masters: the same thing applies to you. Give up threatening because you have a Master in Heaven who is without partiality. Henceforth be empowered in the Lord's strength. Put on the full armor of God. You will be able to stand against the schemes [see 1:22] of the schemer [see 1:22]. It is not wrestling against blood and flesh, but against cosmic powers of darkness, the spiritual [pneumatika] of evil [ponerias] in the Heavenly Realms. Because of this, take up the complete armor of God, so that you may be able to withstand in the day of evil [ponera]. Having done all things, stand dressed in readiness with truth, having put on the breastplate of righteousness and shoes of (the) readiness of the Gospel of peace; and the helmet of salvation, with the sword of the Spirit [Pneumatos] which is the word [rhema] of God through prayer. Praying in the Spirit [Pneumati] and watching everything with perseverance and supplication for all the Saints; and also for me that I may be given the Divine Spirit [logos] to speak with boldness the mystery of the Gospel for which I am a chained ambassador [major part of the definition of Apostle]. May I be bold as I am moved to speak so that now you may also know my concerns. Tychicus, the Beloved [agapetos] brother and faithful servant [diakonos] in the Lord, I have sent for this purpose; that you may know our concerns and for your encouragement. Peace to the brothers and Love [agape] with faith from God the Father and Lord Jesus Christ. Grace with all Loving [agaponton] our Lord Jesus Christ in incorruptibility.

A SIMPLIFIED VERSION:

CHAPTER ONE:

Paul, an Apostle, To "God's People" in Ephesus. God chose Jesus. Jesus predestined us for adoption. He will bring all things into unity. You were sealed with the Holy Spirit. I pray that God will give you the Spirit of Wisdom and revelation (in order that) you may know the inheritance of the Saints. God raised Christ far above all other authority. God appointed Him Head over everything for the Church.

CHAPTER TWO:

You were dead in sin. God made us alive with Christ by grace. God raised us [past tense] in order that He might show His grace in Christ Jesus. This is the gift of God, not as a result of works. God has prepared good works for us.

Therefore remember, Gentiles were excluded from Israel. You have been brough near by Christ's blood. He is our peace. He destroyed the hostile barrier. He annulled the Law (of Moses). His purpose was to create a new man in Himself (Jew and Gentile) reconciling both to God through the Cross. He preached peace to both, for through Him we both have access to the Father through the Spirit. By the One Spirit [Pneumati]. Saints and the Household of God [one noun/title/entity], are together, the whole building is a Holy Temple. You are being built together for the Habitation of God in the Spirit [Pneumati].

CHAPTER THREE:

I am a prisoner of Christ Jesus for you Gentiles. You may have my insights into Christ not revealed to earlier. Now it has been revealed (that) Gentiles are joint-partakers [WITH JEWS] of the promise in

Christ Jesus through my Gospel. I became a deacon [diakonos -servant] by God's grace. I preach Christ to Gentiles. Now the rulers in Heaven may see God's Wisdom in the Church. In Christ we have access by faith. Therefore, don't lose heart at my tribulations. It is glory for you. I worship the Father, in order that [my words] he might give you the strength of the Spirit [Pneumati], in order that [my words] that Christ may dwell in your hearts. Be filled with the fulness of God. To the One able to do all things according to the power [dynamin] working in us, be glory in the Church [ekklesia] and in Christ Jesus to all generations. Amen.

CHAPTER FOUR:

Therefore [Parakaleo], I exhort you to walk worthily (of) your calling, with humility, gentleness (and) patience. Bear with one another in Love [agape]. Keep unity of Spirit [Pneumatos] and peace: one Body (should be "soul")[soma/ not sark, meaning "one soul"] and one Spirit [Pneumati]. You have one Hope [elpidi], one Lord, one faith, one baptism, one God.

Each one has been given grace. Christ led captive captivity [ended sin/alienation from God]. He descended into the lower regions of Earth? The descended one is the same as the ascended one. He appointed some to be Apostles, some Prophets, some Evangelists, some shepherds and teachers for upbuilding of the Body of Christ until we may attain to unity of faith. We might no longer be subject to deceitful men. We should grow up for the upbuilding of (the Body) in Love [agape]. You should no longer be alienated from God, working impurity. This is not what you learned from Christ. The Truth is in Christ. You are to put off corrupt desires. You are to be renewed in the spirit [pneumati] of your mind [noos]. Put on the new humanity [antthropon]; created in truth. Therefore, speak truthfully [to each other]. We are fellow members. Be angry but don't let the sun set on your anger. Give no opportunity to the slanderer [diabolo: a slanderer]. The thief shall no longer steal. Let him work good with his hands to impart (good) to the needy. Do not allow an unwholesome Word [logos] to go forth from your mouth. Speak what is good for edification and grace. Do not grieve the Holy Spirit. Bitterness rage, anger, clamor, blaspheming and malice must be removed. Be tender-hearted and kind forgiving each other. God forgave you.

CHAPTER FIVE:

Be imitators of God. Walk in Love [agape]. Sexual immorality, impurity, covetousness gone from among you. Filthiness, foolish talk and crude jokes are not fitting. Rather thanksgiving. You know that no fornicator [pornos] or covetous person (an idolater) has an inheritance in the Kingdom. Do not deceive with empty words [logois] because the wrath of God comes to the disobedient. Once you were darkness. Now you are light. Children of the Lord of light. The fruit of Light is in goodness, righteousness and truth. Do not have fellowship with unfruitful darkness. Expose the things done secretly by them. Everything exposed to the light [becomes light]. Be careful how you live. The days are evil [pornerai]. Don't be foolish. Understand what the Lord's will is. Don't be drunk or debauched. Be filled with the Spirit [Pneumati]. Give thanks for everything. Submit yourselves to one another in reverence for Christ. The husband is head of the wife similar to Christ the Head of the Church [see 1:22]. As the Church is subject to Christ, so wives to their husbands [see 1:22]. Husbands Love [agapate] the wives just as Christ Loved [agapesen] the Church so that He might sanctify [hagiase: make holy], cleansed by washing of water and word [rhemati]. The Church is blameless. Just so, husbands (are) to Love [agapan] their wives as their own bodies.

The one Loving [agapon] his wife himself Loves [agapa]. No one hates his flesh. One nourishes and cherishes it just as Christ the Church. We are members of the Body. Because of this a man leaves his father and mother and be joined to the wife...and the two into one flesh will become. This great mystery is to speak of Christ and the Church. Let each man Love [agapato] his wife as himself, that the wife may respect the husband.

CHAPTER SIX:

Children: obey your parents-in-the-Lord. Honor your father and mother. That is the first commandment with a promise: that it will be well with you and you will be long-lived upon the Earth. Fathers: do not provoke your children. Bring them up in (the) discipline and admonition of the Lord. Slaves: obey the masters as if to Christ, doing God's Will. Know that (you) will receive good from the Lord. Masters: the same thing applies to you. Give up threatening, You too have a Master. He is without partiality. Henceforth be empowered in the Lord's strength. Put on the full armor of God. You will be able to stand against the schemes [see 1:22] of the schemer [see 1:22]. It is not wrestling against blood and flesh, but against the spiritual [pneumatika] of evil [ponerias]. Take the armor of God, so that you may be able to withstand in the day of evil [ponera]. Stand with truth. Put on the breastplate of righteousness, shoes of readiness, the Gospel, the helmet of salvation, the sword of the Spirit [Pneumatos] which is the word [rhema] of God. Praying in the Spirit [Pneumati] and watching with perseverance and supplication for all the Saints. Pray for me that I may be given the Divine Spirit [logos] to speak the Gospel. Now you know my concerns. Tychicus, the Beloved [agapetos] brother and faithful servant [diakonos] in the Lord, I have sent that you may know our concerns.

Peace to the brothers and Love [agape] with faith from God the Father and Lord Jesus Christ. Grace with all Loving [agaponton] our Lord Jesus Christ in incorruptibility.

AN EVEN SIMPLER OUTLINE

God chose Jesus. Jesus predestined us for adoption.

I pray that God will give you the Spirit of Wisdom and revelation

God made us alive with Christ by grace.

His purpose was to create a new man

You are being built together for the Habitation of God in the Spirit [Pneumati].

Now it has been revealed (that) Gentiles are joint-partakers [WITH JEWS] of the promise in Christ.

Therefore [Parakaleo: THIS IS THE MAIN POINT OF THE LETTER]... Keep unity of Spirit [Pneumatos] and peace: one Soul [soma] and one Spirit [Pneumati].

We should grow up for the upbuilding of (the Body) in Love [agape].

You should no longer be alienated from God, working impurity.

Be tender-hearted and kind forgiving each other. God forgave you.

Be imitators of God. Walk in Love [agape].

(Husbands and wives) Submit yourselves to one another in reverence for Christ.

Children: obey your parents-in-the-Lord.

Fathers: do not provoke your children.

Slaves: obey the masters as if to Christ (It is God's Will).

Masters: You too have a Master.

Henceforth be empowered in the Lord's strength. (Armor of God)

Pray for me.

ANALYSIS

Paul's purpose in writing this epistle is summed up in chapter four, verses one through five: **Therefore** [Parakleo]**, I exhort you to walk worthily according to your calling, with humility and gentleness (and) patience, bearing with one another in Love** [agape]**. Be diligent to keep unity of Spirit** [Pneumatos] **and peace: one Soul** [soma] **and one Spirit** [Pneumati] **just as you have been called into one Hope** [elpidi]**, one Lord, one faith, and one baptism, one God and Father who is over all, through all, and in all.**

The word translated as "therefore" is different from all the other instances in which Paul's word is thus translated. The Greek word for the source of all the other "therefore(s)" is "dio", which means "looking backward". In chapter four, verse one, the source word is "parakaleo", which means: "I beseech, entreat, beg, I exhort, admonish". Clearly, when St Paul invokes parakaleo, he intends the reader to pay close attention.

If we simplify his "exhortation" even more, it becomes: "Hey all y"all! I exhort, and again exhort you, to live up to your Holy Spirit calling, with Godly Love, hope, and peace."

Why would Paul take the time to write such a letter? One doesn't exhort a couple, who live like they are on a permanent honeymoon; "Hey you two! Learn to get along with each other!"

There must have been a division within the Church at Ephesus. The main tension, during the ministry of Paul, was between Jewish and Gentile Christians. If this was the issue, the entire letter makes sense.

Paul began by reminding the entire congregation of the blessings they hold in common. Both Jew and Gentile were saved from sin by grace through faith and marked by the Holy Spirit [1:3-14]. This mark is an indelible stamp, as might a king put his seal on a document like a deed of ownership.

Focusing on the Gentile Christians, Paul reminded them that God had a purpose in saving them. God is going to use their salvation as an "in-order-that" He might demonstrate grace to future generations.

Where ever Paul uses the words "in-order-that", he points out a powerful spiritual dynamic. Christians often miss the importance of these dynamics. Pointedly, God seldom causes something for its own sake. Everything is tending toward the glorious fulfillment of His Purpose. That Purpose is the Unity of all things in Christ [4:13]. This unity must begin in Ephesus among Jew and Gentile.

In order to accomplish that, God is going to use that unity to demonstrate His Wisdom to the Powers in Heavenly Places [4:11]. Christian, did you ever suppose that your salvation has cosmic importance? It is as if God has a bet on against Heavenly Powers; "I bet I can get sinners to turn to me, learn Godly Love for each other, and live in peace and harmony".

Paul found it very hard to understand. He required a kick off a horse on the way to Damascus before he could even entertain such a thought. It took him fifteen years of Bible Study in Arabia before he was ready to begin his training with Barnabas. To him, God's Wisdom is synonymous with "Mystery". The Mystery of salvation by grace through faith, must have been almost secondary to the mystery of the how and why God chose him (least of all the Saints) [3:8]. It is through this double mystery that the Ephesian Gentile Christians have access to God's Household.

And so, Gentiles must remember that at one time the "Household of God" (meaning Israel, the Chosen People) was off limits to all other than the Jews. This is another "grace". Gentiles bless the Jews by their presence, and Jews bless Gentiles in the same way. Unity is better than disunity. Gentiles had no hope. Unless salvation is possible, life has no purpose, no goal, no meaning. Only by the sacrifice of Jesus Christ and by faith in Him, could Gentiles join the Household. More of this when we look at the word "grace" as used throughout this letter.

In the first two chapters, "Grace" is singular and refers to the gift of salvation in Christ [2:8]. In chapter three, Paul testifies to the "grace" given him to preach good news to Gentiles. Again, it is a singular gift [3:7]. In both cases, Grace is a spiritual power. In the first instance it provides the pathway of redemption to sinners. In the second, that pathway is facilitated by the calling of St Paul to preach Good News to Gentiles.

However, in chapter four, Paul gives the word a different meaning. Gift becomes plural. Christ gives graces to each Christian. Again, it is an in-order-that spiritual dynamic. I love the way Paul said it, "Christ apportioned" his gifts. Methodists attribute special meaning to "apportioned". Each full member of the United Methodist Church is apportioned a tiny percentage of the costs of the Church beyond his or her congregation. We each have a share in the ministries of the General Church; in missions, education, witness, and extension. Paul wrote that the Body of Christ has had God's "Grace-Gifts" apportioned to Apostles, Prophets, Evangelists, Preachers, and Teachers: for the work of building up the Body of Christ [4:11]. See how that Grace begins with Jesus Christ, is apportioned to the Body-Builders, as an in-order-that the Grace-Gift of salvation may reach the heart of each Christian, and again as an in-order-that God may demonstrate His Wisdom to Powers in Heavenly Places?

Finally, Paul explained how this Grace functions among members of the Body.

First and foremost; Gentile Christians must put away their former way of life. There pagan worship and way of life was filled with sexual immorality, obscenity, greed and pointlessness. Instead the Body of Christ must be characterized by thanksgiving and modesty. As John Wesley put it, we are to sing songs of faith just as powerfully as we sang the drunken songs of the tavern.

Then specifically: Marriage must be a caricature of the relationship between Christ and the Church (His Body and Bride). A husband must give up his life for his wife just as Christ gave up His life for the Church. Wives must be obedient to their husband as the Church is obedient to Christ.

Children must obey their parents. And parents (he actually only wrote "fathers", but we can forgive him this oversight) must not aggravate or provoke their children to rebellion. Instead, parents are to teach and discipline their children with grace, just as Christ treats them.

Slaves must obey and serve their masters as if serving Christ. Masters must treat their slaves well, remembering that they too have a Master who will not be impressed by the difference between the two.

But God does not leave us without resources in these endeavors. He provides spiritual armor. One should note that freedom of choice exists in Heaven. There are those who dwell in what St Augustine called the City of God. And, there are wicked forces elsewhere. These are the same ones to whom God will demonstrate His Wisdom through our salvation. It is with them that we have "our" struggle. We should note that the source word for evil is the source of our word "pornography" (an unhealthy fascination with the things of the flesh). Does the word "our" mean only us? Or, does it mean God and us? It seems we are teamed with God in this cosmic effort.

And so, God provides us with faith, Gospel (good news), Truth, and (here is a very special word) "rhemati". It literally means the words God speaks directly to a person of Faith. Rhemati can be comfort, instruction, insight, encouragement... but always intended directly and importantly for a particular Christian: a "For your ears only" communication.

We are urged to pray constantly. It is to be a way of life, a witness, a power granted for us to use. If all that Paul wrote in this letter is true, how can we not continually pray? It is our calling, our participation in the Body. It is the basis for unity, and the prerequisite to rhema.

I think the letter may be easily summed up. Paul wanted the Jews and Gentiles in his beloved congregation to live in unity, demonstrating God's Love and Presence.

PHILIPPIANS

Philippians is an affectionate, joy-filled response to a gift of money sent by the Saints in Philippi to the Apostle Paul. He tosses out an admonition to beware of those who would require circumcision [3:2-4], but the main gist of the letter is more "spiritual" than doctrinal.

Many theologians focus on details rather than on the spiritual dynamics of this epistle. And those dynamics are the real treasure that makes this letter so important.

In order to understand the letter most profitably, we must "get into Paul's mind". He was in prison [1:12-14]. We can fruitlessly debate which prison, and when the letter was written. And how the date of his imprisonment relates to the periods of historic persecutions. More than a few people have gotten their PHD speculating about that. But such is the stuff of the back shelves of the library. Is there any profit for the Christian, knowing whether Paul was writing from Rome, or Caesarea, or even Ephesus?

If you have not read about Bonhoeffer imprisoned by the Nazis, or Martin Luther King, Jr. in the Birmingham Jail, or Martin Niemöller in the Berlin Jail, you might be surprised to learn that they each shared a deep happiness and a spiritual joy.

"Joy" is a word the Apostle used four times in this very short letter. I always pray with joy [1:4]; I will continue with all of you for your progress and joy in the faith [1:25]; Make my joy complete … having the same love, being one in spirit and of one mind [2:2]; welcome him [Epaphroditus] in the Lord with great joy [2:29]. And "joy" is not the only happy word. "Rejoice" appears six times.

Happy in jail? What is their secret? That is the key to this letter, and the greatest of spiritual dynamics. This is it: The greatest Christian JOY comes to the saint only after he/she gives up on him/her self. We must abandon our ambitions and earthly desires. Only our life in Christ has any meaning or profit. That is what Paul wanted to communicate. One must resign as captain of his/her own ship, and leave everything up to the Lord of all. Listen to these passages.

For to me, to live is Christ and to die is gain [1:21]. Paul had transferred his focus from the concerns of "apparent life", to the concerns of "Ultimate Life".

I will know that you stand firm in the one Spirit striving together as one for the faith of the gospel without being frightened in any way by those who oppose you. This is a sign to them that they will be destroyed, but that you will be saved—and that by God. For it has been granted to you on behalf of Christ not only to believe in him, but also to suffer for him, since you are going through the same struggle you saw I had, and now hear that I still have [1:27-30]. Within that new viewpoint (Ultimate Life) Paul was absolutely fearless in his persecutions and suffering. He had the assurance of salvation. He knew himself to be a "sacred vessel". Those who opposed him or sought to do harm to him would be destroyed.

And then:

Have the same mindset as Christ Jesus: Who, being in very nature [Gk:morphḗ (say: more-fay) – properly, form (outward expression) that embodies essential (inner) substance so that the form is in complete harmony with the inner essence]. **God, did not consider equality with God something to be used to his own advantage; rather, he made himself nothing by taking the very nature [see above] of a servant, being made in human likeness. And being found in appearance** [schema (say: skhay'-mah) - properly, exterior shape (form); (figuratively) the outer "shape" (manner, appearance)] **as a man, he humbled himself by becoming obedient to death— even**

death on a cross! Therefore God exalted him to the highest place and gave him the name that is above every name, that at the name of Jesus every knee should bow, in heaven and on earth and under the earth, and every tongue acknowledge that Jesus Christ is Lord, to the glory of God the Father [2:5-11]; This is the great "Kenosis passage". The Christ emptied Himself in obedience. Jesus is exalted above all others because He was obedient even to a violent, painful, death. The pathway to exaltation, for each Christian, is through obedience under persecution.

And then again: **But even if I am being poured out like a drink offering on the sacrifice and service coming from your faith, I am glad and rejoice with all of you. So you too should be glad and rejoice with me** [2:17-18]; **I consider everything a loss** [business term: profit and loss] **because of the surpassing worth of knowing Christ Jesus my Lord, for whose sake I have lost all things. I consider them garbage** [3:8 lit: dung]**; and I press on to take hold of that for which Christ Jesus took hold of me** [3:12].

Paul had learned the greatest of life-lessons. Control over one's own fortune is a sham and a delusion. None of us knows what tomorrow will bring. Just as Jesus insisted that we look to the lilies and the birds [Matthew 6:26ff], so Paul has learned that, even in the direst of circumstances, God is in control and will use us to bring forth the Kingdom.

I know of a combat veteran who spoke of the freeing nature of giving up hope for a future. He discovered, under fire, that he was able to function without fear. Just so, Paul expects Christians to be fearless. It is not that we have no hope of a future. Rather it is the knowledge that nothing here can interfere with our glorious and eternal future.

I also know that only when I gave up my own ambitions was I available to the Lord for His Purposes. The difference in the fruitfulness of my ministry was dramatic. My life-path was never what I anticipated, but always into places where my unique set of skills and insights were needed. Only as I was obedient to the Spirit (working in others as well as within myself) was I able to take both weal and woe as gifts of the Lord's good will.

And so, if Paul had advice to share it was this: Whatever happens, conduct yourselves in a manner worthy of the Gospel of Christ. Then, whether I come and see you or only hear about you in my absence, I will know that you stand firm in the one Spirit, striving together as one for the faith of the Gospel without being frightened in any way by those who oppose you. This is a sign to them that they will be destroyed, but that you will be saved—and that by God. For it has been granted to you on behalf of Christ not only to believe in him, but also to suffer for him, since you are going through the same struggle you saw I had, and now hear that I still have [1:27-30].

We are to have an "eternal perspective". We are citizens of the Heavenly City, and what happens here is of little value by comparison. But our citizenship is in heaven. And we eagerly await a Savior from there, the Lord Jesus Christ, who, by the power that enables him to bring everything under his control, will transform our lowly bodies so that they will be like his glorious body [3:20].

And so, fellow Christians: Rejoice in the Lord always. I will say it again: Rejoice! Let your gentleness be evident to all. The Lord is near. Do not be anxious about anything, but in every situation, by prayer and petition, with thanksgiving, present your requests to God. And the peace of God, which transcends all understanding, will guard your hearts and your minds in Christ Jesus [4:4-7].

COLOSSIANS

This letter is a summary of St. Paul's teachings. He was not the founder of the Church at Colossae. The Christians there had never met him [2:1]. The letter is evidence that Paul wanted his teachings to be circulated, and used as the template of the Good News. The reason he presents for writing this letter is: **We continually ask God to fill you with the knowledge of his will through all the wisdom and understanding that the Spirit gives, so that you may live a life worthy of the Lord and please him in every way: bearing fruit in every good work, growing in the knowledge of God** [1:9-10].

So, what does he teach? I have edited the letter. One of the reasons so few are able to point out the main ideas, is that Paul's letter is full of the deepest sentiment. His letters are so beautiful, one is tempted to give equal importance to every phrase. By eliminating the grammatical duplication, of which St. Paul is so fond, we have a much more concise "note".

The Son is the image of the invisible God [1:15]. **For God was pleased to have all his fullness dwell in him, and through him to reconcile to himself all things, by making peace through his blood, shed on the cross. Once you were alienated from God and were enemies in your minds because of your evil behavior. But now he has reconciled you by Christ's physical body through death to present you holy in his sight, without blemish and free from accusation— if you continue in your faith** [1:19-23]. **God has chosen to make known among the Gentiles the glorious riches of this mystery, which is Christ in you** [1:27].

See to it that no one takes you captive through hollow and deceptive philosophy, which depends on human tradition and the elemental spiritual forces [basic principles] **of this world rather than on Christ** [2:8].

For in Christ all the fullness of the Deity lives in bodily form, and in Christ you have been brought to fullness [2:9-10].

Your whole self, ruled by the flesh [sark] was put off when you were circumcised by Christ, having been buried with him in baptism, in which you were also raised with him through your faith [2:11-12].

God made you [or, "us"] **alive with Christ. He forgave us all our sins, having canceled the charge of our legal indebtedness, which stood against us and condemned us; he has taken it away, nailing it to the cross** [2:13-14].

Therefore [Gk: "oun" – not parakaleo], **do not let anyone judge you by what you eat or drink, or with regard to a religious festival, a New Moon celebration or a Sabbath day** [2:16].

Such a person (has) lost connection with the head [2:18, edited].

Since you died with Christ to the elemental spiritual forces of this world, why, as though you still belonged to the world, do you submit to its rules: "Do not handle! Do not taste! Do not touch!" [2:20-21]**?**

Since, then, you have been raised with Christ, set your hearts on things above, where Christ is, seated at the right hand of God. Set your minds on things above, not on earthly things [3:1-2].

Put to death, therefore [Gk: "oun" -not parakaleo]**, whatever belongs to your earthly nature: sexual immorality, impurity, lust, evil desires and greed, which is idolatry** [3:5]**. You must also rid yourselves of all such things as these: anger, rage, malice, slander, and filthy language** [3;8].

Here there is no Gentile or Jew, circumcised or uncircumcised, barbarian, Scythian, slave or free, but Christ is all, and is in all [3:11]**. Clothe yourselves with compassion, kindness, humility, gentleness and patience. Bear with each other and forgive one another if any of you has a grievance against someone. Forgive as the Lord forgave you. And over all these virtues put on love** [agape]**, which binds them all together in perfect unity** [3:12-14].

Let the peace of Christ rule in your hearts [3:15]**. Wives, submit yourselves to your husbands, as is fitting in the Lord. Husbands, love [agape] your wives and do not be harsh with them. Children, obey your parents in everything, for this pleases the Lord** [3:18-20]**. Fathers, do not embitter your children, or they will become discouraged** [3:21]**. Slaves, obey your earthly masters in everything; and do it, not only when their eye is on you and to curry their favor, but with sincerity of heart and reverence** [3:22]**. Masters, provide your slaves with what is right and fair, because you know that you also have a Master in heaven** [4:1]**. Devote yourselves to prayer, being watchful and thankful** [4:2].

Pretty simple to us Protestants. You are saved by grace through faith in Christ. Therefore, do not allow anyone to require that you engage in some sort of required ritual, or accept some secular philosophy. Instead, since God has fully dwelt in Christ, and through Him brings you to complete fullness, cancelling out your debt of sinfulness, put to death all the evils that affect humanity. Get rid of sexual immorality, impurity, lust, evil desires and greed, anger, rage, malice, slander, and filthy language. In their place clothe yourselves with compassion, kindness, humility, gentleness and patience. Forgive as the Lord forgave you. And over all these virtues put on God's Love. Let the peace of Christ rule in your hearts [3:15]. Wives, submit yourselves to your husbands. Husbands, love your wives and do not be harsh with them. Children, obey your parents. Fathers, do not embitter your children. Slaves, obey your earthly masters in everything. Masters know that you also have a Master in heaven. Devote yourselves to prayer, being watchful and thankful.

So why is this letter important enough to be in the Cannon? Probably because of Paul's beautiful ability with language. He includes so many insightful dependent clauses that our attention rises from the simplicity of the message to the contemplation of the divine. His language brings us right into the Presence of God.

For instance: "you may live a life worthy of the Lord and please him in every way: bearing fruit in every good work, growing in the knowledge of God, being strengthened with all power according to his glorious might so that you may have great endurance and patience, and giving joyful thanks to the Father, who has qualified you to share in the inheritance of his holy people in the kingdom of light." [1:10-12] is a spiritual dynamic. To find other dynamics, look for sentences or phrases that can carry an "if-then". IF you live a life worthy of the Lord and please him in every way: bearing fruit in every good work, growing in the knowledge of God, being strengthened with all power according to his glorious might so that you may have great endurance and patience, and giving joyful thanks THEN the Father has qualified you to share in the inheritance of his holy people in the kingdom of light. Let's simplify that. If you live a life worthy of the Lord, and do good works, grow in Godly knowledge (in other words, lead an active Christian life), then God equips you for endurance, and has qualified you for an inheritance in the Kingdom.

Here is another dynamic: **Once you were alienated from God and were enemies in your minds because of your evil behavior. But now he has reconciled you by Christ's physical body through death to present you holy in his sight, without blemish and free from accusation— if you continue in your faith, established and firm, and do not move from the hope held out in the gospel** [1:21-23]. Restated and simplified, we have: "If you continue in faith, Christ has reconciled you and will present you free from accusation". That is truly good news for those of us who must rely on our faith.

The next one is astonishing. **Now I rejoice in what I am suffering for you, and I fill up in my flesh what is still lacking in regard to Christ's afflictions, for the sake of his body, which is the church. I have become its servant by the commission God gave me to present to you the word of God in its fullness— the mystery that has been kept hidden for ages and generations, but is now disclosed to the Lord's people** [1:24-26]. How is "the Word of God presented in fullness"? The answer is difficult to accept. It is through suffering...adding in one's own flesh "the afflictions of Christ".

Poor Laodicea. Tagged by John in Revelation [Revelations 3:14-21] as a lukewarm congregation, and one for which Paul was deeply concerned. **I want you to know how hard I am contending for you and for those at Laodicea** [2:1]. If there is a dynamic here it is this: any congregation that is self-contented will die. Any congregation that loses its zeal for the salvation of those outside its walls will die. Any congregation that is concerned with anything that hinders its focus on salvation by grace through faith will die. And this one did.

The next one is too often ignored by the modern Church: **having disarmed the powers and authorities, he made a public spectacle of them** [2:15]. How many of us consider the "powers and authorities" when we think about our Church? In the twentieth century, the main-line churches decided they didn't exist. All evidence of them was attributed to psychological disturbance. We gave up our power and gave them free-reign. The result has been a powerless Church that turned to politics rather than face its own spiritual bankruptcy. The result has been a Laodicean demise. Remember this rule: the only goal Satan has for you, is to separate you from Christ. If Satan can use a good political goal, to divide you from the spiritual battle raging around us, Satan has won the day.

Since you died with Christ to the elemental spiritual forces of this world, why, as though you still belonged to the world, do you submit to its rules: "Do not handle! Do not taste! Do not touch!"? These rules, which have to do with things that are all destined to perish with use, are based on merely human commands and teachings. Such regulations indeed have an appearance of wisdom, with their self-imposed worship, their false humility and their harsh treatment of the body, but they lack any value in restraining sensual indulgence [2:21-23].

This is a negative spiritual dynamic. Paul tells us that morality by rules doesn't work. Morality by peer pressure doesn't work. The kind of morality required of us must be internal. It isn't enough to obey the law when the cops are watching. It is what is in our heart and mind when nobody is looking that makes the difference. **Instead: Set your minds on things above, not on earthly things** [3:2].

The rest of the instructional part of the letter suggests the outward expressions of that inward righteousness: compassion, kindness, humility, gentleness and patience, God's Love and the peace of Christ.

John Calvin took one verse [3:23] from this part of the letter to develop the Protestant Work Ethic: Whatever you do, work at it with all your heart, as working for the Lord, not for human masters. Note that we are to do this because of our faith, our love for God. It is an inward thing. Calvin was essentially the ruler of Geneva. His theology became the law of the city. Isn't that an interesting contradiction? Yet here it is for us today; not part of our secular law, but still a part of our faith. Unfortunately, it is less and less a part of our faith today. We ignore its corollaries: "I will not take a full day's pay for less than a full day of Godly work" and "I will not accept recompense for anything other than my Godly labor". The first prohibits sloth, and the second gambling. But, again, it is a motive from the Love of God and love of my neighbor, rather than a regulation.

The parts of the letter which I have ignored deal mostly with the stuff of church history: who did what, when and where. One important note about Paul is found here. Apparently, Saint Mark proved himself after having caused the separation of Paul and Barnabas [Acts 15:37-39]. **Aristarchus my fellow prisoner greets you, as does Mark the cousin of Barnabas, concerning whom you have received instructions—if he comes to you, welcome him** [Colossians 4:10. This is further demonstrated by 2 Timothy 4:11]**; he** [Mark] **is useful in my ministry.**

FIRST THESSALONIANS

Paul's visit to Thessaloniki was part of one of the most important "turning points" in human history. As recounted in Acts [Acts 16:6-10]. Thessaloniki is very near Philippi. Paul's work in those little communities marks the change from Christianity being a small middle-eastern cult to the beginning of a world-spanning faith. These two little communities were possibly the first "European" churches. And so, this letter is an account of the Gospel he preached there. And, as such, is the pattern for us today.

Paul's experience in Philippi had not been happy. You know, brothers and sisters, that our visit to you was not without results. We had previously suffered and been treated outrageously in Philippi, as you know, but with the help of our God we dared to tell you his gospel in the face of strong opposition [1 Thess. 2:1-2 (NIV)]. They, apparently, had accused him of selfish motives in his appeal [1 Thess. 2:3-6]. He defended himself saying, Instead, **we were gentle among you. Just as a nursing mother cares for her children, so we cared for you** [1 Thess. 2:7-8]. As a result, the people of this congregation had "become God-Loved" [agapētoi]. People are eventually able to discern whether the good news is proclaimed to them by someone who seriously values them, or is self-interested. - And there is no lack of the latter. Perhaps that is why Paul refused to depend on his "authority" [1 Thess. 2:6] or flattery.

The other side of his insight is that, out of a surplus of God's Love [agape], we are called to express the Good News without regard for its authoritative truth. The Truth of God is what it is. Those who hear may accept or reject according to their own interests. The Truth remains the Truth.

Indeed, Paul's visit to Thessaloniki was very short [only a few weeks according to Acts 17:1-10]. But he was so successful in converting some of the Jews from adherence to the traditional Jewish faith to this "new" Gospel, along with a number of Gentiles, that he had to escape to Berea [Acts 17:1-10].

Undoubtedly, that "stub" of a congregation remembered the risks he had taken to present them with the Gospel of Salvation. And they honored him.

From Athens he sent this letter to his "children" in Thessaloniki. It had not been a long separation, and his intention was to reinforce what he had preached. He had tried again and again to go back to visit them, but Satan interfered [1 Thess. 2:18]. We may infer that those who had stirred up resentment toward Paul were continually active. It was simply too dangerous for Paul to return. And so, he sent Timothy in his place. Timothy had returned with the news that the congregation had continued faithfully [1 Tess. 3:6].

Whether this letter is a blend of two or not is of no consequence. What is before today's Christian is Paul's message.

He was concerned with sexual immorality. We may believe that the pagan culture was promiscuous. Christians must not be so. He demanded that each Christian man view adultery as a violation of God's Love toward his brother. Each Christian woman should see adultery as a violation of God's Love toward a sister [1 Thess. 4:6]. And the penalty is the loss of the Holy Spirit.

He was concerned about grief [1 Thess. 4:13-18]. We may infer that some of the original band had died, probably through violent persecution [1 Thess. 4:13], because it had been such a short time since Paul had fled the city. But from this we have gleaned the doctrine of the rapture. Not only has the Christian the comforting hope of resurrection for those who have passed away, Paul believed that all true believers would soon rise to meet Christ in His Return [1 Thess. 4:16-17].

And this observation led him to expound on the Second Coming of Christ.

His first point is that he does not know when it will happen [1 Thess. 5:1-4]. Christ will surprise the world, as labor pains arrive without warning [1 Thess. 5:3], or as "a thief" [1 Thess. 5:4].

His second point is that while the pagans do not expect Christ's Return, we Christians are aware of the promise and ought to be ready [1 Thess. 5:6, 8-10].

His "therefore" in chapter five, is not the emphatic parakaleo. He used the ordinary dio [1 Thess. 5:11], as if to say that his instructions simply follow this readiness as water from a spring. His instructions are that Christians ought to build each other up [1 Thess. 5:11], acknowledge those who continue to work at their daily jobs [1 Thess. 5:12]. Some commentaries suggest that, because of Paul's doctrine of the Second Coming of Christ, some members of the community had given up daily pursuits. They were idle while awaiting the rapture. Paul would not countenance such a life-style. He also urged them to live in peace with each other [1 Thess. 5:13], admonish the idle and troublemaker [1 Thess. 5:14], and **"Rejoice always, pray continually, give thanks in all circumstances; for this is God's will for you in Christ Jesus. Do not quench the Spirit. Do not treat prophecies with contempt but test them all; hold on to what is good, reject every kind of evil"** [1 Thess. 5:16-22]. With that, the God of peace will sanctify, that is, make and keep holy, all of His faithful people.

Thus, this letter is a reproduction of the Truth he proclaimed there during those few weeks of his ministry.

SECOND THESSALONIANS

Let us deal with the "plan of God" as Paul expressed it to the congregation at Thessalonica (today: Thessaloniki). While many like to concentrate on the apocalyptic doctrine that flows from this letter, we really ought to consider at it in the context of why Paul wrote this letter, and what was happening to the faithful recipients.

In plain words; the Christians in Thessalonica were being martyred. Paul had spent only three weeks in the city before he fled for his life [Acts 17:1-9]. That some of them were being persecuted and possibly martyred is an inescapable implication of Paul's first letter to them [1 Thess. 2:14-16]. And so also in his second missive. Paul expressed his admiration for them. He was aware that, should he return to the city, he would quickly join them in the ultimate persecution. And so, all he could do was to encourage them at a distance.

The "plan of God" begins with suffering: **We are not trying to please people, but God who tests our hearts** [2 Thess. 2:4]. Suffering for Christ has a two-fold purpose. It is the ultimate witness to the worth of Christ, and it is the means by which God tests His Saints. Indeed, according to St. John, those who pass the test of martyrdom have a very special place in Heaven [Revelation 6:9-11]. St. Paul wanted to give encouragement to his congregation. He wrote that God is just and will pay back trouble to those who were the persecutors [2 Thess. 1:6]. He wrote that the faithful will share in the Glory of Christ when He returns [2 Thess. 1:9-10].

It may well be true that the doctrine of the Second Coming was given great emphasis among the people of the Early Church because of their sufferings and martyrdom. The "Greek World" did not give the Good News a fond welcome. That the apocalyptic portions of the Bible continue to be much favored in many places may be because that persecution continues to this day. Christians continue to be the most persecuted people on Earth.

Equally, those who are not persecuted, and those who doubt the doctrine of the Second Coming, usually generalize the doctrine to give a different kind of moral encouragement. Their emphasis tends toward the general principle that patience, morality, and goodness will "win out in the end".

However, a clear interpretation of Paul's letter requires that we take seriously what he wrote. For our persecuted family, we must pray, earnestly and often [2 Tess. 1:11 (NIV)]. With this in mind, we constantly pray for you, that our God may make you worthy of his calling, and that by his power he may bring to fruition your every desire for goodness and your every deed prompted by faith.

We, who are seldom if ever, persecuted ought not play the silly game of, "This part of Scripture is inspired and true, while that part is not". The result will always be the weakening of our proclamation.

A liberal pastor once said, "I want to make the Gospel accessible to more people"; by which he meant that he wanted to reach people who didn't accept that there is such a thing as a Holy Spirit, or that God is really involved in one's life. To him, the Gospel was simply a lofty moral code. Paul would have utter disdain for such ideas. Paul understood the nature of the conflict between the Kingdom of God and the kingdoms of this world. He experienced the worldly powers, and he knew the Heavenly Power.

Thus, Paul anticipated an early return of the Christ. Indeed, his encouragement to the persecuted congregation at Thessalonica leaned heavily on the doctrine. He emphasized it enough that some of the members had given up their daily pursuits. And so, Paul had to correct them. He had not claimed that the Day of the Lord had already come [2 Thess. 2:1-2]. Indeed, he continued, a rebellion, a falling away [apostasies], from which we have apostacy, or rejection of the True Faith], led by a "man of Sin" [2 Thess. 2:3]. He will oppose and will exalt himself over everything that is called [edit]a god or object that is worshipped, so that he sets himself up in God's temple, proclaiming himself to be God [2 Thess. 2:4 (NIV)]. In a time when the Emperor claimed to be a god, such an assumption could easily have been believed. Also today, when we discuss "the Antichrist", we often assert that he (or she) may be a world leader of some sort. His tactics are easy to predict: **The coming of the lawless one will be in accordance with how Satan works. He will use all sorts of displays of power through signs and wonders that serve the lie, and all the ways that wickedness deceives those who are perishing. They perish because they refused to love the truth and so be saved** [2 Thess. 9-10].

But we must rejoice because we are Paul's brothers and sisters loved by the Lord, **because God chose you as first-fruits to be saved through the sanctifying work of the Spirit and through belief in the truth** [2 Thess. 2:13].

Do you see how meaningless this whole letter must seem to those who reduce Christianity to a moral community? They have no idea of the actual sanctifying work of the Holy Spirit. To them "belief in the truth" consists only of an intellectual assent. That leaves it open for debate, doesn't it? But Paul and his followers were faced with an evil much more deadly than the debate of dilatants in a college. To them, belief in Christ was gained only at deadly peril. But they were not discouraged, because they knew Him in whom they gave their full measure of trust.

FIRST TIMOTHY

Much of the New Testament is intended to instruct a second and third generation of Christian leaders [1 Timothy 3:15 ...you will know how people ought to conduct themselves in God's household, which is the church of the living God, the pillar and foundation of the truth.]. The Acts of the Apostles is a book of transitions. Jude is a repudiation of Jewish-Christian leaders who did not display the Presence of the Holy Spirit. First Timothy is a textbook for the organization and policies of the increasingly complex Gentile Christian Community. It is, also, Paul's "charge to that next generation" in the name of Timothy.

Saint John seems to have repudiated some of the second-generation leaders because they were teaching an early form of Gnosticism. Just as did John in his letters, so Paul seems to have had issues with some of the early second-generation leaders, though it is too early for Gnostic ideas. Among them he named Hymenaeus and Alexander [1 Timothy 1:20]. They had, apparently, legalist attitudes, while Paul's understanding of grace suggested: holding on to faith and a good conscience [1 Timothy 1:19].

Paul stated the issue succinctly: **The goal of this command is love** [agape]**, which comes from a pure heart and a good conscience and a sincere** [GK: anupokritos (an-oo-pok'-ree-tos); unhypocritical, unfeigned] **faith. Some**

have departed from these and have turned to meaningless talk. They want to be teachers of the law, but they do not know what they are talking about or what they so confidently affirm [1 Timothy 1:5-7].

His opposition was based on his understanding of law and grace. Did they require obedience to the Law of Moses? Most likely so. But that modifies his statement about the purpose of law [1 Timothy 1:9-11]. **"We also know that the law is made not for the righteous but for lawbreakers and rebels, the ungodly and sinful, the unholy and irreligious",** ought to be the completed sentence. But he continued with a partial list of sinful and unholy people: sexually immoral, practicing homosexuals, slave traders [This is interesting in view of his expressed tolerance of the practice of slavery, though modified by demands for good treatment of slaves. He apparently did not approve of "trading" human beings.], **parricides, and perjurers** [1 Timothy 1:10-11]. The list is incomplete and intended as examples, not as a doctrinal list. There are certainly other sins that could be added. As examples, they do not achieve a high level of doctrinal authority. One may be any of those, and still be granted God's saving grace through Christ Jesus. They are not the unforgivable sins, and they do not bar one from salvation.

Indeed, Paul put himself in that list. **Even though I was once a blasphemer and a persecutor and a violent man, I was shown mercy because I acted in ignorance and unbelief. The grace of our Lord was poured out on me abundantly, along with the faith and love that are in Christ Jesus** [1 Timothy 1:13-14].

His purpose in listing those awful sins was to exalt the power of the "grace of our Lord"! Paul expressed the purpose of Christ in an unforgettable verse: **Here is a trustworthy saying that deserves full acceptance: Christ Jesus came into the world to save sinners—of whom I am the worst** [1 Timothy 1:15]. The legalists could have had no lucid response to his criticism if they accepted his premise.

The charge to the next generation includes prayer for great sinners like kings and government officials [1 Timothy 2:1-2]. But not for their own sake. This is a minor, but important, "in-order-that", of which Saint Paul was very fond. It was in-order-that the Christian Community might live in peace without fear. Unfortunately, we know that the prayer was not answered in the way Paul hoped.

Along with that prayer, Paul hoped that quiet and un-troubling behavior would help avoid trouble with the authorities. Men should pray, women should bedeck themselves with modesty [something our generation of Christians ought rediscover], decency, and good deeds, rather than with jewelry and silks [1 Timothy 2:8-10]. Remember, this is an "in-order-that" recommendation. It is one we should take seriously. It is not a new law.

One of the errors contemporary Christians often make, it they take these verses out of context, is a prohibition of women having any kind of teaching or authority in the church. When our translators parse verses using "woman" they ignore the plain Greek meaning of wife and husband [1 Timothy 2:11-12]. A better translation is: **A wife should learn in quietness and full submission. I do not permit a woman to teach or to assume authority over a husband** [1 Timothy 2:11-12; Gk: anér (an'-ayr), a man, a husband]. Again, remember this is an in-order-that. It is not a new law.

[An aside: I have been the recipient of some very bad female leadership; bishop, district superintendent, associate pastor, and lay members of committees. I have also experienced bad leadership and erroneous decisions by men. It seems to me that humility, wisdom, and ability is more important than gender.]

Also on the subject of leadership, Paul addressed a very important topic. What kind of person should have episcopal authority over a congregation? **Now the overseer** [Gk: episkopé, i.e., bishop, synonymous to elder] **is to be above reproach, faithful to his wife, temperate, self-controlled, respectable, hospitable, able to teach, not given to drunkenness, not violent but gentle, not quarrelsome, not a lover of money. He must manage his own family well and see that his children obey him, and he must do so in a manner worthy of full respect** [1 Timothy 3:2-4; "respect" Gk: semnotés (sem-not'-ace) seriousness, dignity, honor, gravity]. **He must not be a recent convert, or he may become conceited and fall under the same judgment as the devil** [1 Timothy 3:6-7].

Viewing the multitudinous variations in the organization of denominations and congregations, one is tempted to affirm again that this is an in-order-that. **He must also have a good reputation with outsiders, so that he will not fall into disgrace and into the devil's trap** [1 Timothy 3:7]. Disgrace? With whom? Surely not just within the congregation, though that is bad enough. The aim is for the church to be quietly present within the larger population. Scandal within the congregation reflects badly and will prevent good evangelistic outreach.

The practice in the Methodist Church [1939-1968] was to ordain first as deacon and after a time of testing and further education and training, a second ordination as elder. And even with that, of the twenty men with whom I was ordained a deacon, after ten years I was one of two still serving in the pulpit. Clearly, the deaconate is an important testing ground. In the same way, deacons are to be worthy of respect. They must first be tested; and then if there is nothing against them, let them serve as deacons [1 Timothy 3:8 and 10]. But a greater issue than the trust placed in them by the congregation is the reputation of the entire church reflected in their service.

This is made clear by Paul. Not only does he address the reputation of bishops and deacons, he stipulated that the women [probably refers to wives of deacons] are to be worthy of respect. And that is for the same reason. That he referred to deacon's wives is clear because the next sentence regards the marital fidelity of deacons (and I suppose elders and bishops too).

The case is made about the behavior and reputation of the church leadership, but I doubt very much that all who read the epistle also understood that it applies to each member of the church.

Among the false teachings (of Hymenaeus and Alexander [1 Timothy 1:20]?) was a renunciation of marriage. They taught that the [general] Resurrection had already occurred [2 Timothy 2:17; Paul named a third: Philetus]. Some have seen this as part of the growing heresy called Gnosticism. The Gnostics believed themselves to be spiritual beings, freed from the illusion of flesh. Later the Gnostics would teach that this life is an evil illusion which interferes with understanding ourselves as god. Other scholars have taught that ascetics (ala Essenes etc.) were infiltrating the congregations. I reject both in view of what Paul wrote to the Corinthian church [1 Corinthians 7]. His concern was two-fold. First, he wrote, **What I mean, brothers and sisters, is that the time is short** [1 Corinthians 7:29]. **Married or not, the goal is that you may live in a right way in undivided devotion to the Lord** [1 Corinthians 7:35]. Instead of their false renunciation, Paul affirmed that **everything God created is good, and nothing is to be rejected if it is received with thanksgiving, because it is consecrated by the word of God and prayer** [1 Timothy 4:4-5].

In a different, more general way, Paul answered a question that has vexed Christians from the earliest days. Why should I make the moral sacrifices and endure the limitations of the Christian life, if I am confident that my sins are forgiven in the grace of Christ? Not only should all church leaders understand, this is true for all of us: **we labor and strive, because we have put our hope in the living God, who is the Savior of all people, and especially of those who believe** [1 Timothy 4:10].

Not to disparage or even differ with the great Apostle, I think it wise to affirm that the disciplines of Christian life have their own reward in the here and now. I once asked my octogenarian pastor-father whether "the sacrifices of the Christian life (e.g., tithing, abstinence, etc.-) were worth it". He spent two weeks considering the question and then answered "yes". That has been my experience also, as I approach the status of octogenarian. Not just "pie in the sky bye and bye" but the "joy of the Holy Spirit day by day".

The rest of the letter concerns itself with the dignity and fairness Timothy owes to others. The one passage that gives pause for consideration is toward the end: **The elders who direct the affairs of the church well are worthy of double honor, especially those whose work is preaching and teaching. For Scripture says, "Do not muzzle an ox while it is treading out the grain"** [Deuteronomy 25:4] **and "The worker deserves his wages"** [Luke 10:7]. **Do not entertain an accusation against an elder unless it is brought by two or three witnesses. But those elders who are sinning, you are to reprove before everyone, so that the others may take warning. I charge you, in the sight of God and Christ Jesus and the elect angels, to keep these instructions without partiality, and to do nothing out of favoritism** [1 Timothy 5:17-21].

This is the issue of the place of clergy in the church. By contextual association, the "double honor" means a double wage. We have experience in modern times. It seems the church was more effective when pastor salaries were on the lower end of middle class. Wealth seems to compromise the willingness to go where one is needed. Comfort seems to rule out sacrifice. As the wealth of the clergy has increased, the honor attributed by society has decreased. Clergy today are seen as "professionals" and are due no more honor than a dentist or a lawyer.

Today clergy are more subject to public condemnation for sexual sins and/or gender discrimination. In the past, discipline was behind closed doors, and public scandals few. It may be that the Church failed in its duty to protect the congregation from clergy violations; however, one must wonder whether the Church is stronger because of the present litigious process.

My sense is that honor is earned. Clergy, as a group, will be given honor when it is deserved because of the sacrifices required. Honor may also be extended to individuals for effectiveness. And, perhaps over time, the clergy will be so aware of the penalties for sin that its incidence will be restricted. The Church may grow stronger as a result. In the meantime, as congregations grow smaller, salaries are of necessity growing smaller. And that may well increase the willingness of the public to take note of services rendered sacrificially.

Our Bible editors have ended the chapter with an apropos adage: **The sins of some are obvious, reaching the place of judgment ahead of them; the sins of others trail behind them. In the same way, good deeds are obvious, and even those that are not obvious cannot remain hidden forever** [1 Timothy 5:24-25].

I wonder whether in Paul's mind, clergy were "slaves of Christ". He mixes the advice about clergy with advice about slaves. It could be that, in his mind, both served under compulsion and mostly in poverty. Of course, Paul could also be simply observing a list of contemporary issues. The subject that connects them all (widows, clergy, and slaves) is contentment in the time of waiting for the Second Coming.

But godliness with contentment is great gain. For we brought nothing into the world, and we can take nothing out of it. But if we have food and clothing, we will be content with that. Those who want to get rich fall into temptation and a trap and into many foolish and harmful desires that plunge people into ruin and destruction. For the love of money is a root of all kinds of evil. Some people, eager for money, have wandered from the faith and pierced themselves with many griefs [1 Timothy 6:6-10].

Paul's final charge to Timothy rightly applies to all Christians. But you, man of God, flee from all this, and pursue righteousness, godliness, faith, love, endurance and gentleness. Fight the good fight of the faith. Take hold of the eternal life to which you were called when you made your good confession [Jesus is Lord] in the presence of many witnesses [1 Timothy 6:11-12].

SECOND TIMOTHY

Saint Paul's farewell address to his adoptive son, Timotheo, reveals much about how the Christian faith was, and is supposed to, be passed from one to another; and from one generation to another. The key is in one proper noun: The Holy Spirit. **For this reason I remind you to fan into flame the gift of God, which is in you through the laying on of my hands. For the Spirit God gave us does not make us timid, but gives us power, love [agape] and self-discipline** [2 Timothy 1:6-7].

Paul "laid hands on" Timothy, and prayed that he receive the Holy Spirit. We have learned by experience since then, that Jesus is the baptizer, and the laying on of hands is not an absolute requirement. And, unfortunately, the Church has separated the laying on of hands, and the reception of God's Holy Spirit. What is apparent in this letter is that the Holy Spirit is the "necessary ingredient", and not just the laying on of hands.

Often, the laying on of hands facilitates the indwelling of the Spirit, but not always. The Spirit has Its own Will, and so does the person on whom hands have been laid. The evidence must present itself before one may adjudge the recipient. Those evidences include "power, Love [agape], and self-discipline".

If the leaders of the Church are to properly express the Gospel, and properly guide the fellowship, those evidences must be present. **Rather, join with me in suffering for the gospel, by the power of God. He has saved us and called us to a holy life—not because of anything we have done but because of his own purpose and grace** [2 Timothy 1:8-9].

Was suffering one of the evidences? Is that the same as being so obnoxious as to provoke abuse? Probably not. The Gospel, even gently but truthfully presented, will be opposed. Indeed, it is opposed in the churches today, just as it was in the time of Paul and Timothy. And it was those within the fellowship whose opposition caused the suffering to which the Great Apostle directed Timothy's attention.

Paul wrote that: **I was appointed a herald and an apostle and a teacher. That is why I am suffering as I am** [2 Timothy 1:11-12]. Why does it seem apropos to put the emphasis on "herald"? Paul was one shouting his faith in the agora. He seldom waited for permission to speak.

An aside: I conversed with a Muslim from India, who was raised in a Christian Mission School. He was aggressively evangelistic about his faith. He said, "Even some of your scholars say Jesus wasn't raised from the dead!" The proper response would have been, "But they are not Christians. Only we who know the Risen Lord and have received His Spirit, are Christians". But that does not typically come to the mind of a tolerant American Christian. It would be, in our mind, impolite.

What is Timothy to speak? **What you heard from me, keep as the pattern of sound Spirit** [Gk: Logon]**, with faith and love** [Gk: agape] **in Christ Jesus** [2 Timothy 1:13].

Guard the good deposit that was entrusted to you—guard it with the help of the Holy Spirit who lives in us [2 Timothy 1:14]. What is the "good deposit" if not the True Gospel? And, how is it guarded? Only by the Holy Spirit's assistance.

Paul's letter provided advice to Timothy about how to pass the baton on to the third generation of church leaders. Timothy was to pass on to reliable people who will also be qualified to teach others, **the things you have heard me say** [2 Timothy 2:2]. But then he returned to the subject of suffering: **Join with me in suffering, like a good soldier of Christ Jesus** [2 Timothy 2:3]. One of the truest of maxims is that "the army most willing to suffer will be victorious".

However, Paul presented the "carrot" as well as offering the "way of suffering". **The hardworking farmer should be the first to receive a share of the crops** [2 Timothy 2:6]. The "share of the crops", to which he referred, should not be associated with earthly wealth. It is the Heavenly reward due a worker in God's Vineyard.

Paul compared the theologians' practice of arguing about words (as I do) to his instruction that Timothy be a worthy teacher; that is one who rightly handles the Spirit of Truth [2 Timothy 2:15; Gk: logon; The contrast is between academic theorizing and practical expression of God's Spirit].

How may we evaluate today's candidates for leadership in the Church? One measure, according to the Apostle, is the nature of their life. Have they matured and turned away from the common obsessions of youth [2 Timothy 2:22-25]? His/her teaching methodology must be gentle and wise, just as the Spirit is gentle and wise. They must have a clear understanding of the possible sacrifices and suffering the future may bring in an increasingly anti-Christ world.

Indeed, St. Paul pointed to the Timothy's future: **There will be terrible times in the last days. People will be lovers of themselves, lovers of money, boastful, proud, abusive, disobedient to their parents, ungrateful, unholy, without love, unforgiving, slanderous, without self-control, brutal, not lovers of the good, treacherous, rash, conceited, lovers of pleasure rather than lovers of God— having a form of godliness but denying its power** [2 Timothy 3:1-5].

One must define the "last days". Paul expected Timothy to live them. History has given us a different view. The "last days", for us, must mean "now". And history has illustrated the world's antipathy toward Christ and His people.

Verses six through nine are a denunciation of wicked teachers who use guilt to gain immoral advantage. In the context of both the letters to Timothy, Paul was probably addressing the issue of Gnosticism again. The amoral implications could be terribly destructive. Their presence seems to have been, historically, universal. There has never been a time when the Church was free of charlatans. Nor has there ever been a moment free of persecution. Paul set out a spiritual dynamic of fundamental importance, when he wrote: **In fact, everyone** [especially clergy, see 3:17 "servant of God"] **who wants to live a godly life in Christ Jesus will be persecuted, while evildoers and impostors will go from bad to worse, deceiving and being deceived** [2 Timothy 3:12-13]. The antidote for this poison is the written word of God: **All Scripture is God-breathed and is useful for teaching, rebuking, correcting and training in righteousness, so that the servant of God** [lit. "man of God" e.g., clergy] **may be thoroughly equipped for every good work** [2 Timothy 3:16-17].

Paul's deepest hope was that his adoptive son would carry on his efforts. He anticipated serious opposition because of what he had already suffered. And Church Tradition holds that Timothy was martyred in 97 A.D. He was beaten by a mob engaged in a Dionysian celebration. He was Episkopé of Ephesus and would have known that St. John had recently (95 A.D.) been exiled to Patmos. That would be the beginning of the persecution ordered by Domitian. Not only Paul, but Timothy too, **fought the good fight, ...finished the race, ...kept the faith. Now there [was] in store for [them] the crown of righteousness, which the Lord, the righteous Judge, ...award[ed] to [them] on that day—**; but the promise continues: **and not only to [them], but also to all who have longed for his appearing** [2 Timothy 4:7-8 edited].

TITUS

Titus was a contemporary "son" of Saint Paul. He held a place higher than Timothy. He was an assistant to Paul from the earliest days of the Apostle's Christian ministry. Paul took note of his company during the Apostle's "second trip" to Jerusalem [Galatians 2:2]. His presence in Jerusalem was notable because, even though he was Greek, circumcision was not required of him [Galatians 2:3]. Sometimes he was Paul's "Area Advance Manager". For instance, when Paul arrived in Troas, he was discomfited by the absence of Titus, and so went on to Macedonia [2 Corinthians 2:12-14] even though the opportunities in Troas were promising. In Macedonia, God, who consoles the downcast, consoled us by the arrival of Titus [2 Cor 7:5-6].

Such was Paul's estimation of Titus that it was he who carried the Corinthian letters from Paul. And he was placed in charge of the great offering for the "Poor in Jerusalem". However, a serious objection arose in that congregation, becoming the basis for one of the later letters embedded in Second Corinthians. Someone accused Paul of using Titus to raise money the Apostle intended to divert to his own use. **Here I am, ready to come to you this third time. And I will not be a burden, because I do not want what is yours but you; for children ought not to lay up for their parents, but parents for their children. I will most gladly spend and be spent for you. If I love you more, am I to be loved less? Let it be assumed that I did not burden you. Nevertheless (you say) since I was crafty, I took you in by deceit. Did I take advantage of you through any of those whom I sent to you? I urged Titus to go, and sent the brother with him. Titus did not take advantage of you, did he? Did we not conduct ourselves with the same spirit** [2 Cor 12:14-18]? The issue was resolved, and Titus returned to the task [2 Corinthians 8:5-7].

Later, Titus made an exploratory solo mission trip up the Dalmatian Coast into what is now Croatia [2 Timothy 4:10].

Titus's final place of service was Crete. Paul left him in Crete and the Apostle continued on to Rome and his death. It is to Titus in Crete that this letter was sent.

Church Tradition suggests that he was the first episkopé of Crete. This letter seems to be his "brief" or his instructional credentials. The Early Church leaders must have thought a lot about organization. Paul, in his Corinthian correspondence wrote much about how the tasks ought to be divided according to God given abilities [see 1 Corinthians 12]. Paul made a great distinction between "spiritual gifts" and ordinary, every-day jobs. But the spiritual gifts were necessary before one could understand his or her "calling". And, misapplied spiritual gifts compromised the performance of those callings. One who was called to works of charity was not expected to be a teacher or an evangelist.

This letter is extremely important to one who wishes to understand how Titus was to organize the Christians on the island of Crete.

The Early Church naturally copied from the Jewish tradition. The Sanhedrin was comprised of "male elders", and each synagogue was ordered by "male elders", and so, each fellowship was to be regulated by elders [presbuteros; one advanced in age and experience, implies wisdom]. What is most notable in these instructions is that the word "presubteros" (elders) and "episkopé" seem to be used interchangeably. In our English usage, that would mean that elders and bishops are the same order of leader, and that each elder is equal to that of an episkopé. The distinction seems to be, that elders are plural, and episkopé is singular. In other words, each congregation may have had more than one elder, but only one bishop. Was the bishop the "senior pastor"? And, if so, might he have charged one or more of his elders to lead a second or third fellowship while continuing under the direction of the singular episkopé? Titus may well have exercised authority over the more than sixty fellowships on the island [according to church tradition].

The opponent identified, against which Titus was to be vigilant, was the part of the Christian fellowship that insisted on compliance with the Law of Moses. There are many rebellious people, full of meaningless talk and deception, especially those of the circumcision group. They must be silenced, because they are disrupting whole households by teaching things they ought not to teach [Titus 1:10-11]. Paul accused them of seeking "dishonest gain" [Titus 1:11]. He must have been in a foul mood, because he went on to accuse all Cretans of dishonesty and gluttony [Titus 1:12]. His point was to distinguish between proper and improper leaders for the churches.

Appropriate leaders are sober-minded, clean-living, serious men [This is historic, not a commentary on today's ethical standards]. Indeed, all the members lived under that expectation.

The urgency of the work Paul assigned was illuminated by his expectation of the early return of Christ; **For the grace of God has appeared that offers salvation to all people. It teaches us to say "No" to ungodliness and worldly passions, and to live self-controlled, upright and godly lives in this present age, while we wait for the blessed hope—the appearing of the glory of our great God and Savior, Jesus Christ** [Titus 2:11-13].

Perhaps he realized how disparaging were his words, because he wrote a few words of humility [Titus 3:3]. In those words, he best illuminated the character he expected in a Christian. And it all derived from Christ. **He saved us through the washing of rebirth and renewal by the Holy Spirit, whom he poured out on us generously through Jesus Christ our Savior, so that, having been justified by his grace, we might become heirs having the hope of eternal life. This is a trustworthy saying. And I want you to stress these things, so that those who have trusted in God may be careful to devote themselves to doing what is good. But avoid foolish controversies and genealogies and arguments and quarrels about the law, because these are unprofitable and useless** [Titus 3:5-9].

PHILEMON

The way this letter is read in church seems, to me, to miss the profound and urgent tenor hidden in polite words. The subject is slavery. It provides the means by which we are to understand Paul's attitude toward slavery in the other letters.

First notice that Onesimus had fled his "owner" Philemon. In those times, as in our own history, a slave that flees his master is subject to some serious penalties. The penalty Onesimus faced is unknown. It would have begun with a branding of "FUG" on his forehead. "FUG" is from "fugititivs", from which we get fugitive. The penalty may also have included the lash (thirty-nine strokes would be the maximum), and possibly an iron weight attached to his ankles.

Paul, obedient to Roman law, sent him back to his "owner". Some might have seen this as an act of kindness (since the penalty for harboring a slave would fall on both Paul and Onesimus). Others will see it as an act of betrayal. But notice how Paul sent him back. Onesimus was to be a brother...no longer a slave. Paul "expected and anticipated" that Philemon would free Onesimus and allow him to serve voluntarily.

The other scriptural references we have on the subject are Ephesians 6:5 [Slaves, obey your earthly masters with respect and fear, and with sincerity of heart, just as you would obey Christ.] and 9 [masters, treat your slaves in the same way. Do not threaten them, since you know that he who is both their Master and yours is in heaven, and there is no favoritism]; Colossians 3:22 [Slaves, obey your earthly masters in everything; and do it, not only when their eye is on you and to curry their favor, but with sincerity of heart and reverence for the Lord.], and Colossians 4:1 [Masters, provide your slaves with what is right and fair, because you know that you also have a Master in heaven.] There are other passages, in his advice to Timothy, but they are absolutely consistent with these.

With these before us, we can see that anticipating a quick return of Christ, Paul did not want his readers to involve themselves in political issues. Leave everything as it is, and God will sort it out.

Now Paul was confronted with the uglier side of slavery. And still he sent Onesimus back. But the letter is not to be read with a gentle voice. Paul was angry with Philemon, and lent him some heat. He sent it as today we might send a memo, with carbon copies to witnesses. The gist of it is this: "Philemon, I brought Christ to you, by whom you are freed from slavery to sin its death penalty. I taught you that you ought to treat Onesimus as a dear brother. You have treated him badly enough that he ran away from you. I send him back expecting you to free him of obligation, simply because you owe me more than the property value of Onesimus. See to it! The grace of Christ to you...."

I have removed all the extra words to make the letter more like a modern memo.

1Paul, and Timothy, To Philemon:

Cc: Apphia and Archippus, and the church:

3 Grace and peace to you [plural] from God our Father and the Lord Jesus Christ.

I always remember you [singular for the rest of the letter] in my prayers. I hear about your love [Gk: agape] **for people. 6 I pray that your partnership with us in the faith may be effective** [Gk: energés (en-er-gace'); may function properly, producing the correct outcome]. **7 Your love** [Gk: agape] **has given me great joy. You, brother, have refreshed the hearts of the Lord's people.**

8 Therefore [Gk: dio; tentative conclusion, "wherefore"], **though I could order you to do what you ought, 9 I prefer to appeal to you on the basis of love** [Gk: agape]. **It is Paul 10 that appeal** [Gk: paracaleo; emphatic therefore] **to you for Onesimus** [means "useful"]. **11 Formerly he was useless to you, but now he has become useful. 12 I am sending him back to you. 13 I would have liked to keep him with me. 14 I did not want to do anything to appear as "of necessity", rather that any favor you do would appear to be voluntary. 15 Perhaps the reason he was separated from you for a little while was that you might have him back forever** [Gk: aiónios (ahee-o'-nee-os) eternally] **— 16 no longer as a slave, but better than as a slave, rather as a dear brother. He is very dear to me, even dearer to you, as a fellow and a brother in the Lord.**

17 So, welcome him as you would welcome me. 18 If he has wronged you in anything, charge it to me. 19 I, Paul, am writing this with my own hand. I will pay it back—not to mention that you owe me your very self. 20 I do wish, brother, that I may have some profit from you in the Lord. 21 I write to you, knowing that you will do even more than I ask.

22 I hope to be restored to you.

23 Epaphras sends you greetings. 24 Also Mark, Aristarchus, Demas and Luke.

25 The grace of the Lord Jesus Christ be with your spirit.

HEBREWS

Some scholars think Hebrews was written by Barnabas [Cf. Tertullian's De Pudicitia, 20]. I think so to. The theology of the book is similar, but not identical to that of St. Paul, whom Barnabas mentored. The differences, I think may be due to the differing emphasis of the two Apostles. Barnabas was more concerned than Paul to adapt the Gospel to the needs of the Jewish/Hebrew people.

The author introduced his rationale for this new faith by saying that God had sent His Son, through whom the universe was created. Therefore we, Hebrews/Jews, ought to "pay attention" [Hebrews 2:1] because penalties exist for failure to embrace so great a salvation [Hebrews 2:3]. But that is not the end of it. God has proven this good news by signs, wonders and various miracles, and by gifts of the Holy Spirit [Hebrews 2:4].

His technique was that of a rabbi. He "proof-texted" the books we call the Old Testament.

Psalm eight, he insisted was proof that the Creator had put all of nature under the authority of humanity [Lit Heb: "man", masculine noun], but that not all of nature responded to man's authority. For instance, "death". Man has no authority over death. And so, Jesus was sent by the Creator to "taste death" on behalf of humanity [Hebrews 2:9]; so that by his death he might break the power of him who holds the power of death—that is, the devil— and free those who all their lives were held in slavery by their fear of death [Hebrews 2:14-15].

Here is a cute twist. Jesus had to become fully human in order to become a priest: fully human in every way, in order that he might become a merciful and faithful high priest in service to God, and that he might make atonement for the sins of the people [Hebrews 2:17].

The use of the word "apostle" [Hebrews 3:1] in reference to Jesus, is not the same as when applied to The Eleven or Paul. Here the definition is "one who is sent". Its use is appropriate, though confusing, in that the others were commissioned and sent by, and in service to, Jesus.

Barnabas suggested that Jesus was superior to Moses [Hebrews 3:3] in that Moses was a servant in "the house", but Jesus is the "son" in the house [Hebrews 3:5-6]. Barnabas, writing on behalf of the Holy Spirit quoted Psalm 95, in which the Psalmist begged the Hebrew People to not quarrel or test God [Psalm

95:8]. To do so invalidates the promise. Just as the people following Moses were denied entry into the Promised Land by their disobedience, so refusal to accept that Jesus is the Son would result in denial into this new Promised Land, i.e., "God's Rest", or, Heaven [Hebrews 3:11]. "Unbelief" locks one out of God's rest [Hebrews 3:19]. They had the "good news" of release from slavery in Egypt, and now his readers have had the "good news" of release from slavery to death.

Perhaps the confusion about Hebrews is due to Barnabas' tendency to leap from one conclusion to another, all of which are foreign to our understanding. A case in point is the jump from the promise of the Holy Land (Israel), to the promise of a new "holy land": Heaven; with Sabbath as the definition [Hebrews 4:1-7]. The common theme is "rest". The Exodus ended in the "rest" of the Holy Land. God "rested" from His labors on the Seventh Day. And our "rest" is to be Heaven.

Barnabas saw that even with Sabbath in Israel, the Hebrew did not fully rest. Only when all our "works" are done shall we rest. The same was true with the Hebrew. There remains, then, a Sabbath-rest for the people of God; for anyone who enters God's rest also rests from their works, just as God did from his [Hebrews 4:9-10]. That "Sabbath-rest" is Heaven.

The big problem is that we are sinners. We make "every effort" [Hebrews 4:11], and we fall short. A judgment awaits us. Everything is uncovered and laid bare before the eyes of him to whom we must give account [Hebrews 4:13]. We, therefore, require an offering of atonement. Barnabas assumed that this is so apparent, he needn't write it. He simply went on.

His "therefore" is like that of Saint Paul. In this case it is a preliminary "therefore" [Gk: oun, "by extension"], but it is a pointer, a "see this"! **Therefore, since we have a great high priest who has ascended into heaven, Jesus the Son of God, let us hold firmly to the faith we profess. For we do not have a high priest who is unable to empathize with our weaknesses, but we have one who has been tempted in every way, just as we are—yet he did not sin. Let us then approach God's throne of grace with confidence, so that we may receive mercy and find grace to help us in our time of need** [Hebrews 4:14-16].

Now, Barnabas turned to the definition of the Priest who is able to make a sufficient sacrifice on behalf of our sins.

As a pastor, (since Christ there are no priests; only those who claim to be priests) I find the next passage comforting. **Every high priest is selected from among the people and is appointed to represent the people in matters related to God, to offer gifts and sacrifices for sins. He is able to deal gently with those who are ignorant and are going astray, since he himself is subject to weakness. This is why he has to offer sacrifices for his own sins, as well as for the sins of the people. And no one takes this honor on himself, but he receives it when called by God, just as Aaron was** [Hebrews 5:1-4]. Aware of my own weakness and sin, I do (of necessity) have a "gentle" attitude toward the sins of others. Even those of which I am not guilty, I will say, "There, but for the grace of God, go I" [Attributed to Rev. John Bradford, martyred 1555; George Whitefield, etc.]. I suspect Barnabas felt the same way.

Barnabas, however, made a distinction between Jesus and all other priests. He wrote that Jesus was a priest according to [Hebrews 5:6; Gk: kata, meaning "down from", "along the way"] the order of Melchizedek [Hebrews 5:5]. Melchizedek was a resident of Salem (later Jerusalem) to whom Abraham gave a tenth of the booty he had collected after rescuing Lot from Chedorlaomer of Elam [Genesis 14]. He offered Abraham bread and wine. He was a "Priest of the Most High" [Genesis 14:18], but he was a priest in an order of one. There were no others noted. Scripture notes no predecessor, and none after him, though that might be a modern interpretation. More to the point is that Melchizedek was a priest of "the Most High", as was Jesus.

All priests receive authority from one who has held that authority. But Jesus' Authority came directly from God, who designated [Hebrews 5:10; Gk: prosagoreuó, (pros-ag-or-yoo'-o), called by name] him such.

Barnabas was frustrated by the apparent lack of understanding by those whom he addressed [Hebrews 5:10-14]. Perhaps he didn't understand why his teaching is confusing. At any rate, he set aside these "fundamental" underpinnings of his Gospel in order to teach about the Holy Spirit. It seemed to identify these teachings as of greater importance than the prior. He pointedly did not want to discuss the rituals of the new Christ Community [Hebrews 6:1-2; especially re: baptism, cleansing rites]. Instead, he wanted to focus on the errors of the Jewish legalists who insisted on obedience to the entire Law of Moses.

Those who, after having received the Holy Spirit, and experienced direct, personal, communication from God [Hebrews 6:5: "word" Lit Gk: rhema], and then insist on the efficacy of ritual (or salvation by magic formula) are beyond salvation [Hebrews 6:4-6]. But then he "goes back on his word" to say that God is merciful and will remember all the good things those people had done for the benefit of the community [Hebrews 6:9-12].

The gentle personality of Barnabas shows through. He continued his mentoring ministry to Saint Mark when Paul would have nothing more to do with the young man [Acts 15:37-39]. They were his "dear friends" [Hebrews 6:9]. He was the consummate peacemaker. It is more than possible that his Letter to the Hebrews was intended as the means by which a reconciliation between the so-called "Judaizers" and the Gentiles might be effected.

Even though he had written that restoration was impossible, the Apostle attempted to accomplish that very goal. He asserted, we have a priest after the order of Melchizedek, who has entered the Holy of Holies. It all depends on Him, not on our rituals or our obedience to the Law of Moses. God provided, first, the promise to Abraham, and second our Priest, Jesus [Hebrews 6:18-20].

The identification of Jesus and Melchizedek was of great importance to Barnabas. He extensively made the point that Melchizedek was superior to Abraham, as the Priest who collects the tithe is superior to the one who donates. Among the esoteric references, Barnabas noted that Melchizedek was "King of Salem" or "King of Peace" [Hebrews 7:2] and that Levi the Priest gave the offering to Melchizedek because he was **in the body of his ancestor** [Hebrews 7:10]. Thus Melchizedek, and Jesus, are superior to Abraham.

Apparently, Barnabas believed there had been only two perfect offerings of atonement. The first, by Abraham to Melchizedek, and the second by Jesus to God. All of the offerings of the order of Aaron (Levitical priests), were required repeatedly. And thus, the Levitical system is laid aside: because it was weak and useless (for the law made nothing perfect), and a better hope is introduced, by which we draw near to God [Hebrews 7:18-19].

One of the extraordinary passages in the Old Testament is addressed clearly to King David. Psalm begins with **The Lord says to my lord, "Sit at my right hand until I make your enemies your footstool"** [Psalm 110:1]. But Barnabas decided it was addressed to Messiah. He changed the identity of the second "lord" by insisting that David is the speaker, instead of someone addressing David.

And because of that, Jesus rather than David, is a priest forever [Psalm 110:4]. And as a result, Barnabas claims: because Jesus lives forever, he has a permanent priesthood. And therefore [Gk: hothen (hoth'-en) "wherefore"], he is able to **save completely** [Gk: pantelés (pan-tel-ace') forever or utterly] **those who come to God through him, because he always lives to intercede for them.**

"Lives to intercede" begs a question: Why must He intercede continually for those who are already cleansed by His Sacrifice? The answer is that he need not. Unlike the other high priests, he does not need to offer sacrifices day after day, first for his own sins, and then for the sins of the people. He sacrificed for their sins once for all when he offered himself [Hebrews 7:27].

This is the most contentious difference between Catholicism and Protestantism. The Catholic Mass is considered a repeat of the sacrifice of Christ, and is presided over by a Priest. But Barnabas told us that the Sacrifice of Christ is "once and for all". Moreover, priesthood has been superseded by that event. No sacrifice is needed, and thus no priesthood is needed.

One of the esoteric parts of Barnabas' logic is in the word "oath". He used the word five times, to denote that Jesus is a greater Priest than the human priests of Jerusalem. Human contracts are bound by oath [Hebrews 6:16]. God established the Covenant by oath [Hebrews 6:17]. The Jerusalem priests served without God's oath [Hebrews 7:20], and were thus not bound by and to the Covenant. The ministry and Priesthood of Jesus was confirmed by God's oath [Hebrews 7:21] thus making Christ part of the Covenant when the Jerusalem priests were not.

This is the beginning of a New Covenant, one that is superior to the Old Covenant [Hebrews 8:6]. However, that a New Covenant is established requires proof. Why is it required? By whose authority is it established? How is the new better than the old? Does it have a termination date?

First and second: If there had been nothing wrong with that first covenant, no place would have been sought for another. But God found fault with the people and said: **The days are coming, declares the Lord, when I will make a new covenant with the people of Israel** [Hebrews 8:7-8, quoting Jeremiah 31:31]. Remembering that Barnabas addressed Jewish Christians, he wrote: **By calling this covenant "new," he has made the first one obsolete; and what is obsolete and outdated will soon disappear** [Hebrews 8:13].

Third: Only the High Priest could enter the Holy of Holies in the Temple, and only once each year. The Holy of Holies contained the Ark, over which were the Cherubim guarding the place of Atonement. The Priest offered a blood sacrifice on behalf of himself and those of the people done **"in ignorance"** [Hebrews 9:7]. **The Holy Spirit was showing by this that the way into the Most Holy Place had not yet been disclosed as long as the first tabernacle was still functioning** [Hebrews 9:8]. In other words, even the regulations of the Temple were prophetic of a new and superior covenant, one that goes beyond our ignorance, and beyond the Jerusalem Temple into the Heavenly Temple of which Jerusalem is only a copy [Hebrews 8:5].

Jesus as the Christ was able to go into the Temple which is not a copy: **He entered the Most Holy Place once for all by his own blood, thus obtaining eternal redemption** [Hebrews 9:12], in order that, **He would cleanse our consciences from acts that lead to death,** [Literal Gk: **purify the conscience of us from dead works (or rituals) in order to serve the living God**] **so that we may serve the living God** [Hebrews 9:14]!

Fourth: Barnabas had a logical mind, but his preferences were different from ours. Having dealt with the reasons for the New Covenant, he turned to "the inheritance" Jesus gained for the Jews.

He had died, and after death, one's estate must be divided equitably among the heirs. So, we must ask; "What is the Estate?" And "Who are the heirs?"

When our translators have us read **"In the case of a will"** [Hebrews 9:16], the word they translate "will" is a Greek word meaning "Covenant" or "Contract".

Barnabas' argument appealed to Jews who understood that the law requires that nearly everything be cleansed with blood, and without the shedding of blood there is no forgiveness [Hebrews 9:22]. So, the death of Jesus, the shedding of His Blood, was a requirement of the Law of Moses. The sacrifice, and its benefits are half of the estate to be divided. The sacrifice means the atonement for sin, the satisfaction of judgment, and the defeat of death. Salvation, of course, is the term that includes "all of the above". But he has appeared once for all at the culmination of the ages to do away with sin by the sacrifice of himself. Just as people are destined to die once, and after that to face judgment, so Christ was sacrificed once to take away the sins of many; and he will appear a second time, not to bear sin, but to bring salvation to those who are waiting for him [Hebrews 9:26-28]. Salvation is yet to come, according to Barnabas. It is a sure promise (Covenant), but we wait in faith for the consummation. In other words, we faithful Christians have salvation as a promise, but not yet as a reality. The Real will arrive only when the Temporary passes away.

The rituals of the Temple never quite removed the memory of sin, or the sense of guilt. Indeed, the regular sacrifices at the Temple reminded the faithful of their sinfulness. In the same way, our prayers of confession remind us that even though we have salvation as a promise, we continue to "miss the mark of perfection" [In this regard, one might want to read Wesley's sermon "On Perfection" which is based on Hebrews 6:1.].

Barnabas' insight is that God desires something other than our regret for our sinfulness. God desires to put my laws in their hearts [Hebrews 10:16, quoting Jeremiah 31:33]. It is as Jeremiah wrote: **No longer shall they teach one another, or say to each other, "Know the Lord," for they shall all know me, from the least of them to the greatest, says the Lord; for I will forgive their iniquity, and remember their sin no more** [Jeremiah 31:34]. Neither God, nor the faithful will remember sin in the glory of God's Law written on the heart, i.e., God's Love [Again Wesley: Perfection consists of being filled with God's Perfect Love to the exclusion of all else]. And thus: sacrifice for sin is no longer necessary [Hebrews 10:18].

Therefore, brothers and sisters, since we have confidence to enter the Most Holy Place by the blood of Jesus, by a new and living way opened for us through the curtain, that is, his body, and since we have a great priest over the house of God, let us draw near to God with a sincere heart and with the full assurance that faith brings, having our hearts sprinkled to cleanse us from a guilty conscience and having our bodies washed with pure water [Hebrews 10:19-22].

This is an exciting insight. Because of our faith, we have no fear of the Judgment. Because Christ has already entered the real Holy of Holies, and invites us, we have no fear of that either. The High Priest must have felt great trepidation as he went through the curtain, but we have none.

I thought, "Aha, this must be the great 'therefore', but it is not. The Greek word at 10:19 is "oun" which is a pointer but not a "parakaleo" [to call to, exhort]! Something better is still to be revealed by our Apostle.

This is, however, a very serious insight. **If one continues in sin [def: alienated from God] after we have received the knowledge of the truth, no sacrifice for sins is left** [Hebrews 10:26]. However, let us not make the common mistake. Remember that the audience is the body of Early Christian Jews who continued to insist on obedience to the Law of Moses. It is not aimed at Gentile Christians who never were given the system of forgiveness by sacrifice through Moses. We might better paraphrase this passage; If we continue to trust in the System of Temple Sacrifice after we have received Christ, then His Sacrifice is null and void to us. (Even so, St. Paul and I think it a good warning to Gentile Christians, that we strive to cease our sins after we come to Salvation by grace through faith.)

The succeeding verses paint a picture of the hard times faced by the Early Christian Jews; times of persecution and confiscation of property [Hebrews 10:32-35]. Barnabas promised an early return of Christ and a fulsome reward [Hebrews 10:36-39].

Chapter Eleven is the great "Faith Chapter": **Faith is confidence in what we hope for and assurance about what we do not see** [Hebrews 11:1]. It consists of example after example of ancient Hebrews who lived and died in faith; Abel, Enoch, Noah, and Abraham. They lived as foreigners and strangers on Earth [Hebrews 11:13; grammar corrected]. They were longing for a better country—a heavenly one. Therefore [Gk: de; a weak adversative particle] God is not ashamed to be called their God, for he has prepared a city for them [Hebrews 11:16]. That is a lesson appropriate to all, not just Jewish Christians.

Hero after hero is named. The conclusion was appropriate for all Christians who lived (or live) in times of persecution.

These were all commended for their faith, yet none of them received what had been promised, since God had planned something better for us so that only together with us would they be made perfect [Hebrews 11:39-40].

Barnabas has come to his conclusions. The "If this and if that" has become the "therefore".

Chapter twelve begins with "therefore". Unfortunately, it also is not "parakaleo", which means, "I beg you". Instead, Barnabas used "toigaroun" [say: toy-gar-oon'] which means: "wherefore" or "consequently". Perhaps he saw his appeal as a natural logical result of what he'd already written.

Therefore, since we are surrounded by such a great cloud of witnesses, let us throw off everything that hinders and the sin that so easily entangles. And let us run with perseverance the race marked out for us, fixing our eyes on Jesus, the pioneer and perfecter of faith. For the joy set before him he endured the cross, scorning its shame, and sat down at the right hand of the throne of God. Consider him who endured such opposition from sinners, so that you will not grow weary and lose heart [Hebrews 12:1-3]. I think this must be my favorite passage. It brings forth images from my experience as a marathon runner. I must pursue my salvation in Jesus, partly because my ancestors are watching (four generations of Methodist clergy), and partly because I can identify the tedium and effort required to be ready for a marathon race.

However, the meaning of the passage is often missed by modern gentile Christians. He meant: "Consequently, we Jews, in the sight of so many Jews who struggled and persevered in faith, must also pursue salvation by faith, looking to Jesus, who in expectation endured pain, shame, and loss, in order that He (and we Jewish Christians) might sit down at the Throne of God. Considering His example, we Jewish Christians must endure our pain, shame, and loss as we suffer persecution. Never, never, never give up.

Indeed, God is partly responsible for the suffering of the Early Church. Barnabas thought it "discipline": **Endure hardship as discipline; God is treating you as his children** [Hebrews 12:7].

The hardship of persecution must be accounted as within the permissive will of God, as an in-order-that the Church, the Body of Christ, might grow. And the Jewish Christians were experiencing persecution.

Other conclusions include:

Make every effort to live in peace with everyone and to be holy; without holiness no one will see the Lord [Hebrews 12:14].

See that no one is sexually immoral, or is godless like Esau, who for a single meal sold his inheritance [Hebrews 12:16]. I am not sure what connection existed between sexual immorality and Esau...perhaps only free association. Could it have been that Esau gave away his inheritance for the satisfaction of a physical hunger, which could as easily have been a sexual appetite?

You have come to Mount Zion, to the city of the living God, the heavenly Jerusalem. You have come to thousands upon thousands of angels in joyful assembly, to the church of the firstborn, whose names are written in heaven. You have come to God, the Judge of all, to the spirits of the righteous made perfect, to Jesus the mediator of a new covenant, and to the sprinkled blood that speaks a better word than the blood of Abel [Hebrews 12:22-24]. This city is the "real" as compared to the "temporary" Jerusalem with all its implications.

See to it that you do not refuse him who speaks [Hebrews 12:25], that is "one speaking under the influence of the Holy Spirit [this is my interpretation, not explicit in the verse], **because we (Jewish Christians) are witnessing the great transition from Old Covenant to New Covenant: the removing of what can be shaken—that is, created things—so that what cannot be shaken may remain** [Hebrews 12:27], **and, since we are receiving a kingdom that cannot be shaken, let us be thankful** [Hebrews 12:28].

Let family love continue among us [my translation]. Show hospitality to strangers [Hebrews 13:2]. **Minister to those imprisoned for their faith** [Hebrews 13:3]. **Be faithful in marriage** [Hebrews 13:4]. **Do not over-value wealth, instead value contentment because God will never abandon you** [Hebrews 13:5-6]. **Remember (pray for and support) your leaders who have spoken the Spirit Word** [Logon] **to you** [Hebrews 13:7]. **Don't believe strange ideas, remember that those who partake Old Covenant rituals have no place at God's Table** [Hebrews 13:9-10]. **Let us bear the disgrace Jesus bore** [Hebrews 13:13] **and depart from the larger Jewish family** [Hebrews 13:13; "outside the city or camp]. **Submit to the authority of your leaders, remembering that they must give account** [Hebrews 13:17]. **Pray for them** [Hebrews 13:18].

And at last: the great benediction"

Now may the God of peace, who through the blood of the eternal covenant brought back from the dead our Lord Jesus, that great Shepherd of the sheep, equip you with everything good for doing his will, and may he work in us what is pleasing to him, through Jesus Christ, to whom be glory for ever and ever. Amen [Hebrews 13:20-21].

LETTER OF JAMES

This is the most distressing Bible study I have ever done. When I was finished, I was really disappointed, as you will see. Then Susan corrected me. She told me to take another look. She said, "It isn't just the disappointing message that gives it its ultimate value. Consider how many people love this book. What, beside what you have discovered, gives it value today?"

James was the brother of Jesus. He had, as would have had I, serious doubts about the preaching and teaching of his older brother. Most especially, James doubted his brother when those teachings began to focus on the relationship between Jesus and God. Prior to his conversion, he probably had some trouble with the ideas expressed by Matthew, especially Jesus' very negative attitude toward the "Jerusalem establishment". The Scribes and Pharisees were, according to Matthew, the special opponents of Jesus. He called them "White-washed Tombs", with outward righteousness and inward rot.

The Gospel of Mark [3:31-33] proclaims the attitude of James toward Jesus. James accompanied his mother and sisters to "take Jesus home" -an euphemism for "Don't hurt him, we know he is crazy. We will care for him".

And yet, very shortly after the Crucifixion, James was the head of the Church in Jerusalem. He was, so-to-speak, the first Pope. What happened to James? What explains this complete turn-around? The only answer that stands scrutiny, is that, after the Resurrection, Jesus appeared to James. This is not the only time that happened. Saul met Jesus on the road to Damascus. Thousands, if not millions, have met Jesus through the centuries since then. Paul testifies that Jesus did, in fact appear to James: ...**he appeared to Cephas, then to the Twelve. Then he appeared to more than five hundred brethren at one time, most of whom are still alive, though some have fallen asleep. Then he appeared to James, then to all the Apostles. Last of all, as to one untimely born, he appeared also to me** [1 Corinthians 15;5-8].

The key to understanding the Letter of James depends on the date one ascribes to its writing. The best scholars assert that it was written before St. Paul began his work. It was when St. Paul was persecuting the Church; when St. Stephen was murdered, and when much of the "Jesus Sect" fled Jerusalem and went into hiding (in Damascus, for instance) [Acts 8:1].

If this date is correct, then James is the first extant Christian document. It is the earliest expression of the Christian faith we are able to read. Suddenly James becomes perhaps the most important document in the New Testament.

Remember the historical references beginning in Acts 4? Wealthy converts sold their possessions and brought the proceeds to the Church. The Apostles distributed those funds to any in need. They had no investments, they simply distributed what was brought to them.

Then, in Chapter five, Ananias and Sapphira were not fully committed to the idea of "all things in common" and "to each according to need". They withheld some of the proceeds...a kind of earthly insurance program in case the Lord doesn't return next month as expected.

And then, an argument arose between the Hellenists and the more traditional Jewish Christians. One side accused the other of unfair distributions. The result was the appointment of seven deacons, among whom was St. Stephen.

Here we have the basis for the first "Papal Encyclical", which is what the letter of James amounts to. Apparently, the wealthier Hellenists objected that they were not being treated fairly. Perhaps they thought, since they had brought in vastly superior amounts of money, their widows should receive more than the poorer traditionalists. Or, perhaps they were being treated differently because they had accepted Roman and Greek customs. St. James, as head of the Church, was required to respond. He had to make known to all the Christians, whether in Jerusalem or elsewhere, what the policy ought to be.

And so, the outline of the letter suddenly falls into an understandable form.

Count it all joy, my brethren, when you meet various trials, for you know that the testing of your faith produces steadfastness [1:2]. Ananias lacked faith, and failed the test.

[1:6-8] **... he who doubts is like a wave of the sea that is driven and tossed by the wind. For that person must not suppose that a double-minded man, unstable in all his ways, will receive anything from the Lord.** There is a serious penalty for failure to pass the test. Therefore: each member of the Sect had better see to it that all the assets are turned over to the Apostles. We should note here, that the real sin is not so much related to money as it is to failure to do what one promised God that he/she would do. Ananias and Sapphira promised to donate the entirety of their assets, but failed to do what they set out in their promise.

Let the lowly brother boast in his exaltation, and the rich in his humiliation, because like the flower of the grass he will pass away. For the sun rises with its scorching heat and withers the grass; its flower falls, and its beauty perishes. So will the rich man fade away in the midst of his pursuits [1:9-11]. The poor are "exalted, because they will receive, not just out of the charity of the Church, but also the rewards of faithfulness. The rich should take pride in becoming "penniless" because they are joining the poor in the expectation of the glory almost immediately to be revealed.

Speaking as a man of wealth, I have been troubled for years by the urging of Jesus: **go, sell your possessions and give to the poor, and you will have treasure in heaven** [Matthew 19:21]. Recently, while studying Luke, I finally have an insight. Jesus shared the parable of the man who built new barns to hold all his goods [Luke 12:16-21], and I thought I must be the fool, because I have a retirement account. But then I noticed: **But seek his kingdom, and these things will be given to you as well** [Luke 12:31]. I have sought the Kingdom, and God has given these things to me. And then I noticed, **Who then is the faithful and wise manager, whom the master puts in charge...** [Luke 12:42]. Some Christians ought to understand the passage about wealth in this way: God has made us managers for the benefit of the Kingdom.

Every good endowment and every perfect gift is from above [1:17]. God gave each his/her portion in the wealth of the world. It is an endowment intended for use as God gives the opportunity.

Of his own will he brought us forth by the Word of Truth that we should be a kind of first fruits of His creatures [1:18].   We are called to Salvation by the Word of Truth (that is: God's Spirit in my brother: Jesus) and not to wealth: Earthly wealth has little meaning if Jesus is going to return within a few days, or months at the most. We have, in vs 21, the earliest definition of the Holy Spirit [Gk: literally "The Implanted Word"].

Religion that is pure and undefiled before God and the Father is this: to visit orphans and widows in their affliction, and to keep oneself unstained from the world [1:26-27]. This is what God intends for you/us: Righteousness consists of loyalty to the Body of Christ, especially with the donation of your worldly assets, by which the Church is able to provide for the orphans and widows (remember, this is about Ananias).

In Chapter two, James uses the example of a rich man being seated at the front, while a poor man is seated at the rear. Front and rear of what? Of the dining table. Remember that the disciples gathered every day for their meals, and worship took place at the table. To sit at the head, is to have first choice over what is served. To sit at the back, or tail end, is to have the choice of the scraps. He then asks:

Has not God chosen those who are poor in the world to be rich in faith and heirs of the Kingdom which He has promised to those who Love him [2:5]**?**

He goes on to give his answer in the form of a question.

What does it profit, my brethren, if a man says he has faith but has not works? Can his faith save him? If a brother or sister is ill-clad and in lack of daily food, and one of you says to them, "Go in peace, be warmed and filled," without giving them the things needed for the body, what does it profit? So faith by itself, if it has no works, is dead [2:14-17; literally, in the case of Ananias].

In this case, the rich do not profit if "one of the poor", that is the Jerusalem Congregation, is ill clad or hungry. One must see his advantage in the gift that feeds and clothes the brothers and sisters, the widows and orphans of the Sect. Faith, which is the living out the instructions/inspirations of the "Implanted Word", is evidenced in this expression of the Law as expressed by Jesus: **Love your neighbor as yourself** [Matthew 19:19].

The rest of the chapter (two) is devoted to examples of "justification" by doing what the Spirit instructed: Abraham and Rahab, along with the note that even demons believe. The demons shudder, but do not act in accordance with the instructions of the Holy Spirit. If a rich person, e.g., Ananias, fails to turn over their full assets, they become demonic.

Chapter three is ostensibly about teaching and the tongue. Behind that surface, is the discussion going on within the Sect. The Hellenists, the wealthy members, were arguing that they were not being treated with the deference they deserved.

There is an earthly wisdom here, but it is faulty. James noted that, **We all stumble in many ways. Anyone who is never at fault in what they say is perfect, able to keep their whole body in check** [James 3:2]. But we know that no one is able to keep him/her self completely in check. Do you suppose that James intended an oblique criticism on the wealthy members? Did he want to suggest a little humility might be in order. Simply because one has more wealth than others does not imply distinction. Indeed, in addition to James, throughout St. Paul's writings this message is clear. Paul clearly wrote that there is "no distinction, since all have sinned and fall short of the glory of God" [Romans 3:22-23].

Paul engaged in an exercise of "compare and contrast" -just as a high school English teacher might. He contrasted human wisdom with Godly Wisdom. Godly Wisdom always regards the interests and value of "the other" as more important than the self [2 Corinthians 5:16; We no longer regard anyone from a human point of view. And, Philippians 2:3 Regard others as better than yourselves.] We must actually see that other person as one for whom Christ died. And, as a dear friend of mine once said in the midst of a trying circumstance: "If God Loves you and Christ died for you, who am I to judge you?"

He concluded the chapter with: **For where jealousy and selfish ambition exist, there will be disorder and every vile practice. But the Wisdom from above is first pure, then peaceable, gentle,** open to reason, full of mercy and good fruits, without uncertainty or insincerity. And the harvest of righteousness is sown in peace by those who make peace [3:16-18].

That is; peace within the Body, the Sect.

However, there are present in the Body persons whose allegiance is split between this apparent world and the Real World. James used the singular Greek word "philia". It is the only time the word appears in the New Testament [There are 29 times the word is used to indicate friends", all but three in the Gospels]. He wrote: **if you family-love, or friendship-love, the world you are an adulteress** [James 4:4], **if you are a friend of the world, you are an enemy of God.** If that is true of us, James hoped to provoke a correction.

Chapter four is summed up in vs 6-8: **But he gives more grace; therefore it says, "God opposes the proud** [Ananias or the Hellenists?]**, but gives grace to the humble." Submit yourselves therefore to God. Resist the devil and he will flee from you. Draw near to God and He will draw near to you. Cleanse your hands, you sinners, and purify your hearts, you men of double mind.** Remember that the men of "double mind" are men like Ananias. He did not resist the Devil and became demonic. But even now it is not too late for the double-minded. With repentance and with the delivery of the remaining assets, God will forgive and restore.

Chapter five begins with a terrible condemnation of Ananias and others like him [5:1-6]: **Come now, you rich** [Hellenists]**, weep and howl for the miseries that are coming upon you. Your riches have rotted and your garments are moth-eaten. Your gold and silver have rusted, and their rust will be evidence against you and will eat your flesh like fire. You have laid up treasure for the last days. Behold, the wages of the laborers who mowed your fields, which you kept back by fraud, cry out; and the cries of the harvesters have reached the ears of the Lord of hosts. You have lived on the earth in luxury and in pleasure; you have fattened your hearts in a day of slaughter. You have condemned, you have killed the righteous man; he does not resist you.**

He then has some words for the poor [5:7-8]: **Be patient, therefore, brethren, until the coming of the Lord. Behold, the farmer waits for the precious fruit of the earth, being patient over it until it receives the early and the late rain. You also be patient. Establish your hearts, for the coming of the Lord is at hand.**

So now we have a clearer understanding of what was going on in the Church during the time of St. Stephen. Interestingly, it is the poverty of the Jerusalem Church that prompted St. Paul, on his third missionary journey, to seek a collection among the Gentiles for the "poor at Jerusalem".

The holding of all things in common by the Church didn't work out as planned. Thus we, latter day saints, must take other meanings from James. We must ask how those lessons can be extrapolated to our circumstances. And when we do so, our answers will be partly the same, and partly different. We will take, for instance, the lesson about being receptive and responsive to the Implanted Word, even while we understand that the Church is not intended to receive all our worldly possessions. The Venezuela experiment is having the same result as did the early Christian Church. St. Paul had a response. We might do well to emulate his idea when the time comes. But that is well beyond the scope of this lesson.

So what might a disciple learn from James? First: the character of the disciple is grounded and limited by the "Implanted Word" -the Holy Spirit. Second: our earthly loyalty must be to our fellow

Christians...and that is an unlimited commitment. Third: earthly treasure has no bearing on Heavenly Treasure. Fourth: belief without action is null and void. And last: contrary to the opinion of many modern Americans: The Church defines what is True, not the individual. We may differ personally, but do not mistake, the Church has the authority to define the faith...not the individual. One had better be on sure ground before thinking "I am right and the Church is wrong".

FIRST PETER

The subject is not so different from other letters by other authors. It is unique in that it is addressed to a whole region, rather than to one (or two) congregations.

St. Peter addressed the difficulty Christians faced living in a pagan society. It is a lesson today's American Christians may have to learn. **Dear friends, I urge you, as foreigners and exiles, to abstain from sinful desires, which wage war against your soul. Live such good lives among the pagans that, though they accuse you of doing wrong, they may see your good deeds and glorify God on the day he visits us** [1 peter 2:11-12]. The letter is less doctrine and more practical advice about how to live under the threat of mortal persecution. **These (persecutions) have come so that the proven genuineness of your faith—of greater worth than gold, which perishes even though refined by fire—** [1 Peter 1:7]. In other words: endure your troubles now, in order that you may receive a glorious future.

Most scholars believe that the letter was written in the mid-sixties A.D. Nero was Emperor. And Peter considered himself a resident of "Babylon" [1 Peter 5:13; **She who is in Babylon greets you** might be code for himself, might be his wife, or some other famous-to-the-Church woman. In any case, Peter was present.]. Babylon was, of course, code for Rome. And under Nero, Christians were very careful to not betray each other. Babylon was the location of the period of exile among the Hebrew People. Peter taught his friends that for now we live in exile from the new promised land.

So, Peter was in Rome, and his letter was addressed to Christians living in the provinces of Pontus, Galatia, Cappadocia, Asia and Bithynia [1 Peter 1:1]. Historians note that the Neronian Persecution was particularly brutal, and unmatched until Diocletian after 303 A.D.

He began with reasons why one ought to remain faithful to Christ. **In his great mercy he has given us new birth into a living hope... that can never perish... kept in heaven for you... until the coming of the salvation that is ready to be revealed in the last time... though now for a little while you may have had to suffer grief in all kinds of trials** [1 Peter 1: 3-6]. If this is true, then a "therefore" is required. Setting one's mind on Christ: **As obedient children, do not conform to the evil desires you had when you lived in ignorance. But just as he who called you is holy, so be holy in all you do** [1 Peter 1:14-15]. **And, love one another deeply, from the heart** [1Peter 1:22]. **Rid yourselves of all malice and all deceit, hypocrisy, envy, and slander** [1Peter 2:1].

He believed that all Christians constitute a new priesthood, replacing the old Jerusalem priests. Are we a priesthood because our martyrdom amounts to a continuing and connected sacrifice with that of Jesus? He wrote: **But you are a chosen people, a royal priesthood, a holy nation, God's special possession, that you may declare the praises of him who called you out of darkness into his wonderful light** [1 Peter 2:9].

What is interesting about this is the purpose of this new priesthood. **As you come to him, the living Stone—rejected by humans but chosen by God and precious to him— you also, like living stones, are being built into a spiritual temple to be a holy priesthood, offering spiritual sacrifices acceptable to God through Jesus Christ** [1 Peter 2:4-5].

What are those "spiritual sacrifices"? The Christians of those years sacrificed themselves rather than renounce their faith. As Paul wrote to the Colossians: **And now I am happy about my sufferings for you, for by means of my physical sufferings I am helping to complete what still remains of Christ's sufferings on behalf of his body, the church** [Colossians 1:24, Good News]. And today hundreds of Christians face the same dilemma. "Will I be faithful under persecution and even martyrdom, or will I renounce my Lord in fear?"

Peter gave advice about how one might prepare the soul for such an eventuality. **Therefore, with minds that are alert and fully sober, set your hope on the grace to be brought to you when Jesus Christ is revealed at his coming. As obedient children, do not conform to the evil desires you had when you lived in ignorance. But just as he who called you is holy, so be holy in all you do; for it is written: "Be holy, because I am holy"** [1 Peter 1:13-16]. One who does not practice holiness today will not be prepared for the test tomorrow.

His practical advice included that a woman's beauty **should be that of your inner self, the unfading beauty of a gentle and quiet spirit** [1 Peter 3:4]. **A husband should be considerate and treat his wife with gentleness** [1 Peter 3:7]. And, within the Body of Christ, we all ought to be **like-minded, sympathetic, love** [agape] **one another, be compassionate and humble. Do not repay evil with evil or insult with insult. On the contrary, repay evil with blessing, because to this you were called so that you may inherit a blessing** [1 Peter 3:8-9]. He compared the pagan life and the Christian life [1 Peter 4:1-6]. Pagans live for debauchery, lust, drunkenness, orgies, carousing and detestable idolatry. They abuse Christians because those things are rejected by people who are preparing to give an account to the One who is ready to judge such things. And so, Pagans resent, persecute and abuse Christians: **Dear friends, do not be surprised at the fiery ordeal** [Is this a reference to the Christian Martyrs, burnt on crosses in Rome after the fire?] **that has come on you to test you, as though something strange were happening to you. But rejoice inasmuch as you participate in the sufferings of Christ, so that you may be overjoyed when his glory is revealed** [1 Peter 4:12-13]. And: **So then, those who suffer according to God's will should commit themselves to their faithful Creator and continue to do good** [1 Peter 4:19].

For the congregation, his priority is clear. **Above all, love each other deeply, because love covers over a multitude of sins. Offer hospitality to one another without grumbling. Each of you should use whatever gift you have received to serve others, as faithful stewards of God's grace in its various forms. If anyone speaks, they should do so as one who speaks the very words of God. If anyone serves, they should do so with the strength God provides, so that in all things God may be praised through Jesus Christ. To him be the glory and the power for ever and ever. Amen** [1 Peter 4:8-11].

For the pastors? This is a sermon to me and to my fellow clergy. **To the elders among you, I appeal as a fellow elder and a witness of Christ's sufferings who also will share in the glory to be revealed: Be shepherds of God's flock that is under your care, watching over them—not because you must, but because you are willing, as God wants you to be; not pursuing dishonest gain, but eager to serve; not lording it over those entrusted to you, but being examples to the flock. And**

when the Chief Shepherd appears, you will receive the crown of glory that will never fade away [1 Peter 5:1-4]. I fear that my American colleagues, as a group, have neglected this. My father served a church in Newport Minnesota, from 1932 to 1934, starting with no salary and only a summer cabin at a church camp along the Mississippi River. For three generations my family never owned a home (at least until retirement) in honor of Joshua 18:7 [The Levites, however, do not get a portion among you, because the priestly service of the Lord is their inheritance.]. I think I see the Lord acting to make our profession a sacrifice again. Fewer and fewer congregations are able to afford the inflated compensation on the most recent generation.

And finally: **And the God of all grace, who called you to his eternal glory in Christ, after you have suffered a little while, will himself restore you and make you strong, firm and steadfast. To him be the power for ever and ever. Amen** [1 peter 5:10-11].

SECOND PETER

Saint Peter noted that this is his second letter [2 Peter 3:1], and so we conclude that it is addressed to the congregations in Asia Minor (Turkey), just as was the first letter. He intended this to be his "legacy letter" [2 Peter 1:15; …after my departure you will always be able to remember these things.] because the Lord had made clear to him that he was soon to pass into Glory [2 Peter 1:14].

As anyone of considerable age can relate, writing a "legacy letter" is not an easy task. We hope our wisdom will benefit those whom we love. **For if you do these things, you will never stumble, and you will receive a rich welcome into the Eternal Kingdom** [2 Peter 1:10-11]. One expects to put into only a few words what it took a life-time to learn.

Most often one will relate the most important experience of his/her life as evidence. And just so, Peter illustrated his letter with a reference to the Transfiguration [Ref: Matt. 17:5; Mark 9:7; Luke 9:35]. Peter heard God Speak as **The voice** [Of God] **came to him** [Jesus] **from the Majestic Glory, saying, "This is my Son, whom I love** [agape]**; with him I am well pleased". We ourselves heard this voice that came from heaven when we were with him on the sacred mountain** [2 Peter 1:17-18]. While Peter could have written about the Resurrection, he chose this instead, perhaps because he wanted to illustrate his [Peter's] "Authority". After all, we want our readers to take seriously what we proclaim as a sort-of ultimate truth.

Peter said his teachings were confirmed, day to day, by "Prophets". And, to him, those important life-lessons were mixed into the deepest concerns of his present day. So, Peter affirmed his life-long faith understandings as he confronted what he considered the two most pressing issues of the Church during the mid-sixties Anno Domini. They were: false prophets/teachers and the delay in the Return of Christ.

The first issue, for us to consider is the presence of false teachers within the Church. **Truly inspired prophets, though human, spoke from God as they were carried along by the Holy Spirit** [2 Peter 1:21].

There has been an ever-continuing discussion in the Church about whether the Holy Spirit continues to confer the gift of prophecy. I affirm, from my personal experience, that It does. However, just as in the days of the Apostles, so today, false prophecies afflict the Church. But there were also false prophets among the people, just as there will be false teachers among you. They will secretly introduce destructive heresies, even denying the sovereign Lord who bought them—bringing swift destruction on themselves [2 Peter 2:1].

I recall a conversation with a Muslim man in Minneapolis. He rejected the notion of the resurrection, rightly saying "Even some of your theologians deny that it happened". That is emblematic of the corruption of the Gospel in today's world. **Many will follow them** [2 Peter 2:2]. Their future is one of dire judgment and destruction. Peter illustrated what they might expect by pointing to Sodom's destruction and the destructive flood from which the Lord rescued Noah. Even Angels who prove false are fated for terrible destruction [2 Peter2:4]. The Apostle cautioned his readers to not follow those terrible ideas. He identified a sort-of Christian authorized, but pagan-like, worldliness. He used the word "sarx" which we translate as "flesh": This is especially true of those who follow the corrupt desire of the flesh and despise authority [2 Peter 2:10]. But "sarx" was a well-understood term in the early Christian Communities. It meant living as if the meaning and purpose of life is to be found in the senses, including sexuality, greed, envy, anger, etc. One might refer to Paul's list of the "fruits of the flesh" [Galatians 5:19; sarcos]: **sexual immorality, impurity and debauchery; idolatry and witchcraft; hatred, discord, jealousy, fits of rage, selfish ambition, dissensions, factions and envy; drunkenness, orgies, and the like** [Galatians 5:19-21].

As an illustration of today's laxity, one might ask, "When was the last time you heard a sermon against witchcraft?" And today witchcraft has made a remarkable recovery among people who deify "mother nature". Do you know how to differentiate between witchcraft and the "miracle power" of the Holy Spirit? Obviously, this continues to be a relevant issue. And the penalty for false-teaching and false prophecy remains as fearsome.

The Second issue he addressed was the delay in the Return of Christ. **They (Scoffers) will say, "Where is this 'coming' he promised** [2 Peter 3:4]**?** Peter's response was clear and simple: **With the Lord a day is like a thousand years** [2 Peter 3:8]**, and: The day of the Lord will come like a thief** [Matthew 24:44].

His description is eerily appropriate to our time: **The heavens will disappear with a roar; the elements will be destroyed by fire, and the earth and everything done in it will be burnt up** [2 Peter 3:10]**. That day will bring about the destruction of the heavens by fire, and the elements will melt in the heat** [2 Peter 3:12]**. It truly sounds like nuclear war.**

However, the future for true Christians is different. For us, the delay is meant as Grace. **The Lord is not slow in keeping his promise, as some understand slowness. Instead, he is patient with you, not wanting anyone to perish, but everyone to come to repentance** [2 Peter 3:9].

And Peter closes with this caution, this wisdom: Since you are looking forward to this (the Second Coming), **make every effort to be found spotless, blameless and at peace with him (God)** [2 Peter 3:14]**. Dear friends, since you have been forewarned, be on your guard** [against false teaching and worldly behavior] **so that you may not be carried away by the error of the lawless and fall from your secure position. But grow in the grace and knowledge of our Lord and Savior Jesus Christ. To him be glory both now and forever! Amen** [2 Peter 3:17-18].

THE LETTERS OF SAINT JOHN

FIRST JOHN

Want to understand Saint John's personality, experience, Gospel and intention in this letter? He wrote: **My dear children, I write this to you so that you will not sin. But if anybody does sin, we have an advocate with the Father—Jesus Christ, the Righteous One. He is the atoning sacrifice for our sins, and not only for ours but also for the sins of the whole world** [1 John 2:1-2].

Putting that into contemporary language, he tells us: I don't want you to sin, but know you will. And so does Father God. He provided the Righteous Christ as a sacrifice of forgiveness for us Christians, but also available to every human being.

He wrote of his perspective on the world: **(The) truth is seen in him and in you, because the darkness is passing and the true light is already shining** [1 John 2:8]. In other words: the penultimate change in human history has taken place. The ultimate change is about to happen. John believed, as did the other Apostles, that the Second Coming was imminent. The Holy Spirit has indwelt each authentic Christian, and the full light is about to arrive.

Taking his Gospel into view, we can identify "the True Light" as his code for the Holy Spirit. The Spirit is seen in Jesus, and now it may be seen in Christian disciples. That the "darkness is passing" as the Light shines in the darkness [John 1:5] suggests that he end of the world is near, and that the Risen Christ is about to return.

What evidence did he present to assure his readers of the Return of Christ? **Dear children, this is the last hour; and as you have heard that the antichrist is coming, even now many antichrists have come. This is how we know it is the last hour. They went out from us, but they did not really belong to us** [1 John 2:18-19]. A group had left the Church.

One is tempted, without much historical evidence to present, to think that the people who left were tending toward "Gnosticism". That was (and is today) the belief that God is in everything, and that the spiritual person understands that he/she is god. They believed that sin is simply refusal to understand that one is, in fact, god. The most serious problem with Gnosticism is that morality is eliminated in self-love.

John responded: **Anyone who loves their brother and sister lives in the light, and there is nothing in them to make them stumble. But anyone who hates a brother or sister is in the darkness and walks around in the darkness. They do not know where they are going, because the darkness has blinded them** [1 John 2:10-11]. The important word in these verses is "love". John used agape, or God's Love. That is a Love that initiates itself from beyond the individual. John meant it to signify the large difference between friendship or family-love [philia], and erotic attraction [eros]. It is most certainly different from self-love, which is simply "egoism". Speaking of those opposed to the true Gospel a transliteration of John's Greek is: **"Not is the love of the Father in him"** [1 John 2:15]. Our translators had to choose between two possible meanings. The Greek can mean that the believer has no love for God, or that God's Love for others is not in the believer. If John were addressing his congregation on the subject of incipient Gnosticism, both meanings are accurate.

John listed, in poetry, some reasons for his writing. The common theme is that authentic Christians know the God which is beyond the self. **Your sins have been forgiven** [1 John 2:12]**; you know Him who is from the beginning** [1 John 2:13, 14]**; and the Word of God lives in you** [1 John 2:14]. It is God's Holy Spirit the fills the individual. It is not the individual claiming deity for him/her self. You have an anointing from the Holy One [1 John 2:20].

In order to illustrate the wonder and grandeur belonging to the authentic Christian, as opposed to those who thought themselves godly, John calls us **children of God** [John 3:1]! Children of God...not gods. While the Gnostic claims "knowledge" [Gk: Gnosis means knowledge], John allows that we don't know what we will be like, that **has not yet been revealed** [1 John 3:2; Gk: phaneroó (fan-er-o'-o): to make known or clear]. Instead, we look forward to Christ's appearance, when **we shall see him as he is** [1 John 3:2].

The problem of morals was difficult in the Early Church because of the doctrine of freedom from the law. John was quick to point out the inner definition of "law". Everyone who sins breaks the law; in fact, **sin is lawlessness** [1John 3:4]. But the issue continues to be a difficult problem even today. The issue is often put today: "What is the loving thing to do?" Too often, the issue is found in the definition of "love". God's Love is very different from human love. John simply states Anyone who **does not do what is right is not God's child, nor is anyone who does not love their brother and sister** [1 John 3:10].

How shall we know whether what we do is right or not? The answer is subjective. It seems that freedom from the law also means that if we err "in good faith", then our action is "regarded" as right, even if it fails. In other words, we are to do what "we believe" to be the will of God, and leave the judgment to Him. John's words are: **Dear friends, if our hearts do not condemn us, we have confidence before God and receive from him anything we ask, because we keep his commands and do what pleases him….** We know it by the Spirit he gave us [1 John 3:21-22, 24b].

However, that leaves us in a perplexity. There are many voices of spirit. Only one is Holy. How shall we know that what we feel is godly is actually the movement of the Holy Spirit within our hearts. John suggested that we **"test the spirits"** [1 John 4:1]. Recall that John was contesting the Gnostics who thought that their inner voice was the voice of god (since they considered themselves to be god)!

The Gnostics also denied that Jesus was fully human. **Every spirit that acknowledges that Jesus Christ has come in the flesh is from God, but every spirit that does not acknowledge Jesus is not from God. This is the spirit of the antichrist, which you have heard is coming and even now is already in the world** [1 John 4:2-3].

John has given us an answer to a question we did not ask: who is the antichrist? There seems to be an entire industry seeking to provide the answer. But John has given us a simple one. The antichrist spirit denies that Jesus is from God! That spirit has been active since John's time, and still is today. We often misuse the next part of his contention: **the one who is in you is greater than the one who is in the world** [1 John 4:4]. It is the Gnostics who are the "they" in the next sentence: **They are from the world and therefore speak from the viewpoint of the world** [1 John 4:5].

Nowhere in the Bible is the Character of God made more clear than does John. To John, God is God's Love. God's Love is demonstrated in the teaching and self-sacrifice of Jesus. And that Love is the Nature of the Holy Spirit. That Spirit is gifted to each Christian as an "anointing". When that Love/Spirit animates [literally: the deepest source of our existence in action] the Christian, he/she **lives in God, and God in them** [(sic) 1 John 4:16].

A personal note: Over the years I have been infatuated by many different authors of great insight. None of them have been as helpful as St. John. Starting with Love as God's Essential Character, all else derives in proper order. I think John is able to express my faith in one sentence: **God showed his love among us: He sent his one and only Son into the world that we might live through him** [1 John 4:9]. That goes for my ethic as well: **whoever does not love their brother and sister, whom they have seen, cannot love God, whom they have not seen** [1 John 4:20]. Don't agree with my theology? Not a problem. Our theology is not the deciding factor. Only God's Love is important. Don't agree with my politics? Not a problem. Politics is only about this world, and I have (since the night I accepted the Call to Ministry) believed that while politics is about next year's governmental budget, Christ is about eternity. Not a Christian? No problem. I think of them as "pre-Christian". Reprobate? Not a problem. Their sins are no worse than mine, and I have experience God's Love for me. If God Loves me, then God may well Love them too. At any rate, Jesus died for them, even if they have not yet responded to His Grace. A Christian, animated by the Spirit of God's Love must, simply, live out God's Love toward others.

This is the victory that has overcome the world, even our faith. Who is it that overcomes the world? Only the one who believes that Jesus is the Son of God [1 John 5:4-5].

JOHN'S SECOND LETTER

The second of the three letters is addressed to a "dear lady". Scholars are unable to determine who she was. There is simply no evidence. Whether a person or code for a sister congregation makes little difference. The message is the same.

Deceivers have been active in the Church [2 John :4]. Those deceivers were traveling evangelists. They were (in accord with 1 John) Gnostics. They taught that the Creator was a remote Being, and that

Christ only an emissary whose teaching enabled the awakening of human understanding. He was not fully human, and thus did not participate in the sinful flesh of un-awakened humanity. The creed, according to some interpreters of the non-Christian Gnostic gospels, was/is: "God is god, you are god, I am god".

Opposing this heresy, John insisted on the full enfleshment of Jesus [2 John :7], and that before allowing these visiting evangelists into the fellowship do not take them into your house or welcome them. Anyone who welcomes them shares in their wicked work [2 John :10-11].

JOHN'S THIRD LETTER

Apparently, a traveling evangelist named Demetrius [3 John :12] had complained to Saint John that the leader of a congregation named Diotrephes [3 John :9] had refused access to the fellowship. It may be that Diotrephes was mistaken in his evaluation of Demetrius, or else he held heretical views himself. John wrote to a different member, whom he called "Friend Gaius" [3 John :1]. He requested that Gaius, along with other "friends" correct the matter. Gaius was commended for the manner in which he hosted visiting evangelists [3 John :5].

JUDE

Jude was the half-brother of Jesus, brother of James. Tradition suggests that he was active in Judea as an evangelist within the Jewish Christian community. Thus his letter, unlike most others in the New Testament, concerns itself with the problems facing that limited fellowship. His reference to the "rebellion of Korah" [CF Numbers 16] suggests that his issue was among then Jewish Christian leadership. Korah and his followers objected to the priestly leadership of Aaron and Moses. The story is exceedingly bloody. Did the leaders to whom Jude addressed himself object to the leadership of James...and perhaps of Jude himself? This impression is advanced by the additional reference to Cain and Balaam [Jude :11], both of whom resisted Godly Authority. And the angels who did not keep their positions of authority [Jude :6] completes the reference.

The subject may have been sexual amorality. He pointed to Sodom and Gomorrah [Jude :7], insisting that on the strength of their dreams these ungodly people pollute their own bodies [Jude :8]. However, the issue may have been larger. These people are grumblers and faultfinders; they follow their own evil desires; they boast about themselves and flatter others for their own advantage [Jude :16].

The most telling verse is: These are the people who divide you, who follow mere natural instincts and do not have the Spirit [Jude :19].

My suspicion is that, because they had not demonstrated, and in fact had not received the Holy Spirit, they taught freedom from the law, but not obedience to either the Holy Spirit, or to the Jerusalem Council.

APPENDIX

These are studies/lessons that amplify my understandings exhibited in the notes about each book of the New Testament (sans Revelation).

SHEPHERDS, WISE MEN, ANGELS, AND STARS

By Peter Law

Shepherds are just above Buffalo Hunters on the social scale. They stink. They spend so much time alone, they are apt to talk to themselves. They are, however, hardy, self-reliant, brave, and very knowledgeable about nature. It is difficult to fool a shepherd who is out watching his flock by night.

When the Bible speaks of shepherds, it usually is an ambivalent reference. For instance, young David was of no account: he was out watching the sheep. When Jesus compared God to a good shepherd, most of his listeners would have been so offended that they might have wanted to kill him. The meaning of that parable about the lost lamb is that God is like a stupid shepherd who would leave ninety-nine sheep in order to look for one. The arithmetic is all wrong. Sheep alone are gone and done. The shepherd is charged with the care of the rest. Yet, David became King, and God searches out the lost and lonely. Shepherds are a confusing lot. Only two things are certain about that bunch on the hill outside Bethlehem. First, they smelled very bad. Second, they knew what was going on...they were alert.

Now Angels are a different matter. About them we know precious little. From the Old Testament we learn that Angels look like men. There is not one reference to a feminine angel. That there may be feminine angels is not in dispute...only that we have no Biblical account of one. Jesus suggests that angels are non-gender specific; they do not marry in Heaven. Why would they? They are God's Warriors, with a single aim: to secure the Kingdom of God (in Heaven and on Earth). In Daniel chapter eight, Gabriel was sent to explain a vision to Daniel. "One who looked like a man stood before me...and I was terrified and fell prostrate."

We must note the unfortunate reality: Satan is an angel. There is freedom of choice in Heaven, and Satan has chosen the wrong way. Worse, Satan leads a multitude of evil angels. St. Paul wrote that our warfare is against the spiritual forces of evil in the heavenly realms (Eph 6:12). After Satan tried to seduce Jesus into his web of temptation, angels came to minister to the Lord. In Matthew 13, Jesus predicts that He will, at the end of the age, send out His angels to separate the evil from the good. And in Matthew 16, it is written that each will receive from the angels the reward or punishment their deeds deserve.

One thing is certain; they are able to scare the living daylights out of those they visit. One of my favorite images of angels is of Michael hovering triumphant over a bound Satan. It is on the entrance wall of the new Cathedral at Coventry England. Michael is shown as "one terrifically powerful dude"! One can understand why, the first words out of Gabriel's mouth, as he spoke to Mary, were "Do not be afraid". Joseph was approached by angels only in dreams.

What, then, may we say about angels and shepherds. When the angel (only one) appeared and spoke the message to the shepherds, they were "kiss the earth" afraid. They were terrified. They, who had no fear of lions, felt strange things in their bowels. The Angel addressed the group of shepherds: "Don't be terrified, I bring good news to you. In Bethlehem is born this day, the Messiah. There will be great joy among the people!"

Incidentally, we find a reference here to something Methodists don't often know about: the Shekinah Glory of God. After Moses spoke to God, his face glowed. When God led the People of Israel out of Egypt, they followed a fire by night and a column of smoke by day. That fire sat over the Ark and the Tent of Meeting for centuries. There are too many references to list, but know this: when the Shekinah is present, it is symbolic of God's Power and Holiness. God is very close at hand. The Shekinah Glory of God shown around the Angel.

There followed a sudden bursting forth of praise, perhaps spoken, perhaps sung, perhaps chanted, by a multitude of angels. Now a multitude is not a small group. This multitude is composed of more individuals than you and I can imagine. It is an Army of Angels! It is an uncountable throng. The mass of angels stretches off into the infinity of the night sky.

Heaven will be like that for the saints. There will be an uncountable multitude of individuals, all united in the wonder and passion of praise. The experience of God's Presence will be so overwhelming that all one will be able to do is fall down before the Godhead in praise and adoration! And that is exactly what the shepherds did.

After the Angels had "gone away into Heaven", they obediently went into the town...leaving the sheep! They went to the home where Jesus had been birthed by Mary. They gave her the account, through whom it comes down to us. It was an event that Mary treasured in her heart, and told the Church after her Son was resurrected.

Now, in our culture we often mix the star and the shepherds. They don't mix. They are separate.

So, let's look at the star [I am indebted to the late Dr. Karlis Kaufmanis; I highly recommend that you listen to his lecture, found at The Star Of Bethlehem by Karlis Kaufmanis (google.com)]. In the Old Testament, astrologers are found in the list of abominations. They are in the company of enchanters, sorcerers, and magicians. They are ridiculed. For instance: Isaiah 47:13 "Let your astrologers come forward, those stargazers who make predictions month by month, let them save you from what is coming upon you." We would do well to avoid reading the daily astrological predictions. The Bible counts them as demonic. How, then, should we account for the Magi? They were Persian Astrologers.

If I understand it; Matthew was saying to his Jewish audience: even the abominable astrologers understood the signs of the times; why can't you?" That makes sense in the context of the rest of the book.

So, what were the signs in the stars, and can we retrieve them today? We must look for astrological signs, not astronomic signs. The "star" to which the Magi refer was not a nova or a special energy burst. It was something that fit into their star chart. What was that?

Remember that the Magi were members of the Persian Court. They were the scientists of their day. They charted the movement of stars and planets, and tried to deduce meanings. The planet Saturn was considered the defender of Palestine and represented epochal events, the constellation Pisces represented Israel and Syria; Jupiter was the planet of royalty, and finally, Mars was the symbol of bloodshed. So, when, in 7 BC, as they do every 805 years, Jupiter and Saturn traveled close together for almost the full year, the Magi began to think about the birth of a king in Israel or Syria. Syria didn't have a king; remember this is the Roman Empire. Israel, by chance, did have a king. They began to plan a trip to Jerusalem to see whether their prediction of the birth of a king might validate their beliefs. They saw the two planets come together three times in 7BC; in May, in September, and in December. It was time to go. Jerusalem was the destination because that would "of course" be where a king would be born.

Then the "sign" disappeared again. The location of the orbits of the planets came too close to the sun, or were below the horizon during the night-time. But, no matter, the Magi were on a mission. Off to Jerusalem they went.

Now a word about Herod: It is reported that Augustus said, "It is safer to be Herod's dog than Herod's son". Herod was a lethal paranoid. He murdered several of his children. One of the significant astrological absences within the sign that led the Magi to Jerusalem was Mars. Had Mars (the symbol of bloodshed) been seen in the House of Pisces, they might have been more careful with their inquires.

So, they appeared in Jerusalem in January of 6 BC, and innocently asked, "Where's the Baby King?" The gospel tells us that "all Jerusalem was afraid". They would be. Not ten years later, Herod had the leading men of the city arrested, under orders that, should he die, they were all to be put to death. He wanted a great mourning. He did die, and because all his power ended with his last breath, the men were released. There was great rejoicing. Anyway, back to 6 BC. Herod ordered that the Temple scholars determine where a king and defender of Israel ought to be born. Now, if Stalin or Mao asked a question like that, one would not give a quick answer. They went back to the Temple to pray and search. Well, as expected, they found that the great defender of Israel, David, had been born in Bethlehem, and that a tradition had risen among the people that the Messiah would likewise be born there. So, back to Herod they went with the word. I'm confident they were relieved…"In Bethlehem, not Jerusalem", they said. Herod, the "old fox" as Jesus called him, wanted to identify any rival family, and so happily sent the Magi on their way.

Now a wonderful thing happened. As they left Jerusalem, in February, the sign reappeared. However, this time Mars had joined Saturn and Jupiter in the house of Pisces; a clear indication of danger and bloodshed.

And, yet another wonder: the constellation was just barely above the horizon at sundown. This is very important. The road from Jerusalem to Bethlehem is about five miles long. It twists around the hills, and approaches the town from the northwest. As the Magi walked toward the village, the constellation and the three stars touched a dwelling…the very place in which the Magi found Mary and Joseph and Jesus.

Finally, they were warned in a dream (by an angel?) against any return to Jerusalem. Even so, the death of perhaps a dozen little boys couldn't be avoided. Herod would have his pound of flesh.

After leaving their gifts of gold, frankincense and myrrh, symbols of power, royal anointing, and death, they returned to Persia by another route.

And, you know the rest of the story.

Dot and the Universe: HOW STRING THEORY AGREES WITH BIBLICAL TEACHING

Dr. Peter G. Law

Paul, your great learning has made you insane. -Festus

Dimension Zero is Potential but not actualized Dot

A point, which I will name Dot, is the intersection of two "imaginary" lines. Actually, Dot is much more complicated. Dot is identified by arithmeticians in her most simple and elementary form.

However, Dot is the intersection of an infinitesimal number of lines. She is like a universe of her own in two ways. Not only does she contain "infinity", she also contains "eternity". She contains "existence". Existence has an alias: "Location". Location, like eternity, is contained, but not actualized, that is, it has not yet been born. In order to be born, something else must happen. Dot must enter into a relationship with the "Cosmic Artist". The Cosmic Artist chooses to place, or Create, Dot in a singularity; that is, in one Location chosen from among an infinite number of possible locations (see the Tenth Dimension).

Dimension One is a Dot

Existence is the son of Dot. Within him are all the attributes of what we who live in the fourth plane experience are. Existence is the father of Experience. Just as Dot contained all possibility, so each generation following her, contains all the possibilities of eternity and infinity, as well as those capacities which have already been realized. That is, each dimension contains the potential of all other dimensons.

Think of a Cosmic Artist who, with a mindful pen, on a plane of existence, places a Dot. She is there with her Son and her grandson, but only if the Cosmic Artist extends the side of Dot into a "Line". A-line, or "Aline" is her Daughter. Aline may give birth to curves, circles, squares, tetrahedrons, and every manner of shape. She is still like a "Flat Stanley", a paper person taken by children to all sorts of experiences. She is there, but is mindful of nothing. Yet, she contains all "infinity" and all "existence". They are like ova within her womb. In order to be made "real", she must have intercourse with the Cosmic Artist. Her offspring are determined, not by her, but by the Artist.

Dimension Two is a line and or a plane

When the Cosmic Artist draws from Dot an Aline, and, from Aline, shapes; they may be abstract without expressed meaning, or, they may be shaped by "Wisdom". Wisdom (Christian's call this the Holy Spirit) is the personal expression of the Character of the Cosmic Artist. Think of the authors of Pogo or Peanuts. They drew lines into shapes that expressed wisdom, emotion, understanding. And yet, even yet, they are Flat Stanley, expressing, but not experiencing the wisdom contained within their lines. Their wisdom may only be seen (and only possibly understood) if the Cosmic Artist and Dot beget yet another generation of offspring.

Dimension Two (Plane) may be affected from higher planes

These offspring are brought forth from Aline and Existence. Wisdom works within the two bringing about "Aware" (or consciousness). Note that Wisdom has been active from the very first, but is perceptible only to Aware[ness]. Aware is the first of Dot's progeny to be able to begin a journey of self-discovery. By being alert to the individual's environment, Aware may respond. As Dot was passive, Aware is interactive. He is able to act, something Dot was unable to do even though she contained the possibility of action within the boundaries of infinity and eternity.

Dimension Three is a plane with area added.

Volume implies boundaries. There is an edge, a center, an up and down. It is the dimension in which we exist, but it requires the addition of Time to bring self-awareness and self-directed action.

Dimension Four includes Volume, Time, Consciousness and Choice

Consider an amoeba or a virus. They react to their environment. They do not consciously choose an action; their action is "re-active". It is only an automatic response to a stimulus. Yet any reaction is an expression of Aware. Aware may be, as was his Grandmother Dot, only as simple as the intersection of two lines, or as complex as an infinitesimal number of intersections. Aware is the first of Dot's progeny to be capable of yet another attribute: "Choice". Choice may be simple or complex. In the absence of stimulus, an amoeba in a drop of pond water, may move this way or that, may divide or not; without consciously choosing, and yet choosing after all. As stimulating factors increase in number and kind, so does the attribute of choosing.

Consciousness is either a consequence of time, or time is a consequence of consciousness. In either case, Consciousness is the great attribute of the Fourth Dimension. Of course, not all of the Fourth Dimension is conscious, but we are. That is what makes this Dimension so rich in experience. The virus has experience but is not conscious of it. We have both experience and consciousness.

Choice includes Consequences and results in Good and Evil

Prior to this Wisdom has acted only in a creative fashion. As Choice grows to maturity, He encounters the consequences of choosing. They may be reflective of two other flowers in this Garden of Eden. They may reflect the difference between good and evil. Existence falls into an untoward complexity. He has twins: Good and Evil. Good and Evil are inter-actors: expressions of Aware. Some actions lead to the benefit, and some the detriment, of Aware. And, at every enlargement of Aware[ness], the complexity of the interaction also grows more complex. And thus, the Aware[ness] of "life" includes the awareness of "not-life". This is the expression of an interaction between Grandfather Existence and Experience. Experience teaches Choice that Existence is better than non-existence. And, Choice learns the lesson all too well. As Aware matures and becomes "Self-Aware", Choice carries the learned Experience of the virus and amoeba; my Existence is more important to me than your existence. This is the source of morality and all moral codes [See Genesis Chapter Two]. My Existence is the focus [As in Eve, and then Adam], the meaning of all that has transpired since the Cosmic Artist mindfully created Dot. From this, Choice has fathered Good and Evil.

Freedom of Choice between Good and Evil give rise to Will

Good and Evil father Will: A cosmic competition is begun between various expressions of Existence. Each one trying to master what is beyond mastery; the created universe; and even more-so, the Cosmic Artist. The attempt to be equal to, or superior to the Cosmic Artist is the expression of an absolute and unrestrained Evil. The expression of Good, equally absolute, is awareness of the individual's pure relationship to the Cosmic Artist. Dot was perfectly good in that she never rebelled. She was exactly what the Cosmic Artist created (Willed) her to be. The twin progeny of Aware are like Cain and Abel. They are necessary to the outcome designed by Wisdom [Genesis 4:1ff]. Wisdom has provided the only platform in which Choice is able to act meaningfully. "Meaning" is an expression of Wisdom interacting within Location, and His progeny, Experience and Aware.

Freedom of Choice, and Free Will give rise to Meaning

Philosophers have argued for centuries about the boundaries of Meaning; her character, intentions, limits. They have made several things clear. She requires the participation of Will,

Aware[ness], Location, and Choice. Meaning may have the character of either Good or Evil, depending on which Will she chooses: The Will of the Artist, or the Will of Existence. They (the philosophers) have stumbled when they confused the character of the two. One placed his/her continued conscious existence above the continued consciousness of the other, or, placed his/her advancement in wisdom as of greater importance than that of the other. [By and large, the Main-Line churches adopted the false wisdom of the nineteenth century German philosophers like Nietzsche and his "superman" which led directly to the evil of the Nazis; while the Republican Party has found Ayne Rand's superhero equally attractive. Both show little concern for "the other".]

True Wisdom is the Spirit of the Cosmic Artist. She shows concern for each "other". Without that concern, there is no mutuality, and no-one to whom the self-aware may appeal for support. It is perhaps the greatest moral imperative that each self-aware be also "other-aware". This is the great opening to the next generation of Dot's and the Artist's progeny.

We are able to experience Wisdom expressed in Dimension Two as we read comic strips

Just as Dot and her first generation are unable to Experience or to be self-aware, so Existence is unable to reach beyond his limits to view the boundaries of Freedom. Yet, some few have looked into the mystery of Wisdom and have found clues as to her character. It seems true that each generation, is, in some mysterious fashion, able to understand and interact with the previous generation. Thus, Aware is able to see, understand, and perhaps even affect the choices of an un-aware. Or, Aware is able to see the Wisdom in a Flat Stanley like Pogo or Charlie Brown. Just so, Freedom may be able to inter-act with Self-Aware.

Lao Tse found and described Wisdom as the Tau. Moses and Mohammad both sought her hearth through morality of various quality. None has seen a greater image than St. Paul who wrote that he, "in the Spirit was raised to the Third Heaven": [2 Corinthians 12:3-4] And I know that this man...was caught up to paradise (other texts say "Third Heaven") and heard inexpressible things, things that no one is permitted to tell. *This is important later.

Dimension Four is penetrated by higher Dimensions

Saint Paul's description of his present existence included five dimensions. In Ephesians 3:17-19, St Paul wrote: And I pray that you, being rooted and established in (God's) Love, may have power, together with all the Lord's holy people, to grasp how wide and long and high and deep is the love of Christ, and to know this Love that surpasses knowledge—that you may be filled to the measure of all the fullness of God.

One ought to point out that Agape is the means by which one is filled, and is able to experience the fullness of the "Third Heaven". One must also ask, whether the Third Heaven includes three dimensions presently unexperienced in normal human existence.

The Navaho understood this present to be the fourth story in a multi-story pueblo. Thomas Merton named his autobiography, "The Seven Story Mountain" [though his account is of a moral advancement from philosophy and self to communism and social connection to Catholicism (the community of God) to monasticism (losing one's self in God) to the universal experience of monastics]. Others, it seems, have arrived at the same notion. Somehow, in an inexpressible fashion, Wisdom was communicated from a more complex dimension to this present existence. It is as if, Charlie Brown was somehow able to understand his relationship to his author.

Those, and there are many, who have experienced this influx of Wisdom, relate a total Freedom. They witness to a Freedom above and beyond morality. It is a Freedom of perfect acceptance.

No person has expressed the Character of Freedom more perfectly than Jesus. His teachings lead directly to the fullest initiation of Wisdom within the Self-Aware. More than His teachings, His person illuminates the boundaries of Wisdom.

His lessons: It is not what you do, but what you are (or become); Grace and Mercy are more important than revenge and/or power; admiration and devotion to the Artist is the open door, and care for the other is the stairway toward the portal.

To these add the insight of Paul: the gateway to Freedom is open to all who will enter, yet only those who follow the insights of Jesus are prepared to do so. As per above, he described this current reality as having height, width, length and depth. Depth (another euphemism for the Wisdom of Agape/God's Love) is the gateway to Freedom. It is gained by intercourse with Wisdom.

Spirit is the Presence of the Tenth Dimension in all other Dimensions

Paul's friends and fellow teachers, experienced a new boundary when they encountered Wisdom in the Person of Jesus, who already had passed through the portal gateway. They called Wisdom the Holy Spirit. They perceived Spirit as different from self-awareness or emotions. Spirit has an essential reality beyond the physical. Spirit is the radical Freedom of God's Character (the Tenth Dimension).

But what is Freedom like? What does Wisdom teach us?   She enlarges the abilities of Self-Aware. Self-Aware and Wisdom are parents to a New Creation: an exponential increase in LOVE.

Physicists pay attention to the physical characteristics of dimensions. They are important, but not a totality of description. Using these euphemistic words of characteristics, an outline of increasing awareness at each iteration of dimensionality, illuminates the non-physical sibling of the physical (as for instance the "mind" is not the same as the brain, love is not a chemical reaction). Each additional characteristic accompanies an added dimension.

But how may the theories of dimensions illuminate our understanding of how Character might increase at future enlargements of Aware[ness]?

The Fifth Dimension accesses all time within the Fourth Dimension

As described, the fifth dimension (if the present is the fourth) is an enlargement of time. All time is visible or experienced simultaneously. Theologians have previously deduced just such an awareness. The Messiah precedes His birth, and continues past His death. Wisdom was at the beginning of time and is eternal. Many other illustrations are easily available. From this theological perspective, Freedom includes Aware[ness] of one's entire existence within the frame of Eternal Agape. Therefore, since we are surrounded by so great a cloud of witnesses, let us also lay aside every weight and the sin that clings so closely, and let us run with perseverance the race that is set before us, looking to Jesus the pioneer and perfecter of our faith... (Hebrews 12:1-2). In the fifth dimension the individual is aware of, or able to access, all the moments of one's life, along with all the relationships of those moments.

From the Christian perspective, this is the moment of judgement. It is not that an angry God condemns us for our sins. Rather, the individual is able to evaluate his/her own life and choices. Our Gospel proclaims that by Faith and Grace, even though we regret poor choices and sins, we my proceed to the sixth dimension. Freedom allows us that choice. The Biblical witness is that some will desire to remain in the darkness of weeping and gnashing of teeth [see, among others: Luke 13:28]. Within this dimension, one is able to see all that God intended, alongside one's choices. The result will be remorse, or repentance among the faithful.

The sixth dimension includes all possible times and choices.

Here is a hint that characteristics (choice is not just an act, it is a characteristic of Aware[ness]) are fundamental to dimensionality. Here one is able to see the separation of Good and Evil, the Sheep from the Goats, the Wheat from the Weeds. One is able to see the consequences of Choice across the full sweep of Aware[ness]. Christians see this as The Judgment. One is able to see, and understand all one's choices within the context of what God had offered. One condemns one's bad/unfortunate choices as one sees what God's Will would have done. One will choose whether to cede certain previously valued characteristics or not. C.S. Lewis, in The Great Divorce, wonderfully illustrated how some will value intellectual choice over the certainties of Heaven, and some will value their treasures of resentment over the required forgiveness of all others, etc.

Dimension Seven is Heaven/Infinity/Eternity

The Seventh Dimension includes all the possible time lines of an individual life. One is able to see the Meaning of the Person God Created. It is characterized by Wisdom, and Agape. It is as if Charlie Brown met Charles Schultz, and finally understood why Charles created Charlie. Charlie is able to understand why Charles had him do and experience meaning in every strip, some happy and others not happy. Charlie would be amazed by the love and effort of his creator. It would be an infinite bliss to Charlie. And Charles Schultz experienced [I presume] that understanding of himself as he mets his Creator.

The Eighth Dimension includes all possible time-lines within this universe

The eighth dimension is perhaps too far distant for understanding, as it includes the possible jump from one existence to any other existence, or one life to another. It may be the "realm" of "Correction". That is, a platform from which one is able to restore what was lost, or include what was missed, or increase what is Good while eliminating what is Evil. But that is the realm of the Great Artist, not of humans.

"To Infinity...and Beyond"!

The seventh dimension, the one visited by St. Paul, requires infinity to be a singularity. That is, all that is, was, and is to be, within this chosen, created, and single Existence, the one which arose from Dot and the Artist, is brought to full unity of being.

The eighth, ninth, and tenth dimensions are concerned with other singularities*. Prior to any discussion of those dimensions, one must answer two questions. Where is the residence of the Great Artist? And, Does the Artist have complete Freedom of Choice and Will? Various "scientific philosophers" have argued that the Residence is either in the seventh (Third Heaven) or the tenth dimension. However, they assume that if different infinities are possible, they must be existential. Yet if the Great Artist has full freedom of Will, some, if not all, other infinities may have been rejected and do not exist. Not just because they failed to "inflate" but simply because the Great Artist chose to not exercise a willingness to create them. This is, of course, counting "Angels on the tip of a pin"; to no point. Yet it illustrates the futility of any attempt to reach farther than Wisdom is willing to take us. **

8 infinite number of different infinities

9 jump from one infinity to another

10 all infinities as a point, beyond which there is no pathway of inflation.

**

As I grow older, and closer to the ending of this iteration of dimensionality, I have wondered about what I might experience after my demise. There is the Biblical description of bliss, praise and worship; one which I experienced in a 'near-death' episode in 1967. Confronted with string theory, I have tried to complete my understanding by including those scientific postulates in my faith experience. I don't want to go farther than is appropriate to the question: is there life and eternity after death? I believe there is, and look forward to the "last great adventure" in which I shall find out whether there is or is not.